Business

for AS

Ian Marcousé ▪ Andy Hammond
▪ Nigel Watson

Approval message from AQA

This textbook has been approved by AQA for use with our qualification. This means that we have checked that it broadly covers the specification and we are satisfied with the overall quality. Full details of our approval process can be found on our website.

We approve textbooks because we know how important it is for teachers and students to have the right resources to support their teaching and learning. However, the publisher is ultimately responsible for the editorial control and quality of this book.

Please note that when teaching the *AQA AS Business* course, you must refer to AQA's specification as your definitive source of information. While this book has been written to match the specification, it does not provide complete coverage of every aspect of the course.

A wide range of other useful resources can be found on the relevant subject pages of our website: www.aqa.org.uk.

HODDER
EDUCATION
AN HACHETTE UK COMPANY

Although every effort has been made to ensure that website addresses are correct at time of going to press, Hodder Education cannot be held responsible for the content of any website mentioned in this book. It is sometimes possible to find a relocated web page by typing in the address of the home page for a website in the URL window of your browser.

Hachette UK's policy is to use papers that are natural, renewable and recyclable products and made from wood grown in sustainable forests. The logging and manufacturing processes are expected to conform to the environmental regulations of the country of origin.

Orders: please contact Bookpoint Ltd, 130 Milton Park, Abingdon, Oxon OX14 4SB. Telephone: (44) 01235 827720. Fax: (44) 01235 400454. Lines are open from 9.00 - 5.00, Monday to Saturday, with a 24-hour message answering service. You can also order through our website www.hoddereducation.com

© 2015 Ian Marcousé, Andy Hammond, Nigel Watson

First published in 2015 by
Hodder Education
An Hachette UK Company
338 Euston Road
London NW1 3BH

Impression number   10 9 8 7 6 5 4 3 2 1

Year   2019 2018 2017 2016 2015

Cover photo © Sergey Nivens – Fotolia

Illustrations by Aptara, Inc

Typeset in ITC Berkeley Oldstyle Std Book 11/13 by Aptara, Inc.

Printed in Italy

A catalogue record for this title is available from the British Library

ISBN: 978 1471 835803

Contents list

Understanding the nature and purpose of business

Linked to: Issues in understanding forms of business, Chapter 3; Understanding the role and importance of stakeholders, Chapter 10; Decision-making to improve financial performance, Chapter 44.

Definition

According to business guru Peter Drucker, business is the creation of a customer; in other words, conceiving a product or service that people will pay enough for to generate a profit.

1.1 An overview of the subject

Business is best looked at from the boss's point of view. The boss (perhaps the founder or entrepreneur) has an idea or mission. The chief executive of Sainsbury's may decide that a chain of supermarkets in India represents the next big step forward. This is the mission – Sainsbury's succeeding in India. This can then form the basis for setting targets or objectives, such as to open the first ten Sainsbury's supermarkets in India by the end of 2018.

'Business is like a bicycle. Either you keep moving or you fall down.' John David Wright, U.S. businessman

After the chief executive has set that objective, Sainsbury's senior managers must then figure out how to make this happen. What will be needed is a strategy that leads to a plan of action, that is, to set out exactly what needs to happen, and by when. That strategy will have to involve the four main sections of the business (known as the business functions). These are marketing, people, finance and operations (see Table 1.1).

Table 1.1 Introduction to business functions

Marketing	This department advises the business on consumer trends, and on the attitudes and purchasing habits of customers – and decides how to advertise and promote new and existing brands.
People (Human Resources)	Managers of the firm's staff (human resources or HR) plan for and deal with recruitment, training, financial incentives, equal opportunities and also redundancy and dismissals.
Finance	Finance helps to identify what can be afforded and therefore what budgets to set for each of the other functions; it also monitors the spending levels to make sure that costs are kept under control.
Operations	Operations manages the supply chain that starts with buying materials and components, then manufactures a finished product and delivers it to the customer. Service businesses also need to plan the flow of work, so operations management is relevant in a bank or a shop as well as in a factory.

The chief executive will expect the leaders of each of these four functions to come up with their own plan for meeting the overall objective, so there will be a marketing plan, a financial plan and so on. How these things relate to each other can be seen in Figure 1.1.

Figure 1.1 How business works

Having established their own plans, the four functional leaders will now need to meet to make sure that everything fits together. It is no good if marketing decides on an image of Sainsbury's Super-value (a kind of Aldi/Lidl idea) while operations chooses to build stores targeting India's rich elite. Each of the functions must talk to each other and trust each other (see Figure 1.2). This is also the way you are likely to learn this subject. First you study each business function in turn, then you study how the departments work together (and the problems caused if they fail to do so).

Figure 1.2 How business works (2)

Important though it is to understand the internal workings of a business as shown in Figure 1.2, there are many added complications. Much as a chief executive may wish to set optimistic objectives, a series of outside factors can get in the way of success. Most obviously, competitors may have their own ideas; if Sainsbury's finds that the massive Walmart is fighting for every suitable property site in India, opening ten stores will become a lot harder. Figure 1.3 gives an overview of the process of running a business, taking into account external as well as internal factors.

Figure 1.3 How business works (3)

Sainsbury's plc is one of the UK's leading companies, with a 16.5 per cent share of the market for groceries. In 2014 its sales revenue was £26,353 million and profits came to £798 million. Despite these impressive-sounding numbers, the chart below shows how they compare with one of the world's monster businesses – Walmart (which owns Asda). As you can see, Walmart makes more than twenty times more profit per year than Sainsbury's. If Sainsbury's chooses to develop in India, it will probably end up head-to-head with Walmart. That would be tricky.

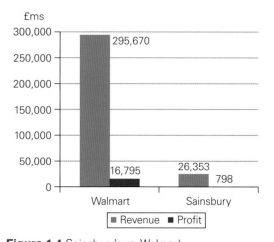

Figure 1.4 Sainsbury's vs. Walmart

2014 figures; Walmart dollars converted at $1.60 to the £

1.2 Why businesses exist

Businesses exist because human spirit and a sense of adventure lead people to 'show what they can do' and to want to find a way to create family income that is not dependent on a specific outside force: a company or a boss. Hundreds of years ago this could be done by being a farmer, running a shop or having independence as a skilled tradesman. Today, starting a business can be the path to riches or to long hours and meagre rewards – but the lure of 'being your own boss' remains powerful.

Figure 1.5 below shows the huge rise in business start-ups in recent years, as shown by the 61.5 per cent growth in company formation between 2008/9 and 2013/14. Part of the spur may have been the recent recession, but it is also testimony to the attractions today of running your own business.

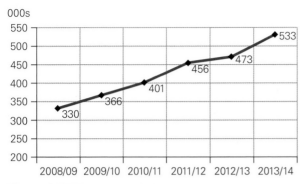

Figure 1.5 UK company start-ups

Source: www.companieshouse.gov.uk

'Entrepreneur: a high-rolling risk taker who would rather be a spectacular failure than a dismal success.' Anon

---

Businesses exist because a complex modern world needs more than simply a buyer, a seller and a market for them to meet. A company such as Rolls Royce Aerospace employs over 20,000 people to design, engineer, build, fit and service more than £5,000 million of sales of engines every year, 75 per cent of which are exports from the UK. Managing this requires huge skills of co-ordination and motivation, all within the Rolls Royce mission 'to provide the finest, most technologically advanced power systems'.

1.3 Mission and objectives

Mission is the aim for the business that is settled upon by the boss (in a small firm) or by the board of directors in a large one. An aim is a general statement of where the business is heading; mission usually takes that statement and makes it sound more evangelical or motivational. An aim might be 'to be No. 1 in the market for advanced engines'. When dressed up as a mission, this becomes: 'to provide the finest, most technologically advanced power systems' (Rolls Royce).

The reason to turn the aim into a motivational statement is to try to excite customers and staff alike – to make them feel part of the project, just as customers once felt that buying innocent smoothies was helping 'to make the world a little fruitier'. Without doubt, if a business has an exciting aim it is great to express it as a motivating mission. Often, though, dull aims are jazzed up as mission statements that mean little or nothing.

From the aims or mission will come the objectives. These will usually be SMART, that is, Specific,

Table 1.2 Good and bad mission statements

Meaningful mission statement	Meaningless mission statement (Would this motivate staff?)
'To become the world's No. 1 online fashion destination for twenty-somethings.' ASOS 2014 (neatly, they call this 'Our Ambition' rather than 'Our Mission')	'We want Tesco to be the most highly valued business by: the customers we serve, the communities in which we operate, our loyal and committed colleagues and of course, our shareholders.' Tesco 2014
'Maintaining a global viewpoint, we are dedicated to supplying products of the highest quality, yet at a reasonable price, for worldwide customer satisfaction. Dreams inspire us to create innovative products that enhance mobility and benefit society.' Honda UK 2014	'To be the world leader in food ingredients and flavours serving the food and beverage industry, and a leading supplier of added value brands and customer branded foods to the Irish and UK markets.' Kerry Foods 2014
'Our product mission drives us to make fantastic ice cream – for its own sake.' Ben & Jerry's 2014	'We create outstanding places which make a positive difference to people's everyday lives.' British Land, 2014

Measurable, Achievable, Realistic and Timebound. For ASOS, an example of a SMART objective might be 'to become one of the Top 3 online clothing sellers in China by January 1st 2017'. Ideally this objective would seem challenging but achievable – and should sit neatly as a stepping stone towards the mission of becoming the world's No. 1.

1.4 Why businesses set objectives

Objectives are set because if you're the boss of 21,300 people running Rolls Royce, you cannot make every decision. Therefore you have to give more junior staff the authority to get on and make middle-ranking decisions, perhaps without letting you know. If managers are clear on the overall objectives they can feel confident in making decisions that contribute towards achieving those goals.

Other benefits from setting objectives include:
- It's motivating to have a clear goal to aim towards – for managers and for staff
- The objectives are the basis for devising the strategy: the medium–long term plan for meeting the objectives.

The plan can be costed both in manpower and money, to know what resources are going to be needed to achieve the objectives.

'Objectives are not fate; they are direction. They are not commands; they are commitments. They do not determine the future; they are means to mobilise the resources and energies of the business for the making of the future.' Peter Drucker, business guru

1.5 Common business objectives

Business objectives are sometimes called corporate objectives because they set targets for the whole organisation, not just one function. Common business objectives include the following:

1. Profit optimisation in the medium-long term. Profit is vital to the long-term health of every company. Profit provides the capital to fund business growth. It also provides the safety blanket that allows a business to take a risk, knowing that even if it flops, the business will not go under. Optimisation means getting the right balance between two or more possibilities: neither so much profit as to risk exploiting the customer, nor so little as to threaten the firm's viability. Good companies appreciate that their long-term position will be helped if their customers believe they are getting value for money.

2. Profit maximisation, that is the attempt by a business to make as much profit as possible, probably as fast as possible. Big companies may follow this approach when they suspect a rival is about to try to buy them out. The higher the profit they can show, the higher the price the company will fetch. The same is likely to be the case for companies about to 'float' their shares onto the stock market.

   Small firms may also be trying to make as much profit as possible, with no concern for their long-term future and therefore no regard for their reputation. Such businesses may end up on investigative TV programmes such as the BBC's *Watchdog*.

Real business

When Candy Crush owner King Digital Entertainment decided to float the business, it had nine months to maximize its profit before the flotation took place. Therefore when the Spring 2014 float happened, it was possible to claim such high profits that a very high share price was justified. The final price of $22.50 per share valued the company at $7 billion. Within six months of the float the shares had lost 40 per cent of their value as King announced that revenues from Candy Crush were lower than expected. The share buyers were certainly crushed. ⇨

Figure 1.6 Candy Crush

3. Growth. The importance of online business has placed growth as one of the most common business objectives. The logic is often to say 'there can only be one giant in this market, so we must make sure it's us'. Therefore decisions are made that focus on rising customer/user numbers instead of rising profits. The assumption is often made that if you get the growth today, the profits will come tomorrow. This is famously true in the console business, in which selling hardware rarely makes a profit – it's the software and the add-ons that bring profits later.

'Growth is a by-product of the pursuit of excellence and is not itself a worthy goal.' Robert Townsend, Avis chief executive and business author.

4. Cash flow. This is rarely a consideration for large firms, but is important for small ones, especially business start-ups. If the objective of a new firm is to ensure that cash flow remains positive, it will be vital that everyone in the business is practising the same approach. So even quite junior staff who have been given some decision-making power (had authority delegated to them) should be clear that they must not risk creating negative cash flow.

Figure 1.7 Logic chain: from mission to decision-making

5. Survival. This relates strongly to the previous point about cash flow. If times are tough, survival may be the key objective; and in that case survival will rely on keeping cash flow high enough. This will be a priority for new, start-up businesses aware that one third of new businesses fail to survive three years.

6. Social and ethical objectives are easy to find on company websites; whether they have any significant influence over business decisions is less clear. All through the period that banks were mis-selling service after service to customers, their websites boasted about their ethical purity. Ultimately, social and ethical objectives only mean something if the business is willing to sacrifice some profit or some market share. Arguably Tesco did just this in May 2014 when it volunteered to remove sweets from near its checkouts (though perhaps it was following Lidl's example, as the German firm did the same earlier in the year). The evidence is that it is fair to be sceptical about whether social and ethical objectives are ever much more than image-related add-ons. Financial objectives remain the overwhelming priority for most businesses.

Five Whys and a How

Question	Answer
Why study business anyway?	Because although some entrepreneurs have no business education, most have quite a lot – and so have most of the world's high-earning chief executives.
Why might a company aim be better expressed as a mission?	If more vibrant, motivating language makes staff care more and work harder, a mission will have paid for itself.
Why do objectives need to be SMART?	Vaguely worded 'objectives' will be too woolly to allow anyone to measure whether they have been achieved or not, so they'd have no motivating force.
Why do new firms struggle with cash flow?	Because retail customers expect generous credit terms (delaying cash inflows) while suppliers demand cash on delivery.
Why may social objectives be easy to boast about but hard to carry through?	Boasts about doing good sit well on a website, but may be ignored by bosses intent on high profits and therefore high bonuses.
How should bosses decide on their company objectives?	By talking to their staff they'll find out what's wrong at the moment and what's possible in the future.

Key terms

Budgets: an agreed ceiling on the monthly spending by any department or manager.

Corporate objectives: targets for the whole business, such as profits to rise by 20 per cent a year for the next three years.

Delegated: having passed authority down the hierarchy so that the local or more expert person makes the decision.

Entrepreneur: a person with the initiative and drive to make a business idea happen.

Mission: a business aim expressed to make it seem especially purposeful and motivating.

Mission statement: a short, powerfully-expressed sentence or two that explains the business aims clearly yet motivationally.

Objectives: targets precise enough to allow praise or blame for the person in charge.

Profit optimisation: that the surplus of revenue over costs should be just right: neither too high in the short term nor too low to finance long-term success.

Strategy: a medium-long term plan for meeting your objectives.

Business is like watching live football. You simply couldn't make it up. The twists and turns for large firms like Tesco or small local firms are remarkably dramatic. One week all is well and the next week there's a crisis.

Both for football managers and company executives, it isn't supposed to be that way. Most football managers want 'a good performance and a clean sheet'. A dull one-nil performance is superior to a frantic 4-3 skirmish. And company bosses yearn for predictability and stability. That's why they set clear objectives and hold managers to account for meeting them. Happily, no matter how much they seek stability, managers are constantly being upset by unexpected results and performances. Studying business should never be boring.

'Entrepreneurs are needed not only to start new business ventures … but also to put life into existing companies, especially large ones.' Anders Wall, Swedish chief executive

Workbook

A. Revision questions

(25 marks; 25 minutes)

1. Explain two differences between mission and objectives. (4)

2. State whether each of the following statements is a mission or an objective.
   a) To become the world's favourite car rental business.
   b) To bring healthy eating to Wigan.
   c) To achieve a 40 per cent market share by the end of 2018. (3)

3. Outline two possible risks if a business such as Sainsbury's sets itself the objective of rapid growth. (4)

4. Outline why 'survival' might be the wisest objective for a brand new start-up business. (3)

5. Why might a business suffering bad publicity emphasise a new set of ethical objectives? (3)

6. Read John David Wright's quotation (see page 1). Explain its meaning in your own words. (4)

7. Outline one strength and one weakness of a business such as Aston Villa FC setting itself objectives for the coming season. (4)

B. Revision exercises
DATA RESPONSE

Snapchat

In late Autumn 2013 two 23-year-old Californians were each offered $750 million in cash by Facebook's Mark Zuckerberg. And they turned it down. Evan Spiegel and Bobby Murphy launched Snapchat in July 2011. Now Facebook wanted to buy the business for $3,000 million. The founders had each retained a 25 per cent stake in the business, hence the $750 m figure.

Snapchat began late one night at Stanford University when Reggie Brown stepped into fellow-student Spiegel's room groaning about a photo he regretted sending. He then said something like 'I wish there was an app to send disappearing photos'. Spiegel saw the potential, calling Brown's remark 'a million dollar idea'. This conversation is now part of a billion dollar lawsuit, as Brown claims his share of the Snapchat goldmine.

Spiegel developed the app as part of a University project. When he presented it, the feedback was, roughly, who wants a disappearing photo? And when it debuted (under the brand name Picaboo) in the Apple App Store on 13 July 2011, no one noticed. Luckily, a bust-up over the share split in August 2011 made Spiegel and Murphy cut Brown out – including the Picaboo name that Brown had put forward. The new name was Snapchat. User uptake remained painfully slow until high school students in California started using it at school – as Facebook had been banned. Then the take-off was spectacular, as shown in Table 1.3

Table 1.3 Growth of Snapchat

	Snapchat users/usage	Snapchat funding
August 2011	127	
October 2011	1,000	
December 2011	2,250	
January 2012	20,000	
April 2012	100,000	$485,000
February 2013	60,000,000	$13,500,000
November 2013	400,000,000	$50,000,000
June 2014	1,000,000,000	

Having turned $3 billion down in 2013, it was perhaps a relief to the founders that Chinese web giant Alibaba talked in August 2014 about an investment that would value Snapchat at $10 billion. This would be an amazing valuation as Snapchat had, at that time, never generated a dollar of revenue. But Snapchat's huge appeal came from demography. Facebook users were now an average of nearly 40 years old, whereas Snapchat's core market was 12–24 year olds, with an average age below 18. Facebook might be the present but Snapchat looked like the future.

The other huge issue for Spiegel and Murphy was Brown's huge lawsuit, demanding his fair share of the company. A similar thing happened with Facebook, making it easy to forecast that lawyers will get rich arguing this case – but it will probably be settled out of court for a very large sum.

Questions (25 marks; 30 minutes)

1. Why do you think that the Snapchat business exists? Explain your answer. (4)

2. With no income, Snapchat's cash flow was dependent entirely on capital investment from outside sources. Analyse the effect this may have on Spiegel and Murphy's ability to run the business. (9)

3. From your own knowledge of Snapchat, do you think the business could ever generate advertising or other revenue to make it worth billions of dollars? Justify your answer. (12)

C. Extend your understanding

1. You have been appointed Chief Executive of Marks & Spencer. Your mission is 'to restore M&S as the clothing store of choice for women over the age of 30'. Discuss how you will set about this task. (20)

2. When faced with crisis in early 2015, a commentator suggested that Morrisons 'might not survive the coming three years'. To what extent do you agree with this statement? (20)

Different business forms

Linked to: Understanding the nature and purpose of business, Chapter 1; Issues in understanding forms of business, Chapter 3; Understanding the role and importance of stakeholders, Chapter 10.

Definition

The legal structure of a business determines the financial impact on the business owners if things go wrong. It also affects the ease with which the business can finance growth.

2.1 Businesses with unlimited liability

Unlimited liability means that the finances of the business are treated as inseparable from the finances of the business owner(s). So if the business loses £1 million, the people owed money (the creditors) can get the courts to force the individual owners to pay up. If that means selling their houses, cars, and so on, so be it. If the owner(s) cannot pay, they can be made personally bankrupt. Two types of business organisation have unlimited liability: sole traders and partnerships.

Sole traders

A sole trader is an individual who owns and operates his or her own business. Although there may be one or two employees, this person makes the final decisions about the running of the business. A sole trader is the only one who benefits financially from success, but must face the burden of any failure. In the eyes of the law the individual and the business are the same. This means that the owner has unlimited liability for any debts that result from running the firm. If a sole trader cannot pay his or her bills, the courts can allow personal assets to be seized by creditors in order to meet outstanding debts. For example, the family home or car may be sold. If insufficient funds can be raised in this way the person will be declared bankrupt.

Despite the financial dangers involved, the sole trader is the most common form of legal structure adopted by UK businesses. In some areas of the economy this kind of business dominates, particularly where little finance is required to set up and run the business and customers demand a personal service. Examples include trades such as builders and plumbers, and many independent shopkeepers.

There are no formal rules to follow when establishing as a sole trader, or administrative costs to pay. Complete confidentiality can be maintained because accounts are not published. As a result many business start-ups adopt this structure.

The main disadvantages facing a sole trader are the limited sources of finance available, long hours of work involved and the difficulty of running the business during periods of ill health (plus unlimited liability).

Partnerships

Partnerships exist when two or more people start a business without forming a company. Like a sole trader, the individuals have unlimited liability for any debts run up by the business. Because people are working together but are unlimitedly liable for any debts, it is vital that the partners trust each other. As a result, this legal structure is often found in the professions, such as medicine and law.

The main difference between a sole trader and a partnership is the number of owners.

2.2 Businesses with limited liability

Limited liability means that the legal duty to pay debts run up by a business stays with the business itself, not its owner/shareholders. If a company has £1 million of debts that it lacks the cash to repay, the courts can force the business to sell all its assets (cars, computers, etc.). If there is still not enough money, the company is closed down, but the owner/shareholders have no personal liability for the remaining debts.

To gain the benefits of limited liability, the business must go through a legal process to become a company. The process of incorporation creates a separate legal identity for the organisation. In the eyes of the law the owners of the business and the company itself are now two different things. The business can take legal action against others and have legal action taken against it. In order to gain separate legal status a company must be registered with the Registrar of Companies.

The key advantages and disadvantages that result from forming a limited company are set out below.

Advantages of forming a limited company:

- Shareholders experience the benefits of limited liability, including the confidence to expand.
- A limited company is able to gain access to a wider range of borrowing opportunities than a sole trader or partnership.

Disadvantages of forming a limited company:

- Limited companies must make financial information available publicly at Companies House. Small firms are not required to make full disclosure of their company accounts, but they have to reveal more than would be the case for a sole trader or partnership.
- Limited companies have to follow more, and more expensive, rules than unlimited liability businesses, for example producing audited accounts and holding

Figure 2.1 Logic chain: sole trader or Ltd?

an annual general meeting of shareholders. These things add several thousands of pounds to annual overhead costs.

2.3 Private limited companies

A small business can be started up as a sole trader, a partnership or as a private limited company. For a private limited company, the start-up capital will often be £100, which can be wholly owned by the entrepreneur, or other people can be brought in as investors. The shares of a private limited company cannot be bought and sold without the agreement of the other directors. This means the company cannot be listed on the stock market. As a result it is possible to maintain close control over the way the business is run. This form of business is often run by a family or small group of friends. It may be very profit focused or, like Global Ethics Ltd, have wholly different objectives than maximising profit.

A legal requirement for private companies is that they must state 'Ltd' after the company name. This warns those dealing with the business that the firm is relatively small and has limited liability. Remember, limited liability protects shareholders from business debts, so there is a risk that 'cowboy' businesspeople might start a company, run it into the ground and then walk away from its debts. Therefore the cheques of a limited company are not as secure as ones from an unlimited liability business. This is why many petrol stations have notices saying 'No company cheques allowed'.

Some of the factors that may determine when a business should start up as a sole trader and when as a private limited company are outlined in Table 2.1.

Real business

One Water

In 2003, Duncan Goose quit his job and founded One Water. He wanted to finance water projects in Africa from profits made selling bottled water in Britain. The particular water project was 'Playpumps': children's roundabouts plumbed into freshly dug water wells. As the children play, each rotation of the roundabout brings up a litre of fresh, clean water.

Duncan thought of forming a charity, but felt that the regulations governing charities might force them to be inefficient. So, for the sum of £125 he founded a limited company, Global Ethics Ltd. This enabled him to set the rules, for instance that the shareholders receive no dividends and the directors receive no fees. But, of course, it ensured that he and other volunteers who put time into One Water are protected, should something go wrong and big debts build up. Today One Water is a major business trading internationally. It has raised more than £10 million, funding more than 900 Playpumps and providing clean water to more than 2 million people, permanently.

Table 2.1 Factors influencing choice between starting a new business as a sole trader or private limited company

Sole trader	Private limited company
When the owner has no intention of expanding, e.g. just wants to run one local restaurant	When the owner has ambitions to expand quickly, therefore needs it to be easier to raise extra finance
When there is no need for substantial bank borrowing, i.e. start-up costs are low	When large borrowings mean significant chances of large losses if things go wrong
When the business will be small enough to mean that one person can make all the big decisions	When the business may require others to make decisions, e.g. when the entrepreneur is on holiday or unwell

2.4 Public limited companies

When a private limited company expands to the point of having share capital of more than £50,000, it can convert to a public limited company. Then it can be floated on the stock market, which allows any member of the general public to buy shares. This increases the company's access to share capital, which enables it to expand considerably. The term 'plc' will appear after the company name, for example Marks & Spencer plc or Tesco plc.

The principal differences between private and public limited companies are:

- A public company can raise capital from the general public, while a private limited company is prohibited from doing so.
- The minimum capital requirement of a public company is £50,000. There is no minimum for a private limited company.
- Public companies must publish far more detailed accounts than private limited companies.

Most large businesses are plcs. Yet the process of converting from a private to a public company can be difficult. Usually, successful small firms grow steadily, perhaps at a rate of 10 or 15 per cent a year. Even that pace of growth causes problems, but good managers can cope. The problem of floating onto the stock market is that it provides a sudden, huge injection of cash. This sounds great, but it forces the firm to try to grow more quickly (otherwise the new shareholders will say: what are you doing with our cash?). Note that the media increasingly uses the U.S. term IPO (Initial Public Offering) instead of the British term 'flotation'.

'I couldn't be more thrilled to have control over my own destiny in a way that is not possible as a public company'. Michael Dell, after paying $25 billion to take Dell Computers private in 2013.

Real business

Poundland

From its origins as a Lincolnshire market stall in the 1990s, on 12 March 2014 Poundland was floated onto the London stock market at a valuation of £750 million. The sellers of the shares included a private equity investor and Poundland's senior management, which reduced its combined holding from 24 per cent to 10 per cent of the shares. One person who gained no benefit was Poundland's founder, Steve Smith, who sold his entire stake in the business for £50 million in 2004. If he felt aggrieved at missing out on the flotation riches, at least he could do so from the comfort of his 13-bedroom mansion.

2.5 Other forms of business organisation

Co-operatives

These can be worker owned, such as JohnLewis/Waitrose, or customer owned, such as the retail Co-op. Co-operatives have the potential to offer a more united cause for the workforce than the profit of shareholders. Workers at John Lewis can enjoy annual bonuses of 20 per cent of their salary, as their share of the company's profits. The Co-op has been less successful, though its focus on ethical trading has made it more relevant to today's shoppers.

Not-for-profit organisations
Mutual businesses

Mutual businesses, including many building societies and mutual life assurance businesses, have no shareholders and no owners. They exist solely for the best interests of members: its customers. In the 1980s and 1990s traditional mutual societies such as Abbey National and the Halifax were turned into private companies. Not one of these businesses survived the 2007–09 credit crunch without being bailed out or taken over. Nationwide now says it is 'proud to be different', as it is still a true building society in that it has no shareholders pressuring it for profits.

'Too many companies, especially large ones, are driven more and more narrowly by the need to ensure that investors get good returns and to justify executives' high salaries. Too often, this means they view employees as costs.' Hilary Clinton, US politician

Charities

Many important organisations have charitable status. These include pressure groups such as Greenpeace and Friends of the Earth. They also include conventional charities such as Oxfam and Save The Children. Charitable status ensures that those who fund the charity are not liable for any debts. It also provides significant tax benefits.

2.6 Private and public sector organisations

All the organisations mentioned above operate in the private sector. This means that they are not owned by the state; neither by national nor local government. Public sector organisations are different. They are owned by the state and therefore may have different obligations and also pressures.

Types of public sector organisation:
Public corporations

These are government-owned organisations that trade mainly with the private sector. There used to be many of these, from British Rail to British Telecom. Now most have been sold to the private sector, often forming a private monopoly such as Thames Water or Virgin West Coast Rail. Among the few remaining public corporations is the Crown Estate, which earns rental income for the government from publicly owned forests, seabeds, farming land and buildings – and also Manchester Airport, which is owned by ten councils around Manchester.

Local authority services

Until recently all local authorities ran services such as care homes for the elderly, even though there was alternative provision from the private sector. The rationale was that the public sector provision of health care was priced below the private-sector level or might even be free. In keeping with other local authorities, hit by spending cuts, Durham County Council closed its last five care homes in April 2014.

Five Whys and a How

Question	Answer
Why might an entrepreneur choose to be a sole trader instead of forming a private limited company?	To minimise administration costs – and presumably on the assumption that there will be very few risks involved in the business
Why would anyone sell goods on credit to a limited liability business?	Because they trust that the proprietors will not close the business down and shelter behind limited personal liability (some have regretted that trust)
Why might a growing business turn itself into a plc and then float its shares on the stock market?	To raise extra capital for expansion – and/or to allow the early-stage investors to sell part of their own holding (perhaps making them millionaires)
Why might 'the divorce of ownership and control' matter to an investor?	It may mean that senior management are more interested in money/power for themselves than building up the business in the long term
Why may a 'mutual' prove no more ethically sound than a profit-seeking company?	Ethics are partly a consequence of personal morality; it may be wrong to assume that those working for mutuals are any different from those working for companies
How do you form a company?	To achieve incorporation you need to complete the memorandum and the articles of association and send them, plus fee, to the Registrar of Companies

Private-public partnerships

Recent governments have promoted the idea that public services will be more efficient if run in partnership with the private sector. This led to the Private Finance Initiative, in which private sector finance was used to initiate public sector investment in hospitals, schools or transport. Although these schemes were supposed to provide better value to taxpayers, House of Commons committee reports show that the record of these schemes is patchy.

Key terms

Bankrupt: when an individual is unable to meet personal liabilities, some or all of which can be as a consequence of business activities.

Creditors: those owed money by a business, for example, suppliers and bankers.

Incorporation: establishing a business as a separate legal entity from its owners, and therefore giving the owners limited liability.

Limited liability: owners are not liable for the debts of the business; they can lose no more than the sum they invested.

Monopoly: where the sales of one business have a dominant share of its marketplace.

Registrar of Companies: the government department which can allow firms to become incorporated. It is located at Companies House, where Articles of Association, Memorandums of Association and the annual accounts of limited companies are available for public scrutiny.

Sole trader: a one-person business with unlimited liability.

Unlimited liability: owners are liable for any debts incurred by the business, even if it requires them to sell all their assets and possessions and become personally bankrupt.

Evaluation: Different business forms

Business organisation is a dry, technical subject. It does contain some important business themes, however, two of which are particularly valuable sources of evaluative comment.

1. The existence of limited liability has had huge effects on business. Some have been unarguably beneficial. How could firms become really big if the owners felt threatened by equally big debts? Limited liability helps firms to take reasonable business risks. It also, however, gives scope for dubious business practices. For example, it is possible to start a firm, live a great lifestyle, go into liquidation leaving the customers/creditors out of pocket and then start again. All too often this is the story told by programmes such as the BBC's *Watchdog*. Companies Acts lay down legislation that tries to make this harder to do, but it still happens. Such unethical behaviour is why government intervention to protect the consumer can always be justified.

2. Short-termism is a curse for effective business decision-making. There is no proof that a stock exchange listing leads to short-termism, only the suspicion that in many cases it does. Massive companies such as Unilever, Nestle and Shell may be above the pressures for short-term performance. In many other cases, though, it seems that British company directors focus too much on the short-term share price. Could this be because their huge bonuses depend on how high the share price is? Worries about shareholder pressures or takeover bids may distract managers from building a long-term business in the way that companies such as BMW and Toyota have done.

'When the operations of capitalism come to resemble the casino, ill fortune will be the lot of many.' John Maynard Keynes, economist

Workbook
A. Revision questions

(25 marks; 25 minutes)

1. Explain two differences between a sole trader and a partnership. (4)

2. In your own words, try to explain the importance of establishing a separate legal entity to separate the business from the individual owner. (4)

3. You can start a business today. All you have to do is tell HM Revenue & Customs (the taxman). Outline two risks of starting in this way. (4)

4. Briefly explain whether each of the following businesses should start as a sole trader, a partnership or a private limited company.

   a) A clothes shop started by Claire Wells with £40,000 of her own money plus £10,000 from the bank. It is located close to her home in Wrexham. (3)

   b) A builders started by Jim Barton and Lee Clark, who plan to become 'No. 1' for loft extensions in Sheffield. They have each invested £15,000 and are borrowing £30,000 from the bank. (3)

5. Explain the risks to a company of moving from a private to a public limited company by floating its shares on the stock market. (5)

6. In what way may the type of business organisation affect the image of the business? (2)

B. Revision exercises
DATA RESPONSE 1

UK business categories

In 2013 the Federation of Small Businesses estimated that there were 5 million businesses in the UK. Use this information plus the pie chart to answer the questions below.

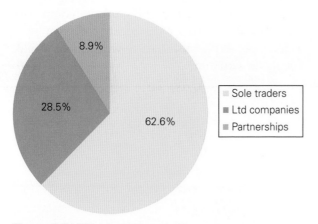

Figure 2.2 UK business organisations
Source: Office of National Statistics, October 2013

Pie chart segments: 8.9%, 28.5%, 62.6%
Legend: Sole traders, Ltd companies, Partnerships

Questions (20 marks; 20 minutes)

1. a) Calculate the number of sole traders in the UK; then calculate the number of limited companies. (3)

   b) Explain two possible reasons why there are so many more sole traders than companies. (6)

2. What proportion of British businesses operate with unlimited liability? (1)

3. In September 2014 the Federation of Small Business announced record confidence levels among its members. A survey of 2,100 small business owners showed that 61 per cent expected growth in the next twelve months. The biggest improvement was in the North East, with September 2014 showing a confidence score of +44 compared with −7 per cent the year before.

   a) Explain two possible reasons why business confidence is important for small firms. (6)

   b) Explain one possible reason why the North East enjoyed such a boost to business confidence. (4)

DATA RESPONSE 2

Starting a new business

Forming a limited company can be time-consuming compared to a sole trader which can be started straight away. According to the World Bank, the number of actions required to get started varies from 1 in New Zealand to 13 in Brazil and China. As a result of the different processes, the number of days it takes to start up varies from 1 day in New Zealand (the world's quickest) to 144 days in Venezuela (the world's slowest).

Figure 2.3 provides data selected from the World Bank's 2013–14 Global Competitiveness Report.

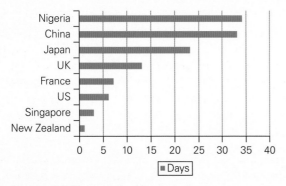

Figure 2.3 Time required to start a business
Source: Global Competitiveness Report 2013–14

Questions (20 marks; 25 minutes)

1. Briefly explain the reasons for it taking longer to set up as a limited company than as a sole trader. (5)

2. To what extent should an entrepreneur be influenced by the length of time to set up when deciding upon the most suitable business structure? (15)

C. Extend your understanding

1. Non-profit organisations such as charities and mutuals run businesses including shops and banks. To what extent would you expect better value for money from a non-profit business than from a profit-seeking business? (20)

2. Sunil Mittal, Indian software entrepreneur, once said: 'We want to manage and grow our companies ourselves. If we give up 51 per cent we might as well get out of the business.' To what extent would you agree with him? (20)

Issues in understanding forms of business

Linked to: Different business forms, Chapter 2; Sources of finance, Chapter 43; Decision-making to improve financial performance, Chapter 44.

Definition

'Forms of business' includes the factors that affect and are affected by business owners, especially shareholders.

3.1 The role of shareholders

Shareholders literally own a share of the business, proportionate to their shareholding. So an individual who has bought 50,000 shares in a business that has issued 5 million shares owns a 1 per cent stake in the company. Therefore he or she has 1 per cent of the voting rights when it comes to decisions to be made at the annual general meeting (AGM). For the company, the role of the shareholder is to provide the capital to get the business going and to keep it growing; for the shareholder, the point of share ownership is the degree of influence it gives, plus the rewards it provides (see Section 3.2).

In theory, shareholders should be proactive, raising important issues with the board of directors. In fact, many have little interest in doing so; they bought shares in the hope of a price rise or rising dividends, and may be more likely to sell shares than to spend time probing what's really happening to the company. Marks & Spencer, for example, has 188,000 shareholders, half of whom have fewer than 500 shares (with a value averaging about £1,000). Even the biggest single private investor in the company has only 3 per cent of the shares, and therefore no real say in key business decisions. Perhaps this is why the directors of Marks & Spencer have been allowed to get away with huge salaries but dismal performance. Profits in 2014 were half the level achieved in 1997/98.

Each year a public limited company must invite all its shareholders to an annual general meeting. There the shareholders have the right to question the board of directors on any aspect of the company's performance or policies. This is often a low-key affair attended by a handful of shareholders, but can sometimes burst into life when there is a controversial issue at stake. In its 2014 AGM, Barclays directors were criticised for their own pay and for the size of the bonuses paid to staff. One shareholder claimed they were 'paying for Manchester United but getting Colchester United', while another said the bank was 'a prisoner to its senior staff'. Despite these criticisms only 24 per cent of shareholders voted against the pay proposals, so the directors got their way.

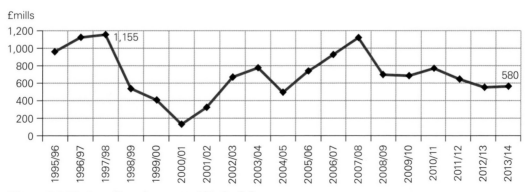

Figure 3.1 Weak profit performance at Marks & Spencer
Source: Marks & Spencer annual accounts

3.2 Shareholder rewards

There are two main financial rewards for company shareholders:

- Annual dividend payments
- A rise in the value of the shares

Annual dividend payments are decided upon by the company directors when they know the final figure for the profit for the year. Most companies have a clearly expressed dividend policy, such as Ted Baker plc's, which is to pay out around half the year's profit to its shareholders. The dividends received are in proportion to shareholdings, that is, they are allocated as a dividend per share figure multiplied by the number of shares each individual owns.

Real business

Example: the individual with a 3 per cent holding in Marks & Spencer is Bill Adderley. He owned 48.5 million M&S shares in 2014, so his annual dividend payment was:

M&S dividend per share 2014: 17p × 48.5 million shares = £8,245,000

For the average holder of 500 shares, it's 500 × £0.17 = £85 dividend for the year

For most, then, dividends are useful but not hugely significant. What a shareholder wants most of all is a rising share price. Figure 3.2 shows that an investor who had bought £1,000 of Marks & Spencer shares in 1998 would have £1,000 × $\left(\frac{434}{444}\right)$ = £977.50 by August 2014, a loss of £22.50 over a 16 year period! Some investment. By contrast the investor in Ted Baker would have turned £1,000 into £1,000 × $\frac{1805}{98.5}$ = £18,325. Sweet.

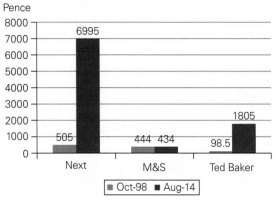

Figure 3.2 Share price growth between October 1998 and August 2014

Source: www.yahoo.finance.com

'A lot of people love Oreos. So their manufacturer is making money. That means more dividends to shareholders.' Maria Bartiromo, US TV journalist

3.3 What influences the price of shares?

What's a share in Apple Inc. worth? In August 2014 the price of one share in Apple rose above $100 in response to investor excitement at the anticipated launch of the iPhone 6 and the iWatch. Does that mean the shares were 'worth' $100? The fact is that nobody knows what a share is going to be worth in future. Nevertheless there are some clear influences on the price of shares.

The value investors place on a share depends on the profit after tax the company makes (known in the UK as its 'earnings') multiplied by the value investors place on those earnings. If investors have a great deal of confidence about the future of the business they'll pay a high multiple (70 times, in the case of Facebook in September 2014). At the same time investors valued Marks & Spencer at just 13 times earnings, i.e. much more lowly.

'With Wrigley chewing gum, it's the lack of change that appeals to me. I don't think it is going to be hurt by the internet. That's the kind of business I like.' Warren Buffett, the world's greatest stock market investor.

3.4 The significance of share price changes

In the short term there is no actual impact on a business of a change in its share price. The share capital of the business was invested *permanently* by the shareholders. So if they lose confidence in the business and want to sell their shares, they have to find another buyer – they cannot demand their money back from the company. Just as, when you buy a new car, you'll then need to find a second-hand purchaser if you want to sell it – the same is true of shares. The media love to write scary headlines about 'share price collapse' as if that means 'company collapse' – but that's not true.

In October 2008 shares in Taylor Wimpey plc hit 10p – an amazing fall from 490p eighteen months before. The collapse in UK house prices put the newly-merged Taylor and Wimpey in a difficult financial position. Amidst all the concern and gloom about whether the company could survive, 10p proved an amazing buying opportunity. By August 2014 the shares hit 117p, giving a glorious 1070 per cent profit. Despite the collapse in Taylor Wimpey's share price, no one panicked, and because the share price has no direct impact on the business, recovery was possible.

In the longer term, however, the share price can matter. If the share price is high, it makes it relatively cheap and easy to obtain more share capital. A business can carry out a rights issue which gives existing shareholders the right to buy more shares at a discount to the market value. If the share price is low and remains low, the company is unlikely to be able to raise any extra share capital, which in turn makes it harder to raise loan capital.

3.5 Issues with different forms of business

1. Unlimited and limited liability

By definition, every 'company' has limited liability. The process of incorporation means that the company is treated as a separate legal entity from those who own the business. So, if the business sells a customer a faulty item, the customer can sue the business but not the owner(s). This becomes important if the business goes into liquidation. Who can then be sued? No one. So consumers have to be wary when dealing with small, limited liability businesses.

The same warning applies to businesses themselves when selling on credit to other businesses. Since 2002 it has been possible for UK firms heading for insolvency to arrange for a 'pre-pack administration'. This allows the business's owners to write off their debts to creditors (including suppliers), yet remain in control of the business. This is how the computer games retailer Game remains in business today even though it, effectively, was bankrupt in 2012. The uncomfortable thing about pre-pack administration is that suppliers lose everything, yet the bosses who presided over a collapsing business remain in charge! After widespread complaints, the UK government spent 18 months consulting over how to make pre-packs fairer to all parties, but in 2014 it was decided to keep the rules as they are. Today, about a quarter of all businesses falling into administration use the pre-pack device. The ethics of this process remain very murky.

2. Ordinary share capital

By definition every company has ordinary share capital that has been issued to at least one shareholder. The company issues the shares in exchange for the investor's capital. The shareholders expect an annual dividend as a reward for their investment, but if the business has a lousy trading year it can choose to drop the dividend. This means that share capital is ideal for a business that naturally has ups and downs, such as one that relies on the British weather (seaside hotels; ice cream parlours, etc.) or one that relies on fashion or new technology.

Table 3.1 Ordinary share capital vs. (bank) loan capital

	Ordinary share capital	**(Bank) loan capital**
Repayment of the capital	Permanent capital therefore never has to be repaid	Lump-sum repayment at the end of the period (perhaps 3 years) strains the cash flow
Annual payments	Flexible: dividends are needed in the long term, but can be scrapped in a difficult year	Inflexible: the bank demands its interest payments every month/year, and penalises hugely those that can't pay
Dilution of control	Selling more shares to raise extra capital might threaten the founder's control of his or her own business	In theory banks have no control (nor do they take a share of future profits) but if interest payments aren't made on time, banks get very heavy-handed

3. Market capitalisation

This is the value the stock market places on the whole business by multiplying the share price by the number of shares issued. Ted Baker has 44 million shares issued and the market values each share at £18, so that's a value of £792 million. That's Ted Baker plc's market capitalisation.

The importance of the figure is that it represents the starting point for any company considering making a takeover bid. After all, if the stock market value is £792 million, any bid has to be above that level in order to persuade existing shareholders to sell. Realistically, any potential buyer of Ted Baker would know that they'd need to find at least £1,000 million to make a successful takeover bid.

4. Dividends

These are the annual reward to shareholders for their investment in the business. They represent an income to shareholders. Given that most companies grow over time, the dividends they declare tend to grow as well. So whereas interest rates on bank deposits go up and down over time (with no upward trend), dividends tend to rise over time, giving a rising income as the years go by. Rising income is especially attractive for retired people, who worry about the real value of their pensions. Figure 3.3 shows that annual dividends can be very valuable for investors who hold on to their shares for a number of years.

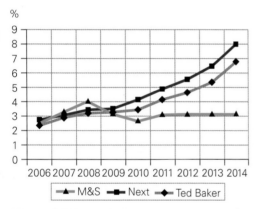

%

Figure 3.3 Rising dividend income over time (except for M&S plc)

An important issue with share dividends, though, is that there is a trade-off. The higher the dividend payout agreed by directors, the lower the amount of retained capital available for reinvestment in the business. This can be measured by looking at the dividend cover. If dividend cover is 1, it would mean the business has paid out all its profits to shareholders, leaving zero for reinvestment. At a figure of 2, half is paid out and half is retained. If you see a firm with a low dividend cover you can wonder:

a) Why are they paying out such high dividends when they're not making very much profit?

b) Will they really be able to go on paying such high dividends?

c) Are the directors propping up the share price in a short-termist way? That is, paying high dividends now at the cost of the future growth prospects (or even survival prospects) of the company.

'Investors systematically overvalue short-term payoffs and pass up investment opportunities that could leave them much better off in the longer term.' Sheila Bair, Chair, Federal Deposit Insurance Corporation

3.6 Effects of ownership on mission, objectives, decisions and performance

Most large companies are plcs and therefore have a large number of outside shareholders who may care little about the business. They simply want rising dividends and a rising share price. Companies such as Marks & Spencer have to report their latest profits every six months – so this becomes a fixation for the chief executive. Short-term thinking is the curse of a company such as Marks & Spencer, which needs plenty of time to come up with a successful new trading strategy.

This can lead to a fundamental problem: whatever the mission statement says, staff will soon learn the real priorities of senior management. If the chief executive shows clear signs of stress in the lead-up to the 6-monthly profit statement, staff will know what matters most. Ultimately, the staff that rise up the career ladder are the ones that respond best to the *real* mission, not the stated one. If the real mission is to get the 6-monthly profit to rise in order to keep the media off the boss's back – that's where the career possibilities lie. The person with an idea to cut costs by 3 per cent will be welcomed much more than another staffer with a plan for cutting greenhouse gas emissions.

'Short-termism is one of the most disturbing problems affecting modern organisations and produces some of the most common unethical behaviours.' Lorenzo Patelli, accounting academic.

Just as a staff member must uncover the real mission, so they must also understand the real business objectives – and their timescale. Every aspect of the business may be more short-term focused than is said or is written down. Naturally, this also affects decision-making and performance within every business. The long-term successes such as Whitbread plc, Ted Baker plc and Next plc have risen above short-term pressures and managed to implement sound long-term strategies. For struggling businesses such as Tesco, Morrisons' and M&S, long-term strategies can be swept aside as City analysts and the media keep their eyes on short-term performance. This can become a deadweight on the shoulders of the business.

Five Whys and a How

Question	Answer
Why might the shares of a successful company fall in price?	Because their success is less than before, leading to dampened expectations; or because a new competitor makes the future look less encouraging
Why might a company hold a rights issue?	Because it wants to raise extra share capital to finance expansion without needing to get into debt to banks
Why might a firm's market capitalisation jump up when a rival makes a takeover bid?	The bid pushes up the share price of the company being bid for, which in turn will boost its market capitalisation
Why might business ownership affect business objectives?	Ownership might affect whether the objectives are long term or short term
Why might short-termism produce unethical behaviours?	Business people may be encouraged to take shortcuts to boost profit, such as painting over cracks that really need to be mended
How do directors decide on the 'right' level of dividends to pay out?	They look at the profit for the year, work out how much capital they'll need in the coming year, and then see what dividend level they can afford

Evaluation: Issues in understanding forms of business

There is a tendency to exaggerate the role of shareholders and the stock market as a whole. The stock market raises relatively little capital to finance business expansion. The majority (about two thirds) of capital for reinvestment comes from business profits. The stock market provides less than 5 per cent of the new capital businesses need for expansion. Despite this, markets have an extraordinary hold over the decision-making by plc bosses because changes in share prices interest the public and therefore business journalists. If a struggling plc came up with an interesting new strategy that might take some years to bear fruit, few would back it.

Perhaps the incredible speed with which businesses such as Snapchat and Instagram became worth billions has strengthened the tendency to look for quick solutions to company problems. In the UK this is a greater problem than in almost every other country because of the huge influence of the City of London. In Germany in particular, the corporate heart of the country is in family business ownership, not in the stock market. This helps them take a longer-term view of the markets in which they operate.

Workbook

A. Revision questions

(35 marks; 35 minutes)

1. Comment on whether each of these questions would be suitable for a company's annual general meeting.

   a) What level of sales are we expecting from the new product you've outlined? (2)

   b) What's been the trend in our industrial accident rate lately? (2)

   c) How does our percentage change in profits compare with that of our closest rival? (2)

2. Why might shareholders argue that a company is setting its dividend levels too high? (3)

3. Another war breaks out in the Middle East, pushing oil prices up sharply. What might be the effect on the share price of these companies?

   a) British Aerospace plc, one of the world's Top 5 arms suppliers. (2)

   b) Thomas Cook, travel agency. (2)

   c) BP plc, oil supplier and retailer. (2)

4. Explain why a short-termist approach to running a business might damage a company in the long term. (5)

5. a) Examine Figure 3.3 (above) then outline two reasons why a long-term investor might be better off buying shares than holding savings in cash. (4)

   b) Despite your answer to 5(a), outline one reason why holding savings in cash may still make sense. (3)

6. Outline the advantages and disadvantages of a family-run private limited company compared with a plc. (8)

B. Revision exercises
DATA RESPONSE

Tesco: Dividend under threat?

Britain's biggest supermarket has had a torrid time in 2014 with its shares falling to a ten-year low. But things could be about to get even worse. Tesco's dividend has been called into question by some analysts, who believe the supermarket giant has no alternative but to cut payments when it next reports to the market on October 1.

Last month Tesco announced the departure of chief executive Phillip Clarke, who will be replaced by Dave Lewis, of Unilever. Mr Lewis is expected to change Tesco's strategy, perhaps to compete with the discounters, such as Aldi and Lidl. To fund the change analysts argue Tesco's only option is to cut the dividend.

The main way investors assess whether a dividend is under threat is the dividend cover. This figure shows the degree to which the dividend payment is exceeded by the company's profits. Those with a low 'cover' score are vulnerable as it means the company is paying out the majority, if not all, of its profits in the form of dividends. The higher the number the safer the dividend, with experts suggesting that a cover of two is reasonably safe. Tesco's dividend cover over the past twelve months has been 1.6, which has come down from 1.8 in 2013.

As the table below shows, Tesco shares looks pretty vulnerable to a cut when looking at the dividend cover compared to its five major competitors. But Morrisons' dividend looks even more insecure. It has been paying out all its profits in the form of dividends. So how can it finance the trading turnaround it needs?

Table 3.2

Supermarket	Dividend cover (last 12 months)	Forecast dividend cover (next 12 months)	Dividend per share
Tesco	1.6	1.8	£0.15
Sainsbury's	2.1	1.8	£0.18
Marks & Spencer	1.9	1.9	£0.17
Morrisons'	−0.8	1	£0.13
Walmart (owns Asda)	2.5	2.7	$1.9

Source: Adapted from *The Telegraph* 20 August 2014

Chris White, who manages the Premier UK Equity Income fund, says: 'We will not know until at least October, if not next year, about the direction Tesco is going to take its businesses, so it is difficult to invest today when there is so much uncertainty. The dividend is at risk, as well as its long-term strategy, so I am not buying,' said Mr White.

Questions (25 marks; 30 minutes)

1. Explain why Tesco's chief executive might be reluctant to cut its dividend. (4)

2. Based on the data in the table, explain why Morrisons' dividend 'looks even more insecure'. (5)

3. To what extent may the questions over Tesco's dividend affect the long-term market capitalisation? (16)

C. Extend your understanding

1. Figures 3.1 and 3.2 show a bleak picture of Marks & Spencer plc over recent years. To what extent may M&S shareholders be able to help the company return to profit growth? (20)

2. Reread the Warren Buffett quote on page 16. To what extent do you think that Warren Buffett is right to have placed a high value on Wrigley's shares because of 'lack of change'? (20)

External factors affecting business

Linked to: Understanding the nature and purpose of business, Chapter 1; Understanding the role and importance of stakeholders, Chapter 10; Marketing and competitiveness, Chapter 12.

Definition

External factors include competition, demographics and environmental issues. Demographic factors involve population composition and trends; environmental factors deal with short- and long-term 'green' issues.

4.1 Introduction

Business thrives on confidence. Confident consumers are willing to dip into their savings for a holiday or to borrow to buy a new carpet or car. Confident investors are willing to put more money into businesses in return for shares. And companies themselves will spend to invest in their future: new factory buildings, new machinery and new computer systems. All this spending can create an upsurge in economic activity.

The reverse also applies: gloom can spread doom. Therefore the economic climate is important (but is dealt with more fully in the second year of the A-level). This chapter covers other external factors that help to create a climate of optimism or pessimism. These factors include:

- market conditions
- competition
- changes in household incomes
- changes in interest rates
- demographic factors
- environmental issues

4.2 Market conditions

Figure 4.1 shows the tricky period for the UK economy between the start of recession in 2008 and the second quarter of 2014, when the economy finally returned to its pre-recession peak. The straight black line shows the GDP trend excluding the recession and the unprecedentedly slow recovery. The graph also shows the normal progress of the UK economy. For more than 200 years it has grown at just under 2.5 per cent per annum, i.e. growth is normal. Therefore the general expectation is that the underlying market conditions will be positive, with the size of markets expanding on a regular basis.

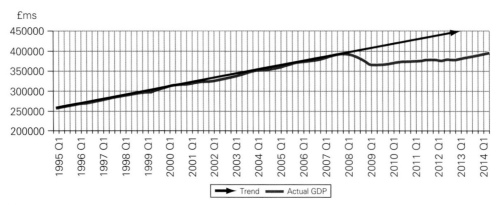

Figure 4.1 UK Gross domestic product 1995-2014

Chained volume measure, quarterly figures, seasonally adjusted

Source: Office for National Statistics

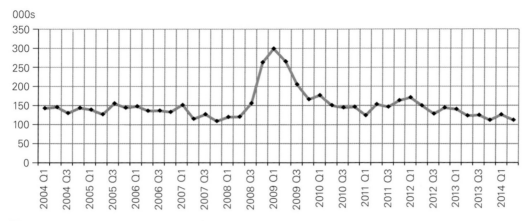

Figure 4.2 UK redundancies per quarter
Source: ILO, quoted by UK Office for National Statistics

When market conditions are as tough as in 2008/09, there are likely to be failures as businesses run out of cash (Woolworths, La Senza and many others went under). There may also be huge pressures placed on company workforces, as people are forced to choose between redundancy and real wage cuts. In the recessions of 1980 and 1990, huge job losses pushed unemployment up above 3 million. The recent recession saw instead a huge squeeze on people's real incomes, meaning that the pain was shared more fairly across the population. Government statistics show that between July 2008 and March 2014 earnings rose 8.6 per cent while prices rose 16.9 per cent. In addition to this squeeze on incomes, Figure 4.2 shows why consumer confidence was hard hit in 2009, with people worried whether they would be next for a redundancy notice. No wonder that, at times, even products like chocolate and chewing gum saw falls in sales volume as market conditions tightened.

In addition to the economy, other important factors affecting market conditions include:

● Customer taste and fashion. In 2012, for no clear reason, consumers became more sceptical of foods with 'diet' claims. One result was that WeightWatchers' yoghurts suffered a sales decline of 13.7 per cent in 2013.

● Disruptive change, resulting from radical innovation or new technology. This can mean that old-established producers are suddenly struggling to remain competitive in the face of radically new market conditions.

● The competitive structure. 70 per cent of the UK chocolate market, for example, is held by three huge firms: Mondelez (Cadbury), Mars and Nestlé. If the

structure changes (if, for example, Mars bought Ferrero of Italy), market conditions would also change – perhaps making it even harder for a new small firm to enter the chocolate market.

'There's no evidence that the business cycle has been repealed.' Alan Greenspan, former Chairman of the US central bank.

4.3 Competition

The tighter the economic and market conditions, the greater the competitive pressures tend to be. In 2009 price cutting was rife within the markets for airline travel, posh hotels, executive cars and more basic things such as furniture and carpets.

Competitive pressures stem from more than price, however. In most modern markets customers are looking for special experiences or product uniqueness to make them part with their cash. Therefore companies need to invest heavily in research and development and in the creativity of their workforce. In April – June 2014 Apple Inc. spent 36 per cent more on R&D than they had in the same period of 2013 ($1.6bn). Analysts concluded that the company was working on new products to be launched in Autumn 2014.

'Competition is the great teacher.' Henry Ford, US auto pioneer.

4.4 Changes in household incomes

According to a 2014 report, real household incomes fell by more than 6 per cent between 2007 and 2013/14. As a result of this squeeze, in the first half of 2014 supermarkets faced an unprecedented fall of 3.2 per cent in their sales volumes. A fall in sales volume had not happened since the Second World War. In addition to this decline in sales volumes, shoppers switched to discount stores to try to maintain their lifestyles. Clearly, changes in household incomes are hugely significant.

Household income is affected by three main things:

1. Changes in the real incomes of the main breadwinners. Generally, economies expand and therefore sales of most goods and services follow suit. The only exceptions are 'inferior goods'.

2. The number within the household who work. Partly this is a function of how many people are in the household at all. One reason consumer spending didn't fall *further* in the recession was that fewer young people left home. So instead of two households, each having to face electricity bills and so forth, more were crammed into one house. This helped to offset some of the spending pressure from falling real wages. Another important factor was the rise in the number of people taking part-time jobs.

3. The impact of government decisions on taxation and benefits. The impact of tax changes has been broadly neutral in recent years, but cutbacks in benefits (especially to the disabled) have hit the spending power of many. In 2014 The Trussell Trust reported that the use of food banks rose from 346,992 people in 2012/13 to 913,138 people in 2013/14.

'The last thing you want to do is raise taxes in the middle of the recession.' Barack Obama, US President.

For every business it is invaluable to forecast the rate of change in household incomes. As with every economic forecast, this is easier to say than to do.

Index numbers and household income

Both economic and business data are often analysed using index numbers. An index means converting a series of data into figures that all relate to a base period where the data is equal to 100. This allows users of the data to see at a glance the percentage changes and trends. In the table below, Column A shows changes in the total price of the average household's shopping basket. As you can see, this rises from £402 in 2005 to £514 in 2014. Column B converts that complex data into an index. This starts by saying 'let £402 = 100', then all the other figures in Column A are related to that base figure of 100 by showing the percentage change from that base figure. For example, the figure for 2014 is $\frac{£514.15}{£402} \times 100 = 127.9$.

The advantage of index numbers is that you can see quickly that, for example, prices rose by 27.9 per cent between 2005 and 2014. So index numbers help you understand trends rather more easily.

Table 4.1 Changes in the average household shopping basket using the Consumer Prices Index

	A. Shopping basket price (£s)	B. Consumer Price Index 2005 = 100
2005	£402	100
2006	£411.25	102.3
2007	£420.90	104.7
2008	£436.20	108.5
2009	£445.40	110.8
2010	£460.30	114.5
2011	£480.80	119.6
2012	£494.45	123.0
2013	£506.90	126.1
2014	£514.15	127.9
2015 est	£524.60	130.5

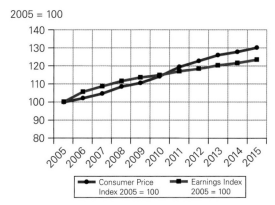

Figure 4.3 Price index vs. earning index
Source: Office of National Statistics, October 2014

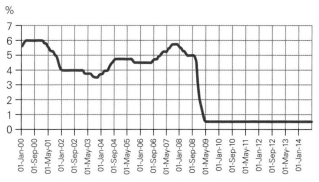

Figure 4.4 UK bank interest rates, 2000–14
Source: www.bankofengland.co.uk

Their other huge benefit is that they enable direct comparisons to be made between different data series. In the case of price changes (shown by the consumer price index), the interesting recent comparison is with household incomes. This data is shown in Figure 4.3. It shows incomes outstripping prices in 2006 and 2007, but then being dragged back until – from 2011 – the income rises fall behind price rises. That means living standards falling – year after year.

If we had tried to plot the actual figures for price increase or earnings on the same graph, the different scales needed would make a comparison difficult.

4.5 Changes in interest rates

The interest rate is the price charged by a bank per year for lending money or for providing credit. Individual banks decide for themselves about the rate they will charge on their credit cards or for the overdrafts they provide. But they are usually influenced by the interest rate that the Central Bank charges high street banks for borrowing money: the bank rate. In Britain, this is set each month by a committee of the Bank of England. As shown in Figure 4.4, the standard rate of interest in the UK has generally been around 4 to 5 per cent. In March 2009, though, the rate was cut to its lowest point in the Bank of England's history: 0.5 per cent. And it remained there as a way of helping to revive an economy hit very hard by the 2009 recession.

'Never has so much money been owed by so few to so many.' Mervyn King, Governor Bank of England, on the £1,000 billion bailout from taxpayers to Britain's banks.

The Bank of England committee is asked to set interest rates at a level that should ensure UK prices rise by around 2 per cent per year. If the committee members decide that the economy is growing so strongly that prices may rise faster than 2 per cent, it will increase interest rates. Then people will feel worried about borrowing more (because of the higher repayment cost) and may cut their spending. This should help to discourage firms from increasing their prices.

For firms, the level of interest rates is very important because:

● It affects consumer demand, especially for goods bought on credit, such as houses and cars. The higher the rate of interest, the lower the sales that can be expected.

● The interest charges affect the total operating costs (that is, the higher the interest rate, the higher the costs of running an overdraft, and therefore the lower the profit).

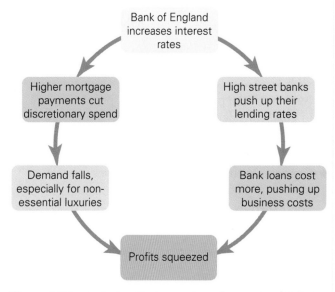

Figure 4.5 Logic chain: effect on costs and revenues of rising interest rates

- The higher the rate of interest, the less attractive it is for a firm to invest money in the future of the business. Therefore, there is a risk of falling demand for items such as lorries, computers and factory machinery.

If interest rates fall, the opposite effects occur, to the benefit of both companies and the economy as a whole.

4.6 Demographic factors

Demographics looks at the make-up of the population. This can usefully start with population size. With a healthy, rising population, the United Nations predicts that the UK will catch up with the population of Germany by 2050. Also interesting is Nigeria's dramatic rise, perhaps to overtake the US, and population decline in Japan, China and Germany. For companies, expanding into Nigeria currently looks more exciting than Japan.

Table 4.2 Population changes predicted by the United Nations in 2012 (all figures in millions)

	2013	2015	2050
Germany	83	81	73
UK	63	67	73
USA	320	351	401
Nigeria	174	240	440
Japan	127	123	108
China	1,386	1,449	1,385
India	1,252	1,419	1,620

For businesses, other key population variables include:

- Age – with the proportion of older people forecast to grow considerably, creating opportunities for the companies that can find the relevant products or services
- Gender – with products such as games consoles tending to be male, while cosmetics remains dominated by female purchasing
- Ethnicity – with opportunities already seized in sectors such as cosmetics, magazines and fast food, there may yet be more opportunities for products targeted at specific ethnicities in the markets for food, soft drinks and confectionery.

4.7 Environmental issues and Fairtrade

With changes in the economy, firms can choose how to react but their decision-making powers are limited. With social or moral questions about green issues or Fairtrade supplies, firms have a great deal more scope to choose what to do. They may decide to do the minimum, focusing on profit-maximisation. This would be entirely understandable if the survival of the business was under threat. Other business, though, might choose to do more than the minimum for moral or ethical reasons. Some bosses, though, see something like Fairtrade as a great marketing tool for selling more chocolate, or coffee or whatever. In other words, they view environmental or ethical issues merely as business opportunities.

There are four factors to consider here.

1. The immediate effect on the environment of actions businesses take, especially the impact on the local community. Some of these represent a straight choice between profit and social responsibility, such as fly-tipping. Because the UK has a landfill tax, it costs builders £80 per tonne to dispose of waste materials. Some are tempted to save their money by dumping waste at the side of roads. This fly-tipping disfigures landscapes and is a grimly cynical way to boost a firm's profit.

2. Sustainability, that is making sure that the actions of your business will not rob future generations of the availability of key resources. Toilet roll brand Velvet states on every pack that they plant three trees for every one cut down to make the paper. Other companies may pay less regard for the long-term future.

3. Global warming. The issue here is the impact of the business on greenhouse gases such as CO_2. In a year, people and businesses globally generate 31,600 million tonnes of CO_2. Some companies make a considerable effort to minimise their own 'carbon footprint'; others do not.

4. Fairtrade supplies, that is whether a business chooses to sign an agreement that all its raw materials will be bought through the Fairtrade organisation. This should guarantee that all supplies will be bought on terms that are more favourable to the farmers/producers than the usual market price. Typically these agreements are for a minimum of five years, thereby helping Fairtrade producers such as Uganda's Gumutindo Coffee Co-operative.

Five Whys and a How

Question	Answer
Why might Aldi and Lidl struggle when the UK economy starts to generate higher real incomes?	Because their sales boom in the 2010-2014 period may have been due to 'downtrading', as people switched to lower suppliers, therefore the reverse may happen as the economy recovers
Why might a rise in competition mean a fall in standards?	Usually consumers benefit from competition, but with complex products such as pensions, suppliers may compete to see who can exploit ('rip-off') customers the most effectively
Why might a rise in interest rates hit profits at a business such as Tesco?	Higher interest rates hit consumers' discretionary income, so spending falls (and so does Tesco revenue); also, higher rates force Tesco to pay more on its bank borrowings/overdrafts
Why may a move to Fairtrade supply damage the profits of a chocolate manufacturer?	If the higher supply costs are not outweighed by higher sales volume or higher consumer prices, Fairtrade supply will inevitably dent profits
Why may fly-tipping rise in recessions?	If builders are struggling to survive, fly-tipping may be a tempting way to cut costs
How are real incomes measured?	By deducting price rises from the changes in people's incomes, for example, 3 per cent more income but prices up 5 per cent - you're 2 per cent worse off in real purchasing power

Evaluation: External factors affecting business

When companies publish their annual results commentators groan if the boss blames disappointing results on external factors such as the weather or the weakness of the economy. Business journalists admire chief execs who achieve their targets no matter what. Yet that may not be realistic. If you're running Coca-Cola you have huge control over your pricing and therefore can probably find a way to boost profits to meet analysts' expectations.

Most firms, though, are vulnerable to external factors. Even monopolies (when a single firm dominates a market) are subject to changing consumer habits, as Microsoft and even Apple have found in recent years. If things seem to be going wonderfully well, and every commentator thinks your business is bulletproof, it's probably time to worry. The one-time boss of monopolist microchip supplier Intel, Andy Grove, once said that 'only the paranoid survive'. That remains grimly true.

Key terms

Consumer demand: the levels of spending by consumers in general (not just the demand from one consumer).

Discretionary income: a person's income after deducting taxes and fixed payments such as rent and utility bills.

Disruptive change: a new initiative that changes the rules within a market or within factory production; its radically different design meant that the iPad did exactly that within the market for tablet computers.

Economic climate: the atmosphere surrounding the economy (for example, 'gloom and doom' or 'optimism and boom').

GDP (Gross Domestic Product) is the value of all the goods and services sold throughout the economy over a period of time (annually or perhaps per quarter), **Inferior goods** suffer falling sales when people are better off, and rising sales when people are worse off. (Think Poundland or Iceland frozen foods.)

Real: changes in money (for example, wages) excluding the distorting effect of changes in prices. So a fall in real wages might mean that wages are unchanged but prices have risen.

Recession: a downturn in sales and production that occurs across most parts of the economy, perhaps leading to six months of continuous economic decline.

Workbook

A. Revision questions

(30 marks; 30 minutes)

1. Explain why a fall in spending in London could have a knock-on effect on the economy in Bradford, Plymouth, Norwich or anywhere else in the country. (3)

2. Explain whether the Bank of England should raise or cut interest rates in the following circumstances:

   a) a sharp recession has hit the UK economy. (3)

   b) house prices have risen by 16 per cent in each of the last two years. (3)

   c) household incomes and spending have been rising rapidly. (3)

3. Outline how an economic downturn could affect the level of unemployment. (5)

4. a) Outline a demographic change that could boost sales at Mothercare. (2)

   b) Explain the possible impact on a supermarket chain of an increase in inward migration to the UK. (5)

5. What is meant by the term 'Fairtrade'? (2)

6. Outline two possible reasons why a manufacturer of chemicals might invest more heavily in anti-pollution measures. (4)

B. Revision exercises

DATA RESPONSE

External pressures on the grocery market

The booming discount supermarket chain Aldi is on the verge of overtaking upmarket Waitrose to become the UK's sixth biggest supermarket as the German-owned grocer continues to open new stores and steal customers from its bigger rivals. Industry data released yesterday shows that while Tesco and Morrisons' continue to decline, Aldi's share of grocery till receipts rose to 4.8 per cent in the 12 weeks to 20 July 2014. A year ago the discounter's market share was 3.7 per cent, according to figures from retail analysts Kantar Worldpanel.

Over the same period, Waitrose's market share edged up to 4.9 per cent from 4.8 per cent last year, while Tesco dropped to 28.9 per cent from 30.3 per cent. The data confirms the trend of shoppers abandoning mid-market players in favour of more upmarket rivals and the discounters, with increasing numbers of shoppers cherry-picking from both ends of the market. 'Waitrose has continued to resist pressure from the competition, testament to its policy of maximum differentiation, and has grown sales by 3.4 per cent. This figure is well above the market average and thereby has lifted its market share', according to Edward Garner, director of Kantar.

Despite this positivity, *The Grocer* magazine has questioned whether Waitrose is now starting to suffer. Its profit margins at 5.4 per cent are well above industry averages, and perhaps shoppers are starting to query its value for money. Partly because of its high prices, Waitrose offers free delivery to online grocery shoppers. With online sales booming it may be that Waitrose profits start to get squeezed by the free delivery, given that picking and delivery is far from free from the shop's point of view.

The numbers come against a backdrop of a challenging market. Kantar says grocery price inflation has fallen for the tenth successive period and now stands at just 0.4 per cent – its lowest level since prices were first measured in 2006. As a result, market growth has fallen to 0.9 per cent.

Tim Vallance, head of retail at property group JLL, said: 'The figures highlight the impact that the big four's response to the rise of the discount retailers is having on the grocery sector, with vicious price cutting leading to shrinking market growth. As shoppers continue to demand a more convenient offer in an increasingly digital world, supermarkets need to think about how and where their customers shop and need to focus on choice, provenance, quality, service and convenience to differentiate from the discounter offering.'

Sources: adapted from *The Guardian*, 30 July 2014 and *The Grocer*, 9 August 2014

Questions (25 marks; 35 minutes)

1. Analyse the market conditions faced by Waitrose at this time. (9)

2. To what extent would Waitrose have been wise, at this time, to have differentiated itself further by switching entirely to Fairtrade supplies? (16)

C. Extend your understanding

1. To what extent may demographic changes influence the future plans of a business that you know? (20)

2. In the last recession, the UK steel company Corus closed its Scunthorpe steelworks, making hundreds redundant. Discuss the strategies Corus, or other companies you have researched, could have adopted to prepare for recession. (20)

What managers do

Linked to: Understanding the nature and purpose of business, Chapter 1; Managers, leadership and decision-making, Chapter 6; Motivation and engagement in theory, Chapter 46; Improving organisational design, Chapter 48.

Definition

Managers organise and galvanise staff into implementing the strategies needed to achieve the business objectives.

5.1 Introduction

A recent study of jobs across Europe showed that a higher percentage of UK employees defined themselves as 'managers' than in any other country. In the UK 11.6 per cent said they were managers; in Germany the figure was 4.7 per cent and in Denmark just 2 per cent. The report's authors concluded that the British are happier describing themselves as managers than in other countries. Elsewhere, the term 'professional' or 'technician' seems more desirable.

So what is this job that the British seem so keen on? Essentially it's about making things happen. For example, a school might employ a company to design a new website. A manager at the school will be put in charge of the project; that person will make sure that the agreed contract will be delivered on time and within budget. This will require meetings, briefings and contacts to make sure everything is running smoothly. At the end of the project, many of the 'sign-offs' will be straightforward, such as agreeing that yes, the site allows downloads and yes, all the hyperlinks work. Others will require judgement, such as the design of the home page: Professional-looking? Distinctive? Well-branded? And so on.

In effect, the professionals or technicians are doing the time-consuming and tricky things; the manager is just the overseer. Does that represent a satisfying job? In fact, recent research suggests that managers do enjoy their jobs. Seven of the top 20 places (out of 274 job categories) were taken up by managers. Table 5.1 shows, among other things, the lack of correlation between job satisfaction and income.

'Management is getting paid for home runs someone else hits.' Casey Stengel, baseball player and manager

Table 5.1 Cabinet Office Research into Jobs and Life Satisfaction, March 2014

Top 3 for job satisfaction	Salary (2013)	Score out of 10
1. Clergy	£20,568	8.291
2. Chief executives and senior officials	£117,700	7.957
3. Managers and proprietors in agriculture and horticulture	£31,721	7.946
Bottom 3 for job satisfaction		
272. Debt and rent collectors	£17,371	6.56
273. Elementary construction occupations	£20,910	6.389
274. Publicans	£25,222	6.38

5.2 The academic study of what managers do

The first significant study of management was by Henri Fayol, a French business executive. His key book General and Industrial Management (1916) suggested that 'to manage is to forecast and plan, to organise, to command, to co-ordinate and to control'. This list reads perfectly well a hundred years later, though in the modern world there would be an attempt to make it sound less like an Army general giving out orders.

Fayol's list formed the basis of Henry Mintzberg's attempt in the 1970s to identify what, exactly, managers did with their time. Was it all spent planning and controlling? In fact careful research showed that, on average, managers were only able to carry out an activity for 9 minutes before being interrupted. He was able to show that instead of management being a careful, intellectual process of planning, managers were fallible humans being interrupted continuously. To describe the work of a manager, Mintzberg identified six characteristics of the role:

1. Managers process large, open-ended workloads under tight time pressure
2. Managerial activities are short in duration, varied and fragmented and often self-initiated
3. Managers prefer action-driven activities and hate letters, (emails) and paperwork
4. They prefer verbal communications through meetings and phone calls
5. They maintain relationships mainly with subordinates and external parties – least with their superiors.
6. Their involvement in the execution of the work is limited though they initiate many of the decisions.

In truth, Mintzberg's list risks understating the relative chaos he identified. He found that management was largely reactive, fighting short-term fires and often failing to put them out.

'If you ask managers what they do, they will most likely tell you that they plan, organise, co-ordinate and control. Then watch what they do. Don't be surprised if you can't relate what you see to those four words.' Henry Mintzberg, academic and author

If Mintzberg had become the expert on what managers do, Peter Drucker remained the key figure in saying what they *should* do. To Drucker, the key was to keep the manager's eyes on the prize – and that prize was reaching the objectives. It is important to bear in mind that Drucker's key research and writing about business was between 1944 and 1950. In other words, towards the end of – and just after – the Second World War. Although Drucker wanted managers to develop staff and use them humanely, he was even more seized by the need to achieve the mission, be it defeating Hitler or finding a way to survive in a tough competitive environment.

So, what should managers do, according to Drucker?

1. Set clear objectives that all staff believe in
2. Find the right team for meeting the objectives. Drucker believed strongly in teamwork, but knew that many individuals would need to be taught/coached to devote their personal strengths to the group.
3. Help ensure that all staff are motivated. He did not regard 'employee satisfaction' as a relevant measure of this; he thought motivation came from within when people were given responsibility. Therefore delegation was a central management task.
4. Drucker was very conscious of the way that factory automation had eliminated certain job roles; he expected this process to grow in future. Therefore, he thought that managers needed to prepare staff for change in general, and specifically help staff learn to learn –thereby being able to adapt to changing job prospects in the future.

'A manager's job should be based on a task to be performed in order to attain the company's objectives… the manager should be directed and controlled by the objectives of performance rather than by his boss.' Peter Drucker, management guru

From the above analysis of the writings of Fayol, Mintzberg and Drucker it is possible to put together a list of the key roles of managers. This is developed in section 5.3.

5.3 The role of managers should include:

Setting objectives: managers need a clear idea of what they want to achieve. This, of course, will depend upon the company-wide (or 'corporate') objectives. The objectives need to be set clearly and specifically – and then put into language that all staff can understand. Especially in the modern world where half the staff may be temporary or part-time, it is vital to boil the objectives down into an easily-remembered phrase.

Analysing: there are three aspects of this that matter:
- Analysing the underlying conditions the business faces (which may lead to new objectives being set)
- Analysing the performance of different staff; in 2012 Morrisons' supermarkets decided to set its checkout staff the target of scanning items in no more than 3 seconds. The company announced that staff who consistently failed to meet the target would be moved to other jobs in-store.
- Analysing how effectively objectives are being met.

Leading: inspiring staff commitment to achieving the goals, in whatever way works for the individual. Some may do this by charisma, that is, by using the power of their personality; others may inspire because of their personal achievements or commitment; finally there may be leadership through effective control and direction – helping staff to see exactly what they must do to be successful. This topic is covered fully in Chapter 6.

Making decisions: though perhaps this should say 'getting decisions made' because it may be that the manager will delegate the task to junior staff. With decision-making, the key is to understand that some decisions have to be made by specific deadlines – even though this may be too early to have all the facts available. Successful managers will have confidence that no one will expect them to get every decision right. A success rate above 50 per cent is pretty impressive in most contexts.

Reviewing: this is hard to do when the outcome from a decision has been poor, therefore it is excellent business practice to insist that every decision be reviewed – perhaps by a small team that should include someone who was not involved in the original decision.

In the long run the businesses that succeed will be the ones that learn most from their mistakes – and from their successes.

'A manager's task is developing and maintaining a culture that promotes work.' Blake and Mouton, *The Managerial Grid.*

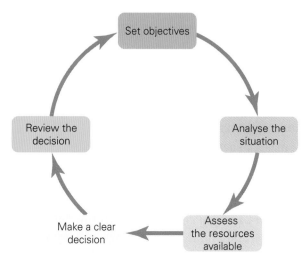

Figure 5.1 Logic chain: how managers make decisions

Five Whys and a How

Question	Answer
Why may management represent a satisfying job?	Because it has responsibility and some autonomy (independence), giving it some important motivators
Why may the clergy find more satisfaction from their job than anyone else?	Presumably they get satisfaction from helping people (their flock); and there's probably a lot of responsibility involved
Why may managers prefer verbal to written communication (according to Mintzberg)?	Perhaps because it makes it easier to get feedback/provoke discussion and also may help in building more team spirit
Why might Drucker have emphasized teamwork?	Because a key lesson of the Second World War was that allies can work effectively with each other – as long as they share a common objective
Why may it be hard for managers to analyse the underlying conditions they face?	Because the constant interruptions they face (every 9 minutes, says Mintzberg) would make it hard to concentrate on the research
How might managers react to Mintzberg's findings about what managers actually do?	They would want to avoid constant interruptions and firefighting; they might demand to work from home one day a week – or close their office door once a week – to create the opportunity to plan

Evaluation: What managers do

Mintzberg's research captured the mismatch between management in theory and in practice. One expects managers to be thinking, planning and controlling. Instead they're having to react to a series of short-term pressures. Are things any different today? Recent research suggests that little has changed since 1973. So managers keep themselves busy, but may not achieve much.

One way to change this is to delegate more – and to truly resist the temptation to meddle. Then you can tell your staff to come back when *they* have sorted out the

problems. Another way to achieve the same objective is to ban people coming to see you on certain days – but realistically that will just build up a lot of pressure for the 'on' days.

What Mintzberg doesn't quite resolve is whether managers like an over-interrupted existence and therefore encourage it (perhaps unconsciously). Not only would it make the manager feel very important, but it would also save her or him from having to do the hard bit: thinking and planning.

'Failing organisations are usually over-managed, but under-led.' Warren Bennis, business academic

---

Key terms

Co-ordinate: the management task of ensuring that staff carrying out different parts of a project are all working to the same time schedule and quality standards.

Subordinates: those working for a manager and therefore under his or her command.

Workbook

A. Revision questions

(25 marks; 25 minutes)

1. **a)** Within the text covering Fayol, distinguish between 'commanding' and 'controlling'. (4)

   b) Explain why each is important to the completion of a project task. (4)

2. Explain in your own words the meaning behind Casey Stengel's quote (see page 30). (4)

3. In relation to Mintzberg, what might be the implications of management activities being 'self-initiated'? (4)

4. Explain in your own words Drucker's view on the implications of rising levels of automation. (4)

5. Other than learning from your mistakes, what else may be the benefit to a business of reviewing activities and decisions? (5)

B. Revision exercises
DATA RESPONSE

In the past 18 months Waterstones bookshops have been following a new strategy. Authority has been delegated to each store manager, allowing each to decide on the right range of books for their local area. So whereas a bookstore in one part of town might stock romance and crime, close to the University there might be academic books plus a big section on pop music. In addition, there has been a huge push to train staff to know more and therefore be more

helpful to customers. The staff member at the till alongside the crime novels should be knowledgeable and interested in these books.

All this might seem obvious, but for the previous 10 years Waterstones' management had done the reverse. All buying decisions were made at Head Office, and all the stores ended up with the same range of stock (mainly based on the Top 50 sellers), sold on a Buy One Get One Half Price promotional model. Waterstones had ended up with this approach when confronted with twin-pincer competition from supermarkets on the one hand ('New Harry Potter for £9.99!') and Amazon on the other. But trying to beat these rivals on the basis of price was a lost cause. The supermarkets would cherry-pick the Top 20 titles and slash their price, while Amazon not only benefited from much lower overheads (no High Street rents) but also from a tax dodge that saw all sales go through Luxembourg, eliminating UK corporation tax. The latter arrangement still exists, giving wealthy Amazon an unfair competitive advantage.

The decision to allow the store managers to choose their own stock preferences might prove highly successful. It will not only make the stores more interesting for customers to visit, but should also provide the store manager with the motivation that comes from responsibility and from the level of challenge that comes with it.

Questions (25 marks; 30 minutes)

1. Analyse whether Drucker would agree with the new strategy at Waterstones. (9)

2. To what extent should Waterstones back up its policy of delegation by offering financial incentives to its store managers? (16)

ASSIGNMENT

Make an appointment to interview a curriculum manager within your school/college (ask your teacher for advice). Then find out:

- Their main areas of responsibility
- How much time they try to devote to each
- How long is it, on average, before they're interrupted from what they're trying to do?

- What they see as the pros and cons of a management role compared with being a classroom teacher.

Write up your findings making comparisons with Mintzberg where helpful. The assignment should be completed in no more than 500 words.

C. Extend your understanding

1. Henry Mintzberg has written that 'the pressures of the job drive the manager to take on too much work, encourage interruption, respond quickly to every stimulus, seek the tangible and avoid the abstract, make decisions in small increments and do everything abruptly.' To what extent does this description fits in with Drucker's view of what the manager's job should be? (20)

2. Within the UK Civil Service, 53 per cent of employees are female and 9.6 per cent are non-white. Among senior management Civil Service grades, 36 per cent are women and 4.8 per cent are non-white. (2013 figures published by the ONS). Discuss what might be done to address the under-representation of women and non-whites in senior management posts in the UK today. (20)

Managers, leadership and decision-making

Linked to: Understanding the nature and purpose of business, Chapter 1; What managers do, Chapter 5; Motivation and engagement in theory, Chapter 46; Improving organisational design, Chapter 48.

Definition

Leadership means taking the initiative to set clear objectives and to motivate or guide staff towards their achievement. Management means organising and galvanising staff to implement the strategies needed to achieve the objectives.

6.1. Introduction

In 2013 the UK's best paid boss was Angela Ahrendts, the Chief Executive of Burberry plc. She received £16.9 million in 2013 and was then 'poached' by Apple, who may be about to pay her close to $100 million a year in future. That's a salary that even Christiano Ronaldo can only dream of (he has to 'get by' on £400,000 a week, way short of $2m a week for Angela). She did a wonderful job for Burberry, building it into a serious global luxury brand – with an especially strong position in China. The main criticism of such pay levels, though, is whether it can be morally right for the boss to be paid 1,000 times as much as shop floor staff. Is leadership ever worth that much?

In recent years business leadership has become an industry in itself. It is assumed that dynamic success comes from dynamic, charismatic leaders. By implication, therefore, these fabulous people are worth fabulous sums of money.

Sometimes, this is unarguably true. What was Sir Alex Ferguson 'worth' to Manchester United? And what was Sir Ken Morrison worth, in building his small supermarket business into a national chain between 1967 and 2008? He was worth lots, undeniably lots. Great leaders exist, and they are worth big financial rewards. Unfortunately, there are many examples of ordinary leaders with ordinary achievements also being paid huge sums. Even though the amount paid may be relatively trivial for a big business, the implications are very significant. The media may over-emphasise the importance of 'the great leader', making it harder for intelligent, but modest, bosses to be given time to succeed.

Real business

In January 2014 the value of Sainsbury's shares fell by £400 million when boss Justin King announced that he would be standing down after a decade as the chief executive. When he arrived Sainsbury's was struggling after:

● losing its 'No. 1' position to Tesco

● wasting £1 billion on a stock control system that didn't work

● a marketing debacle in which they had to scrap a very expensive TV campaign because sales *fell* when the commercial ran!

In the decade that followed Justin King kept completely focused on rebuilding the Sainsbury's UK business. He didn't allow himself to get distracted by overseas adventures, and managed to keep on top of the three big stories in UK grocery in the past ten years: the growth of online ordering; the growth of smaller convenience stores and the continuing concern over diet and health. During his tenure Sainsbury's profits trebled to £750 million a year. King's remuneration was as high as £2.6 million a year – but it is easy to see that his sensibly focused approach meant that he was worth it.

6.2 Introduction to leadership styles

The way in which bosses deal with their employees is known as their leadership style. For example, some managers are quite strict with workers. They always expect deadlines to be met and targets to be hit. Others are more relaxed and understanding. If there is a good reason why a particular task has not been completed by the deadline, they will be willing to accept this and give the employee more time. Although the way in which managers manage will vary slightly from individual to individual, their styles can be categorised under three headings: autocratic, democratic and paternalistic. See Table 6.1.

Autocratic managers

Autocratic managers are authoritarian: they tell employees what to do and do not listen much to what workers themselves have to say. Autocratic managers tend to use one-way, top-down communication. They give orders to workers and do not want feedback.

'You do not lead by hitting people over the head – that's assault, not leadership.' Dwight Eisenhower, US President

Democratic leaders

Democratic leaders, by comparison, like to involve their workers in decisions. They tend to listen to employees' ideas and ensure people contribute to the discussion. Communication by democratic managers tends to be two-way. Bosses put forward an idea and employees give their opinion. A democratic leader will regularly delegate decision-making power to junior staff.

The delegation of authority, which is at the heart of democratic leadership, can be approached in one of two main ways: management by objectives and laissez faire.

Management by objectives

In this situation the leader agrees clear goals with staff, provides the necessary resources, and allows day-to-day decisions to be made by junior staff. These goals will necessarily be SMART, that is Specific, Measurable, Achievable, Relevant and Timebound. As a consequence, junior staff know that their efforts will be monitored against specific targets, such as: 'cut factory wastage costs per unit by 5 per cent within the next 18 months.'

Laissez-faire

Meaning 'let it be', this occurs when leaders are so busy, or so lazy, that they do not take the time to ensure that junior staff know what to do or how to do it. Some people may respond very well to the freedom to decide how to spend their working lives; others may become frustrated. It is said that Bill Gates, in the early days of Microsoft, hired brilliant students and told them no more than to create brilliant software. Was this a laissez-faire style or management by objectives? Clearly the dividing line can be narrow.

Figure 6.1 Manager and employee

Paternalistic leaders

A paternalistic leader thinks and acts like a father. He or she tries to do what is best for their staff/children. There may be consultation to find out the views of the employees, but decisions are made by the head of the 'family'. This type of boss believes employees need direction but thinks it is important that they are supported and cared for properly. Paternalists are interested in the security and social needs of staff.

'As for the best leaders, the people do not notice their existence. The next best, the people honour and praise. The next, the people fear; and the next, the people hate… When the best leader's work is done the people say, "We did it ourselves."' Lao-Tsu, quoted in Townsend, R., and Joseph, M., *Further up the Organisation*

Table 6.1 Assumptions and approaches of the three types of leader

	Democratic	Paternalistic	Autocratic
Approach to staff	Delegation of authority	Consultation with staff	Orders must be obeyed
Approach to staff remuneration	Salary, perhaps plus employee shareholdings	Salary plus extensive fringe benefits	Payment by results, e.g. piece rate
Approach to human resource management	Recruitment and training based on attitudes and teamwork	Emphasis on training and appraisal for personal development	Recruitment and training based on skills; appraisal linked to pay

6.3 Blake's Grid

Following research conducted between 1958 and 1960, Robert Blake and Jane Mouton developed a grid for analysing styles of leadership. The Blake and Mouton Grid looks at two leadership behaviours: 'concern for people' and 'concern for performance'. It then grades people on each of these scales to formulate a judgement on the type of leader they are. If, for example, a leader was obsessed with success at all costs, no matter what the impact on staff, they would be a 9,1 (Highest concern for performance; lowest concern for people). When appointed Fulham manager in the 2013/14 season, Felix Magath was called 'Saddam' and 'The Torturer' by former players. A 9,1 to be sure. By contrast, the best two post-war managers, Brian Clough and Alex Ferguson were both concerned about their people as well as their performance. Both were highly paternalistic; both were 9,9s. That was the combination viewed by Blake and Mouton as the leadership ideal.

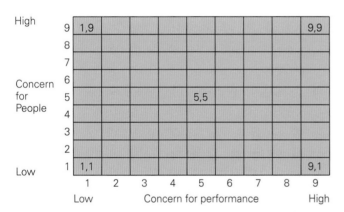

Figure 6.2 The Managerial Grid, Blake and Moulton 1964
Source: Based on *Gridworks* by Robert Blake, Jane Mouton and Walter Barclay, Scientific Methods Inc. 1993

The labels that Blake and Mouton gave for each of the 5 leadership types were:

9,9 – Team management/Teamwork

9,1 – Authority/Obedience

5,5 – Middle-of-the-road management

1,9 – Country club management

1,1 – Impoverished management

To elaborate further, it can be said that:

● 9,9 (Team management): the boss shows interest and trust in staff, with a full belief in the synergy implied by successful teamwork (the whole is greater than the sum of the parts). Despite this, the steely determination to succeed would make it very tough for any team member who wasn't contributing effectively.

● 9,1 (Authority/Obedience): a fanatical drive to succeed, but on the leader's own terms ('my way or the highway'); staff are truly 'human resources', to be used or cast aside like any other resources; strongly linked to an authoritarian leadership style – and perhaps too likely to succeed in the short term only; in the longer term, good staff will leave.

● 5,5 (Middle of the Road): a decent, honest attempt to get the best of both worlds, but struggling to succeed at either; too willing to trade being nice for being successful; think mid-table obscurity or OK-but-not-great performance; when times are good, investors may not realise that it's all a bit second-rate. A famous Warren Buffet saying comes into effect, though, when times are tough: 'Only when the tide goes out do you discover who's been swimming naked.'

● 1,9 (Country Club): the boss is a really nice person; the staff love her or him but can't stop themselves taking advantage of the situation. There's a lack of urgency about getting things done – and probably quite shockingly poor productivity. This situation can only survive if monopoly power is keeping competition away from the business.

● 1,1 (Impoverished management): the boss has neither concern for the staff nor the performance of the business. Some writers have related this to Laissez faire management, but that may be harsh; some laissez faire managers see advantage in letting staff think and work for themselves. In the case of a 1,1 manager, there is absolutely no interest in the business or the people working for it.

In a later development of their theory, Blake and Mouton accepted that a sixth possibility was an entirely opportunistic approach to leadership in which the leader would adopt any style that would help in achieving a specific objective. This might be for no better reason than to maximise the leader's personal remuneration.

'A leader is like a shepherd. He stays behind the flock, letting the most nimble go out ahead, whereupon the others follow, nor realizing that all along they are being directed from behind.' Nelson Mandela

6.4 The Tannenbaum Schmidt Continuum

In 1973 two business academics, Tannenbaum and Schmidt, found a way to present leadership characteristics more dynamically than in the Blake and Mouton Grid. Blake's grid implies that a boss is (and will always be) a 1,9 or a 5,5. By contrast Tannenbaum and Schmidt devised a 'continuum' which suggested that people-centred leadership skills could be learned and developed. This was an attractive idea for Human Resource professionals, who saw an opportunity for devising useful training courses ('learning to lead').

On the continuum (see Figure 6.3) the single issue is a scale relating to the degree to which staff are involved in decision-making. On the left is the purely autocratic process: boss decides. That is steadily softened so that by mid-way, the manager presents the decision but then allows a degree of consultation and discussion in which the decision may change. Further to the right, consultation develops into delegation: getting staff to actually make decisions for themselves.

Tell	Sell		Consult		Delegate	
⇧	⇧	⇧	⇧	⇧	⇧	⇧
Manager makes & announces decision	Manager sells decision	Manager presents ideas & invites questions	Manager presents decision subject to change	Manager presents problem, gets suggestions then decides	Manager defines limits; then asks group for a decision	Manager permits subordinates to decide within defined limits

Figure 6.3 The Tannenbaum and Schmidt Leadership Continuum

Despite the analytic value of the Continuum, Blake's Grid proved to have more of an impact upon managers in general. They found it easier to apply to their own workplaces and to the bosses they knew or had known.

Table 6.2 Blake's Grid vs. Tannenbaum and Schmidt's Continuum

Strengths of Blake's Grid	Strengths of Tannenbaum and Schmidt's Continuum
Blake's Grid measures two factors: concern for people and concern/drive for performance; Tannenbaum and Schmidt only measures one thing: the leader's use of people	The focus on the boss's use of his or her people gives an interesting amount of detail about the range of approaches between the two extremes (autocratic vs. highly democratic)
The understanding that some leaders are driven solely by results/success is perhaps why Blake's Grid is more widely known among managers than the continuum	The continuum gave a basis not only for analysis but also for action, such as persuading new section leaders to get training on how to develop the more democratic aspects of leadership
The labels used – such as 'Country Club' and 'Obedience' – made it easy for managers to visualise the type of person implied by a 5,5 or a 9,1 category; that made them talk about the grid and therefore learn to use it	The continuum also gave bosses a measure by which they could judge their own approach, helping them understand that 'tell' (boss decides; boss announces decision) is an extreme approach, not a normal one

6.5. Leaders and managers

It is important to understand that the role of the leader is not the same as that of the manager. Management guru Peter Drucker once said that: 'Managers do things right; leaders do the right thing.'

In other words, an effective manager is someone who can put an idea or policy into action, and get the details right. By contrast, the leader is good at identifying the key issues facing the business, setting new objectives, and then deciding what should be done, by when, and by whom. It is also sometimes argued that a leader needs to inspire staff. This is often confused with charismatic leadership, that is, when the personal charisma of the leader inspires staff to give something extra or work a bit harder. Although some successful leaders such as Ghandi, Churchill and Mandela had charisma, many others had success despite quite dull personalities. The great British Prime Minister Clement Attlee 'had a lot to be modest about', according to Churchill. Liverpool FC's long period as Britain's top club began with the charismatic Bill Shankly, yet the huge haul of trophies came later, under the leadership of the shy, slightly bumbling Bob Paisley.

'All good leaders have the capacity to create a compelling vision and translate it into action and sustain it'. Warren Bennis, author and organisational consultant

6.6 Effectiveness of different leadership styles

In a BBC poll, Sir Winston Churchill was voted as the 'Greatest Ever Briton'. This accolade was for his achievement as the country's leader in the Second World War. Few would call him the Prime Minister; he was the leader. Yet before the war Churchill's career had been peppered with poor decision-making and difficulties forming political alliances, let alone leading them. Churchill's charismatic, hands-on and paternalistic style proved to be what the country needed at a time of crisis. Immediately after the war Churchill was voted out of office by a country that revered him. People knew he wasn't the leader for the peace.

The effectiveness of a leadership style, therefore, depends greatly on circumstances. At a time of crisis, autocratic and strong paternalistic approaches can work – bringing speedy decision-making at a time when staff want exactly that. Sometimes leaders who have performed well during a crisis are pushed aside shortly after, as the company needs a more democratic, cohesive leader for the good times.

More controversial is whether different leadership styles are needed in different parts of the world. And, if so, is the explanation cultural or due to differences in standards of living and development. This issue is covered more fully in the second year of the A-level course.

Key terms

Autocratic leadership: when the boss keeps all key decisions to him or herself, and gives orders, rather than power, to subordinates.

Charismatic leadership: a leader whose dynamic or magnetic personality makes people willing to follow. The widely held view is that leaders require a dynamic or magnetic personality in order to succeed. Research does not support this.

Democratic leadership: this implies empowering people. That is, delegating full power over the design and execution of substantial tasks.

Laissez-faire leadership: this means allowing people to get on with things themselves, but without the co-ordination and control implicit within democratic leadership.

Paternalistic leadership: this means 'fatherly'. That is, the boss treats staff as part of the family. Typically, this shows through as consultation, but with decision-making remaining at the top ('Dad' decides).

Five Whys and a How

Question	Answer
Why might an uncharismatic leader be successful?	As long as the leader asks the right questions and makes the right calls on the big decisions, charisma is irrelevant
Why might laissez-faire leadership be a problem in a large organisation such as Unilever or Tesco?	Because it would be impossible to co-ordinate a wide range of wholly different approaches by different parts of the business (management by objectives would work far better)
Why might a 9,1 leader be more successful than a 5,5?	The 9,1 leader is a fanatic who drives people on to achieve success, quite possibly against their will; the 5,5 is too woolly, too accepting of compromise
Why might Blake's Grid be better known among business people than Tannenbaum and Schmidt's Continuum?	It gives more insight into the leaders they work with every day because it looks at their drive for success as well as their attitudes to their staff
Why might a leader 'be like a shepherd' (in the words of Nelson Mandela)?	Mandela thought leading from the back was the best approach – that is, letting people show initiative and talent (and only rounding them up if necessary)
How might an autocratic leader learn to be more democratic?	By absorbing the lessons of the Continuum, and seeking a training course designed to encourage more consultative, and then more democratic behaviours

The business writer Robert Townsend suggested that many newly appointed leaders 'disappear behind the mahogany curtain' and are rarely seen again by staff. He thought that 'finally getting to the top' made many leaders focus more on corporate luxuries ('Which jet shall we buy?') than on hard work. Yet he knew that great leaders can make a huge difference to long-term business performance. He advocated a leadership model based on extensive delegation within tight, agreed budgets. Many follow that model today.

Ultimately, judging a leader takes time. The media may find a new 'darling' – perhaps someone who looks and sounds great on TV. That person's achievements may be praised hugely, and they may win 'Business Leader of the Year' awards and a Knighthood. Yet it will be several years before anyone outside the business can appraise the individual's performance. In most businesses it is easy to boost short-term profit: you push prices up here, and make redundancies there. This persuades the media and the shareholders that you are a fine leader. The real question, though, is whether your decisions will push the business forwards or backwards over the coming years. Hold back from rushing to praise (or condemn) a boss on the basis of short-term performance. Big business is a long game. Ninety minutes is a long time in football; a week is a long time in politics; five years is a long time in business.

Workbook
A. Revision questions

(40 marks; 40 minutes)

1. Distinguish between autocratic and **paternalistic leadership**. (4)

2. Outline two types of democratic leadership. (4)

3. Outline one advantage and one disadvantage of an **autocratic leadership** style. (4)

4. Explain why autocratic leaders may be of more use in a crisis than democratic ones. (4)

5. Many managers claim to have a democratic style of leadership. Often, their subordinates disagree. Outline two ways of checking the actual leadership style of a particular manager. (4)

6. How may a paternalistic leader set about generating a clear vision for a business? (4)

7. In your own words, explain what Peter Drucker meant by saying: 'Managers do things right; leaders do the right thing'. (4)

8. A consultancy called Stellar Leadership has a questionnaire for managers to test out where they are on the Tannenbaum and Schmidt Continuum.

Read this multiple choice question then answer parts a-d below:

Choose one of the following:

i. As a general rule, I do not delegate

ii. I delegate occasionally, but when I do I follow up carefully

iii. I delegate regularly, to individuals who have demonstrated that they can handle it.

iv. I use delegation as a means of developing new skills in my people.

    a) Explain what is meant by the Tannenbaum and Schmidt Continuum. (3)

    b) What leadership style would you associate with people who choose answer (i).? (1)

    c) Explain which part of the Tannenbaum and Schmidt Continuum you would associate with answer (iii). (4)

    d) How effective do you think multiple choice questions might be at assessing managers' leadership styles? Explain your answer. (4)

B. Revision exercises
DATA RESPONSE

Curry Karma

Bangalore Balti (BB) started as a small curry house in Leicester. Word of its fresh, fiery food spread rapidly, creating the opportunity for expansion. By 2011 BB had 12 outlets across the Midlands, each run by a member of the owner's family. With plenty of cash in the bank, owner Safiq bought another chain of 16 Indian restaurants and converted them to the Bangalore Balti concept. This pushed the business into needing bank loans, which became a burden at a time when household spending was being held down by falling real incomes.

While Safiq was focusing on the financial pressures, things were slipping operationally. In particular, the managers of the 16 new restaurants showed less respect for the BB menu and seemed much less able to keep costs down and therefore profit margins up. It was also noticeable that labour turnover was higher in the new restaurants than in the original ones.

As the business came to the end of 2014 its profits were below those of four years earlier (See Table 6.3). It was getting hard to pay the interest bills on the loans. Something had to change.

Table 6.3 Data for Bangalore Balti 2011–14

	2011 (%)	2014 (%)
Labour turnover in the previous 12 months	8.4	19.5
Percentage of staff with cooking skills	46.5	28.5
Operating profit margin in the latest 6 months	12.8	4.7
Head office overheads per £ of sales	8.4	22.3

Questions (25 marks; 35 minutes)

1. Explain one internal pressure and one external pressure for change at Bangalore Balti. (6)

2. a) Analyse how Safiq might set about deciding how to change the business in 2015. (10)

   b) Analyse two problems faced by Safiq. (9)

C. Extend your understanding

1. To what extent does autocratic leadership have a place in today's business world? (20)

2. 'Great leaders are born, not made.' To what extent do you agree with this view? (20)

3. Discuss whether it can ever be right to pay a business leader 1,000 times more than the lowest paid in the organisation. (20)

Decision-making: scientific and intuitive

Linked to: What managers do, Chapter 5; Decision trees, Chapter 8; Marketing and decision-making, Chapter 11.

Definition

Most decisions in business are based on hard, probably numerical data and are therefore scientific. Some of the most important, though, are intuitive – a combination of experience and a feel for the future.

7.1 Introduction

Modern managers like to be able to base a decision on numerical evidence. As a consequence, more and more tactical decisions are made by computers. For example, a McDonald's store manager is sent details of how many staff should be employed every hour for next Saturday. The computer makes the 'decision' based on a sales forecast using data from last year and recent weeks. In this way the decision-making can be 'scientific' – in the sense that it is based on objective, numerical data – as opposed to hunch or intuition.

'It is a capital mistake to theorize before one has data. Insensibly one begins to twist facts to suit theories, instead of theories to suit facts.' Arthur Conan Doyle, aka Sherlock Holmes.

When the decision is more strategic, by definition there will be more uncertainty. When Whitbread plc decided to buy Costa Coffee, it couldn't know that it would be able to build the business from 50 outlets to 3,000 (including 350 in China). So computer programmes can't punch out answers. Therefore there is a far greater need for intuition. Whitbread made a brilliant call; Morrisons' made a disastrous one when it bought online site Kiddicare for £70 million in 2011 and sold it for £2 million in 2014!

Scientific decision-making is the goal for most firms because it suggests a method that can be applied in a routine way to measure opportunities or problems. When considering whether to launch a proposed new product, large companies like to have a testing system that they can use for every proposal. Then, over time, enough data is gathered to start to make accurate forecasts.

'Market research will always tell you why you can't do something. It's a substitute for decision-making, for guts.' Laurel Cutler, US business person

Real business

The Grocer magazine regularly features independent research into new product launches using a system called Cambridge Fast Foodfax. It uses various quantitative measures to test the likelihood of sales success. From the answers to those questions a rating score is devised. A look at the data below shows why Marks & Spencer felt optimistic about sales of their new lemonade.

Table 7.1

	Asda Choc Chip Muffin Cheesecake £1.50	Cadbury Dairy Milk Banana Caramel Crisp	M&S Still Blackcurrant Lemonade £1.00
Pre-trial purchase	49 per cent	46 per cent	44 per cent
Post-trial purchase	44 per cent	39 per cent	48 per cent
Better than what's out there	30 per cent	37 per cent	54 per cent
New and different	59 per cent	93 per cent	89 per cent
Overall score	38/50	37/50	41/50

Source: data from *The Grocer*: 2 and 9 August 2014

On these measures experience has shown that a score of 45+ shows a product of huge potential. Between 40 and 44 also shows promise. This approach enables big firms to scrap unpromising new products before taking them to market.

7.2 Scientific decision-making

The desire for a scientific approach to management dates back, at least, to F.W. Taylor and the late 19th century. Taylor wanted managers to find the 'one best way' to do things and then instruct and incentivise workers to follow that one best method. Taylor believed in 'time and motion' studies that measured exactly how and when workers completed certain tasks. He also advocated high division of labour, forcing staff to do simple, repetitive tasks in the workplace. With simple tasks came ease of measurement and from there it was only a short step to the business saying 'measurement is management'. In other words, once you start measuring things in the workplace, staff pay more attention and start behaving differently.

Today managers still want to control business variables, from absenteeism to morale. They also want to control external variables as much as possible. So sales are forecast with great precision and computer software is used to model every foreseeable situation, for example an August bank holiday with cloudy but not rainy weather. Scientific management tries to take the art out of business decision-making – replacing intuition with facts and quantitative forecasts.

Table 7.2 Some good and some awful real business decisions

Good business decisions	Bad business decisions
Coca-Cola buys innocent Drinks – giving it a real competitor to PepsiCo's Tropicana. The £200 million deal was completed in 2013.	Waterstones bookshop decides to stop selling books online, because 'online will never be more than 10 per cent of the market.'
In June 2000 Nick Robertson and Quentin Griffiths launch 'As Seen on Screen'; first year sales are £3.6m. By 2014 'ASOS' has sales of £1,000 million.	Malcolm Walker, owner of Iceland Frozen Foods, takes the business upmarket – focusing on organic products. It didn't last.
Unloved Mondelez (owner of Cadbury) launched Belvita Breakfast Biscuits in 2010. The Grocery trade laughed at the idea, but by 2013 Belvita sales had grown to £58 million – that's more than Jaffa Cakes.	Rupert Murdoch, media mogul, sells MySpace website for $35m, having bought it for $580m six years before.
With recession biting Waitrose launched its 'Essentials' range of lower-priced groceries. By 2013 sales of Essentials are more than £1 billion a year and Waitrose extends the range to 400 more items.	Nestle re-launches its Willie Wonka chocolate bar range in 2013 (sales were poor when it first launched in 2005); time is no healer and the whole range is discontinued in 2014.

'Whenever decisions are made strictly on the basis of bottom-line arithmetic, human beings get crunched along with the numbers.' Thomas Horton, US business leader

'The best class of scientific mind is the same as the best class of business mind. The great desideratum in either case is to know how much evidence is enough to warrant action.' Samuel Butler, British novelist (1835–1902)

7.3 Risk, reward and uncertainty

Uncertainty is the natural state of affairs in businesses where many external factors affect sales and costs. The number of variables makes it impossible to predict what will happen (though some will try, taking their fees prior to the timescale of their predictions). Uncertainty does allow conclusions to be drawn, however. In an uncertain world a business needs a wide-enough range (portfolio) of products to be sure that one flop will not hit the business too hard.

Risk may be quantifiable, at least in some broad ways. If only 1 in 8 Hollywood films brings in more revenue than the cost of making it, it is reasonable to gauge the risk of lossmaking as 7/8 for future films. Then the risk must be set against the potential rewards. With movies, the rewards may be spectacular. *E.T. the Extra-Terrestrial* is believed to have made a 7,000 per cent return; the *Blair Witch Project* a profit of 414,000 per cent!

Figure 7.1 Logic chain: making strategic decisions

For some companies, including those with weak financial positions, low-risk projects are the only ones to consider, even if the returns are quite low too. Other firms are willing to take bigger gambles, figuring that a few failures is not a problem as long as the occasional success proves to be a big one.

7.4 Influences on decision-making

1. Mission. Good business decisions are those that contribute towards the mission of the organisation. This may mean taking decisions that go against the company objectives, perhaps because ethics come into play. So even if a company's 12-month objective is to boost market share from 26 per cent to 29 per cent, it may be ethically wrong to launch a product that attracts consumer interest but is against the consumer's best interests. So a mission such as Google's ('Don't be evil') should ensure that greed for profit does not take precedence over the interests of customers.

2. Objectives. For middle managers intent upon promotion prospects, decision-making is focused on the objectives they have been set. If directors want rising market share, managers will do all they can to deliver. An important factor to consider, though, is the timescale involved. Rising short-term market share can easily be achieved by deciding on price and other sales promotions. Yet this may be at the cost of long-term success. In 2013 Huggies disposable nappies were withdrawn from the UK market, even though sales had been above £100 million a year. The reason was that regular price discounting had undermined the brand. In effect, the company accepted defeat against Procter & Gamble's Pampers. Directors need to be careful to avoid encouraging short-termism. Well-run businesses always look to the medium-long term when setting their objectives. That ensures decision-making based on the true best interests of the company.

3. Ethics. Ethics enter business decisions when they form part of the scientific appraisal of risk and reward. If Marks & Spencer saw a sales opportunity for a 'super-indulgent chocolate moussecake' containing 1,000 calories, the risk of bad publicity would be taken into account. But when you scan the shelves of the store, or queue at a checkout alongside many tempting sweet treats you realise that M&S sells masses of spectacularly fattening foods. No one within the business is saying 'no, we really shouldn't be doing this'.

    With smaller, family-run businesses the same may not apply. If the family wishes to sell fruitcake but not chocolate cake, it can do so. It can allow a decision to be based purely on ethics. For a large, publicly-owned company, that is not a realistic possibility. Public company shareholders want dividend income and to see a rising share price. Putting ethics before profit would find little favour.

Real business

In 2012 a prominent sponsor of the London Olympics was Coca-Cola. To create 'social value' from this expenditure, Coca-Cola worked with the charity StreetGames to get 110,000 youngsters participating in sport. Good though that may be, what about the ethics?

In Mexico 70,000 die each year from diabetes. Mexicans are the fattest people in the world and also drink more Coca-Cola per head than anyone else. When a tax was proposed in Mexico on the sugar in soft drinks, Coca-Cola bottlers warned that 20,000 jobs could be lost. This opposition chimed with the Mexican soft drinks' trade association's hostility to the tax.

So, on reflection, how can one view the aid for StreetGames as anything other than a marketing decision? Ethics do not really enter the Coca-Cola corporate mindset.

4. The external environment, including competition. Big strategic decisions must be rooted in the economic, social, competitive and consumer environment of the time and, even more importantly, of the future. When Domino's Pizza began in 1960, it was not clear to everyone that home-delivery was going to become the dominant way of supplying consumers' love of the product. But founder Tom Monaghan saw through the competition from Pizza Hut and from supermarket cook-at-home pizzas, focusing on home delivery. Today Domino's is the world's biggest pizza delivery company, with sales of more than $1,000 million a year.

    Of all the economic, social and technological aspects of the external environment, none is more important than trends in consumer taste. In 2014 profits at Gillette fell by 17.5 per cent as its male shaving products struggled because of a fashion towards stubble. Less shaving meant less profit. No amount of clever marketing could make up for that.

Another key factor is competition. The issues are twofold: first, how intense is the competition; and second, is that intensity changing? When Scoop ice cream opened in Covent Garden in 2007 it was the first artisan gelato-maker in Central London. According to Time Out magazine August 2014 there are now 22! Three, it is true, are Scoop outlets, but that still leaves 19 competitors. Naturally that makes it harder to run a comfortably profitable business.

5. Resource constraints. Before making a business decision it is crucial to have considered the resource implications. A restaurant chain can only decide to open 20 more stores in the coming year if it has enough capital and the right amount of management talent. Any attempt to expand with insufficient resources is likely to lead to 'overtrading' – expanding more rapidly than your resource-base allows.

Five Whys and a How

Question	Answer
Why is the scientific approach to decision-making easier for tactical than for strategic decisions?	Because tactical decisions are more limited in their scope and effect, often stemming from regular, predictable issues such as a shop asking how many kilos of strawberries are needed for next Saturday?
Why is uncertainty a bigger worry for firms than risk?	Because risk can often be calculated and therefore brought into the decision-making process.
Why might middle managers be inclined to make decisions based on short-term criteria?	Because they are focused more on their next career step than on the long-term best interests of the whole business.
Why might a scientific decision prove wrong?	Either incomplete data were gathered or the interpretation of the data must have been faulty.
Why might a firm's objectives be out of alignment with its mission?	Mission is often influenced by ethics that are more ambitious than the duller, perhaps profit-focused objectives.
How can a firm make sure it takes decisions scientifically?	By gathering as much numerical evidence as possible and weighing it up using a standardized method such as decision trees (see Chapter 8).

Evaluation: Decision-making: scientific and intuitive

Good decisions are those that look good (or even obvious) some time later. They are likely to be made in a collaborative way, using the knowledge and wisdom of the more junior staff who are in day-to-day contact with customers. Of course, if the plan is to make a decision scientifically, the views of staff must be used as part of a calculation (in effect, an equation) that carefully sets the risks out against the rewards.

A training director called Donald Bullock once said that 'Most of our executives make very sound decisions.

The trouble is many of them have turned out not to be right.' This sums up scientific decision-making in particular. The method for making the decision may be perfect but ultimately all that matters is that the decision is right. As shown in Table 7.1, in business there's scope for making huge, multi-million pound decisions. Good executives manage to get the big decisions right most of the time.

Key terms

Intuition: judgement made on qualitative criteria, perhaps experience and strength of market understanding, or perhaps little more than guesswork.

Short-termism: a widespread tendency within a business to focus on short-term results, probably at the cost of long-term success.

Strategic decision: one that is made in circumstances of uncertainty and where the outcome will have a major impact on the medium- to long-term future of the organisation.

Tactical decision: deciding what to do in circumstances that are immediate (short term) and where a mistake is unlikely to have a major impact on the business.

'Participative management is, simply stated, involving the right people at the right time in the decision-making process.' Wayne Barlow, administrator, Federal Aviation Authority

---

Workbook
A. Revision questions

(30 marks; 30 minutes)

1. Explain why intuition may be more important for a strategic decision than for a tactical one. (4)

2. For each of the following decisions, outline whether you believe it to be tactical or strategic. If there is some uncertainty, explain why.

    a) Deciding whether to give an order to supplier A or B. (2)

    b) Deciding whether to move head office from London to New York. (2)

    c) Deciding whether to employ full-time only staff, or whether to go for part-timers. (2)

    d) Deciding whether to put the Bolton FC season ticket price up from £600 to £720. (2)

3. Identify three factors that might undermine the accuracy of the data used in a scientific decision. (3)

4. a) What is meant by the term 'business ethics'? (2)

    b) Why may the desire for high ethical standards conflict with the rewards anticipated from a decision? (5)

5. Based on your best understanding of the current economic position, comment on its possible effect on:

    a) the likely revenue and profit trend at Poundland. (4)

    b) the sales prospects for the newly launched Amira Superior Aromatic Rice, which is priced 50 per cent higher than usual brands. (4)

B. Revision exercises
DATA RESPONSE

Big decisions at Tesco

After his predecessor left in July, new boss Dave Lewis had a few months before starting as Tesco Chief Executive (CEO) in October 2014. This gave him time to think about how to turn the business around. For five years Tesco's market share had been struggling in the UK. But at least it was profitable. Many of its overseas operations were losing money.

Dave Lewis was brought in from outside Tesco, with a strong career at giant Unilever. Lewis was the boss of Unilever's Personal Care division, with annual sales of more than £15 billion (and brands such as Dove and TRESemmé). Before that he had many jobs around the world in a 27-year career with the multinational.

To commentators, Lewis had five main issues to deal with as soon as possible:

- The Tesco brand image, which has been hit hard in the UK
- The perception that Tesco is a relatively expensive store (borne out by *The Grocer's* weekly 'pricecheck')
- Tesco's falling market share in the UK (from 31.2 per cent at its peak to 28.9 per cent by July 2014. NB Each 1 per cent is slightly over £1 billion of sales)
- A series of problems in Tesco's international store portfolio, with sales and profit seeming to struggle post-recession

- More than anything else, should Tesco have all its cost-drivers hacked back to the minimum (scrap Clubcard and so on), in order to take on Lidl and Aldi at the price game?

Questions (30 marks; 35 minutes)

1. Dave Lewis will have to make some big decisions quite soon. Is it a strength or a weakness that he's an outsider to Tesco? Explain your reasoning.   (5)

2. Choose one of the five issues outlined and explain why this should be tackled first.   (9)

3. To what extent would a scientific approach to decision-making help Dave Lewis in the early months of his new job?   (16)

C. Extend your understanding

1. To what extent may there be problems when decision-making is based on clear objectives, but unclear resource constraints?   (20)

2. To what extent can the decisions made by a multinational oil company such as Shell or BP ever be considered ethical?   (20)

Decision trees

Linked to: What managers do, Chapter 5; Decision-making: scientific and intuitive, Chapter 7.

Definition

Decision trees are diagrams that set out all the options available when making a decision, plus an estimate of their likelihood of occurring.

8.1 Introduction

Decision trees provide a logical process for decision-making. The decision problem can be set out in the form of a diagram, like a tree on its side. It can take into account the occasions when a decision can be taken and the occasions when chance will determine the outcome. Chance can be estimated by assigning a probability, such as 0.2 (a 1 in 5 chance). While the estimate of the probability may sometimes be a guess, at other times there may be a logical basis. In the past, the chance of a new product launch surviving two years was 1 in 5, therefore it would be fair to give the probability of success for a new launch at 0.2.

'Compromise is usually bad . . . listen to both sides then pick one or the other.' Robert Townsend, author *Up the Organisation* (1920–1998)

8.2 Step-by-step approach to decision-tree analysis

Step 1: the basics

1. The tree is a diagram setting out the key features of a decision-making problem.

2. The tree is shown lying on its side, roots on the left, branches on the right.

3. The decision problem is set out from left to right with events laid out in the sequence in which they occur.

4. The branches consist of:
    a) a decision to be made, shown by a square (see Figure 8.1)

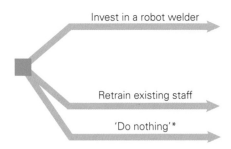

*Note that 'do nothing' is an option for every business decision

Figure 8.1 Decision tree

    b) chance events or alternatives beyond the decision-maker's control, shown by a circle – a node (see Figure 8.2).

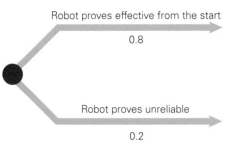

Figure 8.2 Decision tree (2)

Note carefully that a square means a decision and a circle means a chance event, that is, one of two or more events may follow. Therefore:

- there must be a probability attaching to each of the chance events or alternatives

- these probabilities must add up to 1 as one of them must happen.

In Figure 8.2, the decision-maker has allowed for an 80 per cent (0.8) chance that the robot will work well and a 20 per cent (0.2) chance that it will prove unreliable. These figures could be arrived at from experience with robots in the past.

At any square, the decision-maker has the power to choose which branch to take, but at the circles chance takes over. You can choose whether or not to invest in a robot. But there is a chance that the robot may prove unreliable. The full tree so far is shown in Figure 8.3.

The decision-maker will choose which branch provides the better or best value.

If buying costs a net cash outflow of £1,000 per year while hiring costs £800, it is better to hire (see Figure 8.4).

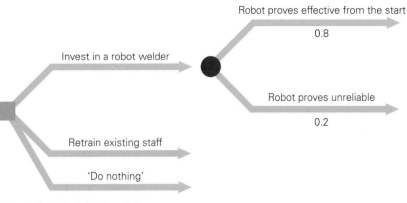

Figure 8.3 Decision tree (3)

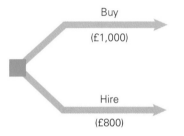

Figure 8.4 Decision tree (4)

Note that the branch not taken is crossed out, as shown in Figure 8.5.

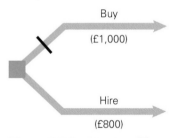

Figure 8.5 Decision tree (5)

Step 2: drawing a decision tree

Bantox plc must decide whether to launch a new product (see Figure 8.6).

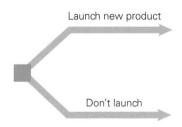

Figure 8.6 Decision tree (6)

Research suggests there will be a 70 per cent chance of success in a new product launch. This would be shown as a probability of 0.7 (see Figure 8.7).

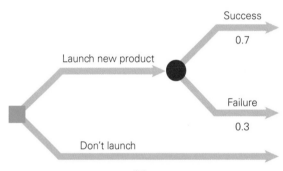

Figure 8.7 Decision tree (7)

Note that, because probabilities must add up to 1, the implied chance of failure is 0.3.

To make a decision based on the tree above, estimates are needed of the financial costs and returns. In this case, let's assume:

- the new product launch will cost £10 million
- a new product success will generate £15 million of positive net cash flows
- a new product failure will generate only £3 million
- no launch means no movements in net cash.

The full decision tree now looks like Figure 8.8.

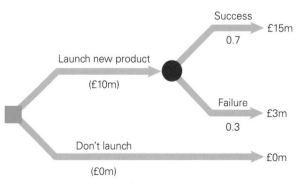

Figure 8.8 Decision tree (8)

Step 3: making calculations

At each probability circle, a calculation is required of the average outcome, given the probabilities involved. If a launch costing £10 million will generate either £15 million or £3 million, what will be the average result, if the same circumstances happened several times over? Sometimes the firm would get £15 million and sometimes £3 million. Usually, to work out an average, you would add the numbers and divide by 2; that is:

$$\frac{£15 + £3\,\text{m}}{2} = £9\,\text{m}$$

That assumes, though, that there is an equal chance of £15 million and £3 million. In fact, the probabilities are not 50/50, they are 70/30. There is a 70 per cent chance of £15 million. So the correct (weighted) average expected value is:

$$£15\,\text{m} \times 0.7 = £10.5\,\text{m}$$
$$£3\,\text{m} \times 0.3 = \underline{£0.9\,\text{m}}$$
Total $\qquad\quad$ £11.4 m

In decision trees, the expected values at probability circles are always calculated by weighted averages.

Calculations on decision trees are carried out from right to left, that is, working backwards through the tree, making calculations at each probability circle.

In the case of Bantox, only one calculation is needed. If there are several circles, it is helpful to number them, and show your weighted average calculations clearly (see Figure 8.9).

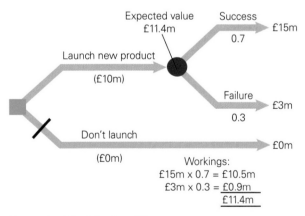

Figure 8.9 Decision tree (9)

Step 4: showing your decisions

Having calculated the expected value (weighted average) at each probability circle, a rational decision can be made. As Figure 8.9 shows, launching the new product will, on average, turn £10 million into £11.4

million; that is, generate a net gain of £1.4 million. Therefore it is preferable to launch. The decision to launch is indicated by crossing out the 'don't launch' option.

8.3 Summary of key points

A decision tree is a diagrammatic presentation of a problem involving decisions (squares) and chance events (circles).

1. The problem is laid out from left to right. Decisions are shown as squares, chance events as circles.

2. Each chance event has a probability estimated for it. The probabilities must add up to 1 since one of them must happen.

3. Two money values are shown:
   a) the cost of the decision (shown as a negative number, that is, in brackets)
   b) the benefit or cost of a specific outcome occurring. These are shown at the end of each branch of the tree.

4. Working from right to left, the decision-maker calculates the expected value at each circle. These values are calculated by multiplying the money value by the probability, then adding the results.

5. Still working from right to left, the decision-maker decides at each square which branches to cross off, leaving only the better or best alternative open.

8.4 Advantages and disadvantages of decision trees

Advantages of decision trees

1. The most important advantage of the technique is allowing for uncertainty. The most common technique for business decision-making is investment appraisal. This is based upon a single forecast of future cash flows, giving a bogus impression of certainty. In reality, every decision can result in a range of possible outcomes, not just one. The decision tree allows for this. By focusing firms on uncertainty, decision trees can help to ensure that managers make more carefully considered decisions.

2. Decision trees also demand that managers consider all the possible alternative outcomes. Although it is important to be single-minded, too many managers adopt a strategy without fully considering the alternatives. They perhaps choose

the approach that worked the last time, or the one adopted by their competitors. Decision trees not only encourage careful consideration of the options, but also require an estimate of the actual outcome for each. This allows 'best-case' and 'worst-case' scenarios to be costed and considered.

Further advantages of decisions trees are set out below.

1. Decision trees set out problems clearly and encourage a logical approach. The discipline of setting out the problem in a decision tree requires logical thinking and can also generate new ideas and approaches.

2. Decision trees encourage a quantitative approach and force assessments of the chances and implications of success and failure.

3. Decision trees not only show the average expected values for each decision but also set out the probability of a specific outcome occurring.

4. Decision trees are most useful when similar scenarios have occurred before, so that good estimates of probabilities and predicted actual values exist.

5. Decision trees are most useful in tactical or routine decisions, rather than strategic decisions.

Disadvantages of decision trees

All quantitative methods can be biased, consciously or unconsciously. Optimism is often a virtue in an executive, but it may lead to exaggerated sales figures or excessively high probabilities for success. This does not mean quantitative methods should be rejected. Only that it is sensible to ask who provided the figures and assess whether they had any reason to want a particular outcome. Cynicism about decision trees is out of place; scepticism is wholly valid.

'We should never allow ourselves to be bullied by an either-or. There is often the possibility of something better than either of these two alternatives'. Mary Parker Follett, business writer (1868–1933)

Further disadvantages of decision trees are set out below.

1. It may be difficult to get meaningful data, especially for estimated probabilities and of success or failure.

2. Decision trees are less useful in the case of completely new problems or one-off strategic problems.

3. It can be relatively easy for a manager seeking to prove a case to manipulate the data. A biased approach to the estimated probabilities or values could 'prove' a pre-desired result rather than a logically determined outcome.

4. Decision trees do not take into account the variability of the business environment.

5. Decision trees may divert managers from the need to take account of qualitative as well as quantitative information when making a decision.

Evaluation: Decision trees

Small firms run by one person benefit from clear, speedy decision-making. The entrepreneur knows the customers, the competition and the staff. Therefore he or she can make effective decisions quickly, with no need to justify them to others. Some may prove faulty, but the quick responses of a small firm should ensure that damage is limited. The business will stand or fall on the hunches and judgements of the boss.

In large firms, the same rules do not apply. A successful career path at a company such as Mars or Unilever often depends upon avoiding mistakes. Therefore it is important to be able to justify why a decision was made. Even if it proves to be wrong, that should not matter as long as the method for making the decision was thorough and analytic.

After all, if four out of five new products prove to be failures, what would be the reason for firing a manager who has just launched a flop?

It can be a matter for regret that methods such as decision trees are used to 'protect the back' of decision-makers. In other words, they may not be valued for themselves, only for their value as a protector. Often, though, the process of trying to protect themselves encourages managers to think hard about their decision-making methods. Those who use decision trees positively may find an improvement in their record of success, and help the big firms to compete with the faster moving small firms.

Five Whys and a How

Question	Answer
Why may decision tree analysis be more useful than investment appraisal?	Because it takes into account alternative possible outcomes and the probability of them occurring (investment appraisal is misleadingly 'certain')
Why are expected values calculated using a 'weighted' rather than a straight average?	Because it is the only way to gain accuracy when there are different probabilities of your possible outcomes occurring
Why may the decision tree technique be useful even if you have no sound basis for estimating the probabilities?	The tree diagram will still indicate the best and worst possible outcomes - a vital part of decision-making (if the worst outcome would threaten the firm's survival, you'd say no)
Why may there be dangers in the apparent 'scientific' precision of the decision tree technique?	People may assume that the technique delivers more accuracy than is true given the degree of estimation involved
Why may decision trees risk sidelining qualitative factors?	Because people are swayed by a 'definite', numerical 'answer' to a problem – so they subconsciously play down qualitative factors
How are calculations done after the decision tree is drawn up?	Working back from right to left, calculating the weighted average at every chance node then cutting off the less profitable decisions

Key terms

Actual values: although known as 'actual values' or 'payoffs', these are the forecasts of the net cash flows which result from following a sequence of decisions and chance events through a decision tree. They should always be shown at the ends of the branches of the tree.

Node: a point in a decision tree where chance takes over. It is denoted by a circle, and at that point it should be possible to calculate the expected value of this pathway.

Expected values: these are the forecast actual values adjusted by the probability of their occurrence.

Although called 'expected', they are not the actual cash flows which result. Expected equals actual × probability.

Net gains (or losses): subtracting the initial outlay from the expected value to find out whether or not a decision is likely to produce a surplus.

Probability: the likelihood of something occurring, usually expressed as a decimal (for example 0.5). The probability of something certain is 1. The probability of something impossible is zero.

Workbook

A. Revision questions

(30 marks; 60 minutes)

1. When drawing a decision tree, what symbol is used to show:

   a) when a decision must be made?

   b) when chance takes over? (2)

2. If the probability of the successful launch of a new product is estimated to be 0.72, the probability of a failed launch must be 0.28. Explain why. (3)

3. State whether each of the following is a decision or a chance event:

   a) choosing between three different new product options

   b) a new product succeeding or failing in the marketplace

   c) good weather on the day of the open air concert

   d) whether to advertise or to cut the price. (4)

4. Explain the difference between an expected value and an actual value. (3)

5. State three advantages and three potential pitfalls of using decision trees. (6)

6. Explain the circumstances in which decision trees are least useful. (4)

7. If the chance of achieving £200,000 is 0.2 and the chance of £20,000 is 0.8, what is the expected value of a decision? (4)

8. Explain how decision trees may help managers to assess the best decision by 'what if?' analysis. (4)

B. Revision exercises

DATA RESPONSE 1

Look at the tree diagram below and answer the following questions.

Questions (20 marks; 20 minutes)

1. Calculate the expected values at nodes 1–4. (12)

2. State your decisions at decision points A–C. Indicate your decisions on the tree diagram. (8)

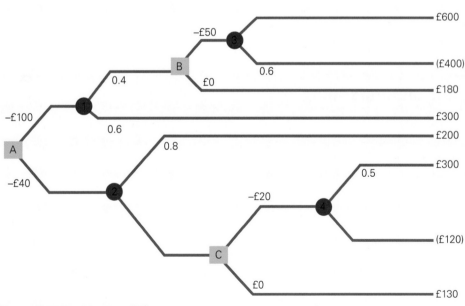

Figure 8.10 Decision tree (10)

DATA RESPONSE 2

Denham Potteries has a capital spending budget of £100,000. The production manager has put in a bid for £100,000 for a new tunnel kiln. The marketing manager has countered with a proposal to spend £80,000 on launching a new product. This new product is in line with the firm's objective of diversifying but may be rather risky given the firm's past record of only one success for every five new products.

Ken Coton, the marketing manager, has provided a handy table of figures to summarise the information. This is set out in Table 8.1

Questions (25 marks; 30 minutes)

1. Draw a fully labelled decision tree to set out the options. (10)

2. What decision should the firm make on purely numerical grounds? (3)

Table 8.1 Denham Potteries

Outcome	Probability (surplus over next 5 years)	Actual value (£)
New product		
Big success	0.1	900,000
Modest success	0.1	500,000
Failure	0.8	30,000
Tunnel kiln		
Success	0.8	200,000
Failure	0.2	60,000

3. Outline the qualitative factors the board should take into account before making the decision. (12)

DATA RESPONSE 3

Mansfield Town FC is considering buying a South American centre forward player for its team. The club knows statistics show that only one in four overseas forwards succeeds in the lower divisions. But things are desperate. The player's contract will cost £500,000 and, if successful, could increase home attendances sufficiently to be worth £1.2 million over the three-year contract. Even if the player is unsuccessful, income from attendances should rise by £200,000.

Questions (20 marks; 15 minutes)

1. Draw the decision tree and label it carefully. (12)

2. On the basis of the tree, what decision should the club take? (4)

3. Outline two reasons why the club might decide to proceed. (4)

C. Extend your understanding

1. Whitbread plc made the brilliant decision in 2000 to move out of the beer market and concentrate on coffee (Costa) and hotels (Holiday Inn). To what extent can decision trees be useful when making long-term strategic decisions such as these? (20)

2. A brilliant fashion designer has been made Chief Executive of Burberry plc. This is a business worth over £1 billion in revenue and in share value. To what extent will the new chief executive's decision-making be improved by using decision trees? (20)

Opportunity cost and trade-offs

Linked to: Understanding the nature and purpose of business, Chapter 1; Decision-making: scientific and intuitive, Chapter 7.

Definition

Opportunity cost is the cost of missing out on the next best alternative when making a decision. For example, the opportunity cost of not going to university may be to risk missing out on £200,000 of extra lifetime earnings (according to 2013 Government data). Similarly, trade-offs look at what you have to give up in order to get what you want most. They may not easily be expressed as a 'cost' (that is, it may not be possible to quantify them).

9.1 Introduction to opportunity cost

This concept will be useful throughout the A-level Business Studies course. It is at the heart of every business decision, from small to multinational companies. Every business faces the same issue: limited resources mean that hiring a marketing manager leaves less money to spend on a marketing campaign. For a start-up business, spending lots of money on a flash opening party means there is less money to pay for staff training.

For a new business the two most important resources are money and time. Both have an opportunity cost. Time spent by an entrepreneur creating a pretty website could mean too little time left for recruiting and training staff, or too little time to sit back and reflect on priorities. The same issue arises with money: it can only be spent once.

It follows that every business decision has an opportunity cost, measured in time, money, and often both. The same is true in other walks of life. A prime minister focused on foreign adventures may lose sight of the key issues affecting people at home. A chancellor who spends an extra £10 billion on education may have to cut back on health care.

For a new business start-up, the most important opportunity cost issues are as follows.

- Do not tie up too much capital in stock (inventory), as this cash could be used more productively elsewhere in the business.
- Do not overstretch yourself: good decisions take time, so make sure you are not doing too much yourself.
- Take care with every decision that uses up cash; at the start of a business it is hard to get more of it, but more is always needed.

9.2 Opportunity costs in developing a business idea

Personal opportunity costs

Starting your first business is likely to be tough. Long hours and highly pressured decisions may cause stress, but the biggest problems go beyond psychology. A difficult cash-flow position is quite normal, yet places a huge strain on the business and its owner(s).

The owner of a first business will probably have come from a background as a salary earner, possibly a very well-paid one. So the first opportunity cost is missing out on the opportunity to earn a regular income. As it could take six months or more to get a business going, this is a long period of financial hardship.

Then comes the investment spending itself, such as the outlay on a lease, on building work, on fixtures and fittings, on machinery and then on the human resources (staff) to make everything work with a human face. All this uses money that could otherwise be used on the proprietor's house, holidays, and so on. The personal opportunity costs add up massively.

Business writers often use the term 'stakeholders', which means all those with a stake in the success or failure of a business. Usually, the key groups are those within the business (internal stakeholders), such as staff, managers and directors; and outside groups (external stakeholders), such as suppliers, customers, bankers and shareholders. In the case of a business start-up, however, there is a whole extra consideration: the wear and tear on the family. Starting a business is a hugely time-consuming and wholly absorbing activity. The restaurant owner might easily spend 80 hours a week on site in the early days, then take further paperwork home. An American business psychologist has said that, 'even when you are home, you're still thinking about the business – it's easy for a spouse to feel neglected, even jealous'.

Despite this, research by a US investment business has shown that, although 32 per cent of new entrepreneurs said that the experience had caused marriage difficulties, 42 per cent of chief executives in fast-growing new firms said that the pressures and exhilarations made their marriages stronger.

'Perpetual devotion to what a man calls his business is only to be sustained by perpetual neglect of many other things.' Robert Louis Stevenson, writer

---

9.3 Deciding between opportunities

Successful business people are those who can make successful decisions. The three founders of innocent Drinks wanted to start a business together, but had no idea what type of business to start. As friends at university they had already run nightclub events together, and two ran an annual music festival in West London. They could have developed a successful festival business, but stumbled upon the idea of a business that made all-fruit smoothies. On finding an investor, in 1999, who could help turn their dream into a reality, they left their salaried jobs, gave up their other business opportunities and concentrated on building the innocent brand. The 2010 sale of a majority of the innocent shares to Coca-Cola for £75 million showed the success of this start-up.

'Alice came to a fork in the road. "Which road do I take?" she asked.

"Where do you want to go?" responded the Cheshire cat.

"I don't know." Alice answered.

"Then" said the cat "it doesn't matter."' Lewis Carroll, *Alice in Wonderland*

When deciding between business start-up opportunities, certain factors are crucial:

Estimating the potential sales that could be achieved by each idea

This is hugely difficult, both in the short term and – even more – in the longer term. Smoothie maker innocent's first-year sales were £0.4 million. Who could have guessed that, eight years later, its sales would be more than 300 times greater? Yet estimates

---

Real business

The opportunity costs of developing one business idea as opposed to another

When 30-year-old Mike Clare opened his first Sofa Bed Centre in 1985 he could raise only £16,000 of capital, even though his estimates showed that £20,000 to £25,000 was needed. Fortunately, hard work plus a great first month's sales brought in the cash he needed to get the business going properly. At that time, none of the banks would lend him any money. In the lead-up to Mike Clare's first store opening, he spent time organising public relations events (to get coverage in the local paper), helping with the building work, wrangling with suppliers over credit terms and making decisions about pricing and display. When the store opened, he spent 18 hours a day 'doing everything'. When the first store took £30,000 in month one, he started looking for a second location, which was open within six months. Quite clearly, there was no possibility of starting more than one business at a time.

Later he built up a bedding business called Dreams, which he sold in 2008 for £170 million. Sadly, Dreams collapsed in 2013, in the aftermath of the great recession. Mike Clare, though, had turned £16,000 into £170m. Given how short of money he was at the start, it would have been impossible for him to have chosen to launch two different businesses at the same time. He had to choose one. Fortunately, he chose wisely.

Given the need for focus, the main opportunity cost arises when an entrepreneur has two ideas. One should be chosen and one rejected. This is possible if the entrepreneur is ruthless. After evaluating the two options carefully, the weaker of the two should be stopped completely. The reason is simple: opening one business is tough enough; two would be impossible.

must be made, either by the use of market research, or by using the expertise of the entrepreneur. Mike Clare of Dreams had previously worked as an area manager for a furniture retailer, so he had a reasonable idea about what the sales might be. Inside knowledge is, of course, hard to beat.

Considering carefully the cash requirements of each idea

The innocent trio were very lucky to find an American investor who put £250,000 into the start of the business in return for a 20 per cent stake. Some new businesses are very hungry for cash (such as setting up a new restaurant in London, which costs over £1 million); other new business ideas (such as a new website) can be started from a back bedroom, keeping initial costs very low.

Deciding whether the time is right

The innocent brand's launch fitted wonderfully with a time of luxury spending and growing concern about diet. In the same year, a small business started in West London focusing on customising cars: 'souping up' the engines to make the cars go faster and give the engines a 'throaty roar'. As rising fuel prices became a greater concern, the business was squeezed out. Five years before, it might have made a lot of money, but it no longer did so.

Deciding whether the skills needed fit your own set of skills

Running a restaurant requires a mix of organisational skills, discipline and meticulous attention to detail. Does that describe you? Or are you better suited to running an online business that can be handled in a relaxed way behind the scenes?

9.4 Trade-offs

In business there are many occasions when one factor has to be traded off against another. An entrepreneur might get huge help at the start from friends, yet realise that these same friends lack the professionalism to help the business grow. The needs of the business may have to be traded off against the friendships. Can a softie be a real business success? Probably not: some inner toughness is clearly important.

Other trade-offs may include:

- when starting in the first place, trading off the start-up against a year's international travel (perhaps with friends); or trading the start-up against going to university
- trading off the aspects of the business you most enjoy doing against those that prove most profitable for the business. The chef/owner may love cooking yet find the business works far better when she or he has the time to mix with the customers, motivate the waiting staff and negotiate hard with suppliers
- trading off time today and time tomorrow. The entrepreneur's ambition may be to 'retire by the time I'm 40'; that may sound great in the long term but, in the short term, her or his spouse and children may see little of them.

Overall, the key to success will be to be clear about what you and your family want from the business. It may be to become outrageously rich, no matter what, or – more likely – to find a balance between the freedom and independence of running your own business and the need to find time for the family. Books on business success assume that success can be measured only in £1,000,000s. Many people running their own small businesses would tell a different story; the independence alone may be the key to their personal satisfaction.

'Strategy is about making choices, trade-offs; it's about deliberately choosing to be different.' Michael Porter, business author/guru

Five Whys and a How

Question	Answer
Why is opportunity cost involved in every business decision?	Because every decision commits resources that can then not be used for other things
Why might an increase in interest rates be relevant to opportunity cost?	Because spending on assets such as inventories or machinery requires taking cash out of the bank – and the higher the interest rate the higher the opportunity cost of that withdrawal
Why might opportunity cost be especially important for a new start-up business?	Because it will almost certainly have little spare capital and even less spare management time – so every wrong decision and every overspend has especially damaging knock-on effects
Why is the projected £42.6 billion price of HS2 criticised both for the cost and for the opportunity cost?	The cost is a problem at a time when Britain's fiscal deficit remains huge; the opportunity cost can be measured in potential cutbacks in NHS, education or welfare spending
Why is time the ultimate opportunity cost?	Because although it's easy to buy the time of lots of staff, there are usually only a few people in a business who make the important decisions, so their time is very limited and very valuable
How might a firm value the opportunity cost of not launching a new product?	Make careful estimates of all the revenues and costs involved in the project, then calculate the potential profit over its lifetime. That's the potential cost of what you're missing out on.

Workbook
A. Revision questions

(20 marks; 20 minutes)

1. Explain in your own words why time is an important aspect of opportunity cost. (3)

2. Give two ways of measuring the opportunity cost to you of doing this homework. (2)

3. Examine one opportunity cost to a restaurant chef/owner of opening a second restaurant. (5)

4. Explain the trade-offs that may exist in the following business situations. Choose the two contexts you feel most comfortable with.

   a) Levi's pushes its workers to produce more pairs of jeans per hour.

   b) A chocolate producer, short of cash, must decide whether to cut its advertising spending or cut back on its research and development into new product ideas.

   c) A football manager decides to double the number of training sessions per week.

   d) A celebrity magazine must decide whether or not to run photos that will generate huge publicity, but probably make the celebrity unwilling to co-operate with the magazine in future. (6)

5. Look at the quote on p. 56. What, according to Robert Louis Stevenson, is the opportunity cost of devotion to business? (4)

B. Revision exercises

DATA RESPONSE 1

James Sutton had a job as a marketing manager paying £55,000 a year. His career prospects looked very good, yet he handed in his notice to start up his own online business. He knew that it would take him away from 9-to-5 work and towards the dedication of 8.00 a.m. to 9.00 p.m. If he took on a member of staff, the wage bill would rise by £16,000.

Questions (15 marks; 15 minutes)

1. Outline three opportunity cost issues within this short passage. (6)

2. Analyse the possible impact on James of the increase in his workload. (9)

DATA RESPONSE 2

In 2002 a co-operative agreement between coffee farmers in 250 Ugandan villages broke down. It had taken years to put together, but disagreements made it collapse. The prize for a successful co-operative was to produce organic coffee beans grown to Fairtrade standards for partners such as Cafédirect. This would ensure significantly higher prices for the raw coffee beans and also much better credit terms (being paid quickly to help with cash flow).

Over the next two years countless hours of work were put into forming a new co-operative. In early 2004 the new Gumutindo Coffee Co-operative was Fairtrade certified. By 2014 7,000 farmers had joined the Gumutindo Co-operative. They receive a guaranteed price of $1.26 per pound of coffee beans, whereas the world price has been as low as $0.80 over the previous eight years. The extra (and stable) income helps the farmers, of whom only 25 per cent have running water and 79 per cent live in mud huts with iron sheet roofing. The Fairtrade organisation has supported the co-operative in starting up its own production plant, converting the raw coffee into packs of coffee ready for sale. Ongoing investments include motorised pulpers and a major investment in solar panels to create electricity in the home as well as the production plant.

Sources: Adapted from www.fairtrade.org.uk and www.gumutindocoffee.co.uk

Questions (30 marks; 35 minutes)

1. What would be the opportunity cost of the farmers who put 'countless hours of work into forming a new co-operative'? (4)

2. Explain one risk for the farmers and one risk for the Fairtrade organisation in forming a new co-operative with high guaranteed prices for coffee beans. (6)

3. Some commentators have suggested that Waitrose should make all its coffee 'Fairtrade', therefore getting rid of brands such as Nescafé Gold Blend. Outline the trade-offs Waitrose management would have to consider before making any such decision. (4)

4. To what extent can one be sure that producing coffee ready-for-sale will increase the income levels of the 7,000 members of the co-operative? (16)

C. Extend your understanding

1. Tesco plc has annual sales of £50 billion and operating profits of over £2 billion a year. To what extent does the leader of such a large business need to consider the concept of opportunity costs? (20)

2. In the 1990s the Chairman of Samsung started to send the company's best and brightest young staff to live abroad for a year to learn about American and European lifestyles. Some directors complained that this was a waste of their time and talent. To what extent might the chairman be right to trade off management time against consumer knowledge? (20)

Understanding the role and importance of stakeholders

Linked to: Understanding the nature and purpose of business, Chapter 1; External factors affecting business, Chapter 4; Decision-making to improve financial performance, Chapter 44; Decision-making and improved human resources performance, Chapter 52.

Definition

A stakeholder is an individual or group that has an effect on, and is affected by, the activities of an organisation.

10.1 Introduction

All firms come into contact, on a daily basis, with suppliers, customers, the local community and employees. Each of these groups has an impact on the firm's success and at the same time is likely to be affected by any change in its activities. If, for example, the managers decide to expand the business, this may lead to:

- overtime for employees
- more orders for suppliers
- a wider range of products for consumers
- more traffic for the local community.

Groups such as suppliers, employees and the community are known as the firm's stakeholder groups because of their links with the organisation. A stakeholder group both has an effect on and is affected by the decisions of the firm. Each stakeholder group will have its own objectives. The managers of a firm must decide on the extent to which they should change their behaviour to meet these objectives. The belief is that a firm can benefit significantly from co-operating with its stakeholder groups and incorporating their needs into the decision-making process. Examples include:

- giving something back to the community to ensure greater co-operation from local inhabitants whenever the business needs their help; for example, when seeking planning permission for expansion
- treating suppliers with respect and involving them in its plans so that the firm builds up a long-term relationship

'Find the appropriate balance of competing claims by various groups of stakeholders. All claims deserve consideration but some claims are more important than others.' Warren Bennis, business author

Despite the benefits that are evident in a stakeholder approach, many managers believe that an organisation's sole duty is to its investors (that decisions should be made in the best interests of shareholders alone). Generally, this means maximising shareholder value (for example, increasing the share price and the dividends paid to shareholders). Even company directors who instinctively want to serve all the stakeholders often find that day-to-day pressures force them to pay primary concern to shareholders' interests – because shareholders are the only people with the power to get rid of the board of directors.

10.2 Stakeholder mapping

In 1991 Professor Mendelow devised a way of analysing the key stakeholders for a specific business. To do this he used the familiar matrix method to measure stakeholder power against stakeholder interest. For instance, if you run a strawberry farm supplying Tesco, your customer may have a huge amount of power over you, but not much interest in you. If you let them down Tesco will walk away and find another supplier. Within this theory there are four stakeholder categories; to help illustrate them, Tesco has been taken as the company whose stakeholders are to be analysed:

- Low power, low interest: such as shareholders with holdings worth less than £750
- Low power, high interest: such as Tesco shopfloor employees
- High power, low interest: such as Tesco's electricity supplier
- High power, high interest: such as the local authorities in Welwyn Garden City (location of Tesco Head Office)

The details of which stakeholders fit which category and what actions the business might take to engage them are given in Figure 10.1:

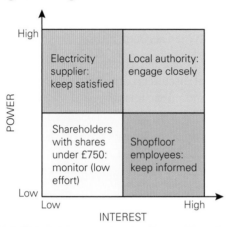

Figure 10.1 Stakeholder map showing the position of each stakeholder and the action a business might take to engage them

Despite the Tesco examples given above, it may be wrong to generalise at all about stakeholder mapping. The essence of the analysis is to assess the specific circumstances of particular businesses and only then decide which stakeholders fall into which category. So although most small shareholders have little interest in the business they 'own' (beyond the dividend and the share price), external shareholders in a business such as Mulberry might be both fashion-conscious and devoted to the company.

The value of this categorisation is that it helps in setting priorities. As shown in Figure 10.1, the company will work hardest to stay in constant communication with high power, high interest stakeholders.

10.3 Overlapping and conflicting stakeholder needs

Certain business circumstances may be to the advantage of all primary stakeholders. If, like Primark, your business concept is working successfully overseas, there are benefits to staff (promotion prospects), the board (bonuses), suppliers, shareholders, financiers and distributors. Even among external shareholders there are potential benefits to Inland Revenue and the wider community. Perhaps the only negative comments might come from environmental pressure groups.

Sadly, this is not often the case. All too often different stakeholders seem unable to stop themselves taking advantage of any weakness in others. In July 2014 Lloyds Bank was fined £105 million by the UK's Financial Conduct Authority and ordered to pay the Bank of England £7.76 million. Lloyds had not only rigged markets but had also deliberately underpaid the British government for help given to keep Lloyds afloat during the tough days in 2009 and 2010. By attempting to benefit its shareholders at the cost of the government and the taxpayer, Lloyds' executives were showing clearly where their stakeholder priorities lay.

'If you look after your customers and you look after your staff then shareholders will do very well . . . If you put shareholder interest – particularly short-term interest – first, you don't create a business.' Ian Gregg, who built Gregg's from one shop to one thousand six hundred.

Table 10.1 Stakeholder needs in different business circumstances

Situation	Overlapping stakeholder interests/needs	Conflicting stakeholder interests/needs
Productivity advance – perhaps coming from new technology	Shareholders, managers and customers	Managers and employees (threats of redundancy)
Fashion or weather turns in your favour	Shareholders, managers, suppliers and employees	Perhaps green campaigners
Recession: creating a strong reason to cut back capacity	Shareholders and managers	Managers and suppliers, employees and perhaps customers
High and rising inflation	Shareholders and managers	Managers and employees; managers and suppliers; managers and retail customers
A new proposal is put to shareholders for a huge incentive scheme for directors	The directors of Co A and the directors of other companies (who are Co A's non-executive directors, and like to see high pay)	The directors and the employees; directors and the customers; (possibly) the directors and the shareholders

10.4 Influences on the relationship with stakeholders

One influence is personal conviction; the boss of the business may reject the notion of stakeholders, believing instead that shareholders should be the board's sole focus. If the firm tried to help the local community, for example, this would take funds away from the shareholders. Similarly, more rewards for the owners would mean fewer resources for employees. In the shareholder view, all these different groups are competing for a fixed set of rewards. If one group has a larger slice of the profits it leaves less for others.

Other possible influences on the relationship with stakeholders:

- Financial pressure: if the business is struggling for survival it would be understandable to focus solely on the internal stakeholders – the ones who can help solve the problems.
- The labour market: when jobs are plentiful, staff demand more pay, better working conditions and (sometimes) job redesign to make things more interesting. In these circumstances conflict between managers and workers is easy to conceive.

10.5 Managing the relationship with different stakeholders

Over the past ten years a criticism of plcs has been excessive executive pay and the extent to which its growth has outstripped both staff pay rises and dividend payments to shareholders. To manage this situation, directors employ financial public relations experts, i.e. they get the company to pay for a service that only really benefits directors. The ability of the 'PR' to smooth over the problems is an essential test of usefulness.

Arguably, this is quite wrong. A debate between directors and shareholders/owners should take place directly, rather than being mediated through a hired PR. Directors should see the company's money as being different from their own, just as one would hope that a head teacher would treat the school's money as completely separate from personal funds.

Generally, companies will produce websites and will generate publicity that suggests that all stakeholders are treated with equal respect. In the banking sector, the energy sector and in all those *Watchdog* programmes, that view has proven a huge simplification.

'We intend to conduct our business in a way that not only meets but exceeds the expectations of our customers, business partners, shareholders, and creditors, as well as the communities in which we operate and society at large.' Akira Mori, Japanese businessman

10.6 Communicating with stakeholders

Today, communicating with stakeholders means electronic communication: a combination of social media, email updates and a website with a 'supplier' section that's as substantial as the customer one. Just as companies talk about employee 'engagement', so they use the same term for 'engagement' of customers when they visit the website. A visit to Unilever's site (www.unilever.co.uk) shows their interest in persuading the outsider to 'follow us on Twitter' and sign up to the Facebook page.

The key issue is whether 'communication' means a two-way process of discussion or whether it's simply a mix of propaganda and public relations. If such communication was open and honest:

- Wouldn't innocent Drinks tell you that it's owned and controlled by Coca-Cola?
- Wouldn't Ben & Jerry's tell you it's owned and controlled by Unilever plc?
- Wouldn't Primark just get on with trying to improve its patchy supply record, instead of making 'Our Ethics' one of four main buttons on its website?

10.7 Consulting with stakeholders

Stakeholder mapping is carried out primarily to identify which stakeholders matter most to a company. In most cases, the internal ones are the most important. Yet if a business has allowed things to slip, external groups may become a priority. For example, Primark probably sees external pressure groups as a huge priority, as the business has so often been accused of lacking ethical standards in relation to its supply chain.

Having identified your most important stakeholders, it is then possible to set up regular consultation links and groupings. For Jaguar Land Rover, which buys key drive-chain components from GKN, regular discussions with GKN make sense in relation to future production levels and also new product development plans. Jaguar Land Rover would expect, in turn, to be given early notice of any bright new products GKN is planning, so that they can appear first in a JLR car.

Five Whys and a How

Question	Answer
Why might it be helpful to a business to use stakeholder mapping?	As part of a process of identifying which of their stakeholders are the most important
Why may it be risky for a business to focus solely on shareholder value?	Because the interests of wider stakeholders may be important to the media, as in the example of Primark and its supply chain
Why may it be difficult for some firms to communicate effectively with their stakeholders?	Because there's a tension between what a shareholder wants to know about the company and what a pressure group wants to know
Why may staff feel that they should be treated as a higher priority than other stakeholders?	Because the staff are actually the heart of the enterprise. It's like football fans and football managers – the latter come and go but the former are there for the long term
Why might a new small company treat customers as their only key stakeholder?	Because the business will stand or fall on repeat purchase and word of mouth from those customers
How might a large clothing retailer establish effective consultation with its stakeholders?	It would be hard because there are potentially so many of them. Perhaps get two representatives from each stakeholder group – then meet regularly (every two months?)

Evaluation: Understanding the role and importance of stakeholders

In recent years, there has been much greater interest in the idea that firms should pay attention to their social responsibilities. Increasingly, firms are being asked to consider, and justify, their actions towards a wide range of groups rather than just their shareholders. Managers are expected to take into account the interests and opinions of numerous internal and external groups before they make a decision. This social responsibility often makes good business sense. If you ignore your stakeholder groups you are vulnerable to pressure group action and may well lose customers and your brightest employees.

It may not be possible to meet the needs of all interest groups, however. Firms must decide on the extent to which they take stakeholders into account. Given their limited resources and other obligations, managers must decide on their priorities. In difficult times it may well be that the need for short-term profit overrides the demands of various stakeholder groups. It would be naive to ignore the fact that TV consumer programmes such as the BBC's *Watchdog* keep exposing business malpractice. Even if progress is being made in general, there are still many firms that persist in seeing short-term profit as the sole business objective.

'Companies, to date, have often used the excuse that they are only beholden to their shareholders, but we need shareholders to think of themselves as stakeholders in the well-being of the society.' Simon Mainwaring, businessman

Workbook

A. Revision questions

(40 marks; 40 minutes)

1. What is meant by a 'stakeholder'? (2)

2. Distinguish between internal and external stakeholders. (3)

3. Some people believe that an increasing number of firms are now trying to meet their social responsibilities. Explain why this may be the case. (3)

4. Outline two responsibilities a firm may have to:
   a) its employees (4)
   b) its customers (4)
   c) the local community. (4)

5. Explain how a firm could damage its profits in the pursuit of meeting its shareholder responsibilities. (4)

6. Explain why a firm's profit may fall by meeting its stakeholder responsibilities. (4)

7. Some managers reject the idea of stakeholding. They believe that a company's duty is purely to its shareholders. Outline two points in favour and two points against this opinion. (8)

8. What factors are likely to determine whether a firm accepts its responsibilities to a particular stakeholder group? (4)

B. Revision exercises

DATA RESPONSE

Market Basket and stakeholder objectives

Figure 10.2 Employees and customers hold a rally in support of Arthur T. DeMoulas and Market Basket, in Tewksbury, Massachusetts, on 25 July 2014.

A protest by thousands of workers at one of New England's largest grocery chains has left store shelves empty and customers scarce as employees demand the return of their fired chief executive. The turmoil is the latest twist in a decades-old feud among members of the DeMoulas family, whose DeMoulas Super Markets Inc. controls 71 Market Basket stores across the North-East of America.

On 23 June, Arthur S. DeMoulas, whose side of the family controls 50.5 percent of shares, fired his cousin, President and Chief Executive Officer Arthur T. DeMoulas, whose side controls 49.5 percent, and replaced him with two co-CEOs (chief executives). Many of the 25,000 employees rose up in support of "Artie T.", who they say is committed to high wages for staff and low prices for customers. Starting wages at Market Basket of $12 an hour are $4 above the minimum wage. Furthermore customers enjoy prices of around 20 per cent below those of rival supermarkets. Kevin Levesque, 53, assistant manager at the Tewksbury store, said his colleagues worry that their compensation won't be nearly as generous in the future. 'They know the changes will come,' he said. 'They have seen it in other companies and businesses in corporate America.'

A groundswell of popular support has followed, with rallies attended by thousands. The protests have been attended by customers as well as staff, especially since eight of the protest leaders were sacked by the new CEOs.

Amid the acrimony within the family, Market Basket has made the various DeMoulas shareholders wealthy. The company has paid out more than $1.1 billion in special dividends since 2001, according to 2013 legal documents. The richest among the family is the ousted Arthur T., who is worth $675 million through his 19 per cent stake and accumulated dividends. Arthur S. is worth about $575 million.

Source: adapted from Bloomberg.com.

Questions (30 marks; 30 minutes)

1. Explain the conflicting objectives among Market Basket's stakeholders. (5)

2. For workers to risk their own jobs to protest in favour of a business leader is unprecedented in recent business history in America or Britain. Explain why the situation at Market Basket may be so rare. (9)

3. To what extent might the sacking of Arthur T. prove right in the long term from the perspective of the majority shareholders in the company? (16)

C. Extend your understanding

1. 'Meeting the objectives of different stakeholder groups may be desirable but it is rarely profitable.' To what extent do you agree with this view? (20)

2. 'A manager's responsibility should be to the shareholders alone.' To what extent do you agree with this view? (20)

Marketing and decision-making

Linked to: Decision-making: scientific and intuitive, Chapter 7; Setting marketing objectives, Chapter 13; Market research, Chapter 15; Market data and analysis, Chapter 18.

Definition

Marketing can be seen either as a way of thinking or as a range of activities. For most modern businesses, marketing is focusing the goals and strategies of the business on an identified market opportunity.

Figure 11.1 Marketing decision-making: the marketing model

11.1 Making marketing decisions

In most firms, marketing is at the heart of the decisions taken by the directors. Not marketing in the sense of price cuts and promotions, but marketing in the sense of analysing growth trends and the competitive struggle within the firm's existing markets, and decisions about which markets the firm wishes to develop in future. Effective marketing decisions stem from a process known as the marketing model. It sets out how to tackle a marketing decision methodically.

Marketing decision-making: the marketing model

Successful marketing is not just about thinking. It is about decisions and action. Marketing decisions are particularly hard to make, because there are so many uncertainties. The procedure shown in Figure 11.1 is one of the most effective ways of ensuring a decision is well thought through.

The intention is to ensure that the strategy decided upon is the most effective at achieving the marketing objectives. In this process, market research is likely to be very important. It is crucial for finding out the background data and again for testing the hypotheses. Test marketing may also be used. This is a way of checking whether the market research results are

accurate, before finally committing the firm to an expensive national marketing campaign.

The marketing model is the way to decide how to turn a marketing objective into a strategy.

11.2 Developments in technology and marketing decisions

In 2014 a social media consultancy boasted that research among 2500 global marketers showed that 34 per cent believed that marketing through social media delivers a positive return on investment. Logically then, 66 per cent doubted that spending on social media was profitable. Why may this be? Part of the problem is embodied in the idea of Facebook 'Likes' or Twitter 'Followers'. Do Starbucks' 6.38 million followers become more loyal to the brand because they signed up to Twitter? No one is quite sure.

Profitable or not, the wind is blowing strongly in the direction of digital marketing. In 2013 UK business spending on social media advertising rose by 71 per cent to £588 million, with the growth in mobile advertising being the most dynamic. For the market as a whole Figure 11.2 shows that UK spending on mobile digital advertising is forecast to overtake spending on TV advertising airtime by 2016, partly at the cost of newspapers and magazines.

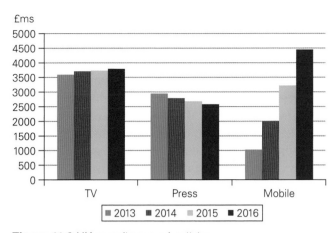

Figure 11.2 UK spending on advertising

Source: *eMarketer* magazine, June 2014

Real business

In 2014, with coffee sales stalling in America, Starbucks decided to broaden its appeal from its target of young professional adults. Parents started to notice their teenage and pre-teen kids showing newfound enthusiasm for Starbucks' 13,000 US outlets. The company had started selling a 'secret menu' of drinks that had gone viral via posts on Instagram and other social media. Only those in the know would think to ask for a 'Grasshopper Frap' or a 'Cotton Candy Frap'. One parent reported that when her tweenaged daughter asked for a Cotton Candy Frap, the shocking pink drink was served with a knowing wink. The thrill of posting a pic to her mates seemed to make up for the vile taste. Apparently McDonald's and others are playing with the secret menu concept after Starbucks' success.

11.3 The use of social media

The use of social media has become a serious alternative to standard press or TV advertising. There are three important benefits to firms from this form of digital marketing:

- The targeting can be especially tightly targeted at the precise tastes and habits of each individual, including noting changes in their behaviour such as when they move from home to University
- Traditional advertising was a one-way process from company to customer. Social media provide the interactivity that may help create some bonding between consumer and brand

- The success of crowdfunding sites such as Kickstarter shows that people are interested in getting involved in businesses, as long as they share the apparent aspirations of the proprietors. This, again, helps create a two-way bond.

From the above come two key benefits. First, social media can provide a way to gain a fuller understanding of what customers really love about the brand and the product range. In other words it can help you gain a fuller understanding of customers and the market you are serving. In the past this was attempted through market research, but the interactions between company and customer now have the potential to be much richer. When innocent Drinks recently introduced their first grass-covered van into Ireland, they asked their social media followers to suggest a name. 'LamborGreeny' was one of many suggestions. The campaign, which also ran in the UK, achieved over 1.4 million impressions for @innocentIreland.

Figure 11.3 innocent tweets: #NameTheVan

The second benefit is derived from the first. Stronger relationships between consumer and brand can cement brand loyalty and, in the long run, there are few more valuable attributes than that. For innocent, fighting directly in a Coca-Cola (innocent) versus PepsiCo (Tropicana) battle over the relatively undifferentiated UK market in orange juice, customer loyalty is especially valuable.

'Profit comes from repeat customers, customers that boast about your product and service, and that bring friends with them.' W. Edwards Deming, quality guru

For companies, the ultimate question is whether spending on social media provides a sufficient return on the money spent. Although this question cannot be answered satisfactorily by most companies, they feel that they are better off being 'in' than 'out'. The company that ignores the digital, online world may become the Morrisons' of its own sector.

Figure 11.4 Logic chain: traditional vs. online advertising

11.4 Relationship marketing

Often known as CRM (Customer Relationship Marketing), the idea is to use the storage capacity of modern IT to be able to build an apparent relationship between consumer and producer. In the past the nearest that could be achieved was to use a database to address letters to customers individually ('Dear Ian…'). Today there are many ways to achieve the same result, starting with what you see the next time you access your computer screen. Without you necessarily realising, the advertisement has been tailored to your tastes and habits; so has the junk mail that comes to your inbox.

'Consumers are statistics. Customers are people.' H. Stanley Marcus, businessman

Software provider Sage promotes its CRM software by saying: 'Make every customer interaction count'. This starts by making sure that there is a central record of all customer contacts, so that any manager can know at any time about past problems or successes (and key facts, such as last year's agreed price deals). The database recording all this knowledge about customers can then be interrogated to decide who might be in the market for this or that newly developed product.

Over time, the idea is to build a relationship with your own customers that makes them feel sufficiently special to stay. In effect, each business is trying to raise the barrier to customer exit. Many businesses believe that it costs five times more to get a new customer than to hold onto an existing one. This is the basis for continuous, heavy investment in CRM. Clever companies put their best sales staff onto their top-spending customers, and make sure that the processes involved in giving high customer satisfaction are all working to the highest possible standard.

'Your most unhappy customers are your greatest source of learning.' Bill Gates, founder of Microsoft

11.5 Dynamic pricing

In July 2014 the Chairman of Center Parcs explained that the company no longer has a price list. The whole business works on 'dynamic pricing', i.e. prices move continually, in line with changes in supply and demand. If a local TV programme features the Sherwood Forest Center Parcs, demand might rise for the forthcoming half-term; Center Parc's computer software will detect the change instantly and push prices up. The computers are programmed to achieve a 97 per cent usage rate – every week of the year. The higher the price they can get for their space the better. That's dynamic pricing.

Table 11.1 The impact of different supply and demand conditions on price

	Supply down	Supply the same	Supply up
Demand up	Price up sharply	Price up	Price unchanged
Demand stays the same	Price up	Price stays the same	Price down
Demand down	Price stays the same	Price down	Price down sharply

Table 11.1 shows the impacts of different supply and demand conditions upon the price of Center Parc holidays (or any other commodity).

The strength of dynamic pricing is that it can achieve high capacity utilisation without requiring banks of skilled staff. No wonder that the same method is used by the low-cost airlines, the rail companies and all the major hotel chains.

11.6 Ethical influences on marketing decisions

In recent years much has been written and said about marketing ethics, especially by companies. They put forward the idea that modern firms are socially responsible in their dealings with consumers (and suppliers). In many cases this may be true, but not in all. When observing companies it is hard to know which is better, their intentions or their PR (public relations).

Ethical marketing requires an honest, open mindset and the willingness to sacrifice profit where it is incompatible with morality. This is hard even for small businesses, but may simply be asking too much within large corporations.

'It horrifies me that ethics is an optional extra at Harvard Business School.' Sir John Harvey-Jones, former boss, ICI

Ethical marketing

Companies today know that boxes have to be ticked: recycling, tick; Fairtrade, tick; low in saturated fats, tick. Because there are so many possible positives a company can use in its packaging and marketing, it simply chooses the ones that happen to score most highly with customers. This is all to do with marketing and nothing to do with ethics.

What of the companies with a conscience, though? Perhaps innocent Drinks with its naïf logo and its talk of doing good? But as it's now owned and controlled by Coca-Cola, few would believe that innocent is a haven of goodness within a multinational that struggles to define itself as a good corporate citizen.

What influences marketing decisions is not ethics but social trends. In other words, companies are desperate to present themselves as moral and responsible, as long as the consumer cares. The problem is that consumers are better at saying they care than they are at acting accordingly. Primark has been associated many times with exploitative terms and conditions for workers at its Far Eastern suppliers but its profit and sales growth figures suggest that low prices trump ethics. Needless to say there are small, niche producers who can command premium prices for their ethically sourced goods but this may simply be clever rather than ethical marketing.

'To know what is right and not to do it is the worst cowardice.' Confucius (551-479 BC) Chinese philosopher

Environmental marketing

The household cleaner Domestos has long announced its purpose through the advertising line: 'Kills germs – dead!' Thoughtfully, though, its website now has a homepage tab on 'Sustainable Cleaning'. No one should doubt that Domestos is the same powerful chemical it always was – and it will be flushed down drains near you – but brand owner Unilever knows it must take into account those interested in the environment.

Far away from that example comes the longstanding but still excellent case of the Toyota Prius. Toyota started developing the Prius when oil/petrol prices were low and persisted with the car for more than ten years before it made any profit. It was an act of faith by the company in a cleaner future and, of course, in Toyota's position at the heart of that future. Overall, it is hard to see the company's actions as anything other than environmentally (and ethically) sound.

When analysing a company that markets itself as environmentally conscious, it is important to consider whether it is 'greenwash' (a green gloss coat over an empty shell) or a genuine attempt to behave responsibly. It would be impressive if the business went ahead with green actions that it felt no need to boast about. And impressive if those actions added to costs (though no one can expect a business to make itself uncompetitive – risking its survival).

Five Whys and a How

Question	Answer
Why might it be helpful to 'form hypotheses' when making a marketing decision (see Figure 11.1)?	In effect they are the alternative strategy options that can then be tested in research or in a **test market**
What might be the effect on press media of the fall in advertising revenue forecast in Figure 11.2?	It might either force magazines to increase their cover prices or – more probably – force some to cut staffing and others to close down
Why might a business decide to double the budget it allocates to relationship marketing?	Perhaps because **benchmarked data** shows that the business is performing relatively poorly at customer loyalty
Why might customers prefer traditional static pricing to dynamic pricing?	Because they can look up prices on a rate card that shows the apparent 'value' of the item; dynamic pricing means today's price is different from yesterdays, which might be unsettling
Why does a rise in demand push prices up (in a dynamic market)?	The hike in demand shows that the available supply can be sold more easily; instead of selling everything at low prices, the computer programme pushes prices up (to ration the supply)
How might a consumer be taken in by 'greenwash'?	A customer might trust that the product is especially environmentally friendly when it is no better than rival products – just more cleverly advertised or packaged

Key terms

Benchmarked data is information on how well one company is performing compared with its peers/competitors, e.g. on customer complaints per 100 sales.

Test market: trialling a new product in an area of the country to get feedback on real sales in the real world.

Evaluation: Marketing and decision-making

Good marketing decisions are made by executives who use logical frameworks such as the marketing model. A former boss of Apple Inc. once said, though, that 'no great marketing decisions have ever been made on quantitative data'. In other words, great decisions require intuition and an understanding of consumer psychology (qualitative data). In the case of Apple, the launch of the iPad was a perfect example.

Another feature of a great decision is that it should not work in the short term but come unstuck further on.

This is why it's so foolish to market products in a less-than-honest manner. At present Coca-Cola is being 'clever' in pretending that innocent Drinks is still a small, quirky company. Eventually people will realise that this is pretty dishonest. The company is just a division of Coca-Cola – and there might be quite a backlash when people realise this. As business guru Robert Townsend wrote 50 years ago: 'Try honesty. . . it really works'.

Workbook

A. Revision questions

(35 marks; 35 minutes)

1. Outline two ways in which a company using the marketing model might 'test the options'. (4)

2. In September 2014 Coca-Cola launched Coke Life in a green can. How might the company judge whether this was the right decision? (5)

3. Explain why digital advertising might be especially cost-effective at reaching target consumers. (5)

4. Why might innocent Drinks want to build a stronger relationship with its customers? (4)

5. In your own words, explain the meaning of the term 'dynamic pricing'. (3)

6. A teacher complained to the Chairman of Centre Parcs that 'holidays with you are too expensive in the holidays'. Explain one reason for and one reason against her argument. (6)

7. Is the price of a commodity likely to rise or fall when:
   a) supply rises while demand is unchanged? (1)
   b) demand falls while supply rises? (1)
   c) supply is unchanged but demand rises? (1)

8. Is it ethical to advertise Wall's Funny Feet ice cream on children's TV? (5)

B. Revision exercises

DATA RESPONSE

Figure 11.5 New product launch: Mars Caramel

The Mars Bar was launched over 80 years ago, created in his kitchen by Frank Mars in 1923. Sold in America as Milky Way (and still is), when it came to Britain in 1932 the decision was made to call it the Mars bar. (Astonishingly, when it started in Britain it was covered in Cadbury chocolate as the new Mars factory at Slough was not yet able to make high quality chocolate.)

The Mars bar has been a fabulous financial success, helping to build the still family-run Mars business to a global turnover of $30 billion by 2011. Nevertheless, sales in Britain have been struggling for the last few years. Whereas customers can kid themselves that an Aero or a packet of Maltesers is a 'light' snack, a Mars always seems a piggy option. In 2011 the whole chocolate confectionery market rose by 2.1 per cent, but sales of Mars bars fell by 0.7 per cent. Nevertheless, with annual sales of £92.6 million, Mars bars still represented a huge, profitable brand.

In September 2012 Mars decided on a new way to boost sales. It came from a successful US test of 'Milky Way Caramel', in effect taking the sludgy bit out of the Mars, leaving just the chocolate and the caramel centre. Given that Mars already marketed Galaxy Caramel over here, it was hard to see where the 'room' was in the market for the new Mars product, which was launched in the UK in September 2012. But Mars had investigated that issue using extensive market research.

Mars marketed Mars Caramel by emphasising that it has 20 per cent fewer calories than the Mars bar. This was expected to make it appeal more to women. But wouldn't consumers simply think: why am I paying the same as a Mars bar for a Mars bar with no 'nougat' centre? If so, they would surely see it as bad value, or even as a 'rip-off'. Mars had to handle the promotion of this new product with great care, steering a path between different ethical issues.

In September 2013 Mars announced that they were re-launching Mars Caramel as an 8-week Limited Edition product supported by a £2.8 million marketing budget. They commented on 'the overwhelming popularity of the original launch'.

Questions (25 marks; 30 minutes)

1. Examine how Mars might have made its decision to go ahead with the launch of Mars Caramel. (8)

2. Explain two 'different ethical issues' in the launch of Mars Caramel. (8)

3. Analyse the possible determinants of whether Mars Caramel proves a success in the long term. (9)

C. Extend your understanding

1. To what extent do you agree that Arsenal F.C. should abandon their current static pricing model (including season tickets) and switch entirely to dynamic pricing for each home game? (By all means substitute your favourite/local football team.) (20)

2. 'It's time for a brand such as Cadbury's Dairy Milk to abandon traditional TV and press media and spend their whole advertising budget on digital and social media.' To what extent do you agree? (20)

Marketing and competitiveness

Linked to: Understanding markets, Chapter 14; Market research, Chapter 15; Segmentation, targeting and positioning, Chapter 19; Marketing mix: the 7 Ps, Chapter 21.

Definition

Competitiveness measures a firm's ability to offer a better combination of price and quality than its rivals.

12.1 Introduction: What is a competitive market?

In the past, markets were physical places where buyers and sellers met in person to exchange goods. Street markets are still like that. Today, some markets are virtual, such as eBay.

Some markets are more competitive than others. The number of firms operating influences the intensity of competition; the more firms there are, the greater the level of competition. However, the respective size of the firms operating in a market should also be taken into account. A market consisting of 50 firms may not be particularly competitive, if, for instance, one of the firms holds a 60 per cent market share and the remaining 40 per cent is shared between the other 49 firms. Similarly, a market with just four firms could be quite competitive because the firms operating within this market may be of a fairly similar size.

Consumers enjoy competitive markets. However, the reverse is true for firms, as prices and profit margins tend to be squeezed. As a result, firms try hard to minimise competition, perhaps by creating a unique selling point (USP) or using predatory pricing.

It could be argued that marketing is vital no matter what the level of competition is within the market. Firms that fail to produce goods and services that satisfy the needs of the consumers will find it hard to succeed in the long term.

'Competition brings out the best in products and the worst in people.' David Sarnoff, US business leader

12.2 Market conditions and competition

One dominant business

In some markets there is no competition because there is only one business operating. This is called a monopoly. The UK market for chewing gum is close to this position, as Wrigley has a 90 per cent market share. For an example of a total monopoly, look at the situation of Virgin Rail – the sole supplier of rail travel between London and Manchester. Monopolies are bad for consumers because they restrict output, pushing up prices and restricting consumer choice. For this reason governments have legal powers to regulate against monopoly power.

Deciding whether or not a firm has a monopoly is a far from straightforward task. First of all, the market itself has to be accurately defined. Camelot has a monopoly to run the National Lottery, but there are many other forms of gambling, such as horse racing and the football pools. So is Camelot really in a dominant market position? Second, national market share figures should not be used in isolation because some firms enjoy local monopolies.

Firms implement their marketing strategy through the marketing mix. In markets dominated by a single large business, firms do not need to spend heavily on promotion because consumers are, to a degree, captive. Prices can be pushed upwards and the product element of the marketing mix can be focused on creating innovations that make it harder for new entrants to break into the market. Apple spends millions of dollars on research and development in order to produce cutting-edge products such as the iPhone 6 (see Figure 12.1). To ensure that Apple maintains its dominant market position new product launches are patented to prevent me-too imitations from being launched by the competition.

Figure 12.1 iPhone 6

Competition amongst a few giants

The UK supermarket industry is a good example of a market that is dominated by a handful of very large companies. Economists call markets like this oligopolistic. The rivalry that exists within such markets can be intense. Firms know that any gains in market share will be at the expense of their rivals. The actions taken by one firm affect the profits made by the other firms that compete within the same market.

In markets made up of a few giants, firms tend to focus on non-price competition when designing the marketing mix. Firms in these markets tend to be reluctant to compete by cutting price. They fear that the other firms in the industry will respond by cutting their prices too, creating a costly price war where no firm wins.

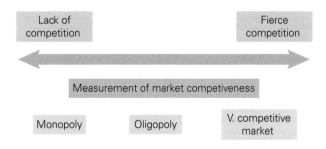

Figure 12.2 Degree of competition

The fiercely competitive market

Fiercely competitive markets can also be fragmented, made up of hundreds of relatively small firms, each of which competes actively against the others. In some of these markets competition is amplified by the fact that firms sell near-identical products, called commodities.

Commodities are products, such as flour, sugar or memory sticks, that are hard to differentiate. Rivalry in commodity markets tends to be intense. In markets such as this, firms have to manage their production costs very carefully because the retail price is the most important factor in determining whether the firm's product sells or not. If a firm cannot cut its costs, it will not be able to cut its prices without cutting into profit margins. Without price cuts market share is likely to be lost.

In fiercely competitive markets firms will try, where possible, to create product differentiation. For example, the restaurant market in Croydon, Surrey, is extremely competitive. There are over 70 outlets within a two-mile radius of the town centre. To survive without having to compete solely on price, firms in markets like this must regularly find new innovations because points of differentiation are quickly copied.

'Without competitors there would be no need for strategy.' Kenichi Ohmae, Japanese business guru

12.3 How marketing decisions may help improve competitiveness

To be competitive, a brand must have a close fit with consumers' tastes and habits. In the period 2009–2014 Coca-Cola found its sales slipping in America and Europe as people turned away from fizzy soft drinks. So in 2014 it launched Coke Life with the proposition: same Coke, fewer calories. If it succeeds it will be by having understood what modern consumers want – and by finding the right market positioning and image to make people want to try it, then buy it regularly. Every aspect of the proposition was researched with care, from the green pack colour to the careful advertising messages (which never mentioned diet or health).

The most important marketing decision concerns positioning: where exactly does the brand fit into the market? If this is achieved successfully, the brand can acquire a clarity or even a personality that makes it easy for consumers to identify with. If the marketing company can get consumers to want to buy a product because of its image, that's perhaps the ultimate business achievement. Some men want to own a BMW because they think the image (successful, sporty) makes them look good; some women want a Chanel bag because it speaks of their classiness and their success. BMW and Chanel charge premium prices almost as a confirmation of their customers' good taste and deep pockets. The result, of course, is huge profit margins for the companies. Chanel's net profit margins of 32 per cent compare with 6 per cent for Mercedes and less than 5 per cent for Tesco and Sainsbury's.

In addition to market positioning, the following are important ways in which marketing can boost competitiveness.

Design

Some firms are highly competitive because they sell products that have been differentiated by their design. In countries such as the UK, where wage rates are relatively high, manufacturers cannot compete on price alone. Production costs are too high compared with rivals in countries where wage rates are lower. By using design as a USP, British manufacturers can compete on quality rather than price, making them less vulnerable to competition from China and India. Good-looking design can add value to a product. For example, the BMW Mini relies upon its retro 1960s styling to command its price premium within the small car market.

Brand image

In many markets brand image is crucial. The results of blind tests indicate that, in many cases, consumers are unable to tell the difference between supermarket own-label products and premium-priced brands. Clever branding and advertising may be the only thing ensuring that Stella Artois carries on outselling Tesco's Premium Lager.

Marketing mix

To pull the marketing strategy together, businesses look to their marketing mix. This is the combination of marketing variables that turns an idea into a practical reality. That is, setting the right price, for the correctly designed product, promoted correctly and distributed in the right places to reach the target market. When this is done with intelligence and creativity (as with the launch of the Samsung Galaxy and the launch of the Sony PS4) the result can be such a highly competitive proposition that rivals struggle to keep up. Six months after launching its Xbox One, Microsoft had to cut its price by $100 to keep up with the all-conquering PS4.

'Competitive advantage is based, not on doing what others already do well, but on doing what others cannot do as well.' Professor John Kay, economist and writer

---

Five Whys and a How

Question	Answer
Why is it hard to compete in a crowded commodity market such as a basic gents' hairdresser?	Because if differentiation is minimal the only way to compete is price, so even though costs are squeezed to the minimum there may be little or no profit
Why is market positioning so important?	Because products succeed best when they have a distinct image/'personality' that fits in with customers' psychology and habits
Why do customers lose out when a firm has a monopoly position?	The company can push prices up yet cut spending on service and innovation to boost its profit at the expense of customers
Why do some firms seem to be able to sustain their competitiveness over many years?	Often, as with Heinz, it's because of a traditional, strong brand and slow-moving markets; with a business such as Sony it's hard to keep coming up with killer innovations
Why was Apple able to gain a net profit margin of 22 per cent in 2014?	Because of the hugely competitive nature of its brand image and the clear positioning of its design-led products
How might a firm's people affect its competitiveness?	Internally, the key decision-makers are middle-managers who need to work collaboratively; externally, the enthusiasm and efficiency of staff can rub off onto customers

Evaluation: Marketing and competitiveness

Competitiveness is a much wider issue than marketing. It is affected by the quality of the design and build of the products, and by the enthusiasm of the staff. These are clearly operations and personnel issues. Nevertheless, marketing is at the heart of competitiveness for many firms. Mars knows how to produce Galaxy chocolate, so the key to the firm's success next year is how well the brand can be marketed. The managers must understand the customers, and then have the wisdom and the creativity to find a way to make the product stand out.

Workbook

A. Revision questions

(30 marks; 30 minutes)

1. What is a competitive market? (2)

2. Explain how the marketing mix of Virgin Trains could be affected by a decision by government to allow other train-operating companies to compete on Virgin's routes. (3)

3. Consider the following:
   a) what is a price war and … (3)
   b) why are they rare? (3)

4. Explain why product differentiation becomes more important as competition within a market increases. (3)

5. Identify four factors that could be used to identify whether or not a business is competitive. (4)

6. How could the size of an organisation affect its efficiency? (3)

7. UK sales of Tropicana fruit juices have struggled in recent years as Coca-Cola's innocent juices have gained market share. Outline two marketing methods Tropicana might adopt to rebuild its competitiveness. (6)

8. Apart from market research, how may a firm achieve its goal of attempting to get closer to the consumer? (3)

B. Revision exercises
DATA RESPONSE 1

Tesco's £9 toaster

The prices of consumer electronics, including toasters, satellite TV set-top boxes and MP3 players, have tumbled in recent years. So, why have the prices of these goods fallen? In part, the price falls reflect the falling price of the components that go into consumer electronics. Low prices also reflect the fact that there is now more competition in the market. In the past, consumers typically bought items such as TVs and computers from specialist retailers such as Currys and Dixons. Today, the situation is somewhat different: in addition to these specialist retailers, consumers can now buy electrical goods over the internet and from supermarkets. Industry analysts also believe that some of the supermarket chains are using set-top boxes and DVD players as loss leaders.

In today's ultra-competitive environment, manufacturers of consumer electronics face intense pressure from retailers to cut costs so that retail prices can be cut without any loss of profit margin. To cut prices without compromising product quality, manufacturers such as the Dutch giant Philips have transferred production from the Netherlands to low-cost locations such as China.

Questions (30 marks; 35 minutes)

1. Describe three characteristics of a highly competitive market. (6)

2. Explain one reason why the market for consumer electronics has become more competitive. (4)

3. How could the degree of competition impact the marketing mix used by a Chinese manufacturer of own-label toasters? (4)

4. In today's increasingly competitive market for consumer electronics, firms must constantly cut costs and prices if they are to survive. To what extent do you agree? (16)

DATA RESPONSE 2

At the beginning of the 1960s Indian food was a niche market business: there were just 500 Indian restaurants in the whole of the UK. As Table 12.1 illustrates, in the two decades that followed, the UK Indian restaurant market grew at a spectacular rate. In more recent times the market has continued to grow; however, the rate of growth has declined. Today, the Indian restaurant market is firmly established. The industry is one of Britain's largest, employing over 60,000 people.

Table 12.1 Number of Indian restaurants in the UK

Year	No. of restaurants	Market growth rate (%)
1960	500	–
1970	1200	140
1980	3000	150
1990	5100	70
2000	7940	56
2004	8750	10
2010	8900	2
2014	10000	12

The Indian restaurant market is made up of thousands of small, independent operators. In most British high streets there are several Indian restaurants that compete aggressively against one another. Indian food is very popular: over 23 million portions of Indian food are sold in restaurants each year. Over the years, growing affluence boosted takings and profits at most Indian restaurants. Most owners chose to use some of the profit to upgrade their facilities. Gradually, Indian restaurants became more sophisticated (for example, air conditioning and with dinner-jacketed waiters).

As more Indian restaurants opened up, however, too many looked the same and had very similar menus. As a result, they were forced into competing against

each other on price. Intense price competition led to falling profit margins. Indian restaurateurs began to realise the importance of product differentiation as a competitive weapon. The first real attempt to create differentiation occurred when a handful of forward-looking Indian restaurants, such as the Gaylord in Mortimer Street, London, imported tandoors. A tandoor is a special type of oven made from clay that gives the food cooked inside it a distinctive taste. Restaurants using tandoor ovens found that they could charge slightly higher prices without emptying their restaurants. Today, Indian restaurants use a variety of tactics to compete, including those listed below.

● Décor and design: in recent times several now famous London-based Indian restaurants, such as the Cinnamon Club (opened at a cost of £2.6 million in the Old Westminster Library) ditched the old-style traditional Indian restaurant décor in favour of a more upmarket-looking, modern design. This change inspired many other Indian restaurants up and down the land to upgrade their fixtures and fittings in the hope that they too could charge Cinnamon Club-style premium prices.

● Exotic-sounding premium-priced menu items: for example, Sea Bass Kaylilan prepared with fenugreek and tamarind.

Other restaurants have adopted a different approach. For example, the Khyber in Croydon has tried to win customers by emphasising its authenticity. The restaurant's website informs the reader that 'Our success is based on more traditional recipes.' The slogan 'It's just how mum would cook it back home' also features prominently on its online menu. It also offers:

● balti cooking, including the super-sized big-as-your-table Nan breads!

Figure 12.3 An Indian restaurant with a contemporary design

- a prestigious imported German lager on draught, or a selection of fine wines

- celebrated curry chefs from the Indian subcontinent flown in for a limited period to cook up special food for a Curry Festival – the equivalent of a nightclub flying in a celebrity DJ.

Questions (30 marks; 35 minutes)

1. Using the table, explain what has happened to the degree of competition within the UK Indian restaurant market over the last 50 years. (4)

2. Explain how efficiency could affect the competitiveness of an Indian restaurant. (4)

3. Identify and explain three marketing approaches an Indian restaurant could adopt to improve its competitiveness. (6)

4. 'Product differentiation is essential if an Indian restaurant is to survive in the long run.' To what extent do you agree with this statement? (16)

C. Extend your understanding

1. To what extent could excellent marketing decisions ensure that a business such as Pizza Express stays in a strong competitive position? (20)

2. To what extent might a small company such as Higgidy Pies be affected if its market becomes dominated by one producer? (20)

Setting marketing objectives

Linked to: Understanding the nature and purpose of business, Chapter 1; Marketing and decision-making, Chapter 11; Market research, Chapter 15; Market data and analysis, Chapter 18.

Definition

Marketing objectives are the targets set for the marketing department to help meet the goals of the organisation as a whole.

13.1 The value of setting marketing objectives

A marketing objective is a marketing target or goal that an organisation hopes to achieve, such as to boost market share from 9 to 12 per cent within 2 years. Marketing objectives steer the direction of the business. Operating a business without knowing your objectives is like driving a car without knowing where you want to go. Some businesses achieve a degree of success without setting marketing objectives; stumbling across a successful business model by accident. But why should anyone rely on chance? If firms set marketing objectives the probability of success increases because decision-making will be more focused.

Marketing objectives must be compatible with the overall objectives of the company; they cannot be set in isolation by the marketing department. Achieving the marketing objective of boosting market share from 9 to 12 per cent will help realise a corporate objective of growth.

To be effective, marketing objectives should be quantifiable and measurable. Targets should also be set within a time frame. An example of a marketing objective that Nestlé might set is: 'To achieve a 9 per cent increase in the sales of Kit Kat by the end of next year.'

'Begin with the end in mind.' Stephen Covey, business writer

13.2 Examples of marketing objectives

Sales volume and sales value

A car manufacturer, such as BMW, could set the following marketing objective: 'To increase the number of BMW 3 Series cars sold in China from 250,000 to 400,000 over the next 12 months'. Setting sales volume targets can be particularly important in industries such as car manufacturing because of the high fixed costs associated with operating in this market. If sales volume can be increased, the high fixed costs of operating will be spread across a greater number of units of output, reducing fixed costs per unit. Lower unit costs will help BMW to widen its profit margins. Higher profit margins will give BMW the opportunity to increase its research and development budgets, raising the likelihood of success for BMW's next generation of new car models.

Nike has benefited from a slightly different way of looking at sales. It set a goal based on sales value rather than volume. In other words, sales measured in money. In 1996 chairman Phil Knight set Nike's sights on being the 'No. 1' supplier of football boots and kit. At the time, Nike was a minor player in the football sector of the sportswear business. Adidas was 'No. 1'. Nike's approach has clearly paid off. In 1996 Nike generated sales of just $40 million from football. In 2014 Nike set, and then subsequently beat, a sales target for its football division of $2,000 million! Nike even outsold Adidas in its German homeland.

Market size

If a business has a large market share, it may worry that boosting its share further may bring investigations from the Competition and Markets Authority.

Therefore, its best way to achieve further growth is by encouraging growth in the market sector as a whole. In the UK, Wrigley has a 90 per cent share of chewing gum sales. So anything it could do to boost the size of the market would help boost its own sales.

In these circumstances businesses might sponsor research by academics into the health-giving properties of the product. Ocean Spray has a 66 per cent share of the UK market for cranberry juice. So research into the supposed benefits of 'cranberries – the superfruit' could boost sales in the market as a whole, from which Ocean Spray would get 66 per cent of the benefit.

Needless to say, for a company with a 25 per cent market share, boosting the market as a whole would make little sense, as 75 per cent of the benefit would be enjoyed by competitors; whereas for Ocean Spray, as for Wrigley, it can make sense to set marketing objectives based on increasing the size of the market as a whole.

Market and sales growth

For public limited companies in particular, pressure from outside shareholders forces them to keep pushing for more growth. This presses the company into finding new opportunities and may lead the marketing department to overreach. For example, marketing departments love to boost sales by 'stretching' brands, by developing more and more variants based on a single brand. Nestle tried to stretch sales of Kit Kat in the UK by launching varieties such as Lemon and Yogurt, Christmas Pudding, Tiramisu and Seville Orange. The net effect was a short-term sales boost followed by a significant sales downturn as consumers lost a clear sense of what the Kit Kat brand meant.

Growth, therefore, must be treated with caution. It is a valid objective, but one that can cause its own difficulties. One UK company that has handled it especially well is the clothing business Ted Baker plc. Sales grew every year between 2003 and 2014, including through the severe recession of 2009–10. It achieved this by keeping growth controlled, focusing one-at-a-time upon new market opportunities such as opening Ted Baker shops in Japan, then America, then China. It never overstretched itself, unlike Tesco with its disastrous expansion into America, or Morrisons' with its failed attempt to grow into the baby clothing market (Kiddicare was bought for £70 m in 2011, but in 2014 Morrisons' cut £163 m from the value of its assets to reflect ongoing losses at Kiddicare, and then sold Kiddicare off for £2m!).

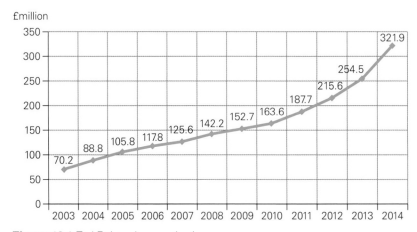

Figure 13.1 Ted Baker plc annual sales revenue
Source: Ted Baker plc accounts

Sensations

Launched in 2002 with celeb backing from Victoria Beckham and Gary Neville, Walkers Sensations once had annual sales of over £100 million in the premium crisps market. But by 2009 sales had flagged seriously, hit by newer, more premium brands such as Kettle Chips. Instead of watching sales continue to drift, Walkers responded by relaunching the brand in early 2010, giving it more striking packaging and launching a wider range of flavours. By 2012 and 2013 the success of this relaunch won the brand new distribution outlets in supermarkets and elsewhere. A well-executed marketing strategy brought the brand back to health (see Figure 13.2).

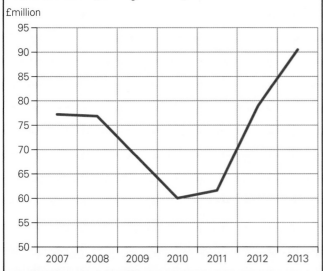

£million

Figure 13.2 Annual sales of Sensations crisps
Source: *The Grocer* Top Products Survey

Market share

Nothing is more important to a marketing department than the market share of its key brands. External factors largely control market size, e.g. the weather or the state of the economy. Market share, by contrast, is largely the product of the marketing department's successes or failures. In 2013 UK sales of Galaxy fell by 5.3 per cent while sales of Cadbury's Dairy Milk rose by 14 per cent. Perhaps Mars (Galaxy) focused too much on a slick new TV advertising campaign with the copy line 'Why have cotton when you can have silk'. Cadbury, by contrast, focused on new product development such as the launch of Dairy Milk with Oreo cookies.

In setting a market share objective, a company needs to be cautiously optimistic, for example, aiming to push a brand such as Snickers from its 2.5 per cent share of the £3.6 billion UK chocolate market to 3.0 per cent

within the next two years. This would be ambitious, but conceivable. Note that a 3 per cent market share would generate annual sales of £108 million, making it perfectly possible to afford a marketing budget of perhaps £10 million, allowing for a substantial TV advertising campaign as well as a significant budget for social media advertising.

Brand loyalty

Brand loyalty exists when consumers repeat-purchase your brand rather than swapping and switching between brands. It is widely agreed that it is far more expensive to have to find a new customer than to keep existing ones happy, so brand loyalty is crucial for achieving high profit margins. For charities, too, it is important to set a marketing objective of improving brand loyalty. If existing donors can be persuaded to set up a direct debit to the charity, its cash flow will improve significantly.

To enhance, or reposition a brand's image

Although some brands stay fresh for generations (Marmite is over 100 years old) others become jaded due to changes in consumer tastes and lifestyles. At this point the firms need to refresh the brand image to keep the products relevant to the target market. A clear objective must be set. For instance: What brand attributes do we want to create? What do we want the brand to stand for?

Repositioning

This occurs when a firm aims to a change a brand's image, so that the brand appeals to a new target market. Twelve years into its life cycle, McVitie's decided to reposition its Hobnobs biscuit brand. Hobnobs had been positioned as a homely, quite healthy biscuit for middle-aged consumers. Research pointed McVitie's in a new direction: younger, more male, and less dull. So new packaging was designed and then launched in conjunction with a new, brighter advertising campaign. In 2013 Hobnobs sales were worth £36 million, 9 per cent up on the previous year.

13.3 Internal influences on marketing objectives and decisions

From within the business there are several pressures on marketing objectives and decisions. In the online grocery business Ocado, the operations department decided in 2014 to build its third, £200 million distribution depot in Salford, near

Manchester. When opened, perhaps in early 2016, this will create the need for Ocado's marketing department to work hard to boost the number of online Ocado shoppers in the North West. So the pressure for market and sales growth will be due to an internal influence.

Among many other possible internal influences are:

● New corporate objectives set by a new chief executive. The new boss may want to boost sales volume, perhaps in response to a perceived short-term opportunity such as the 2016 Brazil Olympics; or there may be a marketing requirement to strengthen brand loyalty as a way to boost pricing power and therefore profit margins.

● The development of an innovative new product. When Apple Inc. devised the iPod in 2001, it ended up forcing the entire business to refocus from IT to consumer electronics. The marketing department needed to gain an understanding of a new, younger, trendier consumer, and to set objectives based on ambitious market share targets and exceptional brand loyalty.

● New financial objectives. If a new finance director demands higher profit margins, this will have an impact upon the marketing department's objectives and decision-making. As long ago as 1999 the multinational Unilever decided to slash 1,200 brands from its portfolio in order to focus on 400 'power brands'. This was to boost profit margins. Amazingly, even in 2013 and 2014 it is still working on achieving this goal. In 2013 it sold off some minor hair care brands and in 2014 sold its Ragu, Bertolli and Slim-fast food brands.

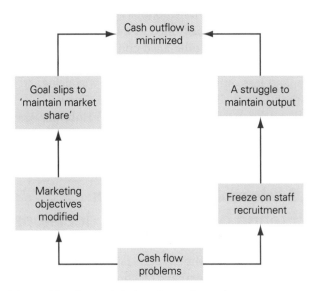

Figure 13.3 Logic chain: how to resolve cash flow difficulties

13.4 External influences on marketing objectives and decisions

It could never make sense to set a marketing objective that ignores the external context of competitors, changing customer tastes, changing economic circumstances and an ever-changing natural environment, from weather to earthquakes to pollutants.

Among many external influences on marketing objectives and decisions are:

● Changes in fashion or consumer taste/habits. The basis for banks' selling and marketing programmes once rested on their high street branches. These days footfall in UK bank branches is falling at a rate of 10 per cent a year as people use online or mobile methods to pay bills or transfer cash. That forces the banks to find new ways to market to their own customers, never mind potential future customers.

● Changing competitive pressures. Colgate is the world's biggest toothpaste-maker, with a 45 per cent global market share (generating sales of $4.5 billion). Its fiercest brand competitor in recent times has been Procter & Gamble's Oral-B brand, which has grown partly through scare tactics in its digital advertising ('Scary things come to those who don't brush' had 7.5 million YouTube hits). In response Colgate has had to rethink its marketing, deciding to increase substantially its budget for digital advertising.

● Changing economic pressures. In 2013 and 2014 continuing pressure on real incomes gave discounters Aldi and Lidl a huge UK market-share boost compared with the flagging Tesco and Morrisons'. This forced Morrisons' to rethink its marketing objectives, opting for the approach 'We're cheaper' which, in turn, forced the business to chop out a whole management layer in order to cut its operating costs.

● Changing natural environment. With a growing consensus about global warming, more companies are placing environmental greenness on their list of marketing objectives. This leads to actions such as Pret a Manger's decision to only use organic milk, or the creation of Green Tomato Cars – a minicab firm that only uses the eco-friendly Toyota Prius.

'A decision is the action an executive must take when he has information so incomplete that the answer does not suggest itself.' Arthur Radford, US Admiral and business consultant

Five Whys and a How

Question	Answer
Why are marketing objectives important?	Because they determine the strategies that the marketing managers choose to adopt
Why may it be better to target sales by value than by volume?	Volume is simply the number bought; value is more important because it includes volume and price, i.e. total revenue
Why might market share rise even though brand loyalty has fallen?	Because of an increase in sales to new customers or an increase in demand from customers who feel no loyalty to any brand
Why might internal influences lead to the wrong marketing objective being adopted?	Pressure for a short-term boost to profits (perhaps coming from Finance) might lead to a mistakenly short-termist marketing objective
Why might external influences clash with internal influences on marketing objectives?	They shouldn't, as insiders should keep an eye on the external context – but internal politics may prevent that from happening
How might a company set marketing objectives for an innovative new product?	By deciding on the long-term goal, then considering the internal and external influences on that goal to determine how realistic it really is

Key terms

Competition and Markets Authority: the renamed Competition Commission, set up in 2014 to intervene where necessary to protect consumers from anti-competitive business practices.

Corporate objective: the targets decided for the company as a whole, usually after boardroom discussion.

Market share: the percentage of total sales in a market held by one brand or company.

Repositioning means tweaking the product, branding and image to shift the proposition to a slightly different place in the market sector, for example, towards younger, more affluent adults.

Short-termist: taking decisions on the basis of short-term need rather than long-term benefit.

Evaluation: Setting marketing objectives

Marketing objectives stem from the corporate goals and from the internal and external circumstances the business faces. The problem for the decision-maker is that there is usually a wide range of contradictory pressures bearing down on the objectives. External forces may point in one direction whereas internal needs suggest a different approach. The expert marketing director will listen to all views and then make a slow, careful decision about what to do. Setting the wrong objectives leads to certain disaster, so it is worth taking time to become as sure as possible about the right step forward.

Workbook

A. Revision questions

(30 marks; 30 minutes)

1. In your own words, explain the meaning of the term 'marketing objectives'. (3)

2. What is meant by the phrase 'target market'? (2)

3. a) In Figure 13.1 on Ted Baker plc, calculate the percentage increase in sales between 2003 and 2014. (3)

b) Inflation between 2003 and 2014 amounted to 33 per cent. How might this figure be used to assess Ted Baker's sales increase? (4)

4. A new Chairman sets the Chief Executive of Tesco the corporate objective of restoring Tesco's UK market share to 32 per cent from its current figure of 28.5 per cent. Outline two possible marketing objectives that might help achieve this target. (4)

5. Explain how a new financial target of boosting short-term cash flow might affect the marketing objectives at fashion retailer French Connection. (5)

6. **a)** If a company operating in a stable market sees its market share fall from 5 per cent to 4 per cent, what would be the percentage impact on its sales revenue? (3)

b) How might the business respond to such slippage in its market share? (6)

B. Revision exercises
DATA RESPONSE

Nākd gains

Table 13.1

	Price per bar	Weight per bar	Price per 100g	Calories per bar	Calories per 100g
Kellogg's Nutri-grain Strawberry bar	59 p	37 g	£1.59	130	351
Nakd Strawberry Crunch bar	75 p	30 g	£2.50	109	363

Source: www.mysupermarket.co.uk. Correct as at 12 July 2014

In 2006 Natural Balance Foods Ltd was founded by Jamie Combs. He saw an opportunity for more honest, natural products in the fast-growing market for cereal bars in the UK (worth £300 million in 2013). The trend towards cereal bars (as a breakfast replacement or as a 'healthy' part of a lunchbox) coincided with one other – a trend towards 'free-from' foods. Although there is little evidence of a widespread need for them, modern consumers like to buy products that are free-from gluten or free-from dairy products. This provided the inspiration behind a very clever brand name: Nākd.

By 2013 sales of Nākd cereal bars put the brand into the top 10 sellers in this sector, with sales of £10 million, up 51 per cent from £6.6 million in 2012. As shown in the table above, these sales stood every chance of being highly profitable given the high value-added in the Nākd brand.

Having created such a successful, growing brand, it was natural to look for new product to launch. So Nākd

Bits was launched in 2013, to offer a 130 g sharing bag in 3 flavours: Cocoa Delight, Berry Delight and Cocoa Orange. The objective was to emulate the success of sharing bags in the chocolate market. Natural Balance Foods Ltd has become a very successful business. Just how far can it grow from here?

Questions (25 marks; 30 minutes)

1. **a)** Calculate Nākd's cereal bar market share in 2013. (3)

b) Comment on that figure. (4)

2. The website for Natural Balance Foods suggests that Nākd's customers are brand loyal. Explain one way in which the company might benefit from this. (4)

3. **a)** Based on the above information, suggest a suitable marketing objective for Nākd in 2016. Explain your reasoning. (5)

b) Analyse two external factors that might prevent the company from achieving the objective you set in 3a). (9)

C. Extend your understanding

1. With reference to a business of your choice, discuss which single factor seems to be the most important influence on the brand loyalty of its customers. (20)

2. Waitrose is a supermarket chain that offers a huge range of well-presented foods, but at distinctly higher prices than its rivals. Discuss the main external influences on the marketing objectives and decisions made by the company and other businesses with which you are familiar. (20)

Understanding markets

Linked to: Market research, Chapter 15; Market data and analysis, Chapter 18.

Definition

A market is where buyers meet sellers. Examples include eBay (digital market) or Smithfield Market, a meat and poultry market (physical).

14.1 Types of market

Local versus national

Most new small firms know and care little about the size of the national market. If you have just bought an ice cream van that you intend to operate in Chichester, it does not matter whether the size of the UK market for ice cream is £500 million or £600 million per year. Your concern is the level of demand and the level of competition locally. And you will probably be delighted if you achieve annual sales of £0.1 million (£100,000).

In the case of the market for ice cream in Chichester, there are several things to consider:

- How do locals buy ice cream at the moment? (Multipacks from supermarkets? Individual cones from ice cream stalls or vans?)

- How many tourists come to the city? Do they come all year round? What type of ice cream do they buy? Where do they buy it?

- How much competition is there? What do competitors offer and charge at the moment? Are there gaps in the market that you could move into?

Other firms are focused more on the national market. For example, Charlie Bigham is a small food company that started in 1996. It produces high-quality, high-priced, ready-to-eat meals. It started by targeting small grocers, but soon found that the sales volumes

were too low to cover their costs. A sales breakthrough in Waitrose supermarkets was followed in 2005 by acceptance by Sainsbury's. This enables the company to deliver to just two warehouses, cutting the business's costs dramatically. Then Waitrose and Sainsbury's distribute to their local shops. So Charlie Bigham Foods has a national presence, even though sales remain well below one per cent of the market for ready meals.

To deal on the national level, Charlie Bigham has to deal professionally with the supermarket buyers, and produce eye-catching packaging that can compete effectively with national and multinational competitors.

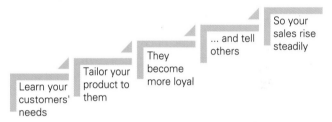

Figure 14.1 Logic ladder: understanding customers

'We were filling a need they didn't know they had.'
Howard Schulz, chief executive, Starbucks

Physical and electronic (virtual)

Markets used all to be physical. The London Stock Exchange was a place where buyers met sellers and face-to-face agreements took place. Similarly, auctions were physical, with bidders having to catch the eye of the auctioneer.

Today an increasing number of markets are digital (or virtual). The stock market exists only on computer screens, and the likes of eBay are transforming auction and other markets worldwide.

From a business point of view the key factors about electronic markets (for example, for finding hotel rooms or flights) are as follows.

Figure 14.2 Bidding on eBay

- They are fiercely price competitive, so the companies supplying services have huge pressure to keep their costs as low as possible.
- They do not rely on physical location, for example, a business can easily be run from a bedroom, such as selling Wii computer games.
- The market is easy and quite cheap to enter, so new competitors can arrive at any time.
- They provide a 'long tail' of competitive, profitable small businesses, able to carve their own little niche in markets. This is very difficult to achieve in the high street, where rents are so high that only big firms can afford them.

14.2 Factors determining demand

Demand is the desire of consumers to buy a product or service, when backed by the ability to pay. It is also known as 'effective demand' (that is, only when the customer has the money is demand effective). Several factors determine the demand for a specific product/service.

Price

Price affects demand in three ways.

1. You may want an £80,000 Mercedes convertible but you cannot afford it; the price puts it beyond your income level. The higher the price, the more people there are who cannot afford to buy.

2. The higher the price, the less good value the item will seem compared with other ways of spending the money. For example, a Chelsea home ticket costing

£48 is the equivalent of going to the movies 6 times. Is it worth it? The higher the price of an item, the more people there will be who say 'it's not worth it'.

3. It should be remembered that the price tag put on an item gives a message about its 'value'. A ring priced at 99p will inevitably be seen as 'cheap' whether or not it is value for money; so although lower prices should boost sales, firms must beware of ruining their image for quality.

Incomes

The British economy grows at a rate of about 2.5 per cent a year. This means that average income levels double every 30 years. Broadly, when your children are aged about 16–18, you are likely to be twice as well off as your parents are today. Economic growth means we all get richer over time.

The demand for most products and services grows as the economy grows. Goods like cars and cinema tickets are 'normal goods' for which demand rises broadly in line with incomes. In some cases it grows even faster; for example, if the economy grows by three per cent in a year, the amount spent on foreign holidays can easily rise by 6 per cent. This type of product is known as a luxury good.

Other goods behave differently, with sales falling when people are better off. These products are known as inferior goods. In their case, rising incomes mean falling sales. For example, the richer we get, the more Tropicana we buy and the less Tesco Orange Squash. As Orange Squash is an inferior good, a couple of years of economic struggle (and perhaps more people out of work) would mean sales would increase as people switch from expensive Tropicana to cheap squash.

Actions of competitors

Demand for British Airways (BA) Heathrow to New York flights does not only depend on their price and the incomes of consumers. It also depends on the actions of their rivals. If Virgin Atlantic is running a brilliant advertising campaign, demand for BA flights may fall as customers switch to Virgin. Or if American Airlines pushes its prices up, people may switch to BA.

The firm's own marketing activities

Following the same logic, if British Airways is running a new advertising campaign, perhaps based on improved customer service, it may enjoy increased sales. In effect, its sales will rise if it can persuade customers to switch from Virgin and American Airlines to BA. One firm's sales increase usually means reduced sales elsewhere.

Seasonal factors

Most firms experience significant variations in sales throughout the year. Some markets, such as ice cream, soft drinks, lager and seaside hotels, boom in the summer and slump in the winter. Other markets, such as sales of perfume, liqueurs, greetings cards and toys, boom at Christmas. Other products that have less obvious reasons for seasonal variations in demand include cars, cat food, carpets, furniture, TVs and newspapers. The variations are caused by patterns of customer behaviour and nothing can be done about it. A well-run business makes sure it understands and can predict the seasonal variations in demand; and then has a plan for coping.

'The aim of marketing is to know and understand the customer so well the product or service fits him and sells itself.' Peter Drucker, business guru

14.3 Market size and trends

Market size is the measurement of all the sales by all the companies within a marketplace. It can be measured in two ways: by volume and by value. Volume measures the quantity of goods purchased, perhaps in tons, in packs or in units. Market size by value is the amount spent by customers on the volume sold. So the difference between volume and value is the price paid per unit.

Take, for example, the figures shown in Table 14.1 for the UK market for sun care products.

Table 14.1 UK market for sun care products

2013 market by value	£198.2 million
2013 market by volume	36.1 million litres
Average price per litre	£5.49 (£198.2/36.1)

Source: *The Grocer*, 12 April 2014

Market size matters because it is the basis for calculating market share (the proportion of the total market held by one company or brand). This, in turn, is essential for evaluating the success or failure of a firm's marketing activities. Market size is also the reference point for calculating trends. Is market size growing or declining? A growth market is far more likely to provide opportunities for new products to be launched or for new distribution initiatives to be successful.

Recent figures and forecasts for the car market in China help to show the importance of market trends. In 2001 the UK car market was four times bigger than that of China. In 2005 China accelerated past Britain. And look at the forecasts for the coming years, shown in Table 14.2.

Table 14.2 Sales of new passenger cars (actual and forecast)

Year	China	Britain
2010	13,800,000	2,000,000
2011	14,470,000	1,940,000
2012	15,500,000	2,050,000
2013	17,500,000	2,225,000
2014 (estimated)	19,100,000	2,380,000
2020 (forecast)	25,000,000	2,400,000

Source: Forecasts by industry experts

In 2009 China became the world's biggest car market. Clearly these figures show that success in China will be far more important to car firms than success in Britain.

14.4 Market share

Market share is the proportion of the total market held by one company or product. It can be measured by volume, but is more often looked at by value. Market share is taken by most firms as the key test of the success of the year's marketing activities. Total sales are affected by factors such as economic growth, but market share measures a firm's ability to win or lose against its competitors. As shown in Table 14.3, high market share can also lead to the producer's ideal of market leadership or market dominance. Cadbury Dairy Milk has market leadership among confectionery brands, but Pampers and Heinz have dominance of their markets.

Table 14.3 Brands with high UK market shares

Leading brand in its market	Sales of leading brand (£ million)	Market size (by value) (£ million)	Market share (%)	Share of nearest competitor (%)
Heinz Baked Beans	216	339	63.7	11.6
Pampers	299	474	63.0	6.4
Coca-Cola	1,188	2,487	47.8	14.4
Cadbury Dairy Milk	506	3,600	14.1	6.0

Source: *The Grocer* 21 December 2013, quoting from Nielsen.

There are many advantages to a business of having the top selling brand (the brand leader). Obviously, sales are higher than anyone else's, but also:

● The brand leader gets the highest distribution level, often without needing to make much effort to achieve it. Even a tiny corner shop stocks Pampers, as well as Happy Shopper own-label nappies. Success breeds success.

- Brand leaders are able to offer lower discount terms to retailers than the number two or three brands in a market. This means higher revenues and profit margins per unit sold.

- The strength of a brand-leading name such Walls Magnum makes it much easier to obtain distribution and consumer trial for new products based on that brand name.

Five Whys and a How

Question	Answer
Why may market share be a better judge of business success than sales?	Sales may rise or fall due to external factors such as recession or new advertising by a rival; market share is a real test of how well the firm has done compared with its rivals
Why do firms draw a distinction between market share by volume and by value?	Ultimately, firms need money to cover costs, therefore the *value* of sales is what matters. In the smartphone business, the iPhone gives Apple a huge market share advantage by *value* because of its high price
Why may online markets be more profitable than traditional, physical markets?	Physical markets have to be located conveniently for consumers, making them expensive to run. Online markets can be located in cheap premises anywhere
Why are seasonal factors important in the market for strawberries?	Because they affect supply and demand, although in different ways (supply in May/June, but demand may jump a little at Christmas)
Why does market decline not have to mean sales decline for a particular brand?	The brand's market share could rise sufficiently to outweigh the effects of the decline in market size
How is market share measured (by volume)?	$\dfrac{\text{Kilos of beans sold by Heinz}}{\text{Kilos of beans sold in total}} \times 100$

Key terms

Inferior goods: products that people turn to when they are 'hard up', and turn away from when they are better off (for example, Tesco Value Beans instead of Heinz Baked Beans).

Luxury goods: Products that people buy much more of when they feel better off, (for example, jewellery, sports cars and holidays at posh hotels).

Normal goods: Products or services for which sales change broadly in line with the economy. That is, if the economy grows by 3 per cent, sales rise by 3 per cent (for example, travel and sales of fast food).

Evaluation: Understanding markets

Almost every large business carries out detailed market analysis on a regular basis. They buy 'retail audits' to find out how retail sales are doing. It can be said, though, that some managers suffer from 'paralysis by analysis'. In other words, they gather so much data (some of it conflicting) that they end up unable to make a decision. Contrast this approach with that of Apple. Boss Steve Jobs focused on understanding customers, not analysing the market as it stood. He believed that Apple could always stay one step ahead by thinking about what customers would want in future. Given Apple's success, it is hard to argue with him.

'Don't find customers for your products; find products for your customers.' Seth Godwin, author

Workbook
A. Revision questions

(35 marks; 35 minutes)

1. Outline three features of the market for fast food near to where you live. (6)

2. Section 14.2 lists five factors determining the demand for a product: price, incomes, actions of competitors, marketing activities and seasonality. Identify which two of these would most heavily affect sales of:

   a) strawberries

   b) EasyJet tickets to Barcelona

   c) tickets to see Newcastle United

   d) DFS furniture. (8)

3. Explain in your own words the difference between market size by volume and market size by value. (3)

4. a) Look at Table 14.2. Toyota's share of the UK car market is about 6 per cent. If it continues with that share, how many UK car sales would that amount to in 2020? How many Toyota cars would be sold in China in 2020, assuming the same market share? (4)

   b) Outline two ways in which Toyota could respond to that sales difference. (6)

5. Why may a shoe shop focusing on 'Little Feat' be able to charge higher prices per pair than a general shoe shop? (2)

6. Look at Table 14.3. Discuss which business should be happier with its market position: Cadbury or Pampers. (6)

B. Revision exercises
DATA RESPONSE 1

Market size, market growth and market shares: the tablet market

Since its launch in early 2010 the Apple iPad has scooped up plaudits, sales and profits. Figure 14.3 shows the sales during what Apple hopes will be as long-lived a product life cycle as the iPod (launched 2002 and still going strong).

Figure 14.4, however, shows how hard it can be to keep ahead of the competition. Few would have expected, in early 2012, that Apple's market share would have halved between the third quarter of 2012 and the same quarter of 2013. Samsung's success has been an important part of that, but so too has been the growth of less-known companies such as China's Lenovo.

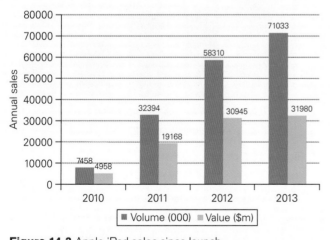

Figure 14.3 Apple iPad sales since launch

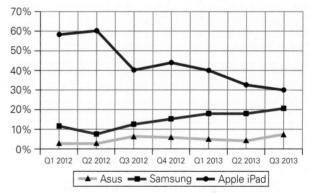

Figure 14.4 Tablet computers: global market shares

Source of all the data: IDC Analysts, Quarterly Reports

Does it matter about falling market share, though, when sales volumes are as solid as those of the iPad, as graphed in Figure 14.4, and world market size is forging ahead, from 28.3 million tablets in Q2 2012 to 47.6m units in Q3 2013?

Questions: 30 marks; 35 minutes

1. Calculate the percentage change in iPad sales between 2012 and 2013:

   a) by volume and   **b)** by value.   (3)

2. Explain the implications for Apple of the difference between your answers to Question 1.   (4)

3. Use Figure 14.4 to help explain why the price of iPads was falling in 2013.   (4)

4. **a)** From the text and Figure 14.4, calculate actual sales of iPads in:

   i. Q2 2012 and

   ii. Q3 2013.   (3)

   b) Experts say that the reason Apple's market share is declining is because it has refused to launch a lower-priced tablet computer. To what extent do you agree that now is the time to launch one?   (16)

DATA RESPONSE 2

Lidl and Aldi winning grocery wars

Discount grocers are the big winners in 2014, Kantar Worldpanel figures show. The grocery market grew by 1.7 per cent year-on-year in the 12 weeks to 2 February 2014. Waitrose, Sainsbury's and Asda all grew slightly, while sales at Tesco and Morrisons' fell. Lidl and Aldi were the big winners with sales growth of 17 per cent and 32 per cent respectively. Perhaps these discount grocers benefited from the continuing squeeze on household living standards.

The changes leave Tesco as the wounded market leader with its 29.2 per cent down sharply from the 31.5 per cent it enjoyed before the recession. Morrisons' suffered a decline from 11.8 per cent in 2013 to 11.3 per cent in 2014. A decline of 0.5 per cent may seem trivial, but as the value of the UK grocery market is £170 billion per year, 0.5 per cent market share represents sales of £850 million!

Questions (30 marks; 35 minutes)

1. **a)** What was the grocery market size and market growth in the 12 weeks to 2 February 2014?   (2)

   b) Identify three possible reasons why sales at Morrisons' actually fell in 2014.   (3)

2. **a)** Show the workings to calculate that a 0.5 per cent share of the UK grocery market equals £850 million.   (3)

   b) Use the figures and the bar chart to work out the value of Aldi's 2014 sales in the UK.   (2)

   c) Analyse two possible reasons why Aldi enjoyed the biggest sales growth within the grocery market in 2014.   (8)

3. Twenty years ago, Sainsbury's was the UK grocery market leader. Discuss whether it could return to that position within the next 20 years.   (12)

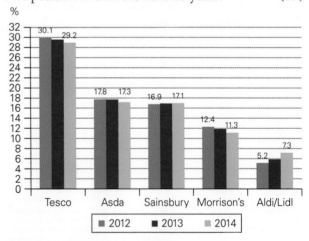

Figure 14.5 UK grocery market-share 2014

Source: Kantar Worldpanel, 12 weeks to 2 February 2014.

C. Extend your understanding

1. A recent report by Mintel forecast that the UK market for bicycles is set to grow by 23 per cent to more than £800 million by 2017. To what extent does this guarantee success for a business such as Halfords, a leading bicycle retailer?   (20)

2. The Cadbury brand Crunchie has a 1 per cent share of the UK chocolate market. Discuss the internal and external factors that might determine whether Cadbury could succeed in doubling Crunchie's market share.   (20)

Market research

Linked to: Different business forms, Chapter 2; Pricing decisions, Chapter 23; Integrating the marketing mix, Chapter 25.

Definition

Market research gathers information about consumers, competitors and distributors within a firm's target market. It is a way of identifying consumers' buying habits and attitudes to current and future products.

15.1 The value of market research

Research shows that the single biggest cause of business failure is failure to understand the market. It is reasonable to suggest that this alone shows why market research has the potential to be valuable to every business.

When opening a first business, the starting point is to discover the marketing fundamentals: how big is the market (market size), what is its future potential and what are the market shares of the existing companies and brands?

Market size means the value of the sales made annually by all the firms within a market. For example, in 2013 the UK market for yoghurts and pot desserts was worth £2,233 million. Market potential can be measured by the annual rate of growth. In the case of yogurt, this has been at a rate of 3 per cent per year, by value. This implies that, by the year 2017, the potential market size will be over £2,500 million.

Market shares are also of crucial importance when investigating a market, as they indicate the relative strength of the firms within the market. In 2013, 25 per cent of the yogurt market was held by Müller, making it the leading brand by far. A benefit it received for its strong market share was a distribution level of almost 100 per cent: nearly every grocery store stocked Müller. If one firm dominates, it may be very difficult to break into the market.

So how can firms find out this type of information? The starting point is secondary research: unearthing data that already exists.

Figure 15.1 The UK market for yoghurt is worth over £2,000 million.

15.2 Methods of secondary research

Internet

Most people start by 'Googling' the topic. This can provide invaluable information, though online providers of market research information will want to charge for the service. With luck, Google will identify a relevant article that can provide useful information.

Government-produced data

The government-funded Office for National Statistics produces valuable reports such as the Annual Abstract of Statistics and Labour Market Trends.

These provide data on population trends, and forecasts; for example, someone starting a hair and beauty salon may find out how many 16- to 20-year-old women there will be in the year 2020.

Having obtained background data, further research is likely to be tailored specifically to the company's needs, such as carrying out a survey among 16- to 20-year-old women about their favourite haircare brands. This type of first-hand research gathers primary data. Some of the pros and cons of primary and secondary research are given in Table 15.1.

Table 15.1 The pros and cons of primary and secondary research

	Secondary research	Primary research
P R O S	• often obtained without cost • good overview of a market • usually based on actual sales figures, or research on large samples	• can aim questions directly at your research objectives • latest information from the marketplace • can assess the psychology of the customer
C O N S	• data may not be updated regularly • not tailored to your own needs • expensive to buy reports on many different marketplaces	• expensive, £10,000+ per survey • risk of questionnaire and interviewer **bias** • research findings may only be usable if comparable 'backdata' exists

'Running a company on market research is like driving while looking in the rear view mirror.' Anita Roddick, founder, Body Shop.

15.3 Methods of primary research

The process of gathering information directly from people within your target market is known as primary (or field) research. When carried out by market research companies it is expensive, but there is much that firms can do for themselves.

For a company that is up and running, a regular survey of customer satisfaction is an important way of measuring the quality of customer service. When investigating a new market, there are various measures that can be taken by a small firm with a limited budget.

● Retailer research: the people closest to a market are those who serve customers directly – the retailers. They are likely to know the up-and-coming brands, the degree of brand loyalty and the importance of price and packaging, all of which is crucial information.

● Observation: when starting up a service business in which location is an all-important factor, it

is invaluable to measure the rate of pedestrian (and possibly traffic) flow past your potential site compared with that of your rivals. A sweet shop or dry cleaners near a busy bus stop may generate twice the sales of a rival 50 yards down the road.

For a large company, primary research will be used extensively in new product development. For example, if we consider the possibility of launching Orange Chocolate Buttons, the development stages, plus research, would probably be as shown in Table 15.2.

Table 15.2 Primary research used in new product development (Orange Chocolate Buttons)

Development stage	Primary research
1. The product idea (probably one of several)	1. Group discussions among regular chocolate buyers (some young, some old)
2. Product test (testing different recipes, different sweetness, 'orangeyness', etc.)	2. A taste test on 200+ chocolate buyers (on street corners, or in a hall)
3. Brand name research (testing several different names and perhaps logos)	3. Quantitative research using a questionnaire on a sample of 200+
4. Packaging research	4. Quantitative research as in item 3
5. Advertising research	5. Group discussions run by psychologists to discover which advertisement has the strongest effect on product image and recall
6. Total proposition test: testing the level of purchase interest, to help make sales forecasts	6. Quantitative research using a questionnaire and product samples on at least 200+ consumers

Real business

The Toyota MR2

When Toyota launched the MR2 sports car, sales were higher than expected. The only exception was found in France, where sales were very poor. The Japanese head office asked the executives of Toyota France to look into this. Why had it been such a flop? Eventually the executives admitted that they should have carried out market research into the brand name MR2 prior to the launch. Pronounced 'em-er-deux' in France, the car sounded like the French swear word *merdre* (crap).

'The aim of marketing is to know and understand the customer so well the product or service fits him and sells itself.' Peter Drucker, business author/guru

15.4 Qualitative research

This is in-depth research into the motivations behind the attitudes and buying habits of consumers. It does not produce statistics such as '52 per cent of chocolate buyers like orange chocolate'; instead it gives clues as to why they like it (is it really because it's orange, or because it's different/a change?). Qualitative research is usually conducted by psychologists, who learn to interpret the way people say things, as well as what they say.

The main form of qualitative research is group discussion (also known as focus groups). These are free-ranging discussions led by psychologists among groups of six to eight consumers. The group leader will have a list of topics that need discussion, but will be free to follow up any point made by a group member. Among the advantages of group discussions is the fact that they:

- may reveal a problem or opportunity the company had not anticipated
- reveal consumer psychology, such as the importance of image and peer pressure.

Real business

Selling luxury in China

A 2013 quantitative study showed that Louis Vuitton, Hermès and Chanel are the luxury brands with the highest reputation in China. But do they share the same image characteristics? To find out, a qualitative study was carried out, depth-interviewing people from three groups: the 'nouveau (super) riche', 'gifters' and 'middle-class luxury'. The study found that the first two groups are price insensitive; indeed, high prices are in some ways attractive. Whereas the third group are very price sensitive within a restricted number of acceptable Western brands. They can be targeted quite differently, for example, online.

Table 15.3 Typical research questions

Qualitative research	Quantitative research
Why do people *really* buy Nikes?	Which pack design do you prefer?
Who in the household *really* decides which brand of shampoo is bought?	Have you heard of any of the following brands? (Ariel, Daz, Persil, etc.)
What mood makes you feel like buying Häagen-Dazs ice cream?	How likely are you to buy this product regularly?
When you buy your children Frosties, how do you feel?	How many newspapers have you bought in the past 7 days?

15.5 Quantitative research

This asks pre-set questions of a large enough sample of people to provide statistically valid data. Questionnaires can answer factual questions such as 'How many 16 to 20 year olds have heard of Chanel No. 5?' There are three key aspects to quantitative research:

- sampling, ensuring that the research results are typical of the whole population, though only a sample of the population has been interviewed. An important factor is the response rate, that is, what proportion of those approached bothered to respond
- writing a questionnaire that is unbiased and meets the research objectives
- assessing the validity of the results.

The value of sampling

The two main concerns in sampling are how to choose the right people for interview (sampling method) and deciding how large a number to interview (sample size).

In 1936, an American magazine attempted to forecast the Presidential election by polling 2.4 million potential voters. The magazine announced that the Republican candidate would win with 55 per cent of the poll. When Democrat F. D. Roosevelt won a landslide, commentators laughed at the 'useless' new science of sampling. Yet a sample of just three thousand by Gallup Poll predicted the result correctly. This proved that the size of a sample is no guarantee of accuracy. The magazine had a huge sample, but it had drawn it from telephone directories and car owners – both affluent populations in the 1930s. Dr Gallup had made sure to find a sample that was truly representative of ordinary Americans. Sampling, then, is more about accuracy than size – though size still matters.

Sample reliability

The key to reliability is to obtain as representative a sample as possible. Dr Gallup's method (still used widely today) was quota sampling. This method involves selecting interviewees in proportion to the consumer profile within the target market. An example of quota sampling is given in Table 15.4.

Table 15.4 An example of quota sampling

Adult:	Chocolate buyers (%)	Respondent quota (sample: 200)
Men	40	80
Women	60	100
16–24	38	76
25–34	21	42
35–44	16	32
45+	25	50

This method allows interviewers to head for busy street corners, interviewing whoever comes along. As long as they achieve the correct quota, they can interview when and where they want to. This ensures a representative sample at relatively low cost. It is the sampling method used most commonly by market research companies.

Sample size

Having decided which sampling method should be used, the next consideration is to determine how many interviews should be conducted. Should 10, 100, or 1,000 people be interviewed? The most high-profile surveys conducted in Britain are the opinion polls asking adults about their voting intentions in a general election. These quota samples of between 1,000 and 1,500 respondents are considered large enough to reflect the opinions of the electorate of 45 million. How is this possible?

Of course, if you only interviewed 10 people, the chances are slim that the views of this sample will match those of the whole population. Of these 10, 7 may say they would definitely buy Chocolate Orange Buttons. If you asked another 10, however, only three may say the same. A sample of 10 is so small that chance variations make the results meaningless. In other words, a researcher can have no statistical confidence in the findings from a sample of 10.

A sample of 100 is far more meaningful. It is not enough to feel confident about marginal decisions (for example, 53 per cent like the red pack design and 47 per cent like the blue one), but is quite enough if the

result is clear-cut (such as, 65 per cent like the name 'Spark'; 35 per cent prefer 'Valencia'). Many major product launches have proceeded following research on as low a sample as 100.

With a sample of 1,000, a high level of confidence is possible. Even small differences would be statistically significant with such a large sample. So why doesn't everyone use samples of 1,000? The answer is because of the cost of doing so: money. Hiring a market research agency to undertake a survey of 100 people would cost approximately £10,000. A sample of 1,000 people would cost three times that amount, which is good value if you can afford it but not everyone can. As shown in the earlier example of launching Orange Buttons, a company might require six surveys before launching a new product. So the amount spent on research alone might reach £180,000 if samples of 1,000 were used.

The concept of confidence intervals

When market researchers present their findings from quantitative research they like to state the level of confidence one can have in the sample finding. In particular, they like to show results to a '95 per cent confidence level'. In other words, the data should be correct 95 per cent of the time, or 19 times out of 20. (Because the data is drawn from a small-ish sample of the whole population there can never be 100 per cent confidence in the findings.)

Let us assume that a research company has conducted a survey to find out how many people like a blue pack-colour for a new detergent. As long as over 50 per cent like the blue, they'll proceed. The research result shows that 60 per cent of the sample like the blue pack. But how confident can one be that this result reflects the views of the whole target market?

The key to this would be the confidence interval. That means how wide the possible range might be from the actual result of 60 per cent. If the confidence interval is no more than plus or minus 9, then the company can be assured that the statistical variability of the sample is no wider than 60+9 on the upside and 60−9 on the downside, that is a range from 51–69. In this case, then, there can be 95 per cent confidence that the of the target market lie between 51 and 69. Therefore more than half like the blue pack and the business can proceed.

The net effect of the above is simply to point out that the results of quantitative market research should be treated with care. The smaller the sample size, the wider the confidence intervals and therefore the lower the level of confidence one can have in the accuracy of the findings.

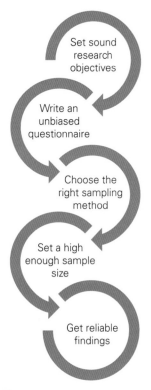

Figure 15.2 Logic chain: getting research right

15.6 Market mapping

Market mapping is carried out in two stages.

1. Identify the key features that characterise consumers within a market; examples in the market for women's clothes would be: young/old and high fashion/conservative

2. Having identified the key characteristics, place every brand on a grid such as that shown in Figure 15.3. This will reveal where the competition is concentrated and may highlight gaps in the market.

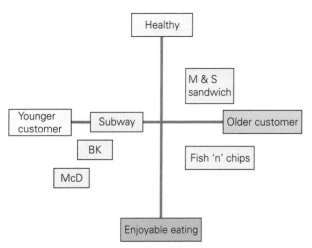

Figure 15.3 Example of a market map for fast food

Using this approach could help in identifying a product or market niche that has not yet been filled. In the market map shown in Figure 15.3 there appears to be an available niche for healthy eating for younger customers within the fast food sector. The market map points to the possibility of this positioning. Then it would be up to the entrepreneur to investigate further. In particular, the entrepreneur will need to investigate whether there may be a niche, but one that is too small to provide an opportunity for a profitable business.

A great example of positioning is Aldi's position within the UK's price-motivated segment of the grocery market. With Asda, Lidl and Iceland as its direct competitors, Aldi has seen its sales boom as a result of persuading middle-Britain that shopping at Aldi is sensible rather than cheapskate. Its slogan 'Spend a little. Live a lot.' is about having a good time, not about 'low, low prices'. Figure 15.4 shows the value to Aldi of astute positioning.

Figure 15.4 UK grocery market year-on-year percentage change, 12 weeks to July 2014
Source: Kantar Worldpanel

Five Whys and a How

Question	Answer
Why may start-up companies struggle to get accurate market research data?	They lack a base of existing customers who can be interviewed, e.g. to find out about changing tastes
Why is secondary data a first step, but not a sufficient step?	Because it only gives general information. For data tailored to your own needs, you need to commission primary research
Why may small samples be dangerous?	Because their findings are subject to high statistical variability, making them unreliable
Why may qualitative research sometimes prove especially important?	Whenever the issues involved are psychological, such as whether a logo strays slightly beyond distinctive towards vulgar
Will 'Big Data' mean that commissioning primary research becomes a thing of the past?	However much data is captured and analysed, it can only be based on past information (such as sales figures). Primary research can ask important hypothetical questions about the future; so 'no' is the answer
How might market mapping help a new company wanting to break into a market?	It places existing brands on a grid based on key consumer variables, to help identify crowded and less-crowded market positions

Key terms

Bias: a factor that causes research findings to be unrepresentative of the whole population; for example, bubbly interviewers or misleading survey questions.

Primary research: finding out information first-hand; for example, Coca-Cola designing a questionnaire to obtain information from people who regularly buy diet products.

Secondary research: finding out information that has already been gathered; for example, the government's estimates of the number of 14 to 16 year olds in Wales.

Sample size: the number of people interviewed. This should be large enough to give confidence that the findings are representative of the whole population.

Sampling method: the approach chosen to select the right people to be part of the research sample; for example, random, quota or stratified.

Standard deviation: sample findings tend to form a bell-shaped curve when shown on a graph. Within this curve, the standard deviation of the data reflects how wide or narrow is the likely variation from the mean average of the findings.

'To steal ideas from one person is plagiarism, to steal ideas from many is research.' Anon

Evaluation: Market research

In large firms, it is rare for any significant marketing decision to be made without market research. Even an apparently minor change to a pack design will only be carried out after testing in research. Is this overkill? Surely marketing executives are employed to make judgements, not merely to do what surveys tell them?

The first issue here is the strong desire to make business decisions as scientifically as possible; in other words, to act on evidence, not on feelings. Quantitative research, especially, fits in with the desire to act on science not hunch. Yet this can be criticised, such as by John Scully, former head of Apple Inc., who once said 'No great marketing decision has ever been made on the basis of quantitative data'. He was pointing out that true innovations, such as the Apple iPad, were the product of creativity and hunch, not science.

The second issue concerns the management culture. In some firms, mistakes lead to inquests, blame and even dismissal. This makes managers keen to find a let-out. When the new product flops, the manager can point an accusing finger at the positive research results: 'It wasn't my fault. We need a new research agency.' In other firms, mistakes are seen as an inevitable part of learning. For every Sinclair C5 (unresearched flop) there may be an iPod (unresearched money-spinner). In firms with a positive, risk-taking approach to business, qualitative insights are likely to be preferred to quantitative data.

Workbook

A. Revision questions

(40 marks, 40 minutes)

1. State three ways in which a cosmetics firm could use market research. (3)

2. Outline three reasons why market research information may prove inaccurate. (6)

3. Distinguish between primary and secondary research. (3)

4. What advantages are there in using secondary research rather than primary? (3)

5. Which is the most commonly used sampling method? Why may it be the most commonly used? (3)

6. State three key factors to take into account when writing a questionnaire. (3)

7. Explain two aspects of marketing in which consumer psychology is important. (4)

8. Outline the pros and cons of using a large sample size. (4)

9. Identify three possible sources of bias in primary market research. (3)

10. Explain how market mapping could be helpful to **two** of the following.

    a) an entrepreneur looking at opening up a new driving school

    b) the brand manager of Werther's Original sweets, worried about falling market share

    c) a private school thinking of opening its first branch in China (8)

B. Revision exercises
DATA RESPONSE

Each year more than £1,500 million is spent on pet food in the UK. All the growth within the market has been for luxury pet foods and for healthier products. Seeing these trends, in early 2014 Town & Country Petfoods launched HiLife Just Desserts, a range of pudding treats for dogs. They contain omega-3 but no added sugar and therefore have no more than 100 calories per tin.

Sales began well, especially of the Apple & Cranberry version. Now sales have flattened out at around £1 million a year and the company thinks it is time to launch some new flavours. Three weeks ago they commissioned some primary research that was carried out using an online survey linked to pet care websites. The sample size was 150.

The main findings were as shown in Table 15.5.

Table 15.5 Findings of online survey

1. Have you ever bought your dog a pet food pudding?				
Ever bought:	Never (%)	Just once (%)	Yes, in the past but no longer (%)	Yes, still do (%)
	61	13	12	14
Which of these flavours may you buy for your dog?				
May try:	Never (%)	May try	May buy monthly (%)	May buy once a week (%)
Muesli yoghurt	61	19	15	5
Rhubarb crumble	43	33	22	2
Apples and custard	52	34	12	2

The marketing director is slightly disappointed that none of the new product ideas has done brilliantly, but happy that there's one clear winner. She plans a short qualitative research exercise among existing HiLife customers, and hopes to launch two new flavours in time for the annual Crufts dog show in three months' time.

Questions (30 marks; 35 minutes)

1. Outline whether the sample size of 150 was appropriate in this case. (4)

2. Analyse the marketing director's conclusion that 'none of the new product ideas has done brilliantly, but happy that there's one clear winner'. (9)

3. a) Explain one method of qualitative research that could be used in this case. (3)

   b) Evaluate two ways in which qualitative research may help the marketing director. Which do you think is the more important, and why? (14)

C. Extend your understanding

1. 'Market research is like an insurance policy. You pay a premium to reduce your marketing risks.' To what extent do you believe this statement to be true? (20)

2. After ten years of rising sales, demand for Shredded Wheat has started to slip. Discuss how the marketing manager could make use of market research to analyse why this has happened and to help decide the strategy needed to return Shredded Wheat to sales growth. (20)

Interpreting marketing data

Linked to: Market research, Chapter 15; Market data and analysis, Chapter 18; Segmentation, targeting and positioning, Chapter 19.

Definition

Today's companies have so much data that the key skill is to identify and draw conclusions from the relatively few nuggets that have yet to be found.

16.1 Correlation

Businesses are always keen to learn about the effect on sales of marketing strategies such as TV advertising, sales promotion or direct mailshots. Often researchers will compare sales volume and advertising expenditure. A good way to do this is on a graph. In Figure 16.1 there is clearly a strong relationship, or correlation, between the two. The correlation is positive: as one increases so does the other. It is important to realise that each point correlating the two variables represents one observation covering a period of time.

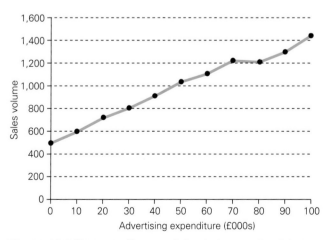

Figure 16.1 Strong positive correlation between advertising expenditure and sales

In Figure 16.2, however, there is not so much linkage, as the diagram is little more than a collection of randomly dispersed points. In this case there is low correlation between advertising and sales, suggesting that the firm should stop wasting its money until it has found a way to make its advertising work more effectively.

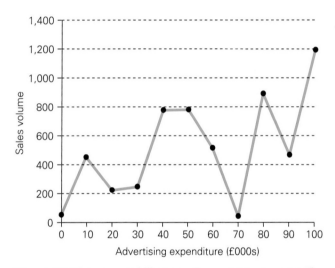

Figure 16.2 Loose correlation: are other variables important?

What the researcher is looking for is cause and effect, namely evidence that the advertising has caused the increase in sales. Now correlation by itself does not indicate cause and effect. The rising of the sun in the morning may be strongly correlated with the delivery of milk, but it does not cause it to be delivered. Strong correlation is evidence that cause and effect *may* be present. Further evidence is needed to know how the variables affect each other. Clearly, the purpose of advertising is to generate sales, so cause and effect may be the explanation. But the sales of a product could rise because of cheaper credit terms, the disappearance of a competitor, or even unusual weather, and not just because of advertising. Where correlation is weak, as in Figure 16.2, researchers should suspect that advertising is not a significant causal factor.

In addition to positive correlation, it is possible to have negative correlation. The most obvious is between price and sales, as a price increase will surely lead to a fall in sales. Other possible negative correlations include:

- the temperature and sales of cold-weather products such as umbrellas, scarves and chocolate (the higher the temperature, the lower the sales)
- consumer incomes and the sales of 'value' products (Poundland's positioning); the better off people are, the fewer they'll buy of these things

---

'The most important thing is to forecast where customers are moving and be in front of them.' Philip Kotler, marketing guru

---

Real business

Correlation

In Britain, the Met Office offers businesses a weather-forecasting service, charging a fee for predicting the sales of products ranging from lemonade to cat food. It uses correlation analysis to predict how demand will vary according to the time of year and the prevailing weather. It has found that lemonade sales rise in the summer, but tail away if the weather is very hot (presumably consumers switch to non-fizzy drinks or to ice lollies). More surprisingly, cat food is weather-affected. Rainy days boost demand (the cats don't go out) while if it's hot, cats eat less.

The website www.metoffice.gov.uk recently featured a producer of hot ready-meals that used the Met Office's correlation software to find out that it lost £70,000 of sales for every 1 degree of temperature increase above 20⁰C. Needless to say, using a weather forecast could enable the business to forecast sales more accurately, and therefore reduce stock losses on its perishable goods.

16.2 Understanding extrapolation

Extrapolation means projecting a trend forward in order to make a forecast of what will happen in the future. Often this is done unconsciously, such as the football fan who assumes that the next game will be easy because the last three have been won. In business, extrapolation should be a more formal affair. Figure 16.3 shows the trend sales data for the Apple iPod. It is easy to see how it can be extrapolated forwards to estimate the possible sales volume in the first quarter of 2015.

The simplest way of predicting the future is to assume that it will be just like the past. For the immediate future this may be realistic. It is unlikely that the economy or demand will change dramatically tomorrow. An assumption that the pattern of sales will continue to follow recent trends may therefore be reasonable. If demand for your product has been rising over the past few months, it is fair to assume it will continue in the foreseeable future. The process of predicting based on what has happened before is known as extrapolation. Extrapolation can often be done by drawing a line by eye to extend the trend on a graph (see Figure 16.4).

'Errors using inadequate data are much less than those using no data at all.' Charles Babbage, father of the computer

---

Here a very steady upward trend over a long period may well continue, and be predicted to continue. However, such stability and predictability are rare. The values of data plotted over time can vary because of seasonal variations or influences and also because of

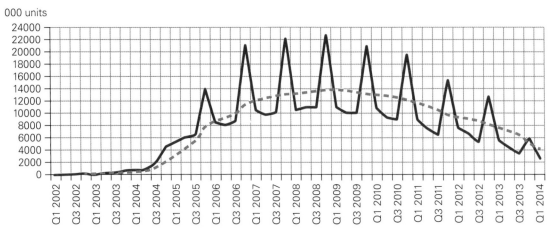

Figure 16.3 Global quarterly sales Apple iPod, 2002–2014

Source: Apple Inc. accounts

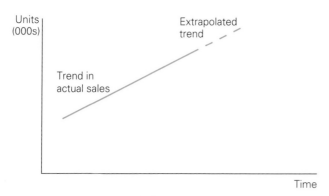

Figure 16.4 An extrapolated sales trend

random factors that cannot be predicted. Despite the uncertainties, predicting sales based on extrapolated trends is the most widely used method.

16.3 How is extrapolation used?

The main use of extrapolation is in sales forecasting. This is crucial because it is at the heart of marketing planning, and key areas such as supply purchasing, production scheduling and staff recruitment and planning.

There are other uses of extrapolation, though. Companies regularly get caught out when believing their own hype. The truly catastrophic purchase by

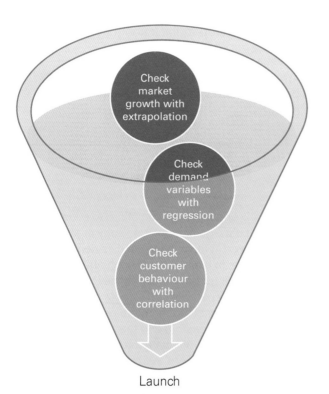

Figure 16.5 Logic chain: data analysis behind product launches

RBS of ABN AMRO Bank was partly because of the success RBS had had with the purchase of NatWest bank. Management assumed thereafter that 'we're good at takeover bids'.

> 'Extrapolations are useful, especially in the art of soothsaying called forecasting trends . . . The trend-to-now may be a fact, but the future trend represents no more than an educated guess.' Darrell Huff, author

16.4 The value of technology in gathering data

In July 2014 Center Parcs opened its newest location at Woburn Forest, near London. The investment had been spread over a 10-year development period, making it tough to recover the £250 million spent. A key to recovering the capital would be through clever enough pricing to replicate the achievement of a 97 per cent occupancy rate throughout Center Parcs UK. This is done through a detailed computer system that checks constantly on the correlation between customer bookings and factors such as time of year, school holidays, big events (such as the World Cup) and customers' previous experience. The particular process used is called regression analysis. This breaks down all the variables affecting data such as sales figures, and then allocates a numerical importance to each one. For customers, the consequence is annoyingly high prices in school holidays (often three times the price in holidays that would be paid outside of them), but Center Parcs sells 97 per cent of their space, so – from a business point of view — it works.

Of course, there are other marketing decisions for which modern technology helps managers:

- Google Adwords allows a company to bid for a word or phrase, so that, for example, searchers for '5 star beach Ibiza' will instantly see advertisements for relevant hotels. This helps advertisers address one of the most famous problems in advertising: 'Half the money I spend on advertising is wasted; the problem is I don't know which half' (attributed to Lord Leverhulme, founder of Unilever). Adwords ensures that the online advertising you see is (almost always) relevant to you.
- The term 'Big Data' describes the extraordinary amount of information available today about people's purchasing behaviour (through card transactions), their likes and dislikes (via Facebook) and the people or companies they follow (via Twitter).

Huge networks of computers are needed to turn this information into general information about the attitudes of different segments of the market and to identify the habits and desires of individual consumers. Technology not only gathers the data but also analyses it by categories decided upon by business managers. The decision about how to analyse the data may be crucial; one company may spot changing attitudes among older consumers; another may not be looking in that direction.

- If technology such as Google Glass takes off, it may be that data gathering becomes even more widespread, with companies being able to know where and how we window shop, thereby learning more about the products we aspire to.

'Human decision about the future . . . cannot depend on strict mathematical expectation.' J. M. Keynes, British economist and writer

Five Whys and a How

Question	Answer
Why might a retailer wish to know the correlation between music and mood?	To decide on the type of music to play at the store entrance, perhaps to help relax customers into staying for longer
Why is it important for a correlation to be strong rather than weak?	Because a weak correlation may mean there is little or no true cause-and-effect relationship between the variables being looked at
Why doesn't correlation prove causation?	Because finding a strong relationship doesn't prove cause and effect; that requires further thought and perhaps analysis
Why may extrapolation of sales data sometimes lead to completely wrong estimates?	Extrapolation assumes that past trends will continue into the future; a break in the trend (fruit juice is no longer good becomes juice is too sugary) causes ever-greater inaccuracy
Why is it important to know and understand extrapolation?	Because many business (and economic) mistakes have been made by people who don't stop to think about how simplistic an idea extrapolation is
How is correlation identified within complex data?	Regression analysis using computer models helps identify the correlation between each variable and the factor being investigated, e.g. sales

Key terms

Regression analysis: breaking sales data down to assess the relative importance of different determinants of the data.

Trend: the general path a series of values (for example, sales) follows along over time, disregarding variations or random fluctuations.

Evaluation: Interpreting marketing data

Today, no marketing manager can afford to sound ignorant about data-gathering technology or about the maths involved in techniques such as correlation and extrapolation. In many ways, though, the most important skills will remain exactly as they have always been: the ability to specify what aspects of the data are the most important (and therefore point data analysis in the right direction) and the ability to interpret and draw conclusions from the gathered information. Human judgement, therefore, will remain at the heart of whether a marketing company launches an inspired innovation or yet another new product failure.

Workbook

A. Revision questions

(30 marks; 30 minutes)

1. What is a sales forecast? (2)

2. Explain how you can show the trend in a series of data? (4)

3. Explain how two of the following Heinz managers could be helped by two weeks' warning that sales are forecast to rise by 15 per cent.
   a) the operations manager
   b) the marketing manager, Heinz Beans
   c) the personnel manager
   d) the chief accountant. (8)

4. What do you understanding by the term 'extrapolation'? How is it used to make a sales forecast? (5)

5. Explain how Coca-Cola may be helped by checking for correlations between the following factors.
   a) sales and the daily temperature
   b) staff absence levels and the leadership style of individual supervisors. (6)

6. Explain why it is risky to assume cause and effect when looking at factors that are correlated. (5)

B. Revision exercises

DATA RESPONSE 1

The US aircraft manufacturer Boeing has predicted that airlines will want more smaller aircraft and fewer large jumbo jets in the next two decades.

Boeing has forecast $2.8 trillion (£1.4 trillion) worth of sales of commercial jets by all manufacturers over the next 20 years, up $200 billion from last year's projections. The company now expects regional, single-aisle and twin-aisle jets for non-stop routes to be the most popular aircraft.

Boeing forecasts a rise of 5 per cent a year in passenger numbers. Cargo traffic will increase by 6.1 per cent, it predicts. The company believes one-third of this demand will come from the Asia-Pacific region, making these developing markets vital for future sales.

The increase in demand for smaller craft is in contrast to an expected fall in demand for jumbos carrying more than 400 people. Boeing says demand for such craft is likely to fall to 960, down from the 990 it forecast a year ago.

The company is banking on its smaller, slimmer 787 plane. It believes this new plane will enable it to triumph over its main rival, Airbus. Twin-engined but with a long range, it will be able to fly direct to more airports in the world, eliminating the need for passengers to make connecting flights to access long-haul flights.

Boeing has forecast the following industry sales over the next 20 years:
- 17,650 single-aisle aeroplanes seating 90–240 passengers
- 6290 twin-aisle jets seating 200–400 passengers
- 3,700 regional jets with no more than 90 seats, up from 3,450 forecast last year
- 960 jumbo jets seating more than 400 passengers.

Adapted from bbc.co.uk

Questions (25 marks; 30 minutes)

1. Analyse the ways in which Boeing might have produced its industry sales forecasts. (9)

2. To what extent do Boeing's findings prove that its success is secure? (16)

DATA RESPONSE 2

Bikes from India

In the 1960s the British motorcycle industry was wiped out by competition from Japan: Honda, Yamaha Suzuki and Kawasaki. An important part of Britain's motorcycle heritage was Royal Enfield, which went bust, though the brand ended up in the hands of an Indian company: the Eicher Group. This group built a substantial business in India based on the brand Royal Enfield. In 2013 around 175,000 Royal Enfield bikes are being produced (that's more than double the entire UK motorbike market).

Figure 16.6 Royal Enfield motorbike

Now, with plans to expand output to 250,000 in 2014, the Eicher Group is eyeing the UK market. It wants to export 5,000 bikes to Britain, which would mean taking a 6 per cent market share. It believes that its market potential is rooted in the fastest growing UK biker demographic: oldie bikers, that is, those aged 55 plus. Today younger people are more likely to ride a bike than a motorbike. Fear of accidents has made motorbikes a tough sell to younger people. Eicher Motor's chief executive, Siddhartha Lal, says that, following secondary research, his group is targeting 'a nostalgic population of older and wealthier leisure riders'. With a price tag set of £5,200 for the October 2013 launch of the Royal Enfield Continental GT, the pitch certainly is at the wealthier end of the market.

In the UK the most obvious direct competitor to the Enfield bike is the rival heritage brand Triumph, the UK's top-selling bike. Although these bikes are made in Thailand, the brand owner has successfully recreated the British image attached to the Triumph brand, which adds value. The Royal Enfield is priced at £1,000 below the equivalent Triumph, but it is yet to be seen whether British bikers will trust the quality standards of bikes from India.

There is another demographic that is not yet being targeted by Eicher. According to a 24-year-old British biker who rented a Royal Enfield during a year-long stay in India, the bikes 'occupy cult status in India. Countless heroes of Bollywood films have been shown riding them . . . The look and feel of the thing, the rawness of the engine, the noise: everyone is obsessed by that'. So perhaps there are also prospects among wealthier Indians living in Britain. Fortunately for Eicher, 56 per cent growth in revenues in 2012 to £120 million has given the group a degree of financial solidity that makes the success of the UK launch desirable but not essential.

One other factor that Eicher will need to face in Britain is the highly seasonal nature of bike sales. In January people think of warm coats, not bikes, so the sales season is limited to the summer months.

All in all, the future of this UK launch seems uncertain. An early review of the Continental GT raises doubts about the 'build compromises', even though it praises the road handling and general modernity of the bike. Siddhartha Lal is hoping that UK success in October 2013 will kickstart a global push by Royal Enfield into export markets. It remains to be seen.

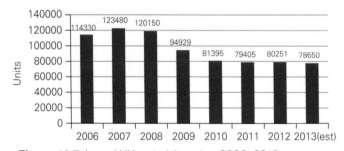

Figure 16.7 Annual UK motorbike sales, 2006–2013

Source: www.mcia.co.uk

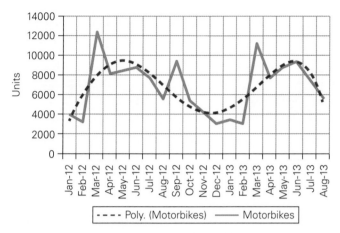

Figure 16.8 Monthly sales of motorbikes in the UK, Jan 2012–Aug 2013

Source: www.mcia.co.uk

Questions (25 marks; 30 minutes)

1. Use Figure 16.7 to identify and explain one reason in favour and one reason against launching into the UK market for motorbikes in 2013. (7)

2. Analyse how a British motorcycle producer might use the sales trend information provided in Figures 16.7 and 16.8. (9)

3. Use Figure 16.8 to analyse the possible difficulties created for a motorbike manufacturer from the strongly seasonal sales pattern in the UK market. (9)

C. Extend your understanding

(20 marks each)

1. 'Since we can never know the future, it is pointless trying to forecast it.' To what extent do you agree with this statement? (20)

2. 'Quantitative sales forecasting techniques have only limited use. Qualitative judgements are needed in a constantly changing world.' To what extent do you agree with this statement? (20)

Price and income elasticity of demand

Linked to: Understanding markets, Chapter 14; Market research, Chapter 15; Segmentation, targeting and positioning, Chapter 19; Niche and mass marketing, Chapter 20; Pricing decisions, Chapter 23.

Definition

Elasticity measures the extent to which demand for a product changes when there is a change in a causal variable, such as price or consumer incomes.

17.1 Introduction

When a company increases the price of a product, it expects to lose some sales. Some customers will switch to a rival supplier; others may decide they do not want (or cannot afford) the product at all. Economists use the term 'the law of demand' to suggest that, almost invariably:

Price up $\longrightarrow$ Demand down

Price down $\longrightarrow$ Demand up

Price elasticity looks beyond the law of demand to ask the more subtle question: When the price goes up, by how much do sales fall? Elasticity measures the extent to which price changes affect demand.

17.2 Price elasticity of demand

In the short term, the most important factor affecting demand is price. When the price of *The Independent* newspaper increased from £1.20 to £1.40 in 2013, sales fell by 9 per cent between May and October; whereas *The Telegraph's* price rise from £1 to £1.20 (the year before) cut sales by just 4 per cent. Readers of *The Independent* proved more price sensitive than readers of *The Telegraph*. Therefore the owners of *The Telegraph* could feel delighted with their pricing decision. Selling 4 per cent fewer papers but receiving 20 per cent more for each one sold meant a significant boost to revenue and profits.

The crucial business question is: how much will demand change when we change the price? Will demand rise by 1 per cent, 5 per cent or 15 per cent following a 10 per cent price cut? Some products are far more price sensitive than others.

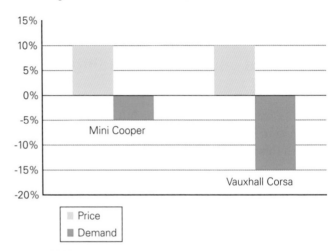

Figure 17.1 Impact of a 10 per cent price rise on car sales

Price elasticity can be calculated using the formula shown below:

$$\text{Price elasticity (PED)} = \frac{\text{per cent change in quantity demanded}}{\text{per cent change in price}}$$

Price elasticity measures the percentage effect on demand of each 1 per cent change in price. So if a 10 per cent increase in price led demand to fall by 20 per cent, the price elasticity would be 2. Strictly speaking, price elasticities are always negative and therefore the actual figure is –2. This is because a price rise pushes demand down, and a price cut pushes demand up. The figure of –2 indicates that, for every 1 per cent change in price, demand will move by 2 per cent in the opposite direction.

17.3 Determinants of price elasticity

Why do some products, services or brands have low price elasticity and some high elasticity? Why is the price elasticity of Branston Baked Beans higher than that of

Heinz Baked Beans? Or the price elasticity of the *Financial Times* as low as −0.05 while the price elasticity of *Look* magazine is as high as −2.0 (that is, 40 times higher)?

The main determinants of price elasticity are as follows.

The degree of product differentiation

This is the extent to which customers view the product as being distinctive from its rivals. *Look* may be an excellent magazine, but it is offering the same mix of fashion, shopping and 'celebs' as many other magazines aimed at young women. So if the cover price is increased, it is easy for readers to switch to an alternative, whereas readers of the *Financial Times* do not have any other option. Therefore, the higher the product differentiation the lower the price elasticity.

Figure 17.2

The availability of substitutes

Customers may see 7 UP and Sprite as very similar drinks. In a supermarket they may buy the cheaper of the two. At a cinema, though, only Sprite may be available. At a train station vending machine, almost certainly Sprite will be the only lemonade. This is because it is a Coca-Cola brand and the distribution strength of Coke places Sprite in locations where 7 UP never goes. When Sprite has no direct competition its price elasticity is much lower; therefore the brand owner (Coke) can push the price up without losing too many customers.

Branding and brand loyalty

Products with low price elasticity are those that consumers buy without thinking about the price tag. Some reach for Coca-Cola without checking its price compared with that of Pepsi, or buy a Harley-Davidson motorcycle even though a Honda superbike may be £4,000 cheaper. Strong brand names with strong brand images create customers who buy out of loyalty.

Real business

Boosting revenue

When *The Telegraph* newspaper increased its price from £1 to £1.20, its daily sales fell by 4 per cent, from 604,000 to 579,000 copies per day. This caused the following effect on daily revenue:

Before price rise: price £1 × sales volume of 604,000 = £604,000

After price rise: price £1.20 × sales volume of 579,000 = £694,800

That is, sales revenue rose by £90,800 per day, a 15 per cent increase. As the slight fall in sales would reduce total variable costs, the impact on profit would have been even greater.

17.4 The value of price elasticity to decision-makers

Being able to estimate a product's price elasticity is a hugely valuable aid to marketing decision-making. At West Ham United, ticket prices for Under-16s vary from £70 in top seats for top games such as Manchester United all the way down to £1 when trying to fill the stadium against less attractive opposition on midweek winter evenings. Unusually for a business, the objective is to fill the stadium rather than maximise revenue. Understanding the price elasticity of demand for junior tickets helps West Ham achieve an average capacity utilisation of 95 per cent or more.

Data on a product's price elasticity can be used for two purposes, as outlined below.

Sales forecasting

A firm considering a price rise will want to know the effect the price change is likely to have on demand. Producing a sales forecast will make possible accurate production, personnel and purchasing decisions. For example, in September 2013 Nintendo cut the price of its Wii U in America by 15 per cent, from $350 to $299. In October–November 2013 sales rose by 150 per cent. At that time, the price elasticity of the Wii U proved to be:

$$\frac{+150 \text{ per cent}}{-15 \text{ per cent}} = -10.$$

Nintendo could then use that knowledge to predict the likely impact of future price changes. Another price cut of 10 per cent could lead to doubling of sales (−10 per cent × −10 = +100 per cent). This information can be passed on to operations and HR, to get the staff in place to produce 100 per cent more stock.

Pricing strategy

There are many external factors that determine a product's demand, and therefore its profitability. For example, a soft drinks manufacturer can do nothing about a wet, cold summer that causes sales and profits to fall. However, the price the firm decides to charge is within its control, and it can be a crucial factor in determining demand and profitability. Price elasticity information can be used in conjunction with internal cost data to forecast the impact of a price change on revenue.

17.5 Classifying price elasticity

Price-elastic products

A price-elastic product is one with a price elasticity of above 1. This means that the percentage change in demand is greater than the percentage change in price that created it. For example, if a firm increased prices by 5 per cent and as a result demand fell by 15 per cent, price elasticity would be:

$$\frac{-15 \text{ per cent}}{+5 \text{ per cent}} \times 100 = -3$$

The higher the price elasticity figure, the more price elastic the product. Cutting price on a price-elastic product will boost total revenue. This is because the extra revenue gained from the increased sales volume more than offsets the revenue lost from the price cut. On the other hand, a price increase on a price-elastic product will lead to a fall in total revenue.

Table 17.1 Summary of price elasticity classification

	Price-elastic product	Price-inelastic product
Characteristic	• Undifferentiated • Many competitors	• Differentiated • Few competitors
Impact of a price cut	Sales rise sharply... so revenue rises	Sales rise, but not much... so revenue falls
Numerically	Between −1 and −5 or more	Between −0.1 and −0.99
Impact of a price rise	Sales fall sharply... so revenue falls	Sales fall, but not much... so revenue rises

Price-inelastic products

Price-inelastic products have price elasticities below 1. This means the percentage change in demand is less than the percentage change in price. In other words, price changes have hardly any effect on demand, perhaps because consumers feel they *must* have the product or brand in question: the stunning dress, the trendiest designer label or – less interestingly – gas for central heating. Customers feel they must have it, either because it really is a necessity, or because it is fashionable. Firms with price-inelastic products will be tempted to push the prices up. A price increase will boost revenue because the price rise creates a relatively small fall in sales volume. This means the majority of customers will continue to purchase the brand but at a higher, revenue-boosting price.

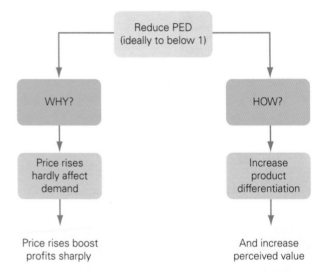

Figure 17.3 Logic chain: lowering price elasticity

17.6 Income elasticity

Another important factor that affects the demand for many products is any change in household incomes. If people are better off they will buy more of most goods, for example, more chocolate, more new cars and more cinema tickets. To measure this effect it is wise to assess the income elasticity (YED) of a product or service. The formula is:

$$\frac{\text{per cent change in demand}}{\text{per cent change in real incomes (incomes after inflation)}}$$

There are three categories a product can be put into:

- a 'normal good', with positive income elasticity, and a YED of between 0.1 and 1.5
- a 'luxury' good, with very positive income elasticity of more than 1.5

- an 'inferior' good, that is, one with negative income elasticity (so, as people get better off, they buy less of it, perhaps including orange squash or Asda Value Milk Chocolate).

Knowing the income elasticity of a product is vital in order to develop a well-balanced product portfolio.

Because inferior goods sell well during recessions, it is helpful for a company to have both inferior goods and luxury goods. Nevertheless, as the UK economy tends to grow at around 2.5 per cent a year in the long term, normal and luxury goods are the most important part of a long-term strategy.

Five Whys and a How

Question	Answer
Why might a company care more about its PED than its sales figures?	Because extra sales do not necessarily boost profit, but control over pricing can transform a firm's profits and prospects
Why do products with high price elasticity not necessarily have high income elasticity?	Price elasticity is about competition and differentiation: income elasticity is about luxury. A Bentley has low price elasticity but high income elasticity
Why may a product's price elasticity change over time?	Because the degree of competition may change, as may the level of differentiation established by advertising
Why are consumers better off buying price elastic products (and services)?	Because the close rivalry between suppliers ensures efficient, value-for-money products
Why may a product's price elasticity vary over its life cycle?	If innovative, it would be low at birth, but increase as rivals catch up, then rise more when it falls out of fashion and into decline
How might a retail dry cleaner reduce its price elasticity?	By finding a USP or strong point of differentiation, e.g. free local collection and delivery

Key terms

Predatory pricing: pricing low with the deliberate intention of driving a competitor out of business.

Price-elastic product: a product that is highly price sensitive, so price elasticity is above 1.

Price-inelastic product: a product that is not very price sensitive, so price elasticity is below 1.

Evaluation: Price and income elasticity of demand

Elasticity is a convenient concept but how useful is it in the real world? Would the average marketing director know the price elasticities of his or her products?

In many cases the answer is no. Textbooks exaggerate the precision that is possible with such a concept. The fact that the price elasticity of *The Telegraph* proved to be −0.2 in 2012 does not mean it will always be that low. Price elasticities change over time, as competition changes and consumer tastes change.

Even though elasticities can vary over time, certain features tend to remain constant. Strong brands such as BMW and Coca-Cola have relatively low price elasticity. This gives them the power over market pricing that ensures strong profitability year after year. For less established firms, these brands are the role models: everyone wants to be the Coca-Cola of their own market or market niche.

Workbook

A. Revision questions

(40 marks; 40 minutes)

1. **a)** If a product's sales have fallen by 21 per cent since a price rise from £2 to £2.07, what is its price elasticity? (4)

   b) Is the product price elastic or price inelastic? (1)

2. Outline two ways in which Nestlé could try to reduce the price elasticity of its Aero chocolate bars. (4)

3. A firm selling 20,000 units at £8 is considering a 4 per cent price increase. It believes its price elasticity is –0.5.

   a) Calculate the effect on revenue. (6)

   b) Outline two reasons why the revenue may prove to be different from the firm's expectations. (4)

4. Explain three ways a firm could make use of information about the price elasticity of its brands. (6)

5. Identify three external factors that could increase the price elasticity of a brand of chocolate. (3)

6. A firm has a sales target of 60,000 units per month. Current sales are 50,000 per month at a price of £1.50. If its products have a price elasticity of –2, what price should the firm charge to meet the target sales volume? (4)

7. Why is price elasticity always negative? (2)

8. Pol Roger sells 10,000 bottles of champagne a month in the UK at £30 a time. Its PED is -0.4 and its YED is +6.

   a) Calculate the value of its UK sales next year if real incomes rise by 2.5 per cent. (3)

   b) Briefly explain how it might use the data on its price elasticity of demand. (3)

B. Revision exercises

DATA RESPONSE 1

A firm selling Manchester United pillowcases for £10 currently generates an annual turnover of £500,000. Variable costs average at £4 per unit and total annual fixed costs are £100,000. The marketing director is considering a price increase of 10 per cent.

Questions (20 marks; 25 minutes)

1. Given that the price elasticity of the product is believed to be –0.4, calculate:

   a) the old and the new sales volume (3)

   b) the new revenue (3)

   c) the expected change in profit following the price increase. (6)

2. Analyse the factors that might affect the price elasticity of pillowcases. (8)

DATA RESPONSE 2

Sauces and sources

Heinz Tomato Ketchup is an iconic brand, more than 100 years old. It dominates the market for ketchup with annual sales of £125 million in the UK. It has a share of UK tomato sauce sales believed to be over 75 per cent. It has no effective branded competition, though sales of supermarket own label ketchups can be considerable.

In 2013 it took a risk by increasing its prices by 10 per cent, even though the average price increase for 'table sauces' was only 3.5 per cent. The result was a 5 per cent fall in Heinz sales volumes.

Figure 17.4 Heinz Tomato Ketchup

Heinz says that the major growth stories in table sauces come from more exotic flavours such as Mexican Chilli and Heinz Sweet Chilli. Perhaps this increased competition explains the collapse in sales of Levi Roots' Reggae Reggae Barbeque sauce, which suffered a 17 per cent fall in 2013 sales volumes following a price rise of 8.5 per cent. The following table sets out the full story.

Figure 17.5 Reggae Reggae Sauce

Questions (25 marks; 30 minutes)

1. **a)** Calculate the price elasticity of Heinz Tomato Ketchup in 2013. (4)

   b) Explain two reasons why this product may have this degree of price elasticity. (4)

Table 17.2 Reggae Reggae Sauce sales 2012 and 2013

	2012	2013
Selling price	£1.55	£1.68
Sales volume (bottles)	3.1 million	2.56 million
Sales revenue (£ millions)	£4.8m	£4.3m

Source: *The Grocer*

Text adapted from *The Grocer* and Mysupermarket.com

2. **a)** Calculate the price elasticity of Reggae Reggae sauce in 2013. (4)

   b) It is believed that the price elasticity of Reggae Reggae sauce is higher now than in the past. Explain two possible reasons why this might have occurred. (4)

3. The figures suggest that Heinz Tomato Ketchup has a significantly lower price elasticity than that of Reggae Reggae Sauce. Analyse the implications of that for Heinz. (9)

C. Extend your understanding

1. WH Smith has found that the price elasticity of its core stationery products (paper, pens, etc.) is quite high. Discuss how it might set about reducing the price elasticity of this part of its business. (20)

2. After its relative failure with Xbox One, Microsoft is preparing to develop and launch Xbox Two. To what extent might it use the concept of price and income elasticity to help it with setting prices and forecasting sales? (20)

Market data and analysis

Linked to: Setting marketing objectives, Chapter 13; Understanding markets, Chapter 14; Market research, Chapter 15; Segmentation, targeting and positioning, Chapter 19.

Definition

Breaking the market down statistically to assess the types of product, consumer and competitor.

18.1 What market are we in?

This sounds like a daft question, but the marketing guru Theodore Levitt considers it vital. Is Liverpool FC in the football business, the sports business or the leisure business? Long ago, Nintendo was Japan's number one producer of playing cards. It decided that its market was the broader games business and experimented with electronic games in the 1970s. Today, despite difficulties in competing with Sony and Xbox, it is a hugely successful producer of games consoles and software. Sales of playing cards represent less than 1 per cent of the modern Nintendo.

Figure 18.1 Nintendo star: Super Mario

'The railroads collapsed because they thought they were in the railroad business, when really they were in the transport business.' Theodore Levitt, business guru.

18.2 The purpose of market analysis

Managers tend to get caught up in the day-to-day needs of the business. A photo of Alexa Chung wearing a silk scarf might make sales leap, forcing clothes store managers to focus 100 per cent on how to find extra stocks of scarves. Market analysis should be a cooler, more thoughtful look at the market's longer-term trends. In 2001 Whitbread decided to sell its pub business to focus on hotels (Premier Inn) and Costa Coffee. It later sold off other businesses such as David Lloyd Health Clubs and TGI Friday's – to focus on where it thought the growth was – in coffee bars especially. Its clever market analysis positioned the business correctly for future growth.

Other clever pieces of market analysis include:

- Danone seeing the opportunity for 'functional foods' (that is, foods bought because they are believed to be good for you), such as Activia yoghurt, then putting more money behind these brands than anyone else. It showed huge confidence in its understanding of the market.
- Harvey Nichols (classic London posh shop) seeing the opportunity for a branch in Leeds, in an era when there was plenty of money in the North. When it made the move, other retailers doubted whether Leeds would be posh enough – it was and it is.

These examples have one thing in common: they are the result of careful analysis of trends within a market, backed by an ability to take bold decisions (and get them right).

'One of the primary objectives of market analysis is to determine the attractiveness of a market.' David Aaker, US writer and businessman

18.3 Consumer usage and attitudes

Market analysis is rooted in a deep understanding of customers. Why do they buy Coca-Cola, not Pepsi? Yet they prefer Tropicana (made by Pepsi) to Minute Maid (made by Coke). And who are the key decision-makers? Purchasers (perhaps parents buying a multipack in Tesco) or the users (perhaps young teenage children slumped in front of the television)? Is the brand decision a result of child pester power, or parental belief in the product's superiority? Knowledge of such subtleties is essential. Only then can the firm know whether to focus marketing effort on the parent or the child.

To acquire the necessary knowledge about usage and attitudes, firms adopt several approaches. The starting point is usually qualitative research, such as group discussions. Run by psychologists, these informal discussions help to pinpoint consumers' underlying motives and behaviour. For example, it is important to learn whether Kit Kat buyers enjoy nibbling the chocolate before eating the wafer biscuit; in other words, to discover whether playing with confectionery is an important part of the enjoyment. This type of information can influence future product development.

Multinational Unilever has set up a Knowledge Management Group to ensure that insights such as this can be spread around the business. Its job is to help Unilever achieve its strategic objectives by 'locating, capturing, sharing, transferring and creating knowledge'. The company believes this helps it benefit from:

- improved decision-making
- fewer mistakes
- reduced duplication
- converting new knowledge more quickly into added value to the business.

Among the other ways to gather information on customer usage and attitudes are quantitative research and obtaining feedback from staff who deal directly with customers. An example of the latter would be bank staff whose task is to sell services such as insurance. Customer doubts about a brochure or a product feature, if fed back to head office, may lead to important improvements.

Quantitative research is also used to monitor customer usage and attitudes. Many firms conduct surveys every month, to track changes in brand awareness or image over time. This procedure may reveal that a TV commercial has had an unintended side effect in making the brand image rather too upmarket, or that customers within a market are becoming more concerned about whether the packaging can be recycled.

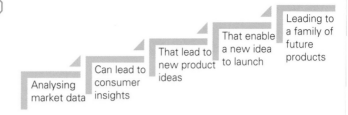

Figure 18.2 Logic ladder: the value of market analysis

18.4 Consumer profiles

Marketing decisions are very hard to make without a clear picture of your customers. Who are they? Young? Outgoing? Affluent? Or not. From product and packaging design, through to pricing, promotion and distribution – all these aspects of marketing hinge on knowing your target market.

A consumer profile is a statistical breakdown of the people who buy a particular product or brand. (For example, what percentage of consumers are women aged 16 to 25?) The main categories analysed within a consumer profile are customers' age, gender, social class, income level and region. Profile information is used mainly for:

- setting quotas for research surveys
- segmenting a market
- deciding in which media to advertise (*Vogue* or *The Sun*?).

A large consumer goods firm will make sure to obtain a profile of consumers throughout the market as well as for its own brand(s). This may be very revealing. It may show that the age profile of its own customers is becoming older than for the market as a whole. This may force a complete rethink of the marketing strategy. The company may have been trying to give the brand a classier image, but may end up attracting older customers.

Real business

The Jaguar XJ

Launched in 2010, the new Jaguar XJ was deliberately designed to restore the company's position within the luxury car sector. In the days when Jaguar was owned by Ford, the American car producer had pulled Jaguar's model range down towards the mass market. The XJ, with prices from around £60,000, would emphasise that Jaguar should be seen alongside Mercedes and BMW, not Ford or Volkswagen. In February 2014 Jaguar announced that booming sales of the XJ in China were an important part of its record-breaking £842 million profit in the third quarter of its 2013/2014 financial year.

Five Whys and a How

Question	Answer
Why is it hard for new firms to break into an established market?	Because the existing firms have rich market understanding that is hard for newcomers to match
Why may it be hard to decide on the boundaries of a market?	Because people and technology change, the boundaries can change. Music and gaming were once separate markets; now mobile hardware has brought them into competition
Why may consumer attitudes be different from usage?	Many consumers disapprove of fattening products, but buy and eat them; consumer psychology is complex
Why does market analysis matter?	Bad day-to-day decisions can waste millions of pounds, but dreadful market analysis (Tesco in America) can waste billions
Why might an ice cream producer benefit from careful analysis of sales data in its market?	It might identify a new trend before competitors, such as a trend towards adult iced lollies (vodka and orange, perhaps?)
How might Jaguar Land Rover build on its success in China?	Work hard at understanding Chinese car buyers to make sure future models are designed to suit their habits, tastes and pockets

Key terms

Product positioning: deciding on the image and target market you want for your own product or brand.

Target market: the type of customer your product or service is aimed at. For example, the target market for Kit Kat Senses is 15- to 30-year-old women.

Evaluation: Market data and analysis

Market analysis is at the heart of successful marketing. All the great marketing decisions are rooted in a deep understanding of what customers really want; from the marketing of Lady GaGa through to the sustained success of the (incredibly pricey) Chanel No. 5 perfume. The clever market stall trader acquires this understanding through daily contact with customers. Large companies need the help of market research to provide a comparable feel. Techniques such as market mapping then help clarify the picture.

Having learnt what the customer really wants from a product, perhaps helped by psychological insights from qualitative research, it is relatively easy to put the strategy into practice. If the marketing insight is powerful enough, the practical details of the marketing mix should not matter too much. The Sony PS4 was a brilliant piece of marketing, but few commentators had anything good to say about the brand's advertising or packaging. The genius came earlier in the process.

Workbook

A. Revision questions

(30 marks; 30 minutes)

1. Reread Section 18.1 and ask yourself 'What if Nintendo had not decided to define its market more widely? What would the business be like today?' (3)

2. Explain how customer 'usage' may be different from customer 'attitudes'. (4)

3. Explain two reasons why it may be important to distinguish 'purchasers' from 'users'. (4)

4. Explain how qualitative research could be used helpfully when analysing a market. (4)

5. When *Look* magazine was launched it announced that its target market was '24-year-old women'. Explain two ways it could make use of this very precise consumer profile. (4)

6. When Apple launched the Apple Watch it believed that its iPhone customers would spend $350 on an extra gadget. Outline two pieces of market analysis that might have led them to that view. (4)

7. Why does market research need to be carried out regularly, not just related to a new product? (3)

8. Explain the importance of market research in achieving effective market analysis. (4)

B. Revision exercises
DATA RESPONSE

What business is Cadbury in? For the first 100 years of the firm's life, the answer would have been chocolate. But in 1989 it bought the Trebor and Bassett's brands to form a large sugar confectionery unit. With Wrigley enjoying uninterrupted growth in chewing gum, Cadbury then bought Adams – a major US gum producer (for £2.7 billion). It followed this up with purchases of other chewing gum producers in countries that included Turkey.

In 2007, Cadbury launched the Trident gum brand in Britain. This was bold because Wrigley enjoyed a market share of more than 90 per cent in the UK. By March 2008 Cadbury was able to announce that 'an astounding £38 million of extra sales value has been added to the gum category, with 75 per cent of this growth delivered by Trident'. Cadbury's management confidently predicted 5 years of growth for Trident of as much as £20 million of sales per year.

By 2009, though, Trident was in sharp retreat, with sales falling to £19 million that year and continuing their slump to reach under £5 million by 2013. By then Cadbury had been submerged into the Kraft food business. So is Cadbury in the food business, the chocolate business, or the confectionery business? It's hard to say.

Table 18.1 UK confectionery market 2013

Confectionery	Market value (£ millions)
Chocolate	3,600
Sugar confectionery	1,147
Chewing gum	272
Total market	5,019

Questions (25 marks; 30 minutes)

1. Explain why companies such as Cadbury need to ask themselves, 'What market am I in?' (5)

2. a) What is meant by the term 'market share'? (2)

   b) Calculate Trident's share of the chewing gum market in 2009 and again in 2013. (4)

   c) Why might Cadbury have been worried about tackling a business with 'a market share of more than 90 per cent'? (5)

3. Analyse what might have gone wrong with Cadbury's understanding of the chewing gum market. (9)

C. Extend your understanding

1. As a generalisation, your grandparents once loved Marks & Spencer and your parents loved Tesco. Now neither is loved. Discuss the problems a business such as Tesco may have in rebuilding customer usage and attitudes. (20)

2. In the past 5 years the boom in China's car market has only been exceeded by the boom in sales of 4 × 4 cars in China. Having analysed the data, Rolls Royce is now developing the world's most expensive 4 × 4. To what extent would you agree with this strategy? (20)

Segmentation, targeting and positioning

Linked to: Understanding markets, Chapter 14; Interpreting marketing data, Chapter 16; Market data and analysis, Chapter 18.

Definition

Segmentation means finding ways to divide a market up to identify untapped opportunities, perhaps among older consumers, or among those who believe they are wheat-intolerant. This offers up the possibility of new target markets and a new positioning within the market.

19.1 Market segmentation

Most markets can be subdivided in several different ways. If you go to WH Smith and look at the magazine racks, you will see the process in action. There are magazines for men and (many more) for women. Within the women's section there are magazines for kids, teens, young adults, those who are middle-aged and some for the elderly. Then there are magazines that target different interests and hobbies, from football to computer consoles to gardening.

Market segmentation is the acknowledgement by companies that customers are not all the same. 'The market' can be broken down into smaller sections in which customers share common characteristics, from the same age group to a shared love of Manchester United. Successful segmentation can increase customer satisfaction (if you love shopping and 'celebs', how wonderful that *Look* magazine is for you!) and provide scope for increasing company profits. After all, customers may be willing to pay a higher price for a magazine focused purely on the subjects they love, instead of buying a general magazine in which most of the articles stay unread.

For new, small companies segmentation is a valuable strategy for breaking into an established market. (Think innocent in fruit juice, first making its mark with smoothies.) For large companies, market segmentation involves two possibilities:

1. Simply to add one niche product to a portfolio otherwise dominated by the mass market
2. Multiple segmentation, in which a wide portfolio of niche brands can add up to a market leading position. This approach would have risked being only marginally profitable in the past, but flexible, high-tech manufacturing systems can make it cost-effective to produce differently targeted products on the same production line. A good example is Ella's Organic – a baby food company which has enjoyed sales growth from £2 million a year in 2009 to £30 million in 2014 by spreading the idea of food good-for-babies across a series of different sectors (and 15 countries overseas).

'In multiple segmentation, a company seeks to appeal to two or more well-defined consumer groups by different marketing plans.' J. Evans and B. Berman, academics and authors

19.2 The process of segmentation

To successfully segment a market, the steps are as follows.

1. Conduct research into the different types of customer within a marketplace; for example, different age groups, gender, region and personality types.
2. See if they have common tastes/habits; for example, younger readers may be more focused on fashion and celebrities than older ones.
3. Identify the segment you wish to focus on, and then conduct some qualitative research into customer motivations and psychology.
4. Devise a product designed not for the whole market, but for a particular segment. This may only achieve a 1 per cent market share, but if the total market is big enough, that could be highly profitable.

In 2003 Camilla Stephens started a pie business that struggled to become profitable. It needed to be refinanced and downscaled in 2004, but from a smaller base it began to grow. Before starting the business, Camilla had been Head of Food at Starbucks UK and also Deputy Editor of Good Housekeeping magazine, so she had a terrific understanding of food trends. Seeing the success of innocent Drinks and Green and Blacks, she focused clearly on hand-made, very high quality, high-priced pies. Think Chicken and Red Pepper rather than Chicken Balti.

In the early years the pie business supplied local cafes and caterers, but in 2006 Camilla (with new partner/husband James Footit) developed the *Higgidy* brand. This proved an incredible turning point. Within 18 months Higgidy was stocked in Sainsbury, Booths and Waitrose supermarkets, giving national distribution and a big boost to sales. By taking their time to understand the market segment for posh pies, Higgidy was put on track to achieve success in the static market for pies and pastries. In the graph below, Higgidy's success is contrasted with the flat sales position of mass-market Pukka Pies.

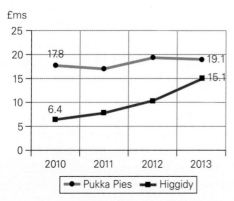

Figure 19.1 Higgidy's sales growth, 2010-13

Source: *The Grocer* magazine

19.3 The value of segmentation

Segmentation offers companies three main benefits.

1. Improved sales volumes. When Xbox 360 and the PS3 were about to be launched, Nintendo surprised the market by bringing out the Wii. Instead of targeting young men, Nintendo had identified market demand for a family console with appeal to young and old. The Wii was a huge success in sales volume terms and in profitability. What Nintendo had expected to be a relatively small segment proved to be a new, differentiated mass-market product. Even for lesser new products, segmentation can build sales volume within a market. In 2013 Cadbury brought out Marvellous Creations – a range of more fun, younger variants on the Dairy Milk theme. Its sales of more than £50 million in 2013 were overwhelming additions to sales of the Dairy Milk brand and of chocolate as a whole. By appealing to a younger segment, more chocolate was sold.

2. Increased prices. When Center Parcs managed to identify a segment in the UK holiday market for a more upmarket version of Butlins and other holiday camps, they effectively became the sole suppliers of this category of holiday. Center Parcs had identified the segment, designed the right product and now enjoy 97 per cent usage, year-round (and made profits of £20 million in 2013/14).

3. Increased diversification and therefore security. It is great to have a blockbuster, mass-market product, but less so if sales start to slip as fashion moves away. Shares in the US shoe brand Crocs fell from $68 in October 2007 to $1.50 in November 2008 as Crocs went from 'hot to what?' Life would have been much more comfortable for the business if it had brands in several segments instead of the one mass-market product.

'In market segmentation a company seeks to appeal to one well-defined consumer group by one marketing plan.' J. Evans and B. Berman, academics and authors

19.4 Methods of segmentation

1. Demographic, in other words by population subset: by age, by ethnic origin or by gender. In the UK market for yoghurt, two of the 'Top Ten' brands are focused on children: Petit Filous (sales of £98 million in 2013) and Munch Bunch (£54.4 million in 2013). Both brands were part of a wave of segmentation that transformed the market from a single product with sales of less than £5 million in 1970 (plain, unsweetened yogurt in glass jars) to today's UK market worth more than £2,000 million (figures from *The Grocer*, 21 December 2013). A glance at daytime TV shows all the products that target the older demographic. And a glance at Figure 19.2 shows the growth to come in this age group.

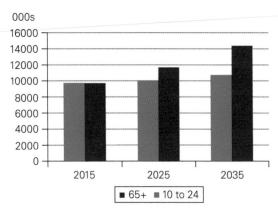

Figure 19.2 UK population by age category
Source: Office of National Statistics Population Projections

2. Geographic, in other words by region or by country (for a UK exporting business). In the UK, sales of the soft drink Irn Bru have always been concentrated in Scotland. But following three years of a marketing push into England, by 2014 57 per cent of the brand's sales came from England and Wales (with 41 per cent drunk by the 8 per cent of the UK population based in Scotland). To brand owners A.G.Barr, geographic segmentation can be seen as a strength (Irn Bru is a must-stock drink in Scotland) as well as offering interesting sales development opportunities.

3. Income; in other words, segmenting markets in relation to household incomes. This is more relevant than ever, because income and wealth distribution has become significantly more unequal over recent decades. The market for eating out is a good example, with (in London) the price of an evening meal varying between £10 per person and £200. This means that businesses have to think hard about whether they want to be involved in every income segment, or whether they would be better off specialising. For example Tragus operates 300 restaurants in the £10-£20 per head sector, under brands such as Strada, Café Rouge and Bella Italia. Another group, D&D London, runs about 30 outlets in Britain at prices of around £50 per head. By specialising in one income-related segment, these groups can learn about their market and therefore make fewer mistakes when opening new restaurants (one of the highest-risk businesses in Britain).

4. Behavioural, that is dividing up a market into how people behave, for example, taking the market for young fashion and dividing it up into fashion leaders and fashion followers. Or subdividing the games market into 'shoot-em-ups' and strategy games. To do this successfully one has to understand the market exceptionally well.

'In the affluent society no useful distinction can be made between luxuries and necessities.' J. K. Galbraith, economist and (outstanding) author

---

19.5 Targeting

Having analysed a market and identified suitable criteria for segmentation, the business then needs to decide which precise segment it wishes to target. Naturally, it will take into account its own strengths, both real (in terms, say, of design skills) and also based on image, such as the association of Porsche with classy sportiness. So when Porsche decided to develop a 4x4 off-road vehicle, it had to look sporty and exude luxury. It did.

In addition to comparing the segments to your own strengths, it would be important to consider:

- the potential size of each segment, by volume and especially by value
- the potential growth rate within each segment
- whether there is a rival business with a better fit with the segment; for example, Saga for the older audience
- whether an existing producer has already got a foothold in the segment. (It may be hugely valuable to be first into a sector.)
- the accessibility of each possible target audience; for example, reaching young adults is less certain than reaching older people. The latter have more predictable behaviours, for example, watching daytime TV, whereas young people may only be reached effectively if, by luck or skill, a social media viral marketing campaign works well.

Having made the decision about targeting, it's time for the final step: positioning.

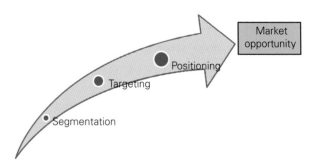

Figure 19.3 Logic chain: STEP towards market opportunity

19.6 Positioning

Having decided which segment to target, there remains the issue of positioning. The decision may be made to aim for the centre of the segment, for example 'for *all* young men'. Or the intention may be to only target the heavily committed shoot-em-up gamers. For Apple consumer electronics, the positioning was clearly 'accessible and easy to use' as opposed to 'for geeks'.

However sure the business is of its segmentation analysis, the decision on positioning will be crucial. A me-too approach works very rarely (though Apple would doubtless argue that Samsung's hugely successful Galaxy model was a me-too of the iPhone). The best approach is to identify a position within the segment that will appeal strongly to a minority, as opposed to appealing a bit to the many.

A great example of positioning is Aldi's position within the UK's price-motivated segment of the grocery market. With Asda, Lidl and Iceland as its direct competitors, Aldi has seen its sales boom as a result of persuading middle-Britain that shopping at Aldi is sensible rather than cheapskate. Its slogan 'Spend a little. Live a lot.' is about having a good time, not about 'low, low prices'. Figure 19.4 shows the value to Aldi of astute positioning.

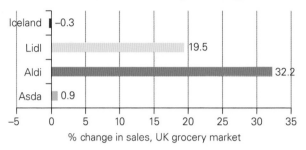

Figure 19.4 Aldi year-on-year percentage change in sales, 12 weeks to July 2014
Source: Kantar Worldpanel

Five Whys and a How

Question	Answer
Why might a company such as Heinz, with a strong mass-market position, choose to segment a market?	Because it's often possible to charge higher prices for segmental products than it is in the mass market
Why might multiple segmentation be preferable to having a big-selling mass-market product?	Because prices and profit margins might be higher and there's less risk than there is having 'all the eggs in one basket'
Why may segmentation by age become more important in the future?	Because of demographic shifts towards more older people
Why might a foreign chocolate company make a targeting mistake if it tried to break into the UK chocolate market?	By not knowing the UK market enough to be able to interpret research findings accurately
Why might it be necessary to use qualitative research before deciding finally on the right positioning for a new biscuit brand?	Because you need insight into consumer psychology, which is what qualitative research should be able to provide
How might segmentation and positioning help Marks & Spencer?	Instead of aiming at everyone it might help them focus more tightly (and more effectively) on specific groups of people

Evaluation: Segmentation, targeting and positioning

In recent years Kellogg's has struggled as breakfast cereal sales have faltered generally in America, Britain and Europe. Its market analysis showed that fewer people eat breakfast, but it struggled to think how to create 'breakfast-on-the-go'. Rice Krispies Cereal Bars do not seem a long-term solution. So the company needs to reposition itself. It made a start in 2012 by buying the Pringles brand for $2.7 billion. But since then it has been unable to see a successful way forward. In the long run, the managements that understand (and are bold enough to implement) a strategy of segmentation, targeting and positioning are the ones that will keep moving from one growth sector to the next.

Workbook

A. Revision questions

(35 marks; 35 minutes)

1. Explain how customer satisfaction might increase as a result of more careful market segmentation. (4)

2. **a)** Look at Figure 19.1. Calculate the percentage sales change between 2010 and 2013 for:
   i. Higgidy (3)
   ii. Pukka (3)

   b) Explain what impact this growth might have had on the unit costs of producing Higgidy Pies. (4)

3. Why might diversification be an attraction for a business planning a segmentation instead of a mass-market strategy? (4)

4. Explain in your own words how the market for shoes could be segmented. (4)

5. Figure 19.2 shows how much population growth is expected in the 65-plus age category. Explain how this might affect a supermarket of your choice. (6)

6. Figure 19.4 might suggest that Iceland Foods needs to reposition itself. How might it set about this process? (7)

B. Revision exercises

DATA RESPONSE

Galaxy Chocolate at 15p head for India

Around the globe, the $100 billion chocolate market is a battle between three multinationals: Mars, Nestlé and Mondelez (the Kraft subsidiary that includes Cadbury). An exception is India, where Mars has no significant foothold. Given that India is the world's fastest-growing market for chocolate, it should be no surprise that Mars is determined to tackle this issue. This November it is launching Galaxy Premium chocolate to take on the might of Cadbury Dairy Milk.

Its approach to the launch shows all the signs of desperation. Although the Galaxy launch is supported by a glossy advertising campaign featuring Bollywood actor Arjun Rampal and model Sapna Pabbi, Mars is pricing Galaxy extremely competitively. In the middle of the market, Cadbury Dairy Milk has a 38g 'value' pack priced at 22p and a 60g Dairy Milk 'Silk' pack for 55p. Mars is to price a 40g pack of Galaxy at 15p.

Figure 19.5 Galaxy's launch in India featured Bollywood actor Arjun Rampal

M.V. Natarajan, general manager of Mars India (Chocolates Division) said: 'India is the world's fastest growing chocolate market and the moulded chocolate segment is the fastest growing sector. India is a very important market for Mars. With this launch we are entering an extremely dynamic segment with our business objective of growing our product range in India.'

The market for chocolate in India has a value of just £555 million at the moment. It is this small because Indians currently eat less than a sixtieth of

the amount of chocolate eaten in Britain (0.165kg a year compared with our 10.2 kgs!). But the market is forecast by Cadbury to grow at 23 per cent a year between 2013 and 2018, which will take it towards the UK's market size.

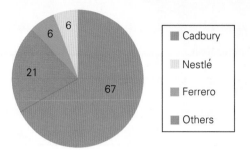

Figure 19.6 Chocolate market-share percentage, India 2013

Mr Natarajan's marketing strategy has two further elements to it. There is a marketing plan targeting the 0–18 age category, based on free distribution of sweets twice a year, on Independence Day and again on Republic Day. 19–35s will also be targeted using a tie-in with Facebook. One week before, Facebook will send the message 'Do you want to send chocolates on your friend's birthday?' There can be no doubt that Mars is determined to succeed.

Questions (30 marks; 35 minutes)

1. Explain two possible reasons why Mars wants to build a market share in India. (5)

2. From the text, analyse how well Mars has used 'segmentation, targeting and positioning' in launching Mars Premium chocolate in India? (9)

3. To what extent do you think the pricing strategy for Galaxy is likely to prove successful for Mars? (16)

C. Extend your understanding

1. Choose one of the following markets (bicycles; shampoos; chicken restaurants or football boots). To what extent would the use of segmentation, targeting and positioning boost the chances of a new company entering the market you've selected? (20)

2. To what extent would companies do better to focus 100 per cent on developing innovative new products than to bog themselves down in segmentation, targeting and positioning? (20)

Niche and mass marketing

Linked to: Market research, Chapter 15; Market data and analysis, Chapter 18; Segmentation targeting and positioning, Chapter 19; Pricing decisions, Chapter 23.

Definition

Mass marketing means devising products with mass appeal and promoting them to all types of customer. Niche marketing is tailoring a product to a particular type of customer.

20.1 Mass marketing

Mass marketing is the attempt to create products or services that have universal appeal. Rather than targeting a specific type of customer, mass marketing aims the product at the whole market. The intention is that everyone should be a consumer of the product. Coca-Cola is a good example of a firm that uses mass-marketing techniques. The company aims its product at young and old alike. Its goal has always been to be the market leader and it still is today. The ultimate prize of mass marketing is the creation of generic brands. These are brands that are so totally associated with the product that customers treat the brand name as if it was a product category. Examples include 'Coke' (cola) and 'Bacardi' (white rum).

Figure 20.1 Mass marketing

As shown in Figure 20.1, when mass marketing is carried out successfully it can be highly profitable. Firms such as Ryanair set out to be high-volume, mass-market operators and achieve handsome profits. However, it is important to note that mass marketing does not have to go hand in hand with low prices. For example, Nintendo, when it launched the DS, decided to become *the* handheld games console. Superb launch advertising and excellent games software development meant that it achieved mass-market sales while keeping its prices high. Even now, with its sales entering the decline phase of its product life cycle (see Figure 20.2), it remains the dominant brand in its market. Mass marketing does not have to aim at the lowest common denominator.

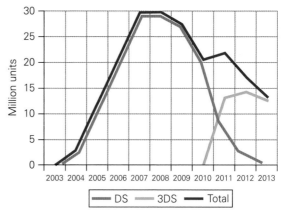

Figure 20.2 Worldwide annual sales of Nintendo handheld consoles, 2003–13

Source: VGChartz.com

'The mass market has split into ever-multiplying, ever-changing sets of micromarkets.' Alvin Toffler, author and social commentator.

20.2 Niche marketing

A niche market is a very small segment of a much larger market. Niche marketing involves identifying the needs of the consumers that make up the niche. A specialised product or service is then designed to meet the distinctive needs of these consumers. Niche-market products tend to sell in relatively low volumes. As a result, the price of a niche-market product is usually higher than the mass-market alternative. Niche market operators often distribute their products through specialist retailers, or directly to the consumer via the internet.

An entrepreneur wanting to set up a niche market business must first identify a group of people who share a taste for a product or service that is currently unsatisfied. A product or a service must then be designed that is capable of meeting this unsatisfied need. To stand a good chance of success, the new niche product will need to be superior to the mass-market equivalent that is currently available. Finally, the niche must be large enough to support a profitable business. Many new niche-market businesses fail because the revenue generated from their niche-market business is not high enough to cover the costs of operating.

A good example is provided by a small neighbourhood restaurant called Bajou that tried, unsuccessfully, to make a business out of selling Cajun food in south Croydon. At the weekend the restaurant was never completely empty, proving that a gap in the market did exist. Unfortunately, this gap in the market was not large enough to cover the overheads of running a restaurant. The restaurant was never full enough to operate above a break-even level. Six months after Bajou opened it was forced to close down. In niche markets entrepreneurs must manage their overhead costs with care if the business is to operate above its break-even point.

Small niche operators lack the economies of scale required to compete on price with larger, established operators. Instead, the small firm could try to find a small, profitable niche. The amount of profit generated by this niche needs to be high enough for the small firm, but too trivial for the big business. Rubicon Exotic has just a 0.6 per cent share of the £2.5 billion UK market for fizzy drinks. Happily, sales of £14 million are profitable enough to satisfy the requirements of Rubicon Drinks, with its low overheads. Small, niche-market businesses survive on the basis that they occupy a relatively unimportant market niche. Larger firms operating in the mass market are happy to ignore the niche businesses because they represent too small an opportunity to be worth their while.

Niche market businesses sell specialised, differentiated products that are designed to appeal to their very specific target market. Firms selling niche-market products can exploit the low price sensitivity created by product differentiation by raising price. Total revenue will rise after the price increase because, in percentage terms, the fall in sales volume will be less than the price increase.

Figure 20.3 Logic chain

'Most large markets evolve from niche markets.' R. McKenna, businessman

20.3 Are niche markets safe havens for small businesses?

In the past many large companies focused on mass markets and ignored small market gaps and the small companies that filled them. To fill lots of small niches would require lots of short production runs (for example, 90 minutes on the printing press producing the Hartlepool FC fanzine, and 60 minutes producing the Darlington one). This has always been expensive, because of the time taken to reset machinery.

This has changed due to technology. As production lines are increasingly set up by computer, they can be reset almost instantly. So large firms can build the sales volumes they need by producing a large variety of low-volume niche-market products. Small-scale producers are coming under threat from larger companies that have begun to target their niches.

Fortunately, small firms are often 'quicker on their feet', so when a large firm 'lumbers' towards the market, the smaller one may still be able to win the competitive war. When the multi-billion dollar PepsiCo bought the smoothie business PJ's, innocent Drinks thought that the market might become very difficult for them. In fact, innocent kept its market share rising within the small smoothie niche within the soft drinks market (but, ironically, sold out to Coca-Cola!).

Real business

Halls Soothers

The £1 billion UK market for sugar confectionery is ferociously competitive. Skittles battle against Jelly Babies, Fruitella against Starburst and so on. In a niche of its own, though, comes Halls Soothers: fruit sweets with a strongly medicinal image, for soothing sore throats. With a recommended retail price of 72p per pack, sales of £17.5 million were achieved in 2013. These sales would have been very profitable as the brand had little direct competition.

Source: Adapted from *The Grocer* Top Products Survey 2013

20.4 Influences on choosing a target market and positioning

Let no-one doubt it: every business would love to have the central, mass-market positioning of Wrigley (90 per cent share of UK chewing gum market) or Pampers (63 per cent of UK market for disposable nappies). Better still might be Colgate, with its 45 per cent share of the world market for toothpaste. Unfortunately, for the vast majority of businesses, this glorious position is not an option. Yes, Branston can take on Heinz's mass-market positioning in the baked bean market, but who would expect this to be profitable?

The conclusion is clear: if someone else has already 'captured' the mass market, you would be wiser to find your own, profitable niche. Then, who knows, in the long term you may be able to move from a strong niche positioning to chip away at the mass-market leader. This is what happened to Twinings tea, which – many years ago – was a tiny, upmarket tea brand in a market dominated by PG Tips and Tetley. In 2013 Twinings came close to toppling Tetley to take second place in the sector, and not too far short of market leader PG Tips. See Figure 20.4

When choosing a niche positioning the key issues are authenticity and the ability to gain a true understanding of the niche. In its sector, Alpro has proved masterful at understanding the consumers who believe that dairy products are bad for them. In a completely different sector, the German company Haribo has proved brilliant at carving out a big, profitable business in the UK's sugar confectionery market.

Additional influences on choosing a target market:

- Any evidence of growth in a sub-sector of the market might encourage a company to launch a

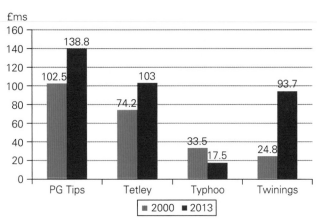

Figure 20.4 UK tea sales 2000–13
Source: *The Grocer* Top Products Survey

niche product now, even if the sector is small, to establish a sizeable market share in case the sector expands. Once, the juice brand Rubicon's exotic flavours made it a tiny seller. Today its sales exceed £20 million, making it one of the UK's Top 10 juice brands.

- Go where the young go. This is not a bad plan, as it positions a business at the forefront of new tastes and habits. Sometimes it will lead to relatively short-term fads that give little scope for profit, but at other times a company may find itself at the centre of a sales boom, such as Crocs or innocent Drinks.

- Follow the young companies. This is the approach taken by the 'once-young-but-now-cash-loaded' IT companies such as Google, Facebook and Twitter. With piles of cash at their disposal they can easily snap up the next Snapchat or WhatsApp.

Evaluation: Niche and mass marketing

Which is better? Is it mass or niche marketing? The answer is that it depends. In the bulk ice cream market, large packs of vanilla ice cream have become so cheap that little profit can be made. It is better by far, then, to be in a separate niche, whether regional (Mackie's Scottish ice cream) or upmarket, such as Rocombe Farm or Häagen Dazs. The latter can cost ten times as much per litre as the mass-market own-label bulk packs.

Yet would a film company prefer to sell a critic's favourite or a blockbuster, smash hit? The answer is the latter, of course. In other words, the mass market is great, if you can succeed there. Businesses such as Heinz, Kellogg's and even Chanel show that mass marketing can be successful and profitable in the long term.

Key terms

Economies of scale: factors that cause costs per unit to fall when a firm operates at a higher level of production.

Generic brands: brands that are so well known that customers say the brand when they mean the product (for example, 'I'll Hoover the floor.').

Price elasticity: the responsiveness of demand to a change in price.

Product differentiation: the extent to which consumers perceive your brand as being different from others.

Five Whys and a How

Question	Answer
Why might a mass-market producer struggle to make a profit?	If the competition is fierce the battle may have to be on the basis of price, making it almost impossible to make satisfactory profits
Why might it be beneficial to target an older customer niche?	Demographic trends are boosting the over-60s, so it could be very profitable to get into the Stena/Tena/Saga market
Why might a large firm benefit from targeting small niches?	With modern, flexible production it is possible to produce small batches tailored to different customer groups, without forcing costs up
Why might a brand new firm benefit from developing a brand new niche?	The first into any market can develop an image of authenticity that can add value in the long term
Why do ethnic brands rarely make it to the mainstream?	Probably because few niche brands become mainstream – though the UK's love of Indian and Chinese food point to the possibilities
How difficult would it be to switch from a niche-market to a mass-market positioning?	It would require a complete rethink of the marketing mix, perhaps including new pack designs and a lower pricing point. Difficult, yes, but Twinings has shown it's not impossible

Workbook

A. Revision questions

(20 marks; 20 minutes)

1. Identify two advantages of niche marketing over mass marketing. (3)

2. Give three reasons why a large firm may wish to enter a niche market. (3)

3. Why may small firms be better at spotting and then reacting to new niche-market opportunities? (3)

4. Give two reasons why average prices in niche markets tend to be higher than those charged in most mass markets. (2)

5. Outline two reasons why technology has made niche marketing a more viable option for large firms. (4)

6. Explain why it is important for a large firm to be flexible if it is to successfully operate in niche markets. (2)

7. In your own words, explain why niche-market products may generate higher profit margins than mass-market products. (3)

B. Revision exercises
DATA RESPONSE 1

The return of mass marketing to the car industry

For many years car manufacturers such as Toyota and Nissan have sought out market niches in an attempt to improve profitability. Cars such as the Toyota Prius, a hybrid electric-powered vehicle, are not intended to sell in high volumes. Instead, niche market cars sell for high prices, delivering a higher profit margin per car than more conventional mass-market models.

However, in the last couple of years, there have been signs that car manufacturers have sought a return to conventional mass marketing, particularly in Asia where rapid rates of economic growth have created a growing middle class. At present both the Indian and the Chinese car markets are unsaturated. For example, only 4 per cent of households in India have a car, whereas the corresponding figure in the US is 88 per cent. Income per head, whilst increasing rapidly, is still low by American and European standards, and so far this has limited the demand for new cars in India.

The car market in India is dominated by Suzuki Maruti, a joint venture between a Japanese and an Indian company. In early 2014 its top seller was the Alto 800 model, with prices starting at £2,600 for a new car. This mass-market car has seen off the unsuccessful attempt by Indian rival Tata to introduce a £1,500 car, the Nano. Indian car buyers are willing to accept compromises on Western safety standards, but still want a degree of comfort and – especially, reliability. Suzuki Maruti, with a market share of more than 40 per cent, provides exactly this.

Environmentalists have expressed their concerns that cheap, mass-market cars such as the Alto add to the problem of global warming and climate change. In 2014 Suzuki Maruti should sell nearly one million cars in India.

Questions (35 marks; 40 minutes)

1. **a)** What is a niche-market product? (2)
   b) Explain why the Toyota Prius is a good example of a niche-market product. (4)

2. Explain two reasons why the Indian car market has grown (6)

3. **a)** What is a mass-market product? (2)
   b) Explain why the Tata Motor's 'People's car' is a good example of a mass-market product. (4)

4. Analyse the implications for European car manufacturers, such as Renault, of mass marketing £2,000 cars in India. (8)

5. Two thousand pound cars can be profitably made in India. Analyse why UK consumers are unlikely to benefit from similar low prices. (9)

DATA RESPONSE 2

Winter melon tea

Mass-market soft drinks like Coca-Cola and Pepsi are very popular in countries such as Hong Kong and Singapore. In an attempt to survive against the imported competition, local producers of soft drinks have managed to establish a flourishing niche market for traditional Asian drinks sold in 33cl cans. Sales of these niche-market products have been rising but from a very low level.

Consumers that make up this niche market are encouraged to believe, through advertising, that traditional drinks such as winter melon tea and grass jelly drink are healthier than their mass-market alternatives. Other firms use economic nationalism to sell their drinks, using slogans such as 'Asian heritage' in their advertising.

However, producers of traditional drinks could now become a victim of their own success. Foreign multinationals have noticed the rapid growth of this market niche, and in response, they have launched their own range of traditional drinks.

Figure 20.5 Winter melon tea

Questions (30 marks; 35 minutes)

1. **a)** What is a mass-market product? (2)
   b) Identify two reasons why Asian traditional drinks are examples of niche-market products. (2)

2. Explain two ways in which the producers of traditional drinks, such as winter melon tea and grass jelly drink, created product differentiation. (4)

3. Niche-market products are normally more expensive than most mass-market products. Using the example of traditional Asian drinks, explain why this is usually so. (6)

4. To what extent will the local producers of Asian traditional drinks be able to survive in the long term given that their products now have to compete against me-too brands produced by foreign multinationals such as Coca-Cola and Pepsi? (16)

C. Extend your understanding

1. Choose one of the following markets: women's fashion retailing; computer console software or chocolate bars. For the market of your choice, to what extent are sales dominated by mass-market or niche-market products/brands? (20)

2. Some commentators think it's virtually impossible to succeed when trying to turn a niche-market into a mass-market product. To what extent would you agree with that view? (20)

Marketing mix: the 7 Ps

Linked to: Setting marketing objectives, Chapter 13; Product decisions: product life cycle and product portfolio, Chapter 22; Pricing decisions, Chapter 23; Place and promotion decisions, Chapter 24.

Definition

The marketing mix is the balance between seven elements involved in a successful marketing strategy. The traditional '4Ps' – product, price, promotion and place – are joined by people, process and the physical environment.

21.1 The elements of the marketing mix

When working out how to market a product successfully, there are seven main variables to consider.

Product

The business must identify the right product (or service) to make the product both appealing and distinctive. To do this, it needs to understand fully both its customers and its competitors. No product will have long-term success unless this stage is completed successfully.

'Don't try to sell a Rolls Royce when the customer wants a Nissan Micra.' Chartered Institute of Marketing

Price

Having identified the right product to appeal to its target market, the business must set the right price. The 'right' price for a Versace handbag may be £1,600; it is a great mistake to think that low prices or special discounts are the path to business success.

'Remember that price positions you in the marketplace.' Chartered Institute of Marketing

Promotion

Marketing managers must identify the right way to create the right image for the product and present it to the right target audience. This may be achieved best by national TV advertising, but specific markets can be reached at far lower cost by more careful targeting (for example, online advertising tailored to the tastes of people who buy from football club websites). 'Promotion' includes both media advertising (TV, press, cinema, radio) and other forms of promotion (including special offers, public relations, direct mail and online promotion).

Place

For products, 'place' is how to get your product to the place where customers can be persuaded to buy. This may be through a vending machine or on a Tesco shelf, or positioned just by the till at a newsagent (the prime position for purchases bought on impulse). For service businesses, place may be online or in the location of a retail outlet (for example, Tesco Direct and Tesco stores).

Real business

Both McVitie's Jaffa Cakes and Burton's Jammie Dodgers are well-known biscuit brands, but the former is distributed in 90 per cent of retail outlets, whereas the latter is in only 64 per cent. Both companies have a similar view of what are the right outlets for their products (for example, supermarkets, corner shops, garages, canteens and cafés), so why may Burton's be losing out to McVitie's in this particular race? Possible reasons include the following:

- Jaffa Cakes have higher consumer demand, therefore retail outlets are more willing to stock the product.
- Jammie Dodgers may have more direct competitors; high product differentiation may make Jaffa Cakes more of a 'must stock' line.
- If Jaffa Cakes have more advertising support, retailers know customers will ask for the product by name while the advertising campaign is running

People

'Anyone who comes into contact with your customers will make an impression, and that can have a profound effect – positive or negative – on customer satisfaction. The reputation of your brand rests in your people's hands. They must, therefore, be appropriately trained, well motivated and have the right attitude,' Chartered Institute of Marketing, www.cim.co.uk.

Process

Process includes every practical aspect of the customer experience, from phoning or trying to use the website, to how effective the signage is in a store or hotel, to the waiting time at a supermarket checkout. Do customers have to wait? Are they kept informed? Is the service efficient? In other words process is the reality of the customer experience. As this is often the responsibility of operations management rather than marketing, it is possible for there to be a big gap between intention and reality.

Figure 21.1 Logic chain: how the mix and the factors relate

Physical environment

However good an advertisement may be, customers pick up clues about a product or service from the physical environment. Arriving to eat at a restaurant, a grubby carpet or dodgy smell might send customers scuttling away. Online, a potential customer may be interested in purchasing, but need a clearer idea of exactly how the holiday cottage looks, or how the dress might look on a person instead of a dummy. Here, too, evidence of the physical environment is needed, perhaps by the ability to take a 360° look at each room in the cottage, or a video clip of the dress being worn in an everyday situation.

Originally the marketing mix focused on 4Ps (product, price, promotion and place). In a world dominated by services and online selling, the further 3Ps have become equally important.

21.2 How is the marketing mix used?

The marketing mix can be used by a new business to develop ideas about how and where to market a product or service. If marketing activity is to be effective, each ingredient needs to be considered and co-ordinated. For each market situation, managers are trying to set the ideal combination of the ingredients based on a balance between cost and effectiveness. A good product poorly priced may fail. If the product is not available following an advertising campaign, the expenditure is wasted. A successful mix is the one that succeeds in putting the strategy into practice (Figure 21.2).

'There is no victory at bargain basement prices.' Dwight D. Eisenhower, US General, then President

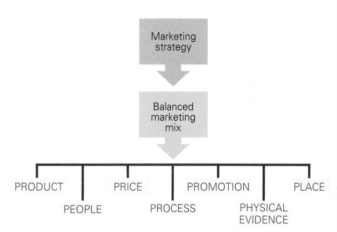

Figure 21.2 A balanced marketing mix

21.3 Influences on the marketing mix

The focus of the marketing mix will vary according to the market in which the firm is operating. Careful market research should reveal the attitudes and tastes of the target market. An important issue will be whether the goods are:

- regular purchases
- impulse purchases
- emergency purchases.

Impulse purchases (such as chocolate brands) are interesting because they require strong branding, great distribution and display, and eye-catching packaging. In other words, the mix focuses on place and promotion. Price is much less important and the quality of the product may not be hugely important. See Table 21.1.

'Don't sell the steak, sell the sizzle.' Advice on advertising from Elmer Wheeler, US business writer

Table 21.1 Different types of purchasing and the marketing mix

Type of purchasing	Important mix elements when buying a product	Important mix elements when buying a service
Regular purchases, e.g. a daily Frappucino	Product, promotion and price	Product, price, people and process
Impulse purchases, e.g. chocolate or a skirt	Place and promotion (including packaging)	Product, people, process and physical environment
Emergency purchases, e.g. bandages	Place and product	Product, place and process

Other influences on the mix:

- whether the product is sold online or face to face. If it's the former, process and evidence of physical environment will be all-important, along with price. If it's sold face to face, people and the product may be more important.
- whether the product/service is targeted at consumers or other businesses (this point is developed further in Section 21.6)
- which stage of its life cycle the product or service is at (see Chapter 22)
- market research: to understand how the mix may need to be tweaked over time, market research is vital. Medium-sized and large firms need primary research to keep the senior managers in touch with the customers they rarely see. Small firms should constantly listen to what customers say – in praise or in criticism.

21.4 Effects of changes in elements of the mix

The traditional view of the marketing mix as being 4Ps had the advantage that all the elements of the mix came largely under the control of the marketing department. So a decision to change the price could be co-ordinated with advertising and promotional campaigns. In the service world of the 7Ps this becomes far harder. The marketing manager does not train the shop floor (customer-facing) staff, and does not get involved in their motivation. Nor does she set up or monitor the processes that try to ensure an efficient customer experience. In the modern world, changes in the marketing mix may be out of the control of the marketing department. So success requires full co-operation from the operations and HR departments.

Table 21.2 Changes in elements of the mix

Possible cause of change	Change in mix for an upmarket London hotel	Effects of these changes in elements of the mix
New visa regulations treble the number of Chinese tourists in Britain	Product tweak: Chinese breakfast option offered; more mix emphasis on Physical Environment; online Process made more China-friendly	Potential Chinese customers will feel more welcome and will enjoy their stay rather more (improving word-of-mouth and online feedback)
Severe economic downturn hits demand, especially from UK leisure customers	To switch focus to business travellers, the product is changed by putting free business magazines and papers in each room; promotion switches media from TV to Google AdWords	The media change uses Google to generate pop-up advertisements for business travellers; the product change should increase the rate of repeat purchasing among this target market
Unforecast torrential rain closes London's commuter train services in the early evening	The traditional 4Ps are pushed aside by the importance of people and process. Can the hotel cope with a sudden surge in demand?	If staff are so well trained that they impress the influx of new customers (and the processes cope), the result could be a long-term boost to demand

21.5 Marketing mix for goods and services

With many 'goods', that is, products, the mix revolves around the product. For example, the marketing mix for the Audi A4 has the car at its heart. The pricing, promotion, physical environment and so on must all fit with the image and 'attitude' of the product.

For services it may be possible to have a purer, broader marketing mix. If one thinks of Tesco compared with Morrisons', the different elements of the mix all come into play in affecting our feelings and actions. Process, for example, may be as important as price. If a customer keeps finding huge queues in Morrisons', they'll eventually settle on Tesco.

It is important to bear in mind that the marketing mix for every product, brand or service will be different from every other. Goods and services do behave differently, but so too do luxury goods versus everyday ones, and presents compared with self-purchased items.

21.6 Marketing mix for B2C and B2B

The key to a successful marketing mix is that every element should be co-ordinated towards delivering a marketing strategy that fits in with the marketing objectives. This is relatively easy to think through in relation to a business that targets the consumer (B2C). Whether it's a product or service, the consumer expects a reality that conforms to the image and therefore delivers value for money. In many cases the image itself may be at the heart of the proposition. If so, keeping that image vibrant and distinctive may be a critical focus of the marketing mix.

Within the category of consumer goods there are three types to be considered:

- Convenience goods are bought out of habit or impulse within a regular process of shopping. Convenience goods are inexpensive, widely available, purchased frequently and with minimal thought or effort. Impulse examples include Coca-Cola, Galaxy chocolate, Wrigley chewing gum and magazines, but the category also includes the regular weekly shop, such as for detergent and shampoo.

- Shopping goods involve a more careful selection process by the buyer, probably because they have a higher unit price than convenience goods and also because they are bought less frequently. Examples include car tyres, mobile phones and clothes.
- Speciality goods are one-off purchases that require a serious purchasing effort, such as a luxury car or an engagement ring. The purchaser will probably shop around a great deal, putting online and shoe-leather time into a research process that should lead to the perfect choice.

By contrast B2B means selling to other businesses, be they retail distributors or businesses that have no direct connection with the public, such as a chemical refinery or a sawmill. A producer of sandwiches for the consumer market might gain a huge order to feed the staff daily at a nearby sawmill employing 800 people. This B2B order carries the financial disadvantage that the customer will want to pay on credit (perhaps 60 days), which hurts the supplier's cash flow. It also means that process will become the critical factor. The sandwiches have to be delivered by a certain time, to a specified quality – and there will be no acceptable excuses for failure.

In some cases companies will be selling homogenous goods to other businesses, for example, 10 litres of white paint or 5,000 light switches. This will make price the most important element in the mix.

Key terms

Homogenous goods: have no points of differentiation and therefore each one is the same as every other (meaning competition is focused on price).

Marketing budget: the sum of money provided for marketing a product or service during a period of time (usually a year).

Marketing mix: the elements involved in putting a marketing strategy into practice; these are product, price, promotion and place.

Marketing strategy: the medium- to long-term plan for meeting the firm's marketing objectives.

Evaluation: Marketing mix: the 7Ps

A successful marketing mix should be matched to the marketing strategy, and that strategy is rooted in how well the product meets the tastes of the market segment being targeted.

Although the 4Ps are presented as a list, there is no doubt that in almost every case the product is the most important ingredient. No amount of marketing effort will make a poor product succeed. However, a good product with weak promotional support may also fail. The balance will vary.

Within the 7Ps it will be helpful to be able to split them into the traditional 4Ps (with their focus on products) and the newer 3Ps than reflect the modern online, service-focused world. Successful writing is always about rethinking how well theory applies in the real world. Be willing to break a theory down into its component parts.

Five Whys and a How

Question	Answer
Why may 'people' be especially important when selling speciality goods?	For expensive, one-off purchases customers will want to be fully confident in the helpfulness and expertise of the salesperson
Why would it be a problem if 'price' was set by the finance director, with no knowledge of the rest of the mix?	If any one element of the mix is out of alignment it's a problem, but especially when it's price. When Xbox One launched at £100 more than the PS4, sales were laughably slow
Why is 'place' still important even in a world of online selling?	Many customers like to look and feel before buying, so 'bricks' are still as important as 'clicks'
Why might a business decide that 'price' is the most important element in their mix?	If goods in their market are homogenous, i.e. little or no product differentiation, then price will be the most important factor
Why may it be hard to co-ordinate the first 4Ps with the final 3?	Because the 4Ps are in the control of the marketing department; the other 3 are controlled by operations and human resources
How does 'place' differ from 'physical environment'?	Place is about getting your products distributed, e.g. in Tesco. Physical environment means giving your potential customers a clue to the quality of a service they want to buy.

Workbook

A. Revision questions

(35 marks; 40 minutes)

1. Explain why it was important to stretch the marketing mix from 4Ps to 7. (3)

2. In your own words, outline each of the three 'new Ps' within the marketing mix. (6)

3. Pick the marketing mix factor (the 'P') you think is of most importance in marketing any **two** of the following brands. Give a brief explanation of why you chose that factor.
   a) *The Sun* newspaper
   b) A Costa latte
   c) Cadbury Creme Eggs
   d) Clothes at Primark. (6)

4. Outline how the marketing mix for Mars bars may affect their level of impulse sales in a small corner shop. (4)

5. What is meant by a market segment? (3)

6. Outline two influences on the marketing mix for the Sony PS4. (4)

7. Explain how changes in elements of the mix might affect the price elasticity of a product such as a motor car. (6)

8. Explain why it might be difficult for a new, small firm to get distribution in a supermarket chain such as Sainsbury's. (3)

B. Revision exercises
DATA RESPONSE

The battle for customers

A leading UK supermarket chain is considering expanding into India. It sees this as a relatively untapped market. The home market is saturated, and price wars and loyalty cards have reduced profit margins. In the UK, the supermarkets have been blamed for the disappearance of the corner shop. In India the situation is very different. A recent survey by an Indian market research firm concluded that small grocery shops will continue to dominate the food retailing market for the foreseeable future. Neither of the two main supermarket contenders has managed to break even in India. They are continuing to expand and hoping that, eventually, economies of scale will permit lower prices and hopefully improve their standing and their profitability.

These new supermarkets have faced several problems.

- The local stores do not stock as many brands as the supermarkets, but they will stock an item if a customer wants it. If they do not have what the customer wants they will get it.
- The local stores offer a free delivery service and allow customers credit.
- The supermarkets cannot match the cost base of the local store. The poor infrastructure makes operational costs very expensive.
- Government laws limiting urban development mean that property prices are high. The smaller stores have often been in the family for generations, and so the initial cost of the site has long since been forgotten.

To try to gain customers, one of the supermarket chains has introduced promotions such as coupons, and has advertised in local newspapers. Another has teamed up with local manufacturers. It obtains staples such as lentils and rice locally. These are then packaged and branded by local manufacturers. This has helped to lower prices for customers and improve margins. A recent entrant into the market is trying to stay ahead of the competition. It has invested in air-conditioning and additional telephone lines to ensure that customers do not have to wait when they call.

The UK chain has looked at the existing market in India and feels it can succeed. However, the managers know they will do this only after a struggle to change customer attitudes.

Questions (30 marks; 35 minutes)

1. What is meant by 'the home market is saturated'? (3)

2. Explain the marketing implications for a business of 'a saturated market'. (4)

3. Why could expansion allow economies of scale? (3)

4. Explain the problems a British retailer could have in marketing its product in India. (4)

5. How important will the marketing mix be in determining the UK chain's chances of success in India? Justify your answer. (16)

C. Extend your understanding

1. An independent clothes shop has decided to switch from targeting consumers to developing a range of work wear and uniforms aimed at business customers. Evaluate the possible impact of this decision on the company's marketing mix. (20)

2. Choose two rival companies or brands you feel familiar with (PS4 vs. Xbox One? Starbucks vs. Costa? Cadbury vs. Mars?). Which element of the mix do you think is the most important for each company/brand? Justify your answer. (20)

Product decisions: product life cycle and product portfolio

Linked to: Setting marketing objectives, Chapter 13; Understanding markets, Chapter 14; Market research, Chapter 15; Interpreting market data, Chapter 16.

Definition

The product life cycle is the theory that all products follow a similar pattern over time, of development, birth, growth, maturity and decline.

22.1 What is the product life cycle?

The product life cycle shows the sales of a product over time. When a new product is first launched sales will usually be slow. This is because the product is not yet known or proven in the market. Retailers may be reluctant to stock the product because it means giving up valuable shelf space to products that may or may not sell. Customers may also be hesitant, waiting until someone else has tried it before they purchase it themselves.

If the product does succeed, then it enters the growth phase of the product life cycle, with new customers buying and existing customers making repeat purchases. However, at some point sales are likely to stabilise; this is known as the maturity phase. This slowing down of the growth of sales might be because competitors have introduced similar products or because the market has now become saturated. Everyone who wants one has bought one, so sales fall back to replacement purchases only.

At some point sales are likely to decline, perhaps because customer tastes have become more sophisticated. So orange squash sales decline as people buy more fresh orange juice. A decline in sales may also be because competitors have launched a more successful model or the original creator has improved

its own product; for example, the iPad drawing sales from the iPhone.

The five key stages of a product's life cycle are known as: development, introduction, growth, maturity and decline. These can be illustrated on a product life cycle diagram. The typical stages in a product's life are shown in Figure 22.1.

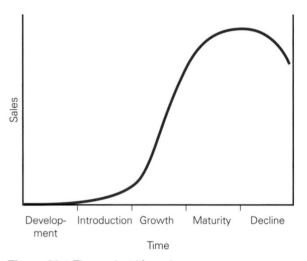

Figure 22.1 The product life cycle

22.2 What is the value of the product life cycle?

The product life cycle model helps managers to plan their marketing activities. Marketing managers will need to adjust their marketing mix at different stages of the product life cycle, as outlined below.

- In the introduction phase the promotion may focus on making customers aware that a new product exists. In the maturity phase it may focus more on highlighting the difference between your product and competitors that have arrived since its introduction.

- At the beginning of the life cycle, a technologically advanced product may be launched with a high price (think of the iPhone). Over time the price may fall

Table 22.1 Examples of how the marketing mix may vary at different stages of the product life cycle

	Development	Introduction	Growth	Maturity	Decline
Sales	Zero	Low	Increasing	Growth is slowing	Falling
Costs per unit	High; there is investment in product development but only a few prototypes and test products being produced	High, because sales are relatively low but launch costs are high and overheads are being spread over a few units	Falling as overheads are spread over more units	Falling as sales are still growing	Still likely to be low as development costs have been covered and reduced promotional costs are needed to raise awareness
Product	Prototypes	Likely to be basic	May be modified given initial customer feedback; range may be increased	Depends – may focus on core products and remove ones in the range not selling well; may diversify and extend brand to new items	Focus on most profitable items
Promotion	As development is nearly finished it may be used to alert customers to the launch	Mainly to raise awareness	Building loyalty	May focus on highlighting the differences with competitors' products	Probably no spending at all
Distribution	Early discussions with retailers will help in finalising the product packaging	May be limited as distributors wait to see customers' reactions	May be increasing as more distributors willing to stock it and product is rolled out to more markets	May focus on key outlets and more profitable channels	Lower budgets to keep costs down
Price	Not needed	Depends on pricing approach, e.g. high if skimming is adopted; low if penetration is adopted to gain market share	Depends on demand conditions and strategy; e.g. with a skimming strategy the price may now be lowered to target more segments	May have to drop to maintain competitiveness	Likely to discount to maintain sales

as newer models are being launched. By considering the requirements of each stage of the life cycle, marketing managers may adjust their marketing activities accordingly.

Managers know that the length of the phases of the life cycle cannot easily be predicted. They will vary from one product to another and this means the marketing mix will need to be altered at different times. For example, a product may be a fad and therefore the overall life of the product will be quite short. Many fashions are popular only for one season and some films are popular only for a matter of weeks. Other products have very long life cycles. The first manufactured cigarettes went on sale in Britain in 1873. By chance, sales hit their peak (120,000 million!) exactly 100 years later. Since 1973 sales have gently declined.

It is also important to distinguish between the life cycle of a product category and the life cycle of a particular brand. Sales of wine are growing, but a

brand that was once the biggest seller (Hirondelle) has virtually disappeared as wine buyers have become more sophisticated. Similarly, confectionery is a mature market but particular brands are at different stages in their life cycles: Mars bars are in maturity while Maltesers are in the growth stage, even though the brand is 80 years old!

22.3 Extension strategies

The aim of an extension strategy is to prevent a decline in the product's sales. There are various means by which this can be achieved, as noted below.

- By targeting a new segment of the market – when sales of Johnson & Johnson's Baby Powder matured, the company repositioned the product towards adults: sales boomed.

- By developing new uses for the product – the basic technology in hot-air paint strippers, for example, is no different from that in a hairdryer.

- By increasing the usage of a product – Actimel's 'challenge' was for consumers to eat one pot a day for a fortnight – a wonderful way to encourage increased consumption.

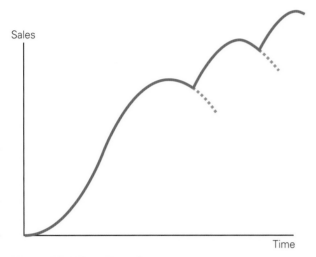

Figure 22.2 The effect of extension strategies

The continued success of products such as Coca-Cola and Kellogg's Cornflakes is not just due to luck; it is down to sophisticated marketing techniques which have managed to maintain sales over many years despite fierce competition. The Kellogg's logo is regularly updated, new pack sizes are often introduced, and various competitions and offers are used on a regular basis to keep sales high.

Given the fact that developing a product can involve high costs and that there is a high failure rate of new products, it is not surprising that if a product is successful managers will try to prolong its sales for as long as it is profitable. Who would have thought, in the 1880s, that a frothy drink would still be a huge seller more than 125 years later? Clever Coke.

22.4 New product development (NPD)

New product development includes the people and processes involved in turning new ideas into products (or services) ready for launch. It is likely to involve research and development (R&D), market research, product engineering and design, plus expertise in packaging, advertising, pricing and branding. It represents all the activities categorised as 'development' in the product life cycle. Some examples of NPD are so excellent (think iPhone, the PS4 or Snapchat) that their life cycles have a remarkably easy start.

Unfortunately even consumer giants such as Cadbury and PepsiCo have poor success rates with new

product launches. The statistics are hard to find, but it seems that fewer than 1 in 5 new products becomes a commercial success. Clearly there must be many reasons why it's hard to create a successful new product, though the single most important is the cautious consumer who would rather buy a trusted product than a new one.

Key influences on successful NPD include:

- a clear understanding of the consumers within a certain market segment, with a special focus on their future needs or wants
- the creativity to be able to see how an everyday problem or issue can be solved innovatively
- enough resources (money and manpower) to be able to develop an idea effectively and market it persuasively.

When a new product succeeds the consequences can be transformational. Nintendo's Wii U was looking down and out before the launch of Mario Kart 8 saw sales of the hardware rise by 600 per cent in June 2014. So the value of NPD cannot be doubted. A successful new product can create its own new life cycle – giving an entire business a morale and profit boost.

Real business

9 out of 10 fail

In July 2014 the Chief Executive of US marketing consultancy Dine was interviewed about the causes of new product launch failures. He said that, in America, the failure rate among new food products is 9 out of 10. He blamed three main causes:

- undercapitalised launches; that is, good idea, but an underfunded marketing campaign
- 'Customer insight is slightly off', for example, launched too early or too late, or slightly wrong market positioning
- overly innovative idea (he cited bubble-gum flavoured milk) where the producer is pursuing disruptive innovation when incremental innovation would be superior.

22.5 The product portfolio

Product portfolio analysis examines the existing position of a firm's products. This allows the firm to consider its existing position and plan what to do next. There are several different methods of portfolio analysis. One of the best known was developed by the

Boston Consulting Group, a management consultancy; it is known as the Boston Matrix.

The Boston Matrix shows the market share of each of the firm's products and the rate of growth of the markets in which they operate. By highlighting the position of each product in terms of market share and market growth, a business can analyse its existing situation and decide what to do next and where to direct its marketing efforts. This model has four categories, as described below.

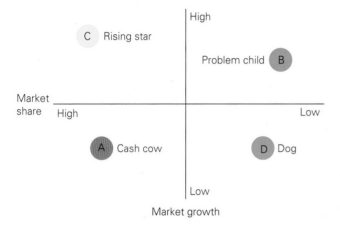

Figure 22.3 Product portfolio: the Boston Matrix

Cash cow: a high share of a slow-growing market

In Figure 22.3, product A has a high market share of a low-growth market. The size of the circle depends on the turnover of the product. This type of product is known as a cash cow. An example of a cash cow may be Heinz Baked Beans. The overall market for baked beans is mature and therefore slow growing. Within this market, the Heinz brand has a market share of more than 50 per cent. This type of product generates high profits and cash for the company because sales are relatively high, while the promotional cost per unit is quite low. Heinz can therefore 'milk' cash from baked beans to invest in newer products such as Heinz Organic Ketchup.

Problem child: a low share of a fast-growing market

Product B, by comparison, is in a high-growth market but has a low market share. This type of product is known as a problem child (also called a 'question mark'). A problem child may well provide high profits in the future; the market itself is attractive because it is growing fast and the product could provide high returns if it manages to gain a greater market share. However, the success of such products is by no means certain and that is why they are like problem children:

they may grow and prosper or things may go wrong. These products usually need a relatively high level of investment to promote them, get them distributed and keep them going.

Rising star: a high share of a growing market

Rising stars such as product C have a high market share and are selling in a fast-growing market. These products are obviously attractive; they are doing well in a successful market. However, they may well need protecting from competitors' products. Once again, the profits of the cash cows can be used to keep the sales growing. Heinz Organic Soups are in this category. They are very successful, with fast-growing sales, but still need heavy promotion to ensure their success.

Dogs: a low share of a stable or declining market

The fourth category of products is known as dogs. These products (like product D in Figure 22.3) have a low share of a low-growth market. They hold little appeal for a firm unless they can be revived. The product or brand will be killed off once its sales slip below the break-even point.

The purpose of product portfolio analysis

Product portfolio analysis aims to examine the existing position of the firm's products. Once this has been done the managers can plan what to do next. Typically this will involve four strategies.

1. Building: this involves investment in promotion and distribution to boost sales and is often used with problem children (question marks).

2. Holding: this involves marketing spending to maintain sales and is used with rising star products.

3. Milking: this means taking whatever profits you can without much more new investment and is often used with cash cow products.

4. Divesting: this involves selling off the product and is common with dogs or problem children.

The various strategies chosen will depend on the firm's portfolio of products. If most of the firm's products are cash cows, for example, it needs to develop new products for future growth. If, however, the majority are problem children then it is in quite a high-risk situation; it needs to try to ensure some products do become stars. If it has too many dogs then it needs to invest in product development or acquire new brands.

Five Whys and a How

Question	Answer
Why does growth slide back towards maturity?	Market saturation is one reason (everyone who wants one has already bought it); the arrival of competition is another
Why do many extension strategies fail?	Because the business has failed to find a new market position for a new type of customer
Why do new product launches have such a low success rate?	Because many consumers are locked into patterns of repeat behaviour, such as always buying Cadbury Dairy Milk
Why may firms struggle to manage their cash flow when their products have short life cycles?	Short life cycles imply a constant need to invest heavily in NPD to develop the next winner to take over from today's fading products
Why do firms find it useful to use both product life cycle and portfolio analysis?	Because the product life cycle helps analyse the progress of a single product while portfolio analysis looks at all a firm's products
How does R&D differ from market research?	R&D is about scientific research and technical development of products or processes; market research is about consumer habits and tastes

Key terms

Cash cow: a product that has a high share of a low-growth market.

Dog: a product that has a low share of a low-growth market.

Extension strategy: marketing activities used to prevent sales from declining.

Portfolio analysis: an analysis of the market position of the firm's existing products; it is used as part of the marketing planning process.

Problem child: a product that has a small share of a fast-growing market.

Rising star: a product that has a high share of a fast-growing market.

Evaluation: Product decisions: product life cycle and product portfolio

The product life cycle model and portfolio analysis are important in assessing the firm's current position within the market. They make up an important step in the planning process. However, simply gathering data does not in itself guarantee success. A manager has to interpret the information effectively and then make the right decision. The models show where a business is at the moment; the difficult decisions relate to where the business will be in the future.

Product portfolio analysis is especially useful for larger businesses with many products. It helps a manager to look critically at the firm's product range. Then decisions can be made on how the firm's marketing spending should be divided up between different products. By contrast, the product life cycle is of more help to a small firm with one or two products.

Workbook

A. Revision questions

(40 marks; 50 minutes)

1. Identify the different stages of the product life cycle. Give an example of one product or service you consider to be at each stage of the life cycle. (4)

2. Explain what is meant by an 'extension strategy'. (4)

3. Explain the importance of new product development. (6)

4. How is it possible for products such as Barbie to apparently defy the decline phase of the product cycle? (7)

5. What is meant by 'product portfolio analysis'? (3)

6. Distinguish between a cash cow and a rising star in the Boston Matrix. (4)

7. Explain how the Boston Matrix could be used by a business such as Cadbury? (5)

8. Firms should never take decline (or growth) for granted. Therefore they should never take success (or failure) for granted. Explain why this advice is important if firms are to make the best use of product life cycle theory. (7)

B. Revision exercises
DATA RESPONSE

Monster life cycle

The market for energy drinks is dominated by Red Bull. First launched in 1987, its UK sales have grown steadily to reach £248 million in 2013. With the market for energy drinks still rising by 10–15 per cent per year, many other companies are determined to take their share of this success.

The attractions are obvious. Not only are sales rising faster than for soft drinks as a whole, but the price per litre is much higher. On 30 December 2013, Tesco charged 49p for a 330ml can of Coca-Cola and £1.58 for 330ml of Red Bull.

As the Coca-Cola Company observed the growth of Red Bull during the 'noughties', it resolved to launch its own rivals. First came Relentless in late 2006, which received its first serious promotional push by being given away at the 2007 Reading and Leeds Music Festivals. Since then it has focused on sponsoring 'extreme' sports. As shown in the graph below, Relentless has achieved significant sales, though sales fell by £5 million between 2011 and 2013.

Perhaps sensing that Relentless was not the answer, in 2010 Coca-Cola took over the distribution of a US energy drink called Monster. The brand holds a 35 per cent share of the $30 billion US market for energy drinks, though there have been questions raised in Congress about the safety of the product.

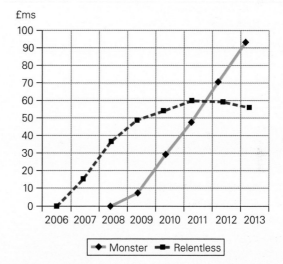

Figure 22.4 Energy drink life cycles; UK annual sales 2006-13

Source: Data from *The Grocer*

Energy drinks are heavy in three ingredients: caffeine, taurine and sugar. In fact the caffeine level is no higher than in coffee, but the combination of ingredients is thought by some to place it in between alcoholic and soft drinks.

Is Monster a real challenger to Red Bull in the UK? With a sales increase of 30 per cent in 2013 compared with 6 per cent for Red Bull, Coca-Cola can hope. But the risk must remain that the Monster life cycle will end up following that of Relentless. Time will tell.

Figure 22.5 Monster energy drink

Questions (30 marks; 35 minutes)

1. Briefly explain the meaning of the term 'product life cycle'. (3)

2. In which stage of its product life cycle was a) Relentless and b) Monster in 2013? (2)

3. Analyse possible extension strategies Coca-Cola might use with Relentless in coming years. (9)

4. To what extent may the future UK life cycle of Monster depend on the marketing of Red Bull? (16)

C. Extend your understanding

1. After many decades of success in the UK, breakfast cereal manufacturers are suffering from a decline in the market size as consumers want to eat breakfast on the move instead of in the kitchen. Discuss a suitable extension strategy for a cereal producer such as Kellogg's. (20)

2. Cadbury has a wide range of chocolate brands including Dairy Milk, Flake, Crunchie, Twirl and Fudge. It wishes to push its UK market share from 34 per cent to 36 per cent within the next two years. To what extent might the Boston Matrix help achieve this goal? (20)

Pricing decisions

Linked to: Understanding markets, Chapter 14; Market research, Chapter 15; Price and income elasticity of demand, Chapter 17; Segmentation, targeting and positioning, Chapter 19; Niche and mass marketing, Chapter 20.

Definition

Price is the amount paid by the customer for a good or service.

23.1 How important are decisions about price?

Price is one of the main links between the customer (demand) and the producer (supply). It gives messages to consumers about product quality and is fundamental to a firm's revenues and profit margins. As part of the marketing mix it is fundamental to most consumer buying decisions. The importance of price to the customer will depend on several factors, as discussed below.

Customer sensitivity to price

Consumers have an idea of the correct price for a product (see Figure 23.1). They balance price with other considerations. These include the factors set out below.

The quality of the product

Products seen as having higher quality can carry a price premium; this may be real or perceived quality.

How much consumers want the product

All purchases are personal; customers will pay more for goods they need or want.

Consumers' income

Customers buy products within their income range; consumers with more disposable income are less concerned about price. Uncertainty about future income will have the same effect as lower income. If interest rates are high, hard-pressed homebuyers will be much more sensitive to price; they need to save money and so they check prices more carefully and avoid high-priced items.

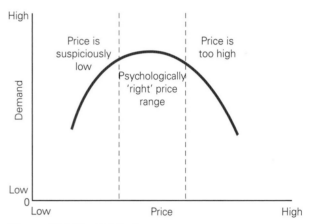

Figure 23.1 The 'right' price

Table 23.1 Price sensitivity in practice

Products, services and brands that are highly price sensitive	Products, services and brands that are not very price sensitive
No-frills air travel	Business-class air travel
Fiat and Ford cars	BMW and Mercedes cars
Children's white school shirts	Babies' disposable nappies
Monday-night cinema tickets	Saturday-night cinema tickets

The level of competitive activity

The fiercer the competition in a market, the more important price becomes. Customers have more choice, so they take more care to buy the best-value item. Whereas, a business with a strong monopoly position is able to charge higher prices.

The availability of the product

If the product is readily available, consumers are more price-conscious. They know they can go elsewhere and find the same product – perhaps cheaper. Scarcity removes some of the barriers to price. This is why perfume companies such as Chanel try to keep their products out of supermarkets and stores like Superdrug.

23.2 Price determines business revenue

Pricing is important to the business. Unlike the other ingredients in the marketing mix it is related directly to revenue through the formula:

Revenue = price × units sold

If the price is not right the business could:

● lose customers: if the price is too high, sales may slump and therefore revenue will be lost. It will depend on the price elasticity of the product (see Chapter 17). If goods remain unsold, the costs of production will not be recovered

● lose revenue: if the price is too low, sales may be high, but not high enough to compensate for the low revenue per unit.

Pricing involves a balance between being competitive and being profitable.

23.3 How do businesses decide what price to charge?

At certain times during a product's life cycle pricing is especially important. Incorrect pricing when the product is launched could cause the product to fail. At other stages in the product's life, pricing may be used to revive interest in the brand.

There are two basic pricing decisions: pricing a new product and managing prices throughout the product life. Both decisions require a good understanding of the market: consumers and competitors.

Pricing decisions require an understanding of costs. These costs must include purchasing, manufacturing, distribution, administration and marketing. Cost information should be available from the company's management accounting systems.

The lowest price a firm can consider charging is set by costs. Except as a temporary promotional tactic (a loss leader), businesses must charge more for the product than the variable cost. This ensures that every product sold contributes towards the fixed costs of the business.

The market determines the highest price that can be charged. The price that is charged will need to take

account of the company objectives. The right price will be the one that achieves the objectives.

There are several ways that businesses obtain market information. These are set out below.

● Market research can provide consumer reactions to possible price changes.

● Competitive research tells the company about other products and prices.

● Analysis of sales patterns shows how the market reacts to price and economic changes.

● Sales staff can report on customer reactions to prices.

Figure 23.2 Determining the price

When making changes to product prices the business needs to understand the relationship between price changes and demand. Demand for some products is more sensitive to price changes than for others. Price elasticity of demand measures how sensitive demand is to price changes. If demand for a product is sensitive to price changes an increase in price could cut total revenue.

Real business

London's Hoxton Hotel

If you put '£1 hotel rooms' into Google, London's Hoxton Hotel pops up in front of you. This 200-room hotel sells five rooms per night at £1 and another five at £29. The other 190 are at the 'normal' rate of £229! The Hoxton uses this device to get customers to register as members of the Hoxton Fan Club. They are the only ones to hear when the £1 sale is taking place. The website boasts that in each sale, 1,000 rooms are sold in 20 minutes. So this pricing trick makes sure that Hoxton has a terrific emailing list of people interested in London hotels.

23.4 Pricing strategies

A pricing strategy is a company's plan for setting its prices over the medium to long term. In other words it is not about deals such as 'This week's special: 40 per cent off!' Short-term offers are known as tactics. Medium- to long-term plans are called strategies.

For new products, firms must choose between two main pricing strategies:

1. skimming
2. penetration.

Some advantages of price skimming and price penetration are shown in Table 23.2.

Skimming

This is used when the product is innovative. As the product is new there will be no competition. The price can therefore be set at a high level. Customers interested in the new product will pay this high price. The business recovers some of the development costs, making sure that enthusiasts who really want the product pay the high price they expect to pay. For example, the first DVD players came onto the UK market at a price of around £1,000. Firms use the initial sales period to assess the market reaction. If sales become stagnant the price can be lowered to attract customers who were unwilling to pay the initial price. The price can also be lowered if competitors enter the market.

Penetration

Penetration pricing is used when launching a product into a market where there are similar products. The price is set lower to gain market share. Once the product is established the price can be increased. It is hoped that high levels of initial sales will recover development costs and lead to lower average costs as the business gains bulk-buying benefits.

Figure 23.3 Logic chain: pros and cons of penetration pricing

Table 23.2 Advantages and disadvantages of price skimming and price penetration

	Price skimming	Price penetration
Advantages	High prices for a new item such as the iPhone help establish the product as a must-have item	Low-priced new products may attract high sales volumes, which make it very hard for a competitor to break into the market
	Early adopters of a product usually want exclusivity and are willing to pay high prices, so skimming makes sense for them and for the supplier	High sales volumes help to cut production costs per unit, as the producer can buy in bulk and therefore get purchasing costs down
	Innovation can be expensive, so it makes sense to charge high prices to recover the investment cost	Achieving high sales volumes ensures that shops will provide high distribution levels and good in-store displays
Disadvantages	Some customers may be put off totally by 'rip-off pricing' at the start of a product's life	Pricing low may affect the brand image, making the product appear 'cheap'
	When the firm decides to cut its prices its image may suffer	It may be hard to gain distribution in more upmarket retail outlets, due to mass-market pricing
	Buyers who bought early (at high prices) may be annoyed that prices fell soon afterwards	Pricing on the basis of value for money can cause customers (and therefore competitors) to be very price sensitive

Real business

After years of dominance by Nike and Adidas, local sports footwear manufacturers made inroads into the Chinese market in 2010. Local brand Li Ning pulled alongside Adidas as the industry No. 2 (market share by volume). The head of JWT, China (advertising agency) said, 'The moment that a local brand can command the same price as a multinational brand is the day that a breakthrough has been made'.

To push further, Li Ning announced a new, higher-priced product range to sit 15 per cent below its foreign rivals. But by 2013 Li Ning was reporting sales slumping by 25 per cent and more than 1,000 store closures. At the same time Nike sales in China slipped by just 3 per cent. The price breakthrough hasn't happened yet.

Figure 23.4 Li Ning trainers/sports wear promotion

Five Whys and a How

Question	Answer
Why should companies be wary of tactical, low pricing, e.g. special offers?	Because of the potential damage to image. Can you imagine a 'special offer' BMW? Or, indeed, buy one BMW, get one free.
Why is price cutting a risk to profits even when it helps increase revenue?	If a 10 per cent price cut boosts demand by 15 per cent, revenue rises; but the price cut hits the profit margin, which may mean that profits actually fall.
Why may firms set lower prices in the growth phase than in the decline phase of the life cycle?	In the growth phase prices may be kept low to attract a large number of potential loyalists; in decline there are few new customers to attract, so prices may be kept high to exploit customer inertia/loyalty.
Why may skimming the market prove the wrong pricing strategy for a new product?	Skimming may generate a good image plus strong profits in the short term, but allow space in the market for new rivals to step in.
Why do music acts not price their tickets high enough to make ticket touting irrelevant?	Because the groups worry that their fans will feel they are being 'ripped off'; much better to blame the touts.
How should a new, independent pizza business set its prices?	It should find out customer reactions to the brand and the product – and set prices accordingly.

Key terms

Complementary goods: products bought in conjunction with each other, such as bacon and eggs, or Gillette shavers and Gillette razors.

Early adopters: consumers with the wealth and the personality to want to be the first to get a new gadget or piece of equipment. They may be the first to wear new fashions in clothes, and the first to get the new (and expensive) computer game.

Monopoly: a market dominated by one supplier.

Price elasticity: a measurement of the extent to which a product's demand changes when its price is changed.

Price sensitive: when customer demand for a product reacts sharply to a price change (that is, the product is highly price elastic).

Evaluation: Pricing decisions

Economists think of price as a neutral factor within a marketplace. Many businesses would disagree, especially those selling consumer goods and services. The reason is that consumer psychology can be heavily influenced by price. A '3p off' sticker makes people reach for the Mars bars, but '50 per cent off' might make people wonder whether they are old stock or have suffered in the sun; they are *too* cheap.

When deciding on the price of a brand new product, marketing managers have many options. Pricing high may generate too few sales to keep retailers happy to stock the product. Yet, pricing too low carries even more dangers. Large companies know there are no safe livings to be made selling cheap jeans, cheap cosmetics or cheap perfumes.

If there is a key to successful pricing, it is to keep it in line with the overall marketing strategy. When Häagen-Dazs launched in the UK at prices more than double those of its competitors, many predicted failure. In fact, the pricing was in line with the image of adult, luxury indulgence and Häagen-Dazs soon outsold all other premium ice creams (though today Ben & Jerry's is No. 1). The worst pricing approach would be to develop an attractively packaged, well-made product and then sell it at a discount to the leading brands. In research, people would welcome it, but deep down they would not trust the product quality. Because psychology is so important to successful pricing, many firms use qualitative research, rather than quantitative, to obtain the necessary psychological insights.

Workbook

A. Revision questions

(35 marks; 40 minutes)

1. Explain why price 'is fundamental to a firm's revenues'. (3)

2. Look at Figure 23.1. Outline two factors that would affect the 'psychologically right price range' for a new Samsung phone. (4)

3. Explain how the actions of Nike could affect the footwear prices set by Adidas. (4)

4. Look at Table 23.1, on the price sensitivity of products, brands and services. Think of two more examples of highly price-sensitive and two examples of not-very-price-sensitive products, services or brands. (4)

5. Explain the difference between pricing strategy and pricing tactics. (2)

6. For each of the following, decide whether the pricing strategy should be skimming or penetration. Briefly explain your reasoning.
   a) Richard Branson's Virgin group launches the world's first space tourism service (you are launched in a rocket, spend time weightless in space, watch the world go round, then come back to earth). (4)
   b) Kellogg's launches a new range of sliced breads for families who are in a hurry. (4)
   c) The first robotic washing machine is launched. It washes, dries and irons the clothes – and places them in neat piles. (4)

7. Is a cash cow likely to be a price maker or a price taker? Explain your reasoning. (3)

8. Identify three circumstances in which a business may decide to use special-offer pricing. (3)

B. Revision exercises

DATA RESPONSE 1

On 1 February 2014, Tesco Price Check provided the information given in Table 23.3 on the prices of shampoo brands. Study the table then answer the questions that follow.

Table 23.3 Prices of shampoo brands in January 2014

Product description	Tesco price (£)	Asda price (£)
TRESemmé Instant Refresh Dry Shampoo 200 ml	4.99	5.00
Pantene Volume & Body 250 ml	2.89	2.68
Head & Shoulders Classic 250 ml	2.99	2.79
Vosene Original 250 ml	1.79	2.00
John Frieda Full Repair 250 ml	5.89	5.89
Own-label* Baby 500 ml	1.00	1.00
Own-label* Budget Shampoo 1000 ml	0.40	0.40
Bob Martin Dog Shampoo 250 ml	-	3.48

Own-label means the supermarket's own brand.

Questions (35 marks; 35 minutes)

1. Explain why it may be fair to describe Vosene shampoo as a price-taker. (4)

2. John Frieda shampoo is priced at more than 40 times the level of supermarket budget shampoos (per ml). Explain why customers may be willing to pay such a high price. (6)

3. Analyse the position of the long-established brand Head and Shoulders within the UK market for shampoo. What pricing strategy does it seem to be using and why may it be possible to use this approach? (9)

4. To what extent could it ever be right for dogs to have 'better' shampoo than babies? (16)

DATA RESPONSE 2

New product pricing strategy

Before the mid-October launch of Maruti Suzuki's new Alto 800, the company set itself a target unprecedented in the history of the Indian automobile industry. Maruti called it the '50/20/10 target'. It meant aiming for 50,000 test drives, 20,000 orders, and 10,000 deliveries - all within the first 10 days.

To make it harder to achieve, the car market was slipping backwards in Autumn 2012 as the Indian economy grappled with 10 per cent inflation and high interest rates. With such high inflation, it would have been understandable if Maruti had priced their new Alto model 10 per cent higher than the previous one. Instead it made headlines by launching at 2 per cent below – even though the specification had been upgraded. Prices for the Alto started at £2,500, with £3,400 for the highest spec.

On the morning of the tenth day, Maruti Suzuki's Managing Executive Officer for Marketing and Sales announced: 'We crossed all three targets. We launched in 821 cities and 1,130 outlets.' That morning, the new Alto had crossed 27,000 bookings and 10,200 deliveries.

Getting the pricing right was critical because Maruti, for so long the dominant force in India with a 45 per cent market share, had lost 3 percentage points in

Figure 23.5 The new Maruti Alto 800

the previous year. This was partly because the Alto model, which had once sold 35,000 cars a month, had seen its sales slip to 18,000 by early 2012. And with small cars such as this making up 70 per cent of the Indian car market, the Alto launch was vital.

When asked whether this pricing might spark a price war, Maruti suggested that it was simply making use of its competitive advantage. An independent auto analyst confirmed that 'Maruti enjoys huge economies of scale, even at lower margins. No other company can do that.'

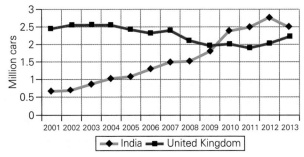

Figure 23.6 Market for new cars: India vs. UK
Sources: OICA & ICCT

The reduced price is intensifying competition in the market in what Abdul Majeed, Partner at PWC, calls the 'volume game'. He explains that Maruti's pricing may initially spark a price war, but it is important to develop the market three or four years down the line, as it would generate high volumes. 'If you can't sell 200,000 to 300,000 cars, you can't make money,' he says. In the short term, margins will feel the pinch, but in the long run the move will be beneficial, as small cars still make up 70 per cent of the Indian car market. 'Car makers will have to take the risk,' says Majeed.

A year on, in September 2013, the Alto was India's top-selling car and Maruti's market share had recovered from 41 per cent to 43.5 per cent since the same month in 2012.

Source: *Business Today* Copyright © 2014, 2014 Living Media India Limited. All Rights Reserved.

Questions (30 marks, 35 minutes)

1. Explain one way in which market trends in new car sales in India (see graph) might have influenced the pricing decision for the new Alto 800. (5)

2. Analyse the possible implications for the Indian car market if Maruti's pricing does 'spark a price war'. (9)

3. To what extent was it wise for Maruti to adopt a penetration pricing strategy for its new Alto model? (16)

C. Extend your understanding

1. At a supermarket, a Mars Bar is priced at 79p and a pack of 3 at £1.00. From the point of view of the consumer and the producer, can both these prices be right? Justify your answer. (20)

2. Research the launch prices and sales of Sony's PS4 and the Microsoft One in 2013/14. To what extent was pricing the key reason for Sony's sales success? (20)

Place and promotion decisions

Linked to: Setting marketing objectives, Chapter 13; Market research, Chapter 15; Segmentation, targeting and positioning, Chapter 19; Marketing mix: the 7Ps, Chapter 21.

Definition

Place is about availability (how to get the product to the right place for customers to make their purchases). It includes physical or online distribution, availability and visibility. Promotion is the part of the marketing mix that focuses on persuading people to buy the product or service.

24.1 Introduction to place

The word 'place' can be unhelpful, because it suggests that manufacturers can place their products where they like (for example, at the entrance of a Tesco store). The real world is not like that. Obtaining distribution at Tesco stores is a dream for most small producers, and a very hard dream to turn into reality. For new firms in particular, place is the toughest of the 7Ps.

Persuading retailers to stock a product is never easy. For the retailer, the key issues are opportunity cost and risk. As shelf space is limited, stocking a particular chocolate bar probably means scrapping another. But which one should the retailer choose? What revenue will be lost? The other consideration is risk. A new, low-calorie chocolate bar may be a slimmer's delight, but high initial sales may slip, leaving the shopkeeper with boxes of slow-moving stock.

24.2 Choosing appropriate distributors

When a new business wants to launch its first product, a key question to consider is the distribution channel; in other words, how the product passes from producer to consumer. Should the product be sold directly, as with pick-your-own strawberries? Or via a wholesaler, then a retailer, as with crisps bought from your local shop? This decision will affect every aspect of the business in the future, especially its profit.

Manufacturers must decide on the right outlets for their own product. If Chanel chooses to launch a new perfume, 'Alexa', backed by Alexa Chung, priced at £69.99, controlling distribution will be vital. The company will want it to be sold in a smart location where elegant sales staff can persuade customers of its wonderful scent and gorgeous packaging. If Superdrug or Morrisons' want to stock the brand, Chanel will try hard to find reasons to say no.

Yet the control is often not in the hands of the producer, but of the retailer. If you came up with a wonderful idea for a brand-new ice cream, how would you get distribution for it? The freezers in corner shops are usually owned by Walls and Mars, so they frown upon independent products being stocked in 'their' space. To the retailer, every foot of shop floor space has an actual cost (the rental value) and an opportunity cost (the cost of missing out on the profits that could be generated by selling other goods). In effect, then, your brand-new ice cream is likely to stay on the drawing board, because obtaining distribution will be too large a barrier to entry to this market.

24.3 Multi-channel distribution

There are three main channels of distribution. These are described below.

Traditional physical channel

Small producers find it hard to achieve distribution in big chains such as B&Q or Sainsbury's, so they usually sell to wholesalers who, in turn, sell to small independent shops. The profit mark-up applied by the 'middleman' adds to the final retail price, but a small producer cannot afford to deliver individually to lots of small shops.

Larger producers cut out the middleman (the wholesaler) and sell directly to retail chains, from Boots to Tesco. This is more cost effective, but exposes the seller to tough negotiation from the retail chains on prices and credit terms.

Direct online

Using this channel of distribution the producer sells directly to the consumer. Manufacturers can do this through mail order or – far more likely today – through a website. This ensures that the producer keeps 100 per cent of the product's selling price. So the benefit of the direct distribution channel is that the producer's higher profits can finance more spending on advertising, on website development or on new product development.

Online retail

Small firms often lack the ability and/or the finance to build a successful e-commerce sales platform. So it can make sense to piggyback on an established platform such as eBay in the West or the amazingly successful TaoBao in China. TaoBao has more than 2 million businesses using the site to sell to China's hundreds of millions of online shoppers. TaoBao is one part of Jack Ma's Alibaba business that had sales, in 2014, of $420 billion – dwarfing Amazon and eBay combined.

'Establish channels for different target markets and aim for efficiency, control and adaptability.' Philip Kotler, marketing guru

Real business

In 2013 internet sales of groceries rose by 19 per cent according to market research agency Kantar. By comparison, sales from grocery shops only rose by 2 per cent. This trend towards online shopping has been developing for ten years and may be accelerating. In the four days leading up to Christmas 2013, 15 per cent of all grocery sales were online. No wonder that Morrisons', the only UK grocery chain with no online presence, was rapidly losing market share. In (belated) response Morrisons' started its first online deliveries in a test market in Warwickshire in January 2014. The same company proved extraordinarily slow to spot the success of smaller, urban grocery outlets such as Tesco Metro.

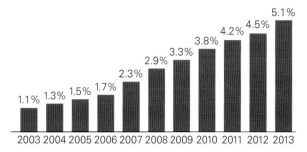

Figure 24.1 E-commerce share of UK grocery spending 2003–13

Source: Kantar Worldpanel, 'Shopping for Groceries,' 6 Aug 2013

24.4 What is promotion?

Promotion is a general term that covers all the marketing activity that informs customers about a product and persuades them to buy it. The different elements of promotion can be grouped into two broad categories: those that stimulate short-term sales and those that build sales for the long term. This distinction provides the basis for analysis of most business situations and questions.

Figure 24.2 Logic chain: place, promotion and sales

24.5 Types of promotion for building long-term sales

These include those described below.

The value of branding

One of the best forms of promotion is branding. Branding is the process of creating a distinctive and lasting identity in the minds of consumers. Establishing a brand can take considerable time and marketing effort, but once a product brand is established it becomes its own means of promotion. The brand name is recognised and this makes it more likely that the customer will buy the product for the first time. If the experience is satisfactory the customer is very likely to continue to choose the brand. Once established, branding has many advantages, such as the following.

- It enables the business to reduce the amount spent on promotion.
- Customers are more likely to purchase the product again (repeat purchases).
- It is easier to persuade retailers to put the products in their stores.
- Other products can be promoted using the same brand name.

'The best advertising is done by satisfied customers.'
Philip Kotler, marketing guru

Persuasive advertising

Persuasive advertising is designed to create a distinctive image. A good example is BMW, which has spent decades persuading us that it produces not a car but a 'Driving Machine'. Advertising of this kind has also helped to create clear consumer images for firms such as McDonald's and L'Oréal (see Table 24.1).

Table 24.1 Examples of persuasive advertising

Company	Slogan	Meaning
innocent Drinks	'Chain of good: tastes good, does good'	'Our smoothies are good for you (whatever the anti-fruit juice folk say) and we give 10 per cent of our profits to charity (please forget we're now owned by Coca-Cola)
L'Oréal	'Because you're worth it'	Go on, spoil yourself; you can afford that bit extra, so buy our products, not our competitors'
McDonald's	'I'm Lovin' it'	Our food may be unhealthy, but it tastes great

Figure 24.3 Corporate sponsorship may be used as a form of promotion

Public relations

This is the attempt to affect consumers' image of a product without spending on media advertising. It includes making contacts with journalists to try to get favourable mentions or articles about your product. It would also include activities such as sponsorship of sport or the arts. (See Figure 24.3) In 2014 Waitrose decided to sponsor the England cricket team. The upmarket image of cricket is the perfect match for the posh image of Waitrose stores.

24.6 Promotional activity needs to fit in with marketing strategy

The type of promotion used and the level of promotional activity will vary not only from company to company and product to product but also in terms of the marketing strategy being

Table 24.2 Marketing strategies and types of promotion

Marketing strategy	Promotion needs to:
Launching a new product	• be informative • reach the target customers
Differentiating the product	• identify the special features of the product • persuade customers that it is different/better than rival products
Extending the life of an existing product	• reinforce the reasons for customers choosing it • highlight any new features • attract new customers
Increasing market share	• attract new customers • reinforce buying in existing customers
Building brand identity	• increase awareness of the company/product name • create customer recognition and loyalty

followed. Different forms of promotion will serve different purposes. Much will depend on what the business is trying to achieve (see Table 24.2).

The correct promotional mix will be achieved only if the business has clear marketing objectives. Once the objectives and strategy are determined it is much easier for the business to develop an effective promotional campaign.

Five Whys and a How

Question	Answer
Why is it hard for a new company to achieve retail distribution for its products?	No retailers have gaps on their shelves, so accepting a new product means dropping an existing one, risking lost revenue
Why might it be a mistake for a company to seek 100 per cent distribution for its products?	Long-term sales success relies on having a clear, positive image. Nike doesn't want its latest sportswear sold cheaply at Sports Direct; the short-term sales would be at a long-term cost
Why do most modern firms pursue multi-channel distribution strategies?	Because today's consumers sometimes want traditional, browsing shopping and sometimes want speedy online purchasing from home
Why may it be a profitable strategy for a producer to offer extra-high profit margins to retailers?	The bigger the slice of a sale taken by the retailer, the less there is for the producer, but high margins attract higher distribution levels and better display at the point-of-sale (e.g. right by the cash till) so sales volumes are boosted
Why may short-term promotions be a mistake in the long term?	No serious business sees short-term sales maximisation as a proper objective; to build for the long term, image has to be built, not exploited
How important is branding for a business-to-business company?	Even business customers like the promise of quality and consistency that are the appeal at the heart of many brands

Barrier to entry: factors that make it hard for new firms to break into an existing market (for example, strong brand loyalty to the current market leaders).

E-commerce: literally, electronic commerce – carried out online.

Impulse purchasing: buying in unplanned way (for example, going to a shop to buy a paper, but coming out with a Mars bar and a Diet Coke).

Evaluation: Place and promotion decisions

Competitiveness is a much wider issue than marketing. It is affected by the quality of the design and build of the products, and by the enthusiasm of the staff. These are clearly operations and personnel issues. Nevertheless, marketing is at the heart of competitiveness for many firms. Mars knows how to produce Galaxy chocolate, so the key to the firm's success next year is how well the brand can be marketed. The managers must understand the customers, and then have the wisdom and the creativity to find a way to make the product stand out.

Place is of particular importance in Business Studies because it can represent a major barrier to entry, especially for new, small firms. The practical constraint on the amount of shop-floor space makes it hard for new products to gain acceptance unless they are genuinely innovative. Therefore, existing producers of branded goods can become quite complacent, with little serious threat from new competition.

Famously, in the nineteenth century Ralph Waldo Emerson said: 'If a man can make a better mousetrap, though he builds his house in the woods the world will make a beaten path to his door.' In other words, if the product is good enough, customers will come and find you. In a modern competitive world, though, the vast majority of products are not that exciting or different from others. So it is crucial to provide customers with convenient access to your products and/or shelf space in an eye-catching location. Getting products into the right place should not be taken for granted.

Successful branding is one way to ensure good distribution and good in-store display. Shopkeepers want to show off the latest and the classiest brands. In this way, promotion and place come together.

Workbook

A. Revision questions

(45 marks; 45 minutes)

1. Outline the meaning of the term 'place'. (2)

2. Explain in your own words why it may be that 'place is the toughest of the 4Ps'. (3)

3. Outline what you think are appropriate distribution channels for:

   a) a new F1 racing game for mobiles and tablets

   b) a new adventure holiday company focusing on wealthy 19 to 32 year olds. (3)

4. Retailers such as WH Smith charge manufacturers a rent on prime store space such as the shelving near to the cash tills.

   a) How may a firm work out whether it is worthwhile to pay the extra? (3)

   b) Why may new, small firms find it hard to pay rents such as these? (4)

5. Explain in your own words what is meant by the phrase 'a better mousetrap'. (3)

6. Outline three reasons for the success of direct online distribution in recent years. (5)

7. Explain what form of promotion you think would work best for marketing:

   a) a new football game for the PS4 (3)

   b) a small, family-focused seaside hotel (3)

   c) organic cosmetics for women. (3)

8. Why is it important for businesses to monitor the effect of their promotional activity? (4)

9. What is meant by the phrase 'promotion needs to be effective'? (4)

10. Explain why promotion is essential for new businesses. (5)

B. Revision exercises
DATA RESPONSE 1

Getting distribution right

Secondary data can be hugely helpful to new companies looking for distribution of their first products. A company launching the first 'Kitten Milk' product has to decide where to focus its efforts. Where does cat food sell? Is it in pet shops, in corner shops or in supermarkets? Desk research company BMRB reports that, whereas 65 per cent of dog owners shop for pet food at supermarkets, 81 per cent of cat owners do the same. A different source (TNS) puts the cat food market size at £829 million. TNS also shows that the market is rising in value by around 2.5 per cent a year.

Further secondary data shows that pet food shoppers spend only 80 per cent of the amount they intend to when they go to a shop. This is because poor distribution stops them finding what they want. And 50 per cent of shoppers will not return to the same store after being let down twice by poor availability.

Questions (25 marks; 25 minutes)

1. State the meaning of the term 'market size'. (2)

2. Consider the following:

a) The Year 1 sales target for Kitten Milk is £5 million. What share of the total market for cat food would that represent? (3)

b) Explain why it might be hard to persuade retailers to stock a product with that level of market share. (4)

3. The marketing manager for Kitten Milk is planning to focus distribution efforts on getting the brand placed in pet shops. To what extent do you agree with this approach? (16)

DATA RESPONSE 2

An arm's length from desire

From its origins in America in 1886, Coca-Cola has been a marketing phenomenon. It was the world's first truly global brand; it virtually invented the red, jolly Christmas Santa, and its bottle design (1919) was the first great piece of packaging design.

Yet a 1950 *Time* magazine article quoted another piece of marketing genius: 'Always within an arm's length of desire.' The marketing experts at Atlanta (home of Coca-Cola) realised nearly 60 years ago that sales of Coca-Cola were limited mainly by availability. Especially on a hot day, a cold Coke would be desired by almost anyone who had it an arm's length away. This led the company to develop a distribution strategy based on maximum availability, maximum in-store visibility and therefore maximum impulse purchase.

From then on, Coca-Cola targeted four main types of distribution:

1. in supermarkets and grocers

2. in any kiosk in a location based on entertainment (for example, a bowling alley or a cinema)

3. in any canteen, bar or restaurant

4. in a vending machine near you. Automatic vending proved one of the most valuable ways of building the market until worries about healthy eating saw them banned in schools. A vending machine is the ultimate barrier to entry.

Overall, though, the Coca-Cola approach to distribution set out in 1950 is what most companies still try to do today.

Questions (25 marks; 30 minutes)

1. Explain how a vending machine can be a 'barrier to entry' to new competitors. (4)

2. Explain what the text means by the difference between 'maximum availability' and 'maximum visibility'. (4)

3. Explain two reasons why 'an arm's length from desire' may be less important for a business that does not rely upon impulse purchase. (8)

4. From all that you know about today's Coke, Diet Coke and Coke Zero, analyse whether Coca-Cola's distribution strategy was at the core of the firm's marketing success. (9)

C. Extend your understanding

1. Heinz has found that its famous brand limits it from expanding its product portfolio, as people won't accept Heinz chilled ready meals or Heinz pizzas. Discuss how it might try to overcome this consumer resistance. (20)

2. You have just developed a new console game that combines the appeal of Candy Crush with the force of Call of Duty. To what extent would obtaining high levels of distribution guarantee the product's success in the UK? (20)

Integrating the marketing mix

Linked to: Marketing and decision-making, Chapter 11; Market research, Chapter 15; Market data and analysis, Chapter 18; Segmentation, targeting and positioning, Chapter 19; Motivation and engagement in theory, Chapter 46; Motivation and engagement in practice, Chapter 47.

Definition

Success comes from a co-ordinated campaign that directs every marketing variable towards the right market positioning for the product or brand.

25.1 The importance of an integrated marketing mix

How do some brands thrive over generations while others arrive, look promising, but then fade away? Do you remember Nokia phones, Strollers (chocolate flop), the McHotel and Virgin Cola (it would wipe out Coke, according to Richard Branson)? In the meantime, some brands keep on going, such as Heinz Tomato Ketchup (born 1888), Marmite (born 1902), Maltesers (born 1932) and the Ford Fiesta (born 1976).

Part of the difference between the successes and the flops is the understanding shown of the mix. Maltesers and Marmite have in common an exceptional level of product differentiation. Therefore the key has been to make the product the central element of the mix, and simply ensure that the other mix factors fit in. Pricing, for example, has generally been quite high, to confirm psychologically the quality of the product. For Heinz Ketchup the degree of differentiation is not as high, but fortunately the image of authenticity has put the brand at the centre of many a table. Only in the case of the Ford Fiesta has the toughly competitive market made it necessary to have a succession of top-notch brand managers making the right decisions about all aspects of the mix.

The reason the mix must be integrated is simple: we the consumers are committing our hard-earned cash in exchange for an uncertain return. Will the dress really look good after a couple of wears? Will the restaurant meal be quite what your fiancé wanted? Therefore we are looking at all the clues surrounding the product or service and weighing them up together. Good-looking menu but prices seem oddly low? No thanks. Good-looking dress but the salesperson can't answer a question about washing? No thanks.

Figure 25.1 Logic chain: links to an effective mix

25.2 Influences on an integrated marketing mix

The brand manager at Mercedes knows that the key is to create an integrated, enveloping image of the car as an aspirational luxury. Customers arriving at a showroom should have an experience in keeping with the brand image: efficient, classy and pampering.

Marketing influences on an integrated mix:

- Position in the product life cycle. In the development stage the central focus is on the product/service and the extent to which it meets existing or new customer needs or wants. Only when market research gives a green light to the product does it make sense to test the appropriate price, packaging and perhaps advertising/promotion. Once those factors have been settled it is time to set out the process that is to be followed by the people who will interact with the customers – and to decide on any physical environment needed to back up the promotional platform. Once the product is launched, the price may change (perhaps increase after penetration pricing at launch).

- The Boston Matrix. When a business has a wide product portfolio (400 'superbrands' in the case of Unilever) it has to prioritise. Cadbury will have sales staff focused on the chocolate market who are to sell perhaps 40 different product lines. Shopkeepers cannot possibly find the time for a hard sell on 40 products, so Cadbury will select two or three to focus on each month. Dairy Milk is such a cash cow (UK 2014 sales of over £500 million) that it will get regular support. In addition, rising stars and the occasional problem child will be selected. A rising star has the twin benefits of a high market share in a growth sector; the problem child is also in the growth sector, but lacks the market share to be strong – yet.

- The type of product. The most important distinction is between goods and services. For the most part the marketing mix for goods is based on the 4Ps, especially if the goods are marketed through traditional retail channels. Services, though, need the extra 3Ps to ensure that there are high-quality people working to highly efficient systems making intelligent use of physical environment where necessary. Other categories to consider are B2B versus B2C, and convenience vs. shopping vs. speciality goods.

- Marketing objectives. If the target for the marketing managers is to boost market share significantly, perhaps as in the case of Müllerlight, from 7.4 to 9 per cent of the £2,200 million market for yoghurts and potted desserts, there will be a need for a big rethink. Going from 7.4 to 9 requires a sales increase of $1.6/7.4 \times 100 = 21.6$ per cent, assuming a static market. Therefore there may be a need for significant new product innovation, or a distribution innovation that competitors cannot easily copy. Either way there may be a significant realignment of the marketing mix in order to achieve the new objectives

- The target market. A posh brand must have all seven mix variables pointing in the same direction, towards aspiration and quality. As mentioned before, the fact that only four of the seven Ps are the direct responsibility of the marketing department can make this a serious challenge. Each week *The Grocer* magazine rates the quality of customer service across all the leading grocers. Given its high prices and posh image, you would expect Waitrose to win this regularly. In fact it wins it less often than Tesco or Morrisons' – far, far behind the 2014 winner Sainsbury. Surely Waitrose customers will notice this at some point.

'You can duplicate the airplanes. You can duplicate the gate facilities. You can duplicate all the hard things, the tangible things you can put your hands on. But it's the intangibles that determine success.' Herb Kelleher, airline chief executive

---

- Competition. Pukka Pies has long been an important brand at football grounds, but it also was developing a useful retail sideline. By 2012 it was selling £3.1 million pies a year in supermarkets. Then Greggs decided to produce its own pies to be sold in supermarkets. Sales of £11 million in 2012 jumped 91 per cent to £21.1 million in 2013. This hit other pie-makers but especially Pukka, which suffered a 12 per cent sales decline in 2013. To survive in this tougher retail environment Pukka will have to think how best to react: reposition the pies, perhaps, to distinguish Pukka more clearly from Greggs, or bring out new, better recipes to beat Greggs on taste.

'Give them quality. That's the best kind of advertising.' Milton Hershey, US chocolate-maker

---

- Market positioning. Today's consumers want something that is targeted tightly at them. This is why Marks & Spencer's clothing is in no man's land; even middle-aged people struggle to think the ranges are targeted at them, because it's all too mass-market. In the clothing sector, this is where Next succeeds (office wear for young adults) and where Zara triumphs worldwide (targeting the under 30s). Clever companies are clear about where their market position is – and focus every aspect of their marketing mix at that positioning. This leads to a co-ordinated, integrated mix.

The all-time biggest-selling games console was Sony's PS2, which sold 158 million units. So when Microsoft chose to launch its second generation Xbox 360 a year before the PS2, there was no doubting its target – young, male game-players: the Sony heartland. Nintendo had been doing some thinking, however. They saw Xbox and Sony hammering the same demographic and decided on an innovative new positioning. Their Wii would target children, girls, families and older adults – in other words, position themselves firmly away from the crowd. The result was a triumph for Nintendo. The Wii sold 101 million consoles compared with PS3's 83 million and Xbox 360's 82 million. Clever market positioning gave Wii the marketing edge.

Among other influences on an integrated marketing mix are:

- Budgets: has the business enough finance to achieve a co-ordinated approach to all seven aspects of the mix? If competitive pressures have forced the business to cut out a whole layer of supervisory management (as happened recently at Asda and at Morrisons') it may be very difficult to deliver People and Processes to the right standard.

- Staff turnover: at McDonalds UK 35 per cent of staff leave each year, having to be replaced. This might make it hard to build consistency into the marketing mix, as new staff will constantly be arriving, each with a lot to learn about service levels. To McDonalds' credit, the business seems well enough managed to be able to overcome this problem.

- External factors, such as changes in the market structure, perhaps introducing fiercer competition; or a switch from good times to recession, causing a rethink in marketing objectives and strategy – and therefore in the marketing mix.

25.3 Digital marketing, e-commerce and the marketing mix

Traditionally, location has been a key factor for retailers. For online retailers it is irrelevant. Yet there are many other potential pitfalls.

In the case of Glasses Direct (see below) outstanding prices combined with a good product, good service and a small investment in advertising to create a highly successful mix. In effect, it was the original idea (high-street glasses at non-rip-off prices) that was the key. In other cases this will not work, because the offer has to be similar to the competition. If you are selling skateboards online, your prices will not be much different to those of other suppliers. This will make it much more important to identify a winning marketing strategy.

Here are some that work well.

- The saturation approach: as used by Moneysupermarket.com to make sure that everyone thinks of you first. The downside, of course, is the huge cost of the TV advertising.

- Google search optimisation: that is, design your website so that it comes very high on the list when people are Googling for something you want to sell. This takes time and a small amount of money, but is much, much cheaper than a multi-million-pound advertising campaign.

- Build a website people will talk about: some good examples are those of BMW (won 2013 'Website of the Year' award) and Ocado. A fun website can provide strong support to a brand image, and get the brand written about in the media, which provides extra, free promotion.

Real business

The £100 million glasses

James Murray-Wells started Glasses Direct at the age of 21, just after completing a degree. He offered pairs of glasses online for £15 instead of the £150 paid in the high street.

James designed the website himself, but – with no money and no publicity – sales in the first month averaged just one or two pairs a day. The only expense he could afford was to get some leaflets printed. This is often a weak form of advertising, but with his incredibly competitive price proposition his leaflets proved highly effective. He took a train from Bristol, handing out flyers to people who would be stuck on a train with nothing else to do but read them. Within days sales started coming through from people living in Bristol. Shortly afterwards came emails of thanks, with people clearly surprised that the glasses were every bit as good as those available on the high street. By the end of the summer, word of mouth had spread and the first articles started appearing in papers. Orders were received for up to 100 pairs a day and the business was booming. Within two years turnover hit £3 million and was rising. By 2013 sales were heading for £40 million a year and there was City talk of floating the business for £100 million. In fact, after selling the business to a German private equity house, Murray-Wells stood down. Having made unknown millions, he is now looking for other business opportunities.

Five Whys and a How

Question	Answer
Why is it important for the marketing mix to be co-ordinated?	So that the consumer gets a single, clear idea and image of the product/service
Why might some brands live forever?	Because the managers might have the ability to keep reinventing the brand to suit new generations
Why might a manager start focusing upon higher and higher prices for a product in its decline phase?	Because the manager believes there's no potential for future growth, making it sensible to maximise revenue from the few remaining loyal customers
Why might a change in target market make it hard to maintain an integrated marketing mix?	It is perhaps easier to change the 4Ps than it is to change the ones that are to do with the efficiency and understanding shown by customer-facing staff
Why might a switch from retailing to online selling lead to a better-integrated marketing mix?	Online selling keeps everything within head office control and may therefore help achieve consistency in dealing with customers
How might a football club learn from the three extra Ps within the marketing mix?	They could learn that the People they employ are supposed to be polite and helpful to fans and that the Process should be efficient enough to minimise queuing and delay

Key terms

Penetration pricing: pricing low enough to attract high sales in order to establish a satisfactory market share

Product differentiation: is the extent to which consumers perceive your product to be distinct from rival products.

Evaluation: Integrating the marketing mix

In an era where the most dramatic business stories are about new technology companies and online businesses, it might seem that the marketing mix is an old-fashioned concept. It is hard to believe that Sergey Brin or Mark Zuckerberg have ever heard of it. Yet it remains an important touchstone – almost a checklist – for middle managers. These days the biggest challenge is to co-ordinate the 7Ps across the three relevant departments: marketing, operations and human resources. Successfully achieving this requires company-wide training and understanding that can only be expected in a very well-run company. If, furthermore, a company has to achieve this across countries worldwide, the challenge is massive indeed.

Workbook

A. Revision questions

(35 marks; 35 minutes)

1. Outline two possible reasons why Maltesers is still selling successfully over 75 years after the brand's birth. (4)

2. Explain why it is important to distinguish between a trend and a fad. Look at the quote by Milton Hershey on page 156. Explain how quality can be the best kind of advertising. (4)

3. Why might new competition in the soft drinks business force Pepsi to rethink its marketing mix? (4)

4. Reread the Real business feature 'The £100m glasses'. Outline two aspects of the marketing mix that were especially important to this business's success. (4)

5. Consider the following:

   a) In February 2008, Cadbury announced the launch of a range of Easter eggs that would not have any outer packaging (they would just be sold in a foil wrapper). Outline one advantage and one disadvantage of this. (4)

   b) In 2012 they admitted that they had returned to full, traditional packaging for Cadbury Easter Eggs. Why might this be? (5)

6. Should a company switching from retail to online distribution consider it a moral duty to cut prices to the consumers? (5)

7. What might be the most important element of the marketing mix for a business such as British Airways? Explain your answer. (5)

B. Revision exercises
DATA RESPONSE

The software triumph

Federico and Cara formed their business (Fedaria Ltd) just two weeks before *Angry Birds* launched in December 2009. The company would develop app games that would be free to download and play, with income to be generated by players choosing to buy extra lives or extra playing time.

By late 2010 Cara developed a brand new game based on a classic game of pirates looking for treasure. Federico knew various journalists who reported on games software, so *Dubloon* received reviews in several paper and digital media. Reviewers loved the game, but sales proved disappointing. Soon after, they produced a successful series of games for the 2012 Olympics: *Shotput*, *Rowing* and – most successful of all: *Javelin*.

By this time – mid 2011 – Fedaria's revenue was hitting £400,000 a month, making it necessary to hire a series of new managers and developers. This made it hard to keep every aspect of the marketing mix co-ordinated, but Federico worked hard to achieve this.

As Britain focused on the Olympics in Spring 2012 downloads went crazy – and so did income. Fedaria *Javelin* became the top Apple app for the UK, and sales were also strong in America and Japan. But in the April 2012 board meeting things went less well.

Cara was unhappy that customer feedback was not as strong as it might be. Customers loved the games but found online ordering difficult and deliveries erratic.

Luckily for the business, Cara's frustration was deflected over the coming weeks as one of her developers came with a near-completed game that she loved. The idea was so simple: stocks. You could download a photo or choose a face to be put in the stocks and then take aim. Tomatoes splattered convincingly; eggs producing dripping yellow yolk and many other options gave lots of idle pleasure. Within three days Cara had a test version on the Fedaria website, where devotees were keen to test out new ideas. Two days after that she knew that – with a few tweaks – this would be a smash.

Now it was time to chat about the game to Federico. He had just finished a meeting with the newly-appointed marketing director (MD). The MD had insisted on a £400,000 advertising budget to 'consolidate the Fedaria brand values in the mind of the target market'. Federico knew that current revenues made this affordable, but his experience made him want to preserve plenty of profit for possible tough times in the future. And now Cara wanted £200,000 to launch *Stocks*. He said no.

Furious, Cara threatened to leave and set up on her own. Federico found a compromise by offering a £50,000 budget to create an online viral PR campaign. Cara accepted and the launch was scheduled for June 2013. By September, *Stocks* was the UK's No. 2 download for mobiles (behind *Candy Crush*), and broke through the £500,000-a-day revenue level.

Questions (30 marks; 35 minutes)

1. Briefly explain how Fedaria handled two aspects of the 7Ps. (5)

2. Analyse the importance of a fully integrated marketing mix in the case of Fedaria Ltd. (9)

3. To what extent does a digital business such as Fedaria hinge on the effectiveness of its marketing mix? (16)

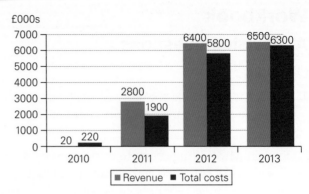

Figure 25.2 Fedaria Ltd: revenues and costs
Figures for 2013 are Jan-Jun only

C. Extend your understanding

1. For a brand you are familiar with, analyse each of the 7Ps then decide which is the most important element of its mix. Justify your answer. (20)

2. No matter how big the brand, there is a limit to its marketing budget. How important is it, therefore to decide which elements of the mix to prioritise? Justify your answer. (20)

Setting operational objectives

Linked with: Efficiency and labour productivity, Chapter 27; Technology and operational efficiency, Chapter 30; Analysing operational performance, Chapter 31; Decision-making to improve operational performance, Chapter 35.

Definition

Operational objectives are the specific, detailed production targets set by an organisation to ensure that its overall company goals are achieved.

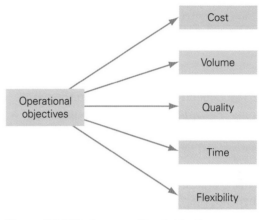

Figure 26.1 The key operational objectives

26.1 Introduction

All organisations share common operational objectives regardless of their size and the sector in which they operate. All firms will attempt to produce goods and services that are 'fit for purpose', delivered quickly and on time. They will also aim to produce the right number of goods as cheaply as possible, bearing in mind the overall strategy.

If, like Ryanair, your target is to be the lowest-cost airline in Europe, every cost will be shaved to the minimum. If your business strategy is to be the highest-rated airline in the world (such as Singapore Airlines), you may accept costs that will seem high to other airlines. The crucial thing is that a firm's operational objectives must be fully in line with its objectives regarding marketing and management of its people.

Finally, there needs to be enough flexibility within operations to allow activities to be varied or adapted quickly, in order to accommodate changes in demand.

26.2 Key operational objectives

The key operational objectives are shown in Figure 26.1 and described below.

Cost

All firms are concerned with keeping costs down, particularly those that compete directly on price. Costs affect what is charged to the customer and therefore the profits that can be generated. During a period of economic downturn, a firm's ability to make further cost reductions can mean the difference between survival and failure. Costs are determined by the efficiency of a business. This can be measured in a number of ways; for example, wastage rates or the productivity of the workforce.

Real business

Will Asda's cost-cutting prove costly?

Faced with ferocious price competition from Aldi and Lidl, in May 2014 Asda announced a plan to cut 4,100 department manager positions at its stores. The result was fury on the part of middle managers who felt their career progression was being blunted. From Asda's point of view, the delayering of its stores was a major part of a £1 billion cost-cutting exercise called 'We Operate for Less'. The company could also defend itself by pointing to a 6-month trial of ⇨

⇒

the flatter organisational structure at two of its stores, which started the previous November. Underlying the decision was the customer shift to online purchasing, putting pressure on the cost structure at large stores such as supermarkets. As one retail analyst explained, the long-term success of the new approach would depend on the difference between cost-cutting and efficiency gains: 'If you can reduce the cost of servicing customers without impacting upon quality, that's efficiency. If you can't, that's cost-cutting'.

Quality

The exact meaning of quality for any individual organisation will depend to some extent on the nature of its operations. Put simply, quality is about getting things 'right' by meeting or beating customer expectations over and over again. Quality has a crucial role to play in guaranteeing customer satisfaction. Not only should firms aim to produce goods or services that are 'fit for purpose', they also need to create a sense of dependability by ensuring that products are ready when customers expect them. Failure to do so is likely to create customer dissatisfaction and encourage customers to switch to rival products. A high degree of quality and dependability is also required within the organisation. Managers need to ensure that quality standards are being met. They also need to synchronize production so that products pass smoothly from one stage to the next. This will help to reduce production time and costs, meaning that goods are ready for dispatch to customers sooner.

Speed of response

This factor is important in many ways, both to the consumer and the producer. Many consumers are 'money-rich, time-poor' as they rush from a well-paid job to pick up the kids, eat, then go out. So operations that save time for the customer can be very successful (for example, Next Directory shopping or pizza delivery). Time-based management is also important to firms in product development. The firm that is first to market is able to charge higher prices than its slower rivals. Speed is also important within the business. The faster items pass through the production process, the lower the costs of warehousing materials and work-in-progress.

'The goal as a company is to have customer service that is not just the best, but legendary.' Sam Walton, founder WalMart.

Flexibility

Firms need to be able to vary the volume of production relatively easily, in order to respond effectively to unexpected increases or decreases in demand. The ability to adapt or modify a standard product range allows a firm to appear to be offering customised products that meet customer needs more precisely, but still benefit from high-volume production, keeping costs down. This flexible approach to production is a form of lean production that has been used successfully by a number of companies, including retail clothing giant Zara.

Real business

Lean production reaches sportswear

Nike became the first sportswear manufacturer to embrace the concept of lean production when it established a new online design facility. Nike iD allows customers to create their own versions of a range of footwear and clothing. Customers follow a step-by-step customisation process, picking from a choice of colours and materials, and adding logos, names and personalised messages in order to create a 'unique' product. The customised goods are manufactured and delivered within four weeks of an order being placed. A 'team locker' version of the service also exists, offering the facility to sports teams and groups. The success of the concept has been followed up with the opening of a number of Nike iD Studios around the world, including London's Oxford Street. Each studio has a team of qualified design consultants on hand to help customers make their choices.

Source: Adapted from www.nike.com

Dependability

These days most large retailers place deliveries straight onto the shelf. They have no stockroom because they have in mind the just-in-time (JIT) goal of zero buffer stock. If a delivery is late, shelves empty and customers are irritated. Therefore dependability is a valuable quality in a supplier. It would be worth paying slightly higher prices to buy from a wholly reliable supplier: one who supplies the correct number of the correct items, on time and to the right quality standard.

Environmental objectives

Most consumer-facing plcs produce annual reports to cover social and environmental aspects of their business. These may include environmental objectives – though they seem more likely to list environmental achievements. The problem with the latter is that they can be self-selected, that is, picking out only the good bits and publicising these.

Next plc is an example of a business that has had clear environmental objectives, set in 2007 and with a target achievement date of the 2015–16 financial year. In its 2013 Corporate Responsibility Report it provided information on one target: cutting waste sent to landfill. As shown in Table 26.1, setting a clear objective has helped Next achieve a remarkable improvement, with the level of waste going to landfill falling from 55 per cent to 15 per cent. But they have some way to go to achieve their objective of 5 per cent.

Table 26.1 Next plc Environmental objectives: waste to landfill

	Target for 2015–16	Actual in 2007–08	Actual in 2011–12	Actual in 2012–13
General waste to landfill	5 per cent	55 per cent	15 per cent	15 per cent
General waste recycled	95 per cent	45 per cent	85 per cent	85 per cent

The adoption of environmental objectives by a firm will have a number of implications for its operations. For instance, it may mean that the business will need to change its supplies of materials to those that come from replenishable or recycled sources. It may need to adopt new processes that are more energy efficient, and produce less waste and pollution. Even the methods of transportation used to bring in materials and deliver goods to customers may need to be investigated in an attempt to reduce congestion. Furthermore, staff will need appropriate training in order to ensure that these policies achieve their objectives.

Added value

To be sustainable in the long term, every business needs added value. That is, the process of turning materials or ideas into a finished product or service must make the selling price higher than all the costs. From that comes the profit the business needs to reinvest in new technologies or higher capacity. Therefore, whether a firm states it or not, it must have added value as a key underlying objective.

Real business

In 2014 the campaign group Make Chocolate Fair estimated that the value added chain on a £1 bar of chocolate was as follows:

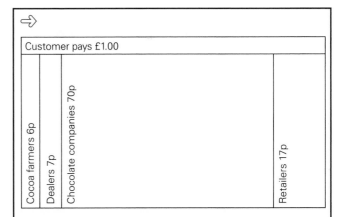

Figure 26.2 Value added chain on a £1.00 bar of chocolate

The charity Oxfam disagreed, saying that the true income to the cocoa farmer was 3 per cent of the value of the bar, not 6 per cent. Both organisations agreed, however, that in 1980 West African cocoa farmers received 16 per cent of the final shop value of the bar. So the value added has steadily been absorbed by the western chocolate companies at the expense of the growers.

'Crisps cost 4 cents more per ounce for every additional 'no' on the packet.' Professor Jurafsky, Stanford University

26.3 The importance of innovation

Innovation means more than merely inventing a new product or process; it involves turning a new idea into a commercial success. Innovation within operations is crucial to the long-term survival and growth of a firm, allowing it to keep ahead of the competition. New products will often require new production methods and machinery. New processes for producing existing goods or delivering services can help to reduce costs and improve the quality and speed of production.

In mid-2014 analysts Research and Markets published a forecast of the future progress of 3D printing (also known as 'additive manufacture'). This technology had grown dramatically as it developed from producing prototype, one-off items to becoming a full-scale way to manufacture economically. According to Research and Markets, continuing innovation in 3D printing will see global sales spiral from $2,200 million in 2013 to $5,600 million by 2019 (see the bar chart).

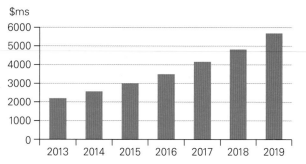

Figure 26.3 Global market for 3D printing, 2013–19

Source: *Research and Markets*

26.4 Internal influences on operational objectives

The nature of the product

The product is at the heart of any firm's operations, so its nature will affect operational objectives. For example, car manufacturers such as BMW and Mercedes have a long-established reputation for high standards of quality, which must be taken into account when developing new models.

The personal characteristics of the operations director

People matter in business, so objectives will differ depending upon the preferences of the boss. In the case of Dyson Ltd, the views of overall founder/owner James Dyson will ensure that any operations director knows that innovation is a primary goal within the business. In plcs such as Unilever, with a less dominant chief executive, it will be the preferences of the operations director that matter. One might feel passionately about the environment, whereas another might be much more focused on profit-related targets connected to speed of response or dependability.

26.5 External influences on operational objectives

Demand

The level and nature of demand will act as a major influence on operational objectives. A business must attempt to predict sales volumes and any likely fluctuations, in order to ensure that customer expectations are met in a cost-effective manner.

Availability of resources

A lack of availability of the right level and quality of resources, including human resources, can act as a major constraint in attempting to achieve operational objectives. For example, skills shortages in a number of industries in the UK, including health care, have led to a reliance on workers from abroad. Similarly, a shortage of financial resources will act as a constraint on the achievement of operational objectives.

Competitors' behaviour

Few firms have the luxury of operating alone in a market and no firm, however successful, can afford to become complacent. Rival firms will strive to increase their market share, and their activities are likely to have a major influence on operational objectives.

Evaluation: Setting operational objectives

The effective management of operations is central to the success of any business, regardless of its size or sector. The key is for all staff to have a clear understanding of what the business is attempting to achieve. The establishment of appropriate operational objectives is only a starting point. At least as important is that they be communicated effectively to everyone: to the part-time and shift workers; to the delivery drivers; to the staff in distribution depots across Europe and so on. In many businesses, the people at the top spend their time setting clear objectives, but the people at the bottom have no idea of what they are or why they matter. Successful operations management hinges on good people management.

Five Whys and a How

Question	Answer
Why is it valuable for a business to set clear operational objectives?	So that all operations staff understand the company's real priorities
Why might a company set the objective of quite low quality standards?	If 'low, low prices' are the marketing approach, low, low costs will be more important than quality, e.g. for a hotel targeting 'hen nights' (low prices are crucial; all the customers seek is a mirror, a bed and a toilet)
Why might operational objectives change if the economy slips into a sharp recession?	Cost minimisation may become a greater priority, perhaps at the cost of quality, speed or innovation
Why might flexibility be an especially important objective for a small business?	Because it's hard to compete with big firms on cost, quality and environmental programmes, so small firms must focus on where they can add value
Why may external influences on operational objectives be more important than internal ones?	Because a factor such as tough competitive pressure can force a business to follow a single approach, as Lidl/Aldi have forced UK supermarkets to cut prices and therefore costs
How might a business such as Gillette increase the added value on its shaving products?	Launching an innovative new shaving system might allow them to charge more for a similar amount of plastic, steel and packaging

Key terms

Buffer stock: is spare stock held just-in-case there's an unexpected demand upturn or an unwanted delay in supplies arriving.

Efficiency: refers to how effectively a firm uses its resources. It can be measured in a number of ways, including labour productivity and wastage rates.

Innovation: this means taking an idea for a new product or process and turning it into a commercial success.

Just-in-time: production is based on zero buffer stocks, that is, new supplies arrive just when they are needed.

Lean production: instead of mass producing, the firm produces goods to order and therefore satisfies the customer while helping to avoid stockpiles of unsold stock.

Productivity: measures how efficiently a firm turns inputs into the production process into output. The most commonly used measure is labour productivity, which looks at output per worker.

Workbook

A. Revision questions

(50 marks; 50 minutes)

1. Explain what is meant by the term 'operational objectives'. (3)

2. Outline two reasons why it is important for a business to keep its costs as low as possible. (4)

3. Analyse the main consequences for a firm of failing to accurately forecast the volume of production required to meet demand. (6)

4. Briefly explain what is meant by quality for a car manufacturer such as Mercedes. (4)

5. Choose one of the following businesses. Outline two possible ways in which it delivers quality to its customers.

   a) electronics manufacturer, Sony

   b) luxury hotel chain, Ritz-Carlton

   c) discount retailer, Aldi. (6)

6. Examine two key benefits for a firm that develops a reputation for quality. (6)

7. Give two reasons why a firm may aim to achieve a high degree of flexibility in its operations. (2)

8. Look at Table 26.1 and explain the value of setting an ambitious environmental objective such as going from 55 per cent to 5 per cent of waste going to landfill. (5)

9. Explain, using examples, what is meant by the term 'lean production'. (4)

10. Analyse two ways in which a business can benefit from a commitment to innovation. (6)

11. Outline one advantage and one disadvantage for a business of establishing environmental objectives. (4)

B. Revision exercises
DATA RESPONSE

Renault targets the cheap mass market

In the first half of 2014 French car maker Renault enjoyed a 25 per cent profit increase, largely thanks to a 35 per cent rise in sales of its low-cost Dacia brand. When Renault bought Dacia in 1999, many commentators thought the French company had made a big mistake. Dacia's productivity was low and profits were non-existent. Now Renault is enjoying a payback on its investment. Dacia's no-frills Logan saloon has a price tag of the equivalent of around £6,000, while the Logan estate sells for the equivalent of £7,500. Both models are targeted at customers who would normally opt to buy a second-hand, rather than a brand-new car.

Until recently, all the cars were made at Renault's Dacia plant in Romania. The Logan was originally intended to be sold in Romania only, but proved to be a huge success in both France and Germany, with waiting lists of customers eager to get hold of the car. Annual output at the plant was increased by the company from 200,000 to 350,000 in 2008. By 2013 the factory was close to its maximum capacity level,

with 342,620 cars rolling off the line. In 2014 Renault expanded its Dacia factory in Morocco from 200,000 to 340,000 cars, to absorb the rising demand for the Dacia. Workers at the Romanian plant are highly skilled, but low paid compared with France. In 2014 a French car worker typically earns £18 an hour, while in Romania it's £6 and in Morocco £3. The low-cost production is matched by low-tech factories, with a much lower investment in robots than in the west.

The Dacia car models are practical and cheap to produce, but with far less production flexibility than achieved today on sophisticated production lines for producers such as Mercedes.

Questions (25 marks; 30 minutes)

1. Analyse Renault's operational objectives in launching its Logan car range. (9)

2. To what extent is it likely that the other major car manufacturers will be forced to follow Renault and target the low-cost segment of the market? (16)

C. Extend your understanding

1. To what extent is the long-term success of an online grocery business dependent on setting the right operational objectives? (20)

2. For a business you know well, how important are the main internal and external influences on their operational objectives and decisions? (20)

Efficiency and labour productivity

Linked with: Technology and operational efficiency, Chapter 30; Analysing operational performance, Chapter 31; Motivation and engagement in theory, Chapter 46; Motivation and engagement in practice, Chapter 47.

Definition

Labour productivity is a measure of efficiency; it measures the output of a firm in relation to the labour inputs.

27.1 Are efficiency and productivity the same thing?

Directly, the answer is no. Productivity is output per worker per time period (hour, month or year). That ignores some other key features of efficiency, notably waste. One super-fast worker may produce a lot of output, but in a wasteful manner. A decorator may paint speedily but messily, wasting 20 per cent of the paint. So productivity may be high but overall efficiency no better than average. And a company may produce chemicals with high productivity, but create pollution locally (waste products leaking out of the chimney, perhaps). Again this would not be efficient.

Overall, though, labour productivity is regarded by businesses as one of the most important tests of management efficiency. Therefore most of this chapter focuses on labour productivity.

27.2 Productivity: what is it?

Labour productivity measures the amount a worker produces over a given time. For example, an employee might make ten pairs of jeans in an hour. Measuring productivity is relatively easy in manufacturing, where the number of goods can be counted. In the service sector it is not always possible to be sure what to measure. Productivity in services can be measured in some cases: the number of customers served, number of patients seen, and the sales per employee. But how can the productivity of a receptionist be measured?

It is important to distinguish between productivity and total output. By hiring more employees a firm may increase the total output, but this does not mean that the output per employee has gone up. Similarly it is possible to have lower production with higher productivity because of a fall in the number of employees. Imagine, for example, 20 employees producing 40 tables a week at a furniture company. Their productivity on average is 2 tables per week. If new machinery enables 10 employees to make 30 tables the overall output has fallen, but the output per worker has risen to 3. This rise in productivity would lower the labour cost per table.

27.3 The importance of productivity

The output per employee is a very important measure of a firm's performance. It has a direct impact on the cost of producing a unit. If productivity increases then, assuming wages are unchanged, the labour cost per unit will fall. Imagine that in one factory employees make five pairs of shoes per day, but in another they make ten pairs per day; assuming the wage rate is the same, this means the labour cost of a pair of shoes will be halved in the second factory (see Table 27.1). With lower labour costs this firm is likely to be in a better competitive position.

Table 27.1 Shoe factory productivity and wage costs

	Daily wage rate (£)	Productivity rate (per day)	Wage cost per pair (£)
Factory	50	5	10
Factory 2	50	10	5

By increasing productivity a firm can improve its competitiveness (ability to equal or beat its rivals). It can either sell its products at a lower price or keep the price as it is and enjoy a higher profit margin. This is why firms continually monitor their productivity relative to their competitors and, where possible, try to increase it. However, they need to make sure that quality does not suffer in the rush to produce more. It may be necessary to set both productivity and quality targets.

'Engineering is the ability to do for $1 what any damn fool can do for $5.' Arthur Wellington, nineteenth century US engineer

---

27.4 How to increase labour productivity

Increase investment in modern equipment

By investing in modern, sophisticated machines and better production processes, it shouldn't be hard to improve output per worker. That, in turn, would improve individual companies' competitiveness and help to boost the country's economic growth. Yet Figure 27.1 is a reminder that Britain consistently invests less than other countries as a share of GDP – despite repeated cuts to corporation tax that are said to encourage greater business investment.

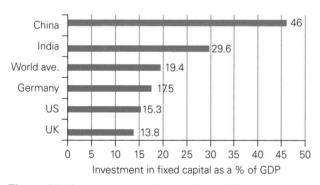

Figure 27.1 Investment spending: too low in UK

Investment in fixed capital as a percentage of GDP

Source: CIA *World Factbook* 2014

'Not everything that can be counted counts, and not everything that counts can be counted.' Albert Einstein, the ultimate boffin.

Improve the ability level of those at work

To increase productivity a firm may need to introduce more or better training for its employees. A skilled and well-trained workforce is likely to produce more and make fewer mistakes. Employees should be able to complete tasks more quickly and will not need as much supervision or advice. They will be able to solve their own work-related problems and may be in a better position to contribute ideas on how to increase productivity further.

However, firms are often reluctant to invest in training because employees may leave and work for another firm once they have gained more skills. There is a danger that the training will not provide sufficient gains to justify the initial investment and so any spending in this area needs to be properly researched and costed. Simply training people for the sake of it is obviously of limited value. However, in general UK firms do not have a particularly good record in training and more investment here could have a significant effect on the UK's productivity levels.

It should also be remembered that elaborate training may not be necessary for a firm that recruits the right people. Great care must be taken in the selection process to find staff with the right skills and attitudes. A firm with a good reputation locally will find it much easier to pick the best people. This is why many firms take great care over their relations with the local community.

Improve employee motivation

Professor Frederick Herzberg, the American psychologist and business management theorist, once said that most people's idea of a fair day's work is less than half what they can give.

The key to success, he felt, was to design jobs that contained motivators to help employees give much, much more. His suggestions on how to provide job enrichment are detailed in the Chapter 46.

There is no doubt that motivation matters. A motivated sales force may achieve twice the sales level of an unmotivated one. A motivated computer technician may correct twice the computer faults of an unmotivated one. And, in both cases, overall business performance will be boosted.

Real business

Motivation on the pitch

When Fulham Football Club appointed a new groundsman, few people even noticed. The fans had always been proud of the pitch, but newly appointed Frank Boahene was not impressed. He thought it needed a dramatic improvement before the start of the new season in August. With no time to reseed the pitch, he decided the best way to strengthen the grass was to cut it three times a day. Doing so first thing in the morning and last thing in the afternoon was not a problem. But he also chose to 'pop back' from his home in Reading (an hour's drive) to do the third cut at 11.00 at night. Every day! That's motivation.

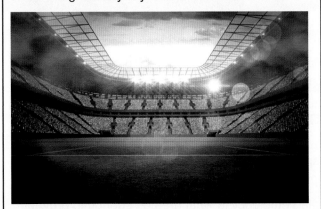

Figure 27.2

'Looking for differences between the more productive and less productive organisations, we found that the most striking difference is the number of people who are involved and feel responsibility for solving problems.' Michael McTague, management consultant.

27.5 Difficulties increasing productivity

The role of management

A serious problem for UK management is that productivity has never been a central focus for directors. In the UK directors focus on profits; elsewhere they look for efficiency first, trusting that profits will follow.

Perhaps the key management role is to identify increasing productivity as a permanent objective. The Japanese bulldozer company Komatsu set a target of a 10-per-cent productivity increase every year, until they caught up with the world-leading American producer, Caterpillar. Today Komatsu is the world No. 2 producer, with annual sales of £11.5 billion.

In many firms, productivity is not a direct target. The focus, day by day, is on production, not productivity. After all, it is production which ensures that customer orders are fulfilled. An operations manager, faced with a 10-per-cent increase in orders, may simply ask the workforce to do overtime. The work gets done; the workforce is happy to earn extra money; and it's all rather easy to do. It is harder by far to reorganise the workplace to make production more effective. Managers whose main focus is on the short term, therefore, think of production not productivity.

As shown in Figure 27.3, productivity has been very weak in Britain since 2007. If this continues the economic recovery will stall.

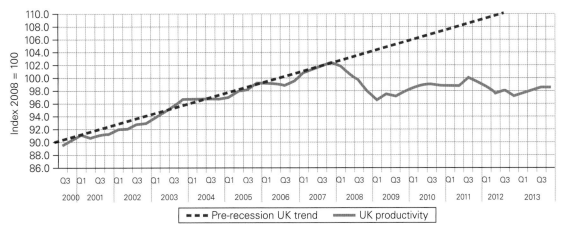

Figure 27.3 UK Productivity Index, output per worker

Source: Office for National Statistics, June 2014

Boosting productivity when markets are static

Everyone in a business is happy when higher sales lead to higher production. Bonuses look more secure and so do the jobs themselves. But productivity is a measure of efficiency, so it is more controversial. If a productivity-boosting production method is introduced to a business in a static market, there is only one possible outcome: job losses. In other words, if production next month is to be 1,000 units, just like last month, better productivity means fewer people will be needed to produce those units. As staff are perfectly aware of this, those working in static markets are very wary of changes to production methods. They resist change because they fear the outcome. In the long term everyone in the business needs to help improve productivity, or else the business will become uncompetitive. But in the short term people worry about their income, their families and so on. So it can be difficult to introduce productivity-boosting measures.

Five Whys and a How

Question	Answer
Why might employees be concerned about moves to increase productivity?	Because if the business operates in a static market, higher productivity probably means fewer jobs
Why might it be hard to measure the productivity of a doctor?	Although you could measure patients seen per month, you couldn't measure the quality of diagnosis and care
Why might it be useful for a manufacturing company to set targets for annual productivity improvement?	Because this would help the business gain competitiveness in relation to UK and overseas rivals
Why may it matter (Fig 27.1) that capital spending in the UK is relatively low?	As capital spending is an important way to boost productivity, low spending is a concern for long-term UK competitiveness
Why (see Fig 27.3) is it a concern that UK productivity growth flattened out between 2007 and 2013?	Because rising efficiency is what creates economic growth. If productivity stays flat Britain's economic growth will be flat as well
How might a service business try to increase productivity?	By getting staff to care more, work smarter and contribute ideas on how the business could work more effectively

Key terms

GDP: Gross Domestic Product is the value of all the goods and services produced in a country in a year.

Job enrichment: giving people the opportunity to use their ability (Professor Herzberg's definition).

Evaluation: Efficiency and labour productivity

Greater labour productivity can lead to greater efficiency and higher profitability. This is because, other things being equal, it lowers the labour cost per unit. However, productivity is only one factor that contributes to a firm's success. A firm must also ensure it produces a good quality product that it is marketed effectively and that costs are controlled. There is little point increasing productivity by 20 per cent if at the same time you pay your staff 30 per cent more. Similarly, there is no point producing more if there is no actual demand. Higher productivity, therefore, contributes to better performance but needs to be accompanied by effective decision-making throughout the firm.

The importance of productivity to a firm depends primarily on the level of value added involved. Top price perfumes such as Chanel have huge profit margins. Production costs are a tiny proportion of the selling price, therefore a 10 per cent productivity increase might have only a marginal effect on profit and virtually none on the competitiveness of the brand. For mass-market products in competitive markets, high productivity is likely to be essential for survival. A 5-per-cent cost advantage might make all the difference. Therefore, when considering an appropriate recommendation for solving a business problem, a judgement is required as to whether boosting productivity is a top priority for the business concerned.

Workbook

A. Revision questions

(40 marks; 45 minutes)

1. What is meant by the term 'unit costs'? (2)

2. What's the difference between 'unit costs' and 'costs per unit'? (3)

3. What would usually happen to unit costs if extra demand led to higher output? (4)

4. Outline three factors that might cause a fall in a firm's productivity. (6)

5. Calculate the change in productivity at AB Co. (see Table 27.2) since last year. (4)

Table 27.2 Productivity at AB Co.

	Output	Number of staff
Last year	6,000	80
This year	7,200	90

6. Explain how capacity utilization and unit costs may be linked. (4)

7. Explain why fixed costs per unit vary as output varies. (4)

8. Calculate the change in productivity at BDQ Co. (see Table 27.3) since last year. (4)

Table 27.3 Productivity at BDQ Co.

	Output	Number of staff
Last year	32,000	50
This year	30,000	40

9. Explain how motivation and productivity may be linked. (4)

10. Explain how productivity might be *too* high. (5)

B. Revision exercises
DATA RESPONSE 1

In developing countries labour is often wasted by employers because it is relatively cheap. The result is workers being profitably employed in low productivity activities such as shoe cleaning, street vending and sandwich boards (a human, walking advertising poster).

Real wages in the UK have fallen sharply over the last decade. This has encouraged some British firms to adopt some of the same methods used by employers in developing countries. Cheap British labour is now being employed in activities that are profitable, but where productivity is very low.

A good example is Domino's pizza. In recent years the takeaway chain has used some of its employees to act as human advertisements. Workers are asked to wave and dance at passing motorists on busy street corners whilst wearing giant pizza boxes featuring the company's brand and details of special promotional prices. The company has defended their use of 'wobble boarding' by claiming that 'it is a key part of our marketing activity'. The use of wobble boards to boost sales of pizza has attracted criticism. In Cambridge local residents wrote letters of complaint arguing that it was demeaning and degrading for young people, including graduates, to be paid minimum wages to act as little more than walking advertisements. Other criticized the adverts on the grounds that they could distract motorists, causing accidents. Presumably, Domino's uses wobble boards because the extra revenue generated from this form of advertising exceeds the wages paid to wobble boarders.

Figure 27.4 Domino's advertising using 'wobble boards'

Questions (35 marks; 40 minutes)

1. How might the manager of a Domino's pizza outlet measure the productivity of their wobble boarders? (4)

2. The manager of a Pizza Express estimates that a team of five wobble boarders working for eight hours daily will boost the restaurant's gross profit by £500 per day. According to the local job centre there will be plenty of people willing to undertake this work at the national minimum wage of £6.50 per hour. Calculate whether it would be profitable for Pizza Express to employ the wobble boarders. (6)

3. Analyse the factors that might cause profitability to be high when productivity is low. (9)

4. To what extent is it ethical to employ graduates to act as human advertisements. (16)

DATA RESPONSE 2

Going potty

Farah Stewart was trying to explain the need to boost productivity to the employees at her ceramics factory, FS Ltd. Relations between Farah and her staff had not been good in recent years. The company was not doing well and she blamed the workers. 'On average you work 8 hours a day at £8 an hour and produce around 160 pots each. Meanwhile at Frandon, I am told, they produce 280 pots a day. Can't you see that this makes it cheaper for them and if things go on like this we'll be out of business? You need to work much harder to get our unit costs down! I know you are expecting to get a pay rise this year, but I cannot afford it until you produce more; then we'll think about it.'

Jeff Battersby, the spokesperson for the employees, was clearly annoyed by Farah's tone. 'Firstly Ms Stewart have you ever considered that if you paid us more we might produce more for you? I'm not surprised productivity is higher at Frandon – they get about £80 a day. There's no point demanding more work from us if you are not willing to pay for it – we're not slaves you know. If you paid us £10 an hour, like Frandon, I reckon we could increase productivity by 50 per cent. However that's not the only issue: they've got better equipment. It's not our fault if the kilns don't work half the time and take an age to heat up. Sort out the equipment and our pay and you'll soon see productivity improve. Why not ask us next time instead of jumping to conclusions?'

Questions (30 marks; 35 minutes)

1. **a)** FS Ltd employs 50 pot makers whilst Frandon Ltd employs 30 people in production. Calculate the total output for each of the two companies. (3)

   b) With reference to FS Ltd and Frandon Ltd explain the difference between 'total output' and 'productivity'. (4)

2. **a)** Calculate the average labour cost per pot at FS Ltd if employees are paid £8 an hour and their daily output is 160 pots each. (4)

   b) What is the wage cost per pot at Frandon? (Assume an 8-hour day.) (3)

3. To what extent might the business benefit from involving employees in discussions about how to improve productivity? (16)

C. Extend your understanding

1. Faced with falling sales and sharply falling market share, the boss at Morrisons' Supermarkets decides to implement a 12-month Productivity Improvement Programme (PIP). Discuss how the boss should set about this task. (20)

2. New competition from Chinese-made cars is undercutting the prices of British-made cars by 35 per cent. To what extent can this problem be overcome by a sustained management programme to boost labour productivity at a British car factory? (20)

Lean production

Linked with: Niche and mass marketing, Chapter 20; Efficiency and labour productivity, Chapter 27; Managing inventory, Chapter 34; Decision-making to improve operational performance, Chapter 35.

Definition

Lean production is a philosophy that aims to produce more using less, by eliminating all forms of waste ('waste' being defined as anything that does not add value to the final product).

28.1 Introduction

The rise of this Japanese approach to production has been unstoppable. The whole approach has been termed 'lean production', though its ideas have been spread more generally to include service businesses as well. It is based upon a combined focus by management and workers on minimising the use of the key business resources: materials, manpower, capital, floor space and time. The main components of lean management are:

- just-in-time (JIT)
- total quality management (TQM)
- time-based management.

Toyota and the origins of lean production

In most industries, new ideas and methods tend to emerge during a period of crisis, when old ideas no longer seem to work. The motor industry is no different. The inspiration came from Eiji Toyoda's three-month visit to Ford's Rouge plant in Detroit in 1950. Eiji's family had set up the Toyota Motor Company in 1937. Now, in Japan's situation of desperate shortages after the Second World War, he hoped to learn from Ford. On his return, Eiji reported that the mass production system at the Rouge plant was riddled with

muda (the Japanese term for wasted effort, materials and time). By analysing the weaknesses of mass production, Toyota was the first company to develop lean production.

Toyota realised that mass production could only be fully economic if identical products could be produced continuously. Yet Henry Ford's statement that 'they can have any colour they want ... as long as it's black' was no longer acceptable to customers. Mass production was also very wasteful, as poor-quality production led to a high reject rate at the end of the production line.

Toyota's solution was to design machines that could be used for many different operations – flexible production. Mass producers took a whole day to change a stamping machine from producing one part to making another. Toyota eventually reduced this time to just three minutes, and so simplified the process that factory line workers could do it without any help from engineers! This carried with it the advantage of flexibility. If buying habits changed in the USA, Ford could not react quickly, because each production line was dedicated to producing a particular product in a particular way. Toyota's multi-purpose machines could adapt quickly to a surge of demand for, for example, open-top cars or right-hand-drive models.

By a process of continuous refinement, Toyota developed the approach to:

- maximise the input from staff
- focus attention upon the quality of supplies and production
- minimise wasted resources in stock through just-in-time.

Above all else, the company was able to turn the spotlight onto product development – to shorten the time between product conception and product launch. With its ability to be 'first-to-market' and its terrific reputation for quality, in 2013 Toyota was the world's No. 1 car producer.

There is nothing so useless as doing efficiently that which shouldn't be done at all.' Peter Drucker, business guru

28.2 The benefits of lean production

Lean production:

- creates higher levels of labour productivity, therefore it uses less labour
- requires less stock, less factory space and less capital equipment than a mass producer of comparable size; the lean producer therefore has substantial cost advantages over the mass producer
- creates substantial marketing advantages: first, it results in far fewer defects, improving quality and reliability for the customer; second, lean production requires half the engineering hours to develop a new product, which means that the lean producer can develop a vast range of products that a mass producer cannot afford to match.

Real business

Pioneered decades ago by carmakers determined to cut waste, those same ideas are now starting to influence modern biotech companies. Innovative R&D is no longer enough, for success there needs to be manufacturing efficiency. So biotech companies are applying 'just-in-time' principles to the equipment and labour aspects of their business.

One example is at the US producer of proteins, Aldevron, which has hired researchers from the University of Wisconsin to study the company's manufacturing processes and outline a strategy for improving efficiency. The company hopes that the university will help shrink the facility's product delivery timeline by at least 25 per cent - shaving a week or two off of a typical four - to five-week process. 'Because our labour force is more expensive, we've got to figure out how to do things faster,' said Aldevron's vice president. The productivity gains from lean manufacturing could help Aldevron fend off overseas manufacturers that provide the same services at cheaper rates.

28.3 The components of lean production

Lean people management

Lean producers reject the waste of human talent involved in narrow, repetitive jobs. They believe in empowerment, team working and job enrichment. Problem solving is not just left to specialist engineers. Employees are trained in preventative maintenance, to spot when a fault is developing and correct it before the production line has to stop. If a problem does emerge on the line, they are trained to solve it without needing an engineer or a supervisor. Teams meet regularly to discuss ways in which their sections could be run more smoothly.

Lean approach to quality

In a mass production system, quality control is a specialised job that takes place at the end of the line. In a lean system, each team is responsible for checking the quality of its own work. If a fault is spotted, every worker has the power to stop the assembly line. This policy prevents errors being passed on, to be corrected only after the fault has been found at the end of the line. The lean approach, therefore, is self-checking at every production stage so that quality failures at the end (or with customers) become extremely rare.

One way to achieve lean quality is total quality management (TQM). This attempts to achieve a culture of quality throughout the organisation, so that the primary objective of all employees is to achieve quality the first time around without the need for any reworking. To achieve total quality, managers must 'make quality the number one, non-negotiable priority, and actively seek and listen to the views of employees on how to improve quality,' (Roger Trapp, in *The Independent*).

Lean design

As consumers become more demanding and technology advances, car design has become highly complex. This threatens to increase costs and development times. Lean producers combat this by simultaneous engineering. This means integrating the development functions so that separate design and engineering stages are tackled at the same time. This speeds up development times, which cuts costs and reduces the risk of early obsolescence.

Lean component supply

The approach to component supply varies greatly from company to company. Mass producers tend to have rather distant relationships with suppliers, often based on minimising the delivery cost per unit. They may buy from several sources to keep up the competitive pressure. The supplier, in turn, may be secretive about costs and profit margins to prevent the buyer from pressing for still lower prices. Lean producers work in partnership with their suppliers or, more often, with a single supplier. They keep the supplier fully informed of new product developments, encouraging ideas and technical advice. This means that by the time the assembly line starts running, errors have been ironed out so there are very few running changes or failures. Both parties are also likely to share financial and sales information electronically. This encourages an atmosphere of trust and common purpose, and aids planning.

'To be competitive, we have to look for every opportunity to improve efficiencies and productivity while increasing quality. Lean manufacturing principles have improved every aspect of our processes.' Cynthia Fanning, general manager, General Electric

---

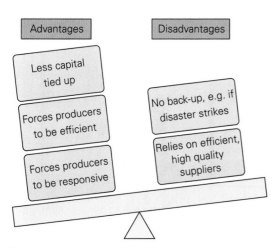

Figure 28.1 Advantages and disadvantages of 'lean' production

28.4 Just-in-time

Lean producers run with minimal buffer stocks, relying on daily or hourly deliveries from trusted suppliers. As there is no safety net, a faulty shipment of components could bring an entire factory to a halt. Mass producers rely on stockpiles, 'just-in-case'.

The just-in-time (JIT) system of manufacturing is perhaps the best-known element of lean production. JIT aims to minimise the costs of holding unnecessary stocks of raw materials, components, work in progress and finished products. The principle that underpins JIT is that production should be 'pulled through' rather than 'pushed through'. This means that production should be for specific customer orders, so that the production cycle starts only once a customer has placed an order with the producer.

Summary of the just-in-time approach

- No buffer stocks of any type are held.
- Production is to order.
- Stock is ordered only when it is needed, just in time.
- Zero defects are essential as no stock safety net exists.
- No 'spare' workers are employed.
- Staff are multi-skilled and capable of filling in for absent colleagues.
- It is used by lean producers.

'Great companies will have strong lean vision in place… and are working daily at getting on with doing a small number of important things consistently – day in, day out.' TXM, Total Excellence Manufacturing

---

The advantages and disadvantages of a JIT system are listed in Table 28.1.

Table 28.1 The advantages and disadvantages of using a JIT system

Advantages of using JIT	Disadvantages of using JIT
- Improves the firm's liquidity - The costs of holding stocks are reduced - Storage space can be converted to a more productive use - Stock wastage and stock rotation become lesser issues for management - Response times to changing demands are speeded up as new components can be ordered instantly	- Any break in supply causes immediate problems for the purchaser - The costs of processing orders may be increased - The purchaser's reputation is placed in the hands of the external supplier

28.5 Time-based management

Time-based management involves managing time in the same way most companies manage costs, quality or stock. Time-based manufacturers try to shorten rather than lengthen production runs in order to reduce costs and to increase levels of customer satisfaction. To do this, manufacturers invest in flexible capital; that is, machines that can make more than one model. Training must also be seen as a priority because staff have to be multi-skilled.

Time-based management creates five benefits:

1. By reducing lead and set-up times, productivity improves, creating a cost advantage.

2. Shortening lead times cuts customer response times, increasing consumer satisfaction as customers receive their orders sooner.

3. Lower stock holding costs: short lead and set-up times make firms more responsive to changes in the market. Consequently there should be less need for long production runs and stockpiles of finished products. If demand does suddenly increase, production can simply be quickly restarted.

4. An ability to offer the consumer a more varied product range without losing cost-reducing economies of scale. Time-based management therefore makes market segmentation a much cheaper strategy to operate.

5. Keeping time under tight control can help achieve first-mover advantage if you can get your new product out before rivals get theirs to market.

Real business

Time-based management

Zara is a fashion retailing phenomenon built on an understanding of the importance of time. When Christian Dior featured a glamorous embroidered Afghan coat on the catwalk, Zara had its own version in its shops within a fortnight. It was able to design, manufacture and distribute the coat to its shops throughout Europe within 14 days – and sell it for just £95. If a style doesn't succeed within a week, it is withdrawn. No style stays on the shop floor for more than four weeks. The immediate result is obvious. Fashion- and price-conscious women flock to Zara.

Less obviously, Zara benefits from a vital secondary factor. In Spain, Zara's home country, an average high-street clothes store expects its regular customers to visit three times a year. Yet the average is 17 times for Zara! As the stock is constantly changing, the store is constantly worth visiting. Zara's owner started the business with €25 in 1963; today he is one of the world's three richest men, with wealth of over $60 billion. Time well spent.

Figure 28.2 Zara

Key terms

First-mover advantage: the benefits to distribution and brand credibility from beating rivals to the market with an innovative new product.

Just-in-time: producing with minimum stock levels so every process must be completed just in time for the process that follows.

Kaizen: continuous improvement (that is, encouraging all staff to regularly come up with ideas to improve efficiency and quality).

Total quality management: a passion for quality that starts at the top, then spreads throughout the organisation.

Five Whys and a How

Question	Answer
Why isn't mass production more efficient than lean production?	Because it relies on everyone wanting the same. In fact, people love products to be tailor-made to their own requirements
Why do mass producers hold stocks of finished goods, 'just-in-case'?	Because they aren't sure what future demand will be, so they keep stocks just in case they're needed
Why are lean producers likely to have higher-than-average profit margins?	Their production methods save costs by cutting out waste, while adding value by customising products to match exact tastes
Why is just-in-time so popular with grocery chains such as Tesco?	Because stock forms a huge part of their total costs, so it's vital to minimise it
Why are lean producers particularly reliant on keen, well-trained staff?	Eliminating waste requires staff involvement, as it's the staff who know best where the production process has weaknesses
How might a business set about moving from mass production to lean production?	It needs to establish a new culture based on trusting and giving authority to staff; it's a mistake to assume it's to do with mechanisation or robots.

Evaluation: Lean production

Some of the arguments put forward above could be criticised for being too black and white (mass production = terrible; lean production = wonderful). The reality of business is often to do with shades of grey, with some lean producers having their own weaknesses. Some trends are unarguable, however. When people first started writing about the Toyota production system, Toyota was a failure compared with the giant US car producers Ford and General Motors. Today Toyota is the world's No. 1 car maker.

However, there is a downside. By definition, lean thinking involves the elimination of waste. This waste could be over-manning. So by switching to a leaner system the consequence could be redundancies. In this context, lean management becomes little more than a 'fig leaf' that a ruthless manager may wish to hide behind when seeking to justify controversial staffing decisions.

Workbook

A. Revision questions

(35 marks; 35 minutes)

1. State the three components of lean production. (3)

2. State three problems of mass production. (3)

3. Distinguish between just-in-time and just-in-case. (4)

4. What advantages are there in using time-based management? (4)

5. Why is it important to reduce machine set-up times? (3)

6. What are the opportunity costs of holding too much stock? (4)

7. Outline possible sources of waste in any organisation with which you are familiar. (Your school? Your part-time employer?) (4)

8. What is reworking and why does it add to costs? (5)

9. Why could it be important to be first to the market with a new product idea? (5)

B. Revision exercises
DATA RESPONSE

Operations management and the Airbus A350

The baker round the corner from my house often grumbles about the impossibility of predicting daily customer demand. He hates being left with unsold bread, but also hates selling out at midday then spending his afternoon apologising to disappointed customers. But compared with the aircraft manufacturing business, baking is a doddle. The bar chart shows the crazily unpredictable sales of the Airbus A350 plane – each one listed at a price of around $275 million. Orders in 2013 alone, therefore, were worth around $63 billion. As Britain receives 40 per cent of the value of each plane (we make the wings and Rolls Royce makes the aero engines) these orders mean huge amounts in terms of orders and exports.

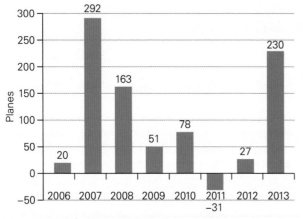

Figure 28.3 Net orders for the Airbus A350 plane

But how does Airbus manage its production in the light of such erratic demand? Well, although Airbus launched the A350 in 2006, it was still in development until the maiden flight in mid-2013. In the meantime it accumulated over 800 firm orders for the plane. Production started in late 2013 at a rate of just 1 plane a month. Although it had only just started, time was taken expanding the assembly line in Toulouse, France, to allow for growth in the future. By the end of 2014 they will be producing 3 per month and by the end of 2015 maximum capacity will have risen to 10 A350s a month. Airbus is very optimistic about this plane, expecting to deliver its first planes early to its first customers. This has surprised many observers because more than 50 per cent of the plane is made from new, light, composite materials – and high technology in aircraft has traditionally been a cause of late rather than early deliveries.

The world's duopoly plane manufacturers have such huge order books that Kuwait's 10 A 350s will not be delivered until 2018 – that is part of the purchase agreement. So even though demand is highly erratic, production works steadily through a huge order book, one plane at a time.

Questions (25 marks; 30 minutes)

1. Given the erratic demand, analyse the significance of the statement: 'by the end of 2015 maximum capacity will have risen to 10 A350s a month'? (9)

2. Based on the bar chart and the text, to what extent would Airbus benefit from a move to JIT plane manufacture for the A350? (16)

C. Extend your understanding

1. To what extent should managers ignore the short-term difficulties faced when switching to lean methods of production? (20)

2. Evaluate why some firms seem far better than others in terms of their ability to successfully implement lean production techniques. (20)

Capacity utilisation

Linked with: Efficiency and labour productivity, Chapter 27; Technology and operational efficiency, Chapter 30; Analysing operational performance, Chapter 31.

Definition

Capacity utilisation measures a firm's output level as a percentage of the firm's maximum output level. A football stadium is at full capacity when all the seats are filled.

29.1 The importance of capacity

Few products have completely predictable sales (baked beans? Marmite?) and therefore there is a fine balance to be struck between using your factory capacity fully and therefore efficiently, and yet having the wiggle room to meet unexpectedly high orders.

So it is vital to have sufficient spare capacity to cope with higher demand, while keeping maximum capacity low enough to keep costs down: a fine balance.

29.2 How is capacity utilisation measured?

Capacity utilisation is measured using the formula:

$$\frac{\text{current output}}{\text{maximum possible output}} \times 100$$

What does capacity depend upon? A firm's maximum output level is determined by the quantity of buildings, machinery and labour it has available. Maximum capacity is achieved when the firm is making full use of all the buildings, machinery and labour available, that is, 100 per cent capacity utilisation.

For a service business the same logic applies, though it is much harder to identify a precise figure. This

is because it may take a different time to serve each customer. Many service businesses cope with fluctuating demand by employing temporary or part-time staff. These employees provide a far greater degree of flexibility to employers. Part-time hours can be increased, or extra temporary staff can be employed to increase capacity easily. If demand falls, temporary staff can be laid off without redundancy payments, or part-time staff can have their hours reduced, thus reducing capacity easily and cheaply.

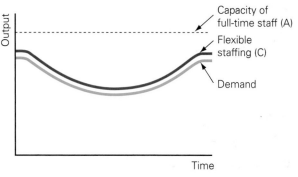

Figure 29.1 How flexible staffing can reduce wastage implied by having under-used full-time staff

29.3 How to utilise capacity efficiently

Fixed costs are fixed in relation to output. This means that whether capacity utilisation is 50 per cent or 100 per cent, fixed costs will not change. So if a football club invests in an expensive playing staff (whose salaries are a fixed cost) but matches are played to a half-empty stadium, the fixed costs will become a huge burden. This is because the very fact that fixed costs do not change *in total* as output changes means that they do change *per unit* of output/demand. A half-empty stadium means that the fixed costs per unit are double the level at maximum capacity (see Table 29.1).

Table 29.1 Fixed costs and capacity

	Full stadium	Half-empty stadium
	50,000 fans	25,000 fans
Weekly salary bill (fixed costs)	£750,000	£750,000
Salary fixed cost per fan	£15	£30
	(£750,000/50,000)	(£750,000/25,000)

When the capacity utilisation of the stadium is at 50 per cent, then £30 of the ticket price is needed for the players' wages alone. The many other fixed and variable costs of running a football club would be on top of this, of course.

The reason why capacity utilisation is so important is that it has an inverse (opposite) effect upon fixed costs per unit. In other words, when utilisation is high, fixed costs are spread over many units. This cuts the cost per unit, which enables the producer either to cut prices to boost demand further, or to enjoy larger profit margins. If utilisation is low, fixed costs per unit become punishingly high. In June 2014 a newspaper in Zimbabwe reported that manufacturing capacity utilisation had fallen in the last year by 10 per cent to 30 per cent. According to the report, firms had reduced output in response to falling demand. This would make fixed costs per unit three times higher than necessary, which is an almost impossible situation.

The ideal level of capacity utilisation, therefore, is at or near 100 per cent. This spreads fixed costs as thinly as possible, boosting profit margins. There are two key concerns about operating at maximum capacity for long, however. These are the risks that:

1. if demand rises further, you will have to turn it away, enabling your competitors to benefit, and
2. you will struggle to service the machinery and train/retrain staff. This may prove costly in the long term and will increase the chances of production breakdowns in the short term.

The production ideal, therefore, is a capacity utilisation of around 90 per cent.

'On a hot summer's day we're churning out ice cream at our absolute maximum. And it hurts.'
Matteo Pantani, founder of Scoop, Covent Garden

Real business

In 2014, suffering from a sharp downturn in sales at its biggest stores, Tesco re-evaluated the size of its car parks. Their average utilisation rate had fallen to an all-time low. In response it invited Avis car hire to take over sections of the big store car parks. For Avis, it could be a winner: 'We think this will work really well for customers who want a convenient place to pick up their hire car and do a quick shop before heading off on their travels.' For Tesco it reduces the waste involved in empty car spaces. It increases Tesco's capacity utilisation and therefore (slightly) reduces costs per customer.

29.4 How to get towards full capacity utilisation

If a firm's capacity utilisation is an unsatisfactory 45 per cent, how could it be increased to a more acceptable level of around 90 per cent? There are two possible approaches, as discussed below.

Increase demand (in this case, double it!)

Demand for existing products could be boosted by extra promotional spending, price-cutting or – more fundamentally – devising a new strategy to reposition the products into growth sectors. If supermarket own-label products are flourishing, perhaps offer to produce under the Tesco or Sainsbury's banner. If doubling of sales is needed, it is unlikely that existing products will provide the whole answer. The other approach is to launch new products. This could be highly effective, but implies long-term planning and investment.

Cut capacity

If your current factory and labour force is capable of producing 10,000 units a week, but there is demand for only 4,500, there will be a great temptation to cut capacity to 5,000. This may be done by cutting out the night shift (that is, making those workers redundant). This would avoid the disruption and inflexibility caused by the alternative, which is to move to smaller premises. Moving will enable all fixed costs to be cut (rent, rates, salaries, and so on) but may look silly if, six months later, demand has recovered to 6,000 units when your new factory capacity is only 5,000.

How to select the best option

A key factor in deciding whether to cut capacity or boost demand is the underlying cause of the low utilisation. It may be the result of a known temporary demand shortfall, such as a seasonal low point in the toy business. Or it may be due to an economic recession, which (on past experience) may hit demand for around 18 to 24 months. Either way, it could prove to be a mistake in the long run to cut capacity. Nevertheless, if a firm faces huge short-term losses from its excess fixed costs, it may have to forget the future and concentrate on short-term survival.

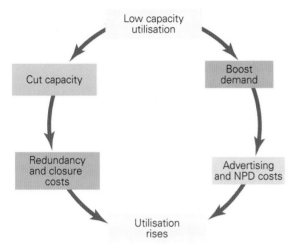

Figure 29.2 Logic chain: improving capacity utilisation

29.5 Capital and labour intensity

A further factor affecting production efficiency concerns the balance struck between capital- and labour-intensive production. Measuring up a bride-to-be and then making a wedding dress by hand is the ultimate in labour-intensive production. However hard the dressmaker works, his or her productivity will be very low. This is because so little can be mechanised or automated. By contrast, a dress designer for Topshop may be able to order 5,000 identical size 10 dresses to be distributed across the Topshop stores. This batch of 5,000 can be produced largely by machine (that is, through capital- rather than labour-intensive production).

The importance of this topic is that it points to a huge opportunity for small firms. In almost every industry there is scope for some labour-intensive production. This is because there are always some people who want – and can afford – an entirely individual product. In addition, there are businesses where labour-intensive production is inevitable, such as plumbing, advertising (creating and producing commercials), legal advice and running a school. Starting a new car-manufacturing firm will be massively expensive and make you compete head-on with huge firms. Starting a new advertising agency has neither problem.

Labour-intensive production

Labour-intensive production:

- means that labour costs form a high percentage of total costs

- has low financial barriers to entry, because it is cheap to start up production
- makes it necessary for management to focus on the cost of labour (making it especially attractive to switch production to a low-cost country such as Cambodia)
- has the advantage of being highly flexible, making it possible for a small firm to operate successfully without direct competition from a large one.

'When a man tells you that he got rich through hard work, ask him whose.' Don Marquis, author and playwright

Capital-intensive production

Capital-intensive production:

- has a large percentage of its total costs tied up in the fixed costs of purchasing and operating machinery
- has high financial barriers to entry
- may be able to keep producing in a high-cost country because labour costs are such a small proportion of the total costs (for example, mass production of Coca-Cola or Heinz Beans)
- can be inflexible, both in terms of switching from one product to another, and in the ability to tailor a product to an individual customer.

'Capital intensive production is great on the way up, but trouble on the way down.' Anon

Figure 29.3 Labour- vs. capital-intensive production

29.6 How to choose the optimum mix of resources

There are three main targets focused on by operations managers:

1. quality targets (for example, to have no more than 1 in 100 customers demand a refund)
2. capacity utilisation targets (such as, that the factory should be working at 85 to 95 per cent of its maximum possible capacity)

3. unit costs (for instance, keeping the average cost per unit at below £1.99 in order to keep the selling price below £2.99).

The optimum mix between these is the best compromise that can be found – which may mean that none of the three targets is met at its ideal point. Companies have to start by choosing the degree of automation they think they require, that is, where on the spectrum between absolute labour-intensive and absolute capital-intensive production, then the actual level of capacity utilisation will kick in. Ideally, the production mix should mean a compromise between cost efficiency and the ability to respond flexibly to changing customer requirements.

Five Whys and a How

Question	Answer
Why is a company's capacity utilisation an important non-accounting ratio?	Because it gives insight into unit costs, the effectiveness of its marketing strategy and the job security of its staff
Why might a company's capacity utilisation vary during the year?	For a seasonal business such as hotels, it will be much harder to sell rooms in the winter than the summer
Why might a struggling business choose not to cut its maximum capacity level during a recession?	It may be confident that the end of the recession will see a recovery in sales, i.e. that it would be short-sighted to cut capacity today, then run out of capacity tomorrow
Why may companies move from labour-intensive to capital-intensive production as they get bigger?	Increased scale of production provides scope for increasing specialisation and then automation of the relatively simple, repetitive tasks
Why are labour-intensive products likely to be made in developing countries?	Labour-intensive means that labour costs will be a relatively high proportion of total costs; so it makes sense to look for production locations where labour is cheap
How might a business boost its capacity utilisation?	Either find a way to increase demand/usage or cut the maximum capacity at the existing premises

Key terms

Downtime: any period when machinery is not being used in production. Some downtime is necessary for maintenance, but too much may suggest incompetence.

Excess capacity: when there is more capacity than justified by current demand (that is, utilisation is low).

Rationalisation: reorganising in order to increase efficiency. This often implies cutting capacity to increase the percentage of utilisation.

Evaluation: Capacity utilisation

Most firms aim to operate close to full capacity but probably not at 100 per cent. A small amount of spare capacity is accepted as necessary, bringing a certain degree of flexibility. In this way, sudden surges of demand can be coped with in the short run by increasing output, or downtime can be used for maintenance.

Firms operating close to full capacity are those that may be considering investing in new premises or machinery. Building new factories takes time, as well as huge quantities of money. Can the firm afford to wait 18 months for its capacity to be expanded? Perhaps the firm would be better served subcontracting certain areas of its work to other companies, thus freeing capacity.

Capacity utilisation also raises the difficult issue of cutting capacity by rationalisation and, often, redundancy. This incorporates many issues of human resource management, motivation and social responsibility. There are fewer more important tests of the skills and far-sightedness of senior managers.

Workbook

A. Revision questions

(40 marks; 40 minutes)

1. What is meant by the phrase '100 per cent capacity utilisation'? (3)

2. At what level of capacity utilisation will fixed costs per unit be lowest for any firm? Briefly explain your answer. (4)

3. What formula is used to calculate the capacity utilisation of a firm? (2)

4. How can a firm increase its capacity utilisation without increasing output? (3)

5. If a firm is currently selling 11,000 units per month and this represents a capacity utilisation of 55 per cent, what is its maximum capacity? (4)

6. Use the information given in Table 29.2 to calculate profit per week at 50 per cent, 75 per cent and 100 per cent capacity utilisation. (8)

Table 29.2 A firm's data

Maximum capacity	80 units per week
Variable cost per unit	£1,800
Total fixed cost per week	£150,000
Selling price	£4,300

7. Briefly explain the risks of operating at 100 per cent capacity utilisation for any extended period of time. (5)

8. Outline two benefits to a business of using labour-intensive production methods. (4)

9. Explain why a business might want to achieve the optimum rather than the maximum when setting operational objectives. (4)

10. Explain why the manufacture of the Mini car might benefit from capital-intensive production. (3)

B. Revision exercises
DATA RESPONSE

Ryanair load factors

The Irish low-cost airline, Ryanair carried over 81 million passengers in 2013, making it the world's most popular airline. The company's success is based on highly efficient operations management. The low fares charged by Ryanair will only generate profit if the company can minimise its costs. To that end the airline only operates with one type of plane, the Boeing 737. This decision enables the company to benefit from a range of economies of scale. Some airlines operate with leased planes, others like Ryanair buy outright. In July 2014 a Boeing 737 could be leased for $463 000 per month or bought outright for $81 million; either way the fixed costs are significant. In these circumstances load factors (the phrase used in the aviation business for capacity utilisation) must be kept very high in order to dilute the punishing fixed costs. The tactics used by Ryanair to achieve high load factors include:

- charging low prices
- reducing seat pitch – by removing some leg room extra rows of seats can be crammed into each plane

- fast turnarounds in-between flights, ensuring the each plane spends as much time in the air as possible earning revenue.

According to the Centre for Aviation in March 2014, the number of passengers carried by Ryanair grew by over 7 per cent compared to the previous year and their load factor averaged 78 per cent.

Questions (30 marks; 35 minutes)

1. a) A Boeing 737 can accommodate 213 passengers when full. Calculate the load factor of a flight carrying 150 passengers. (2)

   b) The operating cost of flying a 737 is approximately £7,000 per hour. What would be the average cost per passenger of a two-hour flight to Ibiza assuming a load factor of 70 per cent. (3)

   c) What would the new average cost per passenger be for the same flight if the load factor can be increased to 95 per cent? (3)

2. Other than price, explain two tactics Ryanair could employ in order to increase its load factors. (6)

3. In recent years Ryanair has been on the receiving end of bad publicity regarding the quality of its customer service. To what extent could this be due to the airline's high load factors/capacity utilisation. (16)

C. Extend your understanding

1. Discuss the implications of a decision by Arsenal FC to increase its stadium capacity from 60,000 to 80,000. (By all means substitute for Arsenal any other sports club with which you are familiar.) (20)

2. Due to a significant change in shopping habits Tesco finds that its huge Tesco Extra shops are 40 per cent under-utilised. Evaluate the strategies Tesco might adopt to overcome this problem. (20)

Technology and operational efficiency

Linked to: Setting operational objectives, Chapter 26; Efficiency and labour productivity, Chapter 27; Analysing operational performance, Chapter 31; Decision-making to improve operational performance, Chapter 35.

Definition

Technology means the computer hardware and software used to automate systems, and to handle, analyse and communicate business data.

30.1 Introduction

Information technology (IT) applications in business are various and rapidly changing. Often, the changes that occur are to processing speed and business jargon; the essential tasks remain the same. Many commentators have pointed out how minor have been the changes brought about by the internet compared with the coming of railways and then the motor car. It may be, though, that the biggest changes are still to come. Certainly an idea such as Google's self-drive car paints a possible future that could be hugely different. Van driving may be automated, leaving drivers unemployed; dramatic cost-reductions in robotics may mean the end of McJobs; and online teaching platforms may cut into that profession. The big changes to operational efficiency may be to come.

Key technology applications that can boost efficiency:

- automated stock control systems
- computer-aided design (CAD)
- 3D printing

- robotics
- communicating with suppliers, including electronic data interchange (EDI).

30.2 Automated stock control systems

Modern stock control systems are based on laser scanning of bar-coded information. This ensures the computer knows the exact quantity of each product/size/colour that has come into the stockroom. In retail outlets, a laser-scanning till is then used to record exactly what has been sold. This allows the store's computer to keep up-to-date records of current stocks of every item. This data can enable a buyer to decide how much extra to order, or an electronic link with the supplier can re-order automatically (see Section 30.6).

All this information will be held in the form of a database. This makes it easy for the firm to carry out an aged stock analysis: the computer provides a printout showing the stock in order of age. Table 30.1 shows a list of stock in a clothes shop, with the oldest first. It enables the manager to make informed decisions about what to do now and in the future. In this case:

- Big price reductions seem to be called for on the first five items; they have been around too long.
- There should be fewer orders in future for size 8 dresses.

'Computers are useless. They can only give you answers.' Pablo Picasso, artist

---

Table 30.1 An example of aged stock analysis

Garment	Received (days ago)	Number received	In stock today
Green *Fabrice* dress, size 8	285	2	1
Blue *Channelle* dress, size 14	241	1	1
Red *Channelle* dress, size 8	241	2	2
Red *Grigio* jacket, size 10	249	4	3
Black *Grigio* dress, size 8	205	3	2
Black *Fabrice* dress, size 12	192	2	1
Blue *Florentine* suit, size 8	179	1	1

30.3 Design technology

Computer-aided design (CAD) has been around for more than 20 years, but is now affordable and hugely powerful. Before CAD, product designers, engineers and architects drew their designs by hand. A CAD system works digitally, allowing designs to be saved, changed and reworked without starting from scratch. Even better, CAD can show a 3D version of a drawing and rotate to show the back and sides.

For multinationals such as Sony, a product designed in Tokyo can be sent electronically to Sony offices in America and Europe, for local designers to tweak the work to make it better suited to local tastes. And when work is behind schedule, designers in Tokyo can pass a design on to London at the end of the Japanese working day; then the design can be sent on to America. The time differences mean that 24-hour working can be kept up.

The benefits of CAD systems to successful design are that:

- The data generated by a CAD system can be linked to computer-aided manufacturing (CAM) to provide integrated, highly accurate production.
- They are hugely beneficial for businesses that are constantly required to provide designs that are unique, yet based on common principles (for example, designing a new bridge, car or office block).
- CAD improves the productivity of designers and also helps them to be more ambitious; the extraordinary buildings of Frank Gehry could not have been produced without CAD (because only computers could calculate whether the unusual structures would fall down in a high wind).

Figure 30.2 A Frank Gehry building which might not have been possible without CAD

30.4 3D printing

3D printers can make three-dimensional solid objects of almost any shape from a digital design/model. The printer works by adding layer after layer of material (such as plastic resin) to build up the shape. This enables businesses to print a prototype of a new car part, or false tooth or high-heeled shoe. In turn, this makes prototyping hugely cheaper than the traditional method of designing and building machines simply to produce a single item. A modern 3D printer costs around £3,000 and would provide the scope to make hundreds of different prototype designs.

In 2014 there was a great deal of discussion about whether 3D printing could become a new method of cost-effective, flexible manufacturing. In particular there was a hope that it would work for small-scale batch production, for example, of 10 pairs of size 7 shoes. If this could be done to the right quality standard it might make it possible for individuals to design and manufacture products at home, then perhaps sell them online.

'The most impressive part (of 3D printing): economies of scale cease to be an issue' Brad Hart, Forbes magazine

Real business

In April 2014 it was reported that a Chinese business called Winsun had produced ten detached houses using 3D-printers and a superfast-drying concrete mixture made of waste materials. Each had been created at a cost of less than £3,000 according to Winsun's chief executive, Ma Yihe, who went on to say: 'We can print buildings to any digital design our customers bring us. It's fast and cheap.' The house may not look great, but in a world where millions need a home, this technology will surely find a market.

30.5 Robotics

Industrial robots are fundamental to the car industry worldwide and are becoming increasingly important in the production of electrical goods such as TVs and computers. Nevertheless, it remains a bit of a surprise that robots have not become a more powerful force in industry. Thirty years ago, people assumed that few workers would be left in factories – the robots were coming. In Britain today there are fewer than 50 robots per 10,000 workers. Even in Japan (with more than

40 per cent of the world's robots) the figure is only 500 robots per 10,000 manufacturing workers.

Figure 30.3 shows that despite the dip in worldwide sales of industrial robots during the 2009 recession, sales have boomed since. The single biggest growth market since 2009 has been China.

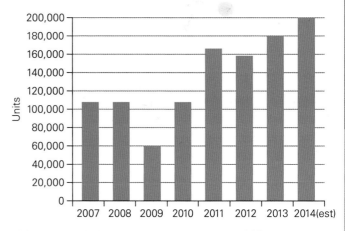

Figure 30.3 Industrial robot sales worldwide, 2007–14

Source: World Robotics Report, IFR Statistical Department

Real business

Toshiba robots

Three Toshiba robots are used at a pet food factory in Bremen, northern Germany. The company has made substantial investment in factory automation in order to improve productivity. Toshiba Machine robots now package birdseed sticks at a rate of 90 per minute. Where once there were seven people working on the application across three shifts, now three Toshiba Machine TH490 robots achieve the same results. The people have been redeployed across the plant.

The robots are part of a production line that manufactures birdseed sticks that are like a fat-based lollypop, embedded with nuts and seeds. The sticks are fed down three conveyors, each with a ceiling-mounted robot at its end. As this happens, the boxes are fed down another conveyor. A robot gripper then picks up the seed sticks and transfers them into boxes on a moving conveyor. Ceiling-mounted SCARA robots make the best use of the available work area.

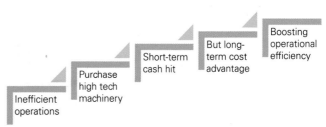

Figure 30.4 Logic ladder: boosting operational efficiency

30.6 Communication with suppliers

Electronic data interchange (EDI)

EDI is a permanent link between computers on different sites, enabling specified types of data to be exchanged. By establishing an EDI link, firms can ensure that the latest information is available instantly to other branches of their business, or even to other businesses. For example, Heinz's link with Tesco enables it to see how sales of soups are going this week. If chicken soup sales have pushed ahead by 20 per cent (perhaps because of being featured on a TV programme), production increases can be planned, even before the Tesco head office phones through with a large order. This makes a just-in-time operation far more feasible.

Five Whys and a How

Question	Answer
Why do workers fear the growth of lower-cost new technologies?	Because they *are* a threat to jobs, especially in the short term
Why may automated stock control systems help with firms' cash flow?	Because accurate stock records and ordering should allow lower buffer stocks and therefore less cash tied up in stock
Why might 3D printing 'democratise' manufacturing?	One day, from their own homes, people may be able to design and 'print' shoes, vacuum flasks or whatever – and sell them online (cutting into the power of big business)
Why might physical shops survive, despite the rise of online shopping?	Because shopping remains an important social/leisure/fun activity for many
Why might it seem surprising that the big growth in industrial robots is in China?	Because Chinese wages have always been very low compared with the West, making it surprising that robots would be cost-effective in China
How might new technology affect schools in coming years?	It is now possible to have one 'super-teacher' leading a class that is taken online by every school in the country. It's hard to imagine that this won't be tried in future.

Evaluation: Technology and operational efficiency

Years ago managers at Guinness thought change management was a technical question. When a change was needed, such as a new distribution system, they hired consultants whose main focus was to establish effective information technology links. Time after time they were disappointed by the results. Improvements began only when they realised that the key variable was not the technology but the people. Not only were results better if staff were consulted fully but, also, the new systems were successful only if staff applied them with enthusiasm and confidence.

Technology is only a set of tools. It can form the basis of a major competitive advantage, as with easyJet's early move into online booking. More often, though, the successful application of IT relies on good understanding of customer and staff needs and wants. This suggests that good management of information technology is no different from good management generally.

'One machine can do the work of fifty ordinary men. No machine can do the work of one extraordinary man.'
Elbert Hubbard, nineteenth century writer

Workbook
A. Revision questions

(35 marks; 35 minutes)

1. A database could be used by an aircraft manufacturer such as Boeing to record the supplier and batch number of every part used on every aircraft. How could this information be used? (3)

2. State two benefits of good database management in achieving efficient stock control. (2)

3. Read the Real business on Triumph. Identify one benefit and one drawback of keeping all design work in the UK. (2)

4. Look at Figure 30.3. Explain one possible implication for:
   a) a UK factory owner feeling under pressure from competition from China (3)
   b) a UK worker, with few qualifications or skills, who is thinking of taking a job in a factory. (3)

5. Explain one benefit and one drawback of computer-aided manufacture (CAM). (4)

6. From your reading of the whole unit, outline three ways in which technology can lead to improved quality. (6)

7. How significant could online shopping become for each of the following types of business?
   a) a music shop specialising in 1980s classic pop and rock (2)
   b) a builders' merchant (selling bricks, cement, etc.) (2)
   c) a firm specialising in made-to-measure 3D-printed hats. (2)

8. From your reading of the whole unit, explain two ways in which technology can reduce waste within a business. (6)

B. Revision exercises
DATA RESPONSE

Printed fashion

Operations management has long required the co-ordination of a complex series of processes: R&D and product development; production engineering; the production process itself, part-internal and part-outsourced; ordering materials and components; storing finished stock; and on-time delivery. Part of the complexity comes from tension between designers who want to create magical new products and engineers who want products that can be manufactured with ease, efficiency and reliability.

All that may be about to change. Suddenly the process of manufacturing may come under the control of the designer. Welcome to the world of 3D printing (also known as 'additive manufacture'). The 3D printer simply adds layer after layer of material that is moulded into a seamless, strong product. In future, young designers will be able to produce finished goods from their own bedrooms, without needing skilled craftsmen to do the work.

Figure 30.5 shows a 3D printed shoe made from woven nylon. The heel is (virtually) unbreakable

Figure 30.5 A 3D printed shoe

and the delicate, thin 'straps' are very strong nylon. Shoes like this are designed using 3D Computer-Aided Design (CAD) software, allowing prototypes to be 3D printed then trialled.

Today, if you want to buy a pair, they will be made to fit your foot size exactly, that is, made-to-measure and printed-to-order. So producers hold no finished goods stock and the designer controls the whole process – from idea to design to finished product.

The *Financial Times* reported on 27 January 2013 that a trends think-tank believed: 'Brands could use it (3D printing) to enhance the in-store experience.

Burberry could invite customers to print their own personalised sunglasses designs and have them ready to go in minutes. The process would still be branded but would invite the customer in'.

3D printing hit Paris Fashion Week in January 2013 with garments such as the dress shown in Figure 30.6. In the past, 3D printing only worked in hard materials such as plastic, but now it's possible with softer polyurethanes.

Figure 30.6 3D-printed clothes at Paris Fashion Week

'The ability to vary softness and elasticity inspired us to design a "second skin" for the body, acting as armour-in-motion,' said co-designer, Neri Oxman. 'In this way we were able to design not only the garment's form but also its motion.'

Questions (30 marks; 35 minutes)

1. Explain how 3D printing might make a business more able to meet customer expectations. (4)

2. Small fashion businesses can find it hard to match production and demand. Examine two ways in which 3D printing might help such businesses. (10)

3. To what extent might 3D printing help a fashion business develop and manage its operations effectively? (16)

C. Extend your understanding

1. Information technology is reducing the need to meet people face to face. To what extent might this change the best way to run a successful business? (20)

2. 'Internet retailing will mean the death of the high street.' To what extent do you agree with this? (20)

Analysing operational performance

Linked with: Efficiency and labour productivity, Chapter 27; Capacity utilisation, Chapter 29; Technology and operational efficiency, Chapter 30.

Definition

Operational performance is monitored regularly by businesses in order to ensure that the business remains competitive.

31.1 What is operational performance?

Ultimately, operational performance can be measured in three ways:

- What's the total unit cost to get the right product to meet the consumer's requirement? And how does that compare with rivals?
- Does the quality of the product and service create customer delight? Or satisfaction? Or mild disappointment? Or 'I'm going to fill social media with my disgust'?
- Does the price charged create enough of a premium over the unit cost to make the business sustainable and profitable in the long term?

To understand competitiveness and unit costs, it is helpful to look at three factors: labour productivity, capacity utilisation and issues surrounding a company's total available capacity.

31.2 Labour productivity

Labour productivity measures the amount produced per worker over a given time. For example, the Nissan factory in Sunderland has a productivity rate of 100 cars per worker per year. Interestingly, though, Nissan first achieved this productivity level in 1998!

By 2014 its productivity level had hardly changed. Fortunately this didn't matter too much to the business, because Nissan in 2014 was making car models such as Qashqai and the all-electric Leaf. These are cars that are so distinctive that customers are thinking about the brand-tag not the price-tag. When the Nissan factory opened in 1990 it employed just 450 people. By 2014 this figure had risen to more than 7,000. Successful operational performance is about profitable sales, not an obsession with productivity (or any other performance measure). For more detail on productivity and how it can be improved, go to Chapter 27.

$$\text{Productivity formula: } \frac{\text{Output per unit of time}}{\text{Number of workers}}$$

Example: 24 staff produce 720 vacuum cleaners a day, so

$$\text{productivity} = \frac{720}{24} = 30 \text{ units per worker per day.}$$

31.3 Difficulties measuring productivity

Productivity is said to be output per worker, per time period. A few moments' thought, though, makes that seem unsatisfactory. Nissan's Sunderland car factory makes 100 cars per worker per year. But what if it's doing little more than assembling sections of cars made at other factories? It may be that a car factory operating at 50 cars per worker per year is really more productive. They may be making some of the parts on-site and doing a great deal more assembly and paint work. Comparing the productivity of different factories is actually very difficult.

The ideal measure for comparison would be added value per worker, such as the value of all the finished cars minus the cost of all the bought-in components and services, divided by the number of workers. Even then there would be problems. As a Range Rover has a higher price tag than a comparable Ford, the value added would be higher – so the marketing achievement of a higher price tag would artificially affect the productivity measure. Oh for a simple life.

The situation can be even harder in service businesses where there is no concrete way to measure output. This is one reason why working at telephone call centres can be so frustrating. 'Metrics' such as calls answered per hour can obstruct an employee who wants to help a caller, but needs time to be able to do so. A really caring approach equates to low productivity and

perhaps a stern word from the boss. And then there's the attempt to apply productivity metrics to the NHS – heart operations per hour, perhaps?

31.4 Unit costs

Unit costs (also known as costs per unit and as average costs) are important in business, but quite tricky to deal with. The problem comes from the nature of fixed costs.

Worked example

Fixed costs per unit

Your sister is in her 'leaving year' at school and is excited about the prom. She wants to go by limo and enquires about the price. The limo will cost £240 for an hour. If she goes by herself that's a lot of money. If she could get three others to come it'll just be £60 each. Actually, there's room for five others. The fixed costs per unit work out as follows.

Table 31.1 Hiring a limo

Number of passengers paying	Total fixed cost	Fixed cost per unit (per person)
1	£240	£240
2	£240	£120
3	£240	£80
4	£240	£60
5	£240	£48
6	£240	£40

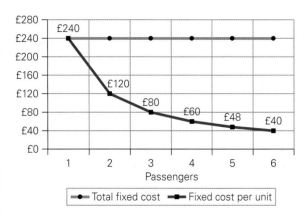

Figure 31.1 Converting Table 31.1 into a line graph

After booking the limo the supplier phones up and offers a special catering option: food and unlimited soft drinks for an extra £20 per person. That would add £20 to the total if your sister goes alone, but £120 if she invites five friends.

Table 31.2 Hiring a limo (2)

Number of passengers paying	Total fixed cost	Fixed cost per unit (per person)	Total cost	Total cost per unit (unit cost)
1	£240	£240	£260	£260
2	£240	£120	£280	£140
3	£240	£80	£300	£100
4	£240	£60	£320	£80
5	£240	£48	£340	£68
6	£240	£40	£360	£60

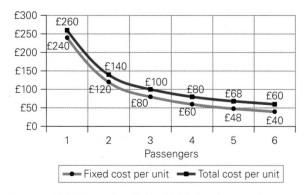

Figure 31.2 Converting Table 31.2 into a line graph

The important things to remember about the above are:

- Fixed costs per unit fall as output increases (the fixed costs get spread more thinly)
- … so fixed costs per unit rise as output decreases
- … which, in turn, means that total unit costs increase as demand/output falls.
- Unit costs and average costs are exactly the same thing.

Fixed costs per unit formula: $\dfrac{\text{Total fixed costs}}{\text{Number of units}}$

Unit costs formula: $\dfrac{\text{Total costs}}{\text{Number of units}}$

Total fixed costs don't change when output changes, but they do change per unit.

31.5 Capacity utilisation

This has been covered in detail in Chapter 29, so just a few points need to be added:

● Capacity utilisation relates directly to fixed and total costs per unit. If poor sales push capacity utilisation rates down to 50 per cent then fixed costs per unit will be twice as high as they need be; that, in turn, will push unit (average) costs higher than they should be. This is why football teams relegated from the Premier League can hit such massive financial buffers: they still have high wage bills and the same large grounds – but now have lower capacity utilisation as supporters stay away.

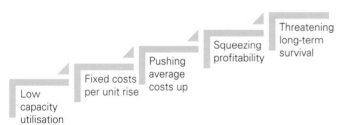

Figure 31.3 Logic ladder: danger of low capacity utilisation

● When capacity utilisation starts to move above 90 per cent, it may be time to increase capacity. In 2014 Renault added 60 per cent to the capacity of its car factory in Morocco to cope with booming demand for its low-cost Dacia car model.

31.6 The use of data in operational decision-making and planning

Right up until the end of 2013 executives at Apple believed that iPad sales would keep growing for several years to come. This was especially the case because Apple had made some important sales breakthroughs in China. Rising sales would spread the fixed costs of running the brand (Apple spends more than $1 billion a year on advertising, for example). Figure 31.4 shows that operational decision-making has to be based on accurate sales forecasts. These rely on a combination of good analysis of actual sales figures plus effective use of market research to anticipate when shifts are going to take place. In this case research into customers' future purchasing plans should have shown that the cult of the iPad was wearing thin.

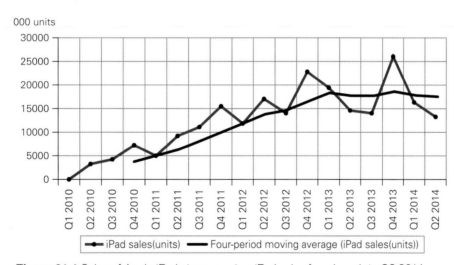

Figure 31.4 Sales of Apple iPad stops growing; iPad sales from launch to Q2 2014

Five Whys and a How

Question	Answer
Why might productivity and quality of service be inversely related in the service sector?	Because rapid, cold-hearted service may be efficient but not pleasant for the customer
Why do average costs rise when demand falls?	Because there are fewer customers, so the total fixed costs rise per unit, pushing up the unit (average) total costs
Why are average costs important?	Because they have to be below the selling price if the company is to make a profit
Why might a seaside hotel decide to close in November and reopen in April?	Because it wants to limit its annual capacity and thereby increase its capacity utilisation
Why is capacity utilisation a most-favoured metric in the airline business?	Because flying has huge fixed costs but not many variable ones, so fixed costs per passenger matter and that is affected by capacity utilisation
How does capacity utilisation have an impact on average costs?	High utilisation spreads the fixed costs per unit thinly, bringing the average (total) costs down

Key term

Metrics: are numerical measures used to determine the performance of an employee or a department.

Evaluation: Analysing operational performance

Greater labour productivity can lead to greater efficiency and higher profitability. This is because, other things being equal, it lowers the labour cost per unit. However, productivity is only one factor that contributes to a firm's success. A firm must also ensure it produces a good quality product, that it is marketed effectively and that costs are controlled. There is little point increasing productivity by 20 per cent if at the same time you pay your staff 30 per cent more. Similarly, there is no point producing more if there is no actual demand. Higher productivity, therefore, contributes to better performance but needs to be accompanied by effective decision-making throughout the firm.

The importance of productivity to a firm depends primarily on the level of value added involved. Top price perfumes such as Chanel have huge profit margins. Production costs are a tiny proportion of the selling price. Therefore a 10 per cent productivity increase might have only a marginal effect on profit and virtually none on the competitiveness of the brand. For mass-market products in competitive markets, high productivity is likely to be essential for survival. A 5 per cent cost advantage might make all the difference. Therefore, when judging an appropriate recommendation for solving a business problem, a judgement is required as to whether boosting productivity is a top priority for the business concerned.

Workbook

A. Revision questions

(40 marks; 45 minutes)

1. What is meant by the term 'productivity'? (3)

2. Why may it be hard to measure the productivity of staff who work in service industries? (4)

3. How does productivity relate to labour costs per unit? (4)

4. Explain how a firm may be able to increase its employees' productivity. (4)

5. How can increased investment in machinery help to boost productivity? (3)

6. Identify two factors which help and two factors which limit your productivity as a student. (4)

7. Outline the likely effect of increased motivation on the productivity of a teacher. (5)

8. Calculate the change in productivity at BDQ Co. (see Table 31.3) since last year. (4)

Table 31.3 Productivity at BDQ Co.

	Output	Number of staff
Last year	32,000	50
This year	30,000	40

9. Explain how motivation and productivity may be linked. (4)

10. Explain how productivity can be linked to unit labour costs. (5)

B. Revision exercises
DATA RESPONSE

Operations management at JCB

Midway through 2014 JCB looked set to break the £3 billion turnover mark for the first time in its history. One of the country's biggest and most important engineering companies, JCB's yellow and black construction vehicles are among the top three bestsellers globally. In its UK heartland of Staffordshire and Derbyshire, JCB employs over 5,000 people in highly skilled, secure jobs.

One of JCB's secrets has been its willingness to invest. Its 1979 decision to start up in India has led to the achievement of a 50 per cent market share in this huge, fast-developing country. India's new government is embarking on a huge programme of investment in roads and other infrastructure which should be great for JCB. Just in 2014 the company has announced:

- a £25 million programme to double production in Germany
- a £45 million investment in a six-cylinder engine to slot into its fuel-efficient Dieselmax range
- and a £150 million plan to expand production in the UK, with the expectation of creating 2,500 more jobs by 2018.

As the bar chart shows, not long ago – in the 2009 recession – the company's plans were thrown into turmoil by a collapse in sales. That year the company was saved by sales growth in India and China. Even so, with an estimated total capacity of 62,000 units in 2009, the rate of utilisation was very poor. To their credit, senior managers kept their heads and kept investing in the firm's future. From a struggle to break even in 2009 the company bounced back to make £365 million in profit in 2012.

In late 2014 JCB was holding to its long-term plan for significant increases in its global capacity. Its factories in India and Brazil are getting greater investment and new factories are being built in Uttoxeter and Cheadle in Britain. JCB believes that developing countries will continue to plough funds into construction investment and that JCB should be at the heart of this business. It shows no fear of its two huge global rivals: Caterpillar of America and Komatsu of Japan.

Another plan for the future is to improve the productivity of the JCB factories worldwide. In 2014 the 12,000-strong workforce were on course to produce 72,000 units. By 2018 the hope is to get annual productivity up to 8 units per worker.

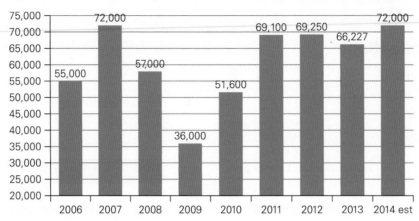

Figure 31.5 JCB annual global sales (in units)

Source: JCB press reports

Questions (25 marks; 30 minutes)

1. **a)** Calculate JCB's capacity utilisation in 2009. (3)

    b) Explain how JCB might have set about rebuilding this figure? (5)

2. Analyse the problems JCB might have faced in matching output to the order levels shown in the bar chart. (9)

3. **a)** Calculate JCB's labour productivity in 2014. (3)

    b) Explain the problems there may be in getting productivity up to 8 units per worker by 2018. (5)

C. Extend your understanding

1. After years of profitable growth Aldi's operational performance is starting to deteriorate. To what extent is this inevitable at a time of rapid growth? (20)

2. British Airways' costs per passenger are five times those of Ryanair. How important is it for British Airways to close that gap? Justify your answer. (20)

Improving quality

Linked with: Setting operational objectives, Chapter 26; Managing supply chains, Chapter 33.

Definition

Quality means providing what the customer wants, at the right time, to the right standard of product and service, and therefore yielding high customer satisfaction.

32.1 The importance of quality

W. Edwards Deming, the American quality guru, said that 'quality is defined by the customer'. The customer may insist on certain specifications, or demand exceptional levels of customer comfort. Another definition of quality is 'fit for use'. Although hard to define, there is no doubt that customers are very aware of quality. Their perception of quality is an important part of the buying decision.

Customers will accept some trade-off between price and quality. There is, however, a minimum level of quality that is acceptable. The customer wants the product to work (be fit for use), regardless of the price. If the customers think that the quality is below a minimum level they will not buy. Above the minimum level of acceptable quality, customers will expect to get more as they pay more.

The importance of quality is related to the level of competitiveness in the market. When competition is fierce, the quality of the product can tip the balance in the customer's decision-making. Yet the consumers' perception of quality can change. For many years computer manufacturer Dell was hugely successful selling directly to customers through the internet or newspaper advertising. Yet when the stunningly successful launch of the iPad turned people back towards Apple computers, Dell's famously high quality manufacture became irrelevant in the face of Apple's high quality design.

For all customers, quality is about satisfying their expectations. The customer will take into account the total buying experience. Customer service and after-sales service may be as important as the product itself. The way the product is sold, even *where* it is sold, all contribute to the customer's feelings about the quality of the product.

Quality is a moving target. A quality standard that is acceptable today may not be in the future. Customer expectations of quality are constantly changing. As quality improves, customer demands also increase.

Quality:

- is satisfying (preferably beating) customer expectations
- applies to services as well as products
- involves the whole business process, not just the manufacturing of the product
- is an ever-rising target.

'Quality has to be caused, not controlled.' Philip Crosby, American quality guru

Real business

Ryanair

Between 1991 and 2013 Ryanair boss Michael O'Leary built up the airline from almost nothing to become Europe's largest carrier. In all that time O'Leary focused on three things: low costs to make low prices possible, plus two aspects of quality: on-time arrivals and fewest bags lost. By 2005 Ryanair was the best in Europe on both these measures of customer quality. Yet in 2013 O'Leary announced that in future Ryanair would be more sensitive to other aspects of customer quality – above all else being friendlier, smilier and keener to give customers a more pleasant flying experience. Customers' quality needs had changed, and quality had become more important in customers' purchasing decisions.

'Reducing the cost of quality is in fact an opportunity to increase profits without raising sales, buying new equipment, or hiring new people.' Philip Crosby, American quality guru

---

32.2 The consequences of poor quality

Where the consumer has choice, quality is vital. A reputation for good quality brings marketing advantages. A good quality product will:

- generate a high level of repeat purchase, and therefore a longer product life cycle
- allow brand building and cross marketing
- allow a price premium (this is often greater than any added costs of quality improvements; in other words, quality adds value and additional profit)
- make products easier to place (retailers are more likely to stock products with a good reputation).

The consequences of a poor product or poor service for the business are shown in Table 32.1.

Table 32.1 Implications of poor product or service quality

Marketing costs	Business costs
Loss of sales	Scrapping of unsuitable goods
Loss of reputation	Reworking of unsatisfactory goods – costs of labour and materials
May have to price-discount	Lower prices for 'seconds'
May impact on other products in range	Handling complaints/warranty claims
Retailers may be unwilling to stock goods	Loss of consumer goodwill and repeat purchase

'Quality is remembered long after the price is forgotten.' Gucci slogan

Figure 32.1 Logic chain: quality is different things to different people

32.3 Methods of improving quality

As the importance of quality for both marketing and cost control has been recognised, there has been a growth in initiatives to control and improve quality. Techniques for quality control, such as inspection and statistical control, continue. They have been supplemented by other policies aimed at controlling and improving quality. These include total quality management, quality control and quality assurance. The pros and cons of each of these policies are set out in Table 32.2.

Total quality management

Total quality management (TQM) was introduced by American business guru W. Edwards Deming. He worked with Japanese firms, and his techniques are said to be one of the reasons for the success of businesses such as Honda and Toyota. TQM is not a management tool: it is a philosophy. It is a way of looking at quality issues. It requires commitment from the whole organisation, not just the quality control department. The business considers quality in every part of the business process – from design right through to sales. TQM is about building-in rather than inspecting-out. For it to be successful, it should be woven into the organisational culture.

Quality control

Quality control (QC) is the traditional way to manage quality, and is based on inspection. Workers get on with producing as many units as possible, and quality control inspectors check that the output meets minimum acceptable standards. This might be done by checking every product; for example, starting up every newly built car and driving it from the factory to a storage area. Or it might be done by checking every two hundredth Kit Kat coming off the end of the factory's production line. If one Kit Kat is faulty, inspectors will check others from the same batch and – if concerned – may scrap the whole batch. The problem with this system is that faulty products can slip through, and it stops staff from producing the best quality: they just focus on products 'good enough' to pass the checks. TQM is therefore a superior approach.

Quality assurance

Quality assurance (QA) is a system that assures customers that detailed systems are in place to govern quality at every stage in production. It will start with the quality-checking process for newly arrived raw

Table 32.2 Pros and cons of TQM, QC and QA

	TQM	QC	QA
Pros	Should become deeply rooted in the company culture (e.g. product safety at a producer of baby car seats)	Can be used to guarantee that no defective item will leave the factory	Makes sure the company has a quality system for every stage in the production process
	Once all staff think about quality, it should show through from design to manufacture and after-sales service (e.g. at Lexus or BMW)	Requires little staff training, therefore suits a business with unskilled or temporary staff (as ordinary workers needn't worry about quality)	Some customers like the reassurance provided by keeping records about quality checks at every stage in production; they believe they will get a higher-quality service and may therefore be willing to pay more
Cons	Especially at first, staff sceptical of management initiatives may treat TQM as 'hot air'; it lacks the clear, concrete programme of QC or QA	Leaving quality for the inspectors to sort out may mean poor quality is built into the product (e.g. clothes with seams that soon unpick)	QA does not promise a high-quality product, only a high-quality, reliable process; this process may churn out 'OK' products reliably
	To get TQM into the culture of a business may be expensive, as it will require extensive training among all staff (e.g. all British Airways staff flying economy from Heathrow to New York)	QC can be trusted when 100 per cent of output is tested, but not when it is based on sampling; Ford used to test just 1 in 7 of its new cars; that led to quality problems	QA may encourage complacency; it suggests quality has been sorted, whereas rising customer requirements mean quality should keep moving ahead

materials and components. Companies have to put in place a documented quality assurance system. This should operate throughout the company, involving suppliers and subcontractors. The main criticism of QA is that it is a paper-based system and therefore encourages staff to tick boxes rather than care about the customer experience.

Improvement

Customer expectations of quality are always changing. It is important that businesses seek to improve quality. Therefore, staff need to be encouraged to put forward ways in which their jobs can be done better. The Japanese term *kaizen* (meaning 'continuous improvement') has become common in British manufacturing.

32.4 Other quality initiatives

Six Sigma

A programme developed by America's General Electric Company, which aims to have fewer defective products than 1 per 300,000. To achieve this, staff are trained to become 'Green Belt' or 'Black Belt' quality experts. Although gimmicky, this has been followed widely by other companies.

'Quality is our best assurance of customer allegiance, our strongest defence against foreign competition, and the only path to sustained growth and earnings.' Jack Welch, General Electric chief

Quality circles

A quality circle is a group of employees who meet together regularly for the purpose of identifying problems and recommending adjustments to the working processes. This is done to improve the product or process. It is used to address known quality issues such as defective products. It can also be useful for identifying better practices that may improve quality. In addition, it has the advantage of improving staff morale through employee involvement. It takes advantage of the knowledge of operators.

Zero defects

The aim is to produce goods and services with no faults or problems. This is vital in industries such as passenger aircraft production or the manufacture of surgical equipment.

Real business

Boeing Dreamliner

In January 2013 all of Boeing's new 787 Dreamliner aircraft were grounded. With each plane having a list price of over $200 million this was a huge and costly embarrassment for the American plane maker and its global airline customers.

The specific problem was a battery on the plane that overheated and sometimes caught fire. In fact, though, the Dreamliner had already suffered far more teething problems than would usually be expected from Boeing.

⇨

The reason proved to be the way Boeing had organised the huge operation of developing and engineering the production process. Due to lack of production capacity, 60 per cent of the design and production of key components had been outsourced to suppliers from around the world. Because Boeing's own quality standards had not been applied uniformly, the company's quality assurance and quality control systems struggled to cope.

32.5 Benefits and difficulties of improving quality

The traditional belief was that high quality was costly: in terms of materials, labour, training and checking systems. Therefore, managements should beware of building too much quality into a product (the term given to this was 'over-engineered'). The alternative approach, put forward by the American writer Philip Crosby, is that 'quality is free'. The latter view suggests that getting things right first time can save a huge amount of time and money.

Benefits when improving quality:

- A great deal of research shows that staff like to take pride in their work, and that working to high quality standards is important. Management focus on quality, therefore, can boost morale and motivation.
- Really high quality standards can boost price levels remarkably. At the time of writing, Waitrose supermarkets has champagne at prices from £20 to £255 for a bottle; so customers are willing to pay £255 for a product they only need to pay £20 for.

Difficulties when improving quality:

- If quality control is to be effective it must balance the costs against the advantages; 100 per cent quality is possible, but it may make the product so expensive that sales suffer.
- Companies that rely on outsourced or temporary staff may struggle to achieve the high levels of quality implied by a TQM culture. True quality is about service as well as the product – which relies on the wholehearted commitment of staff

Five Whys and a How

Question	Answer
Why are some companies able to get away with the appalling quality revealed on TV programmes such as *Cowboy Builders* or *Watchdog*?	Some companies can make high, long-term profits without needing customer loyalty. They rely on finding a steady stream of naïve customers; consumer protection laws try – but often fail – to stop these things happening
Why may companies find it hard to correct an image of poor quality?	Images tend to build up over time, so they can be hard to shift. Change may require consistent quality programmes over several years
Why is quality assurance more popular these days than quality control?	Quality assurance can be used to check the whole supply chain, rather than just the final product. That fits with the needs of Tesco or Waitrose, who want to be sure of provenance
Why does quality matter if you're buying a £10 skirt from Primark?	It still matters, even if the customer may not mind about queues or scruffy displays. The skirt must be cut well enough to fit properly and made of fabrics that look good
Why do new firms sometimes struggle with quality?	They may have a very positive culture, but not yet have the processes in place to ensure quality
How would you set about improving quality at a struggling handbag maker?	First, give each worker a complete unit of work, i.e. producing the whole bag without division of labour, which would be hugely motivating; and drop any piecework payments

Key terms

Competitiveness: the ability of a firm to beat its competitors (for example, Galaxy is a highly competitive brand in the chocolate market).

Right first time: avoiding mistakes and therefore achieving high quality with no wastage of time or materials.

Trade-off: accepting less of one thing to achieve more of another (for example, slightly lower quality in exchange for cheapness).

Zero defects: eliminating quality defects by getting things right first time.

Evaluation: Improving quality

In recent years, there has been a change in the emphasis on quality. The quality business has itself grown. The management section of any bookshop will reveal several titles dedicated to quality management. The growth of initiatives such as TQM and continuous improvement goes on. The number of worldwide registrations for ISO 9000 increases by more than 25 per cent each year. Not all of these are from British businesses; there has been a rapid rise in overseas registrations. With an increase in the international awareness of quality, British businesses will have to ensure that they continue to be competitive.

This growth in emphasis on quality has undoubtedly brought benefits to business. Increased quality brings

rewards in the marketplace. Companies have also found that the initiatives, especially where they are people-based, have brought other advantages: changes in working practices have improved motivation and efficiency, and have reduced waste and costs.

This change in emphasis has not been without problems. The shift to a focus on the customer and the role of the employee could result in additional costs. Unless this results in increased profits, shareholders may feel that they are losing out. Some businesses have found that changing cultures is not easy. Resistance from workers and management has often caused problems.

Workbook

A. Revision questions

(30 marks; 30 minutes)

1. State two reasons why quality management is important. (2)
2. How important is quality to the consumer? (3)
3. Suggest two criteria customers may use to judge quality at:
   a) a budget-priced hotel chain (2)
   b) a Tesco supermarket (2)
   c) a McDonald's. (2)
4. Why has there been an increase in awareness of the importance of improving the quality of products? (3)
5. Give two marketing advantages that come from a quality reputation. (2)
6. What costs are involved if the firm has quality problems? (3)
7. What is Total Quality Management? (3)
8. Outline two benefits of adopting quality circles to a clothing chain such as Topshop. (4)
9. Outline two additional costs that may be incurred in order to improve quality. (4)

B. Revision exercises
DATA RESPONSE

Horsemeat and food quality in 2013

In January 2013 supermarkets were hit by an extraordinary scandal as it emerged that foods made of processed 'beef' actually contained horsemeat. Tesco

was quickly forced to admit that one of its products contained 30 per cent horsemeat. Discounter Aldi also had to endure some tough headlines. Broadly, higher-priced retailers such as Waitrose, Sainsbury and Marks

& Spencer came out of the saga pretty well; Tesco, Asda and Morrisons' fared worse. In the 12 weeks to 17 February Tesco's market share slipped below 30 per cent for the first time in several years.

So how could it happen?

Amazingly, most supermarkets do not check the meat when it arrives at their depots. This task is outsourced ('farmed out') to companies approved by the British Retail Consortium. Inspectors go once to the source of supply, acting on behalf of all retailers. But in evidence to a government committee in February 2013, Paul Smith, a recently retired food inspector told the committee: 'The suppliers can select which "approved inspection body" they use. They also pay for the audit. Yes, they can pick which audit company, the alleged policeman, they wish. In practice they also pick the individual auditor by heaping praise and requesting the same individual for the next visit.'

> **Throughout the world, our customers want safe, affordable products. Many also want to know that what they buy is sourced to robust ethical and environmental standards.**
>
> **We believe it is possible to provide for all our customers, whatever their needs, whilst upholding strong standards across our business and in our supply chains.**
>
> Source: Tesco Social Responsibility Report

So despite the claims it makes in its Social Responsibility Report, Tesco does nothing to check on its food supplies. Other companies such as Waitrose may well do so, as they had no problem with horsemeat contamination.

The consequence of this slack approach to quality is clear in the impact of the scandal on food sales. In the four weeks after the scandal first hit, sales of frozen burgers were down (nationally) by over 40 per cent and sales of all ready meals were down by 12 per cent.

So what should Tesco have done? First, it should have switched its focus from public relations to quality management. Tesco shoppers probably believed that tough Tesco buyers went to suppliers, checked the quality standards, then negotiated toughly on price. Clearly the checking part may have been a bit of a myth. To clear the air, the company should have brought in a new policy of checking at the producer, and then checked as products arrived at Tesco. In effect this would have been a full Quality Assurance regime. Having set the new policy up, it would then have been time to tell the consumer.

> **The meat inspection workforce managed by the Food Standards Agency has shrunk from a high point of 1700 - during the BSE and E. coli crises in the 1990s - to around 800 today. This has been a direct consequence of the deregulatory policies of both the European Commission and UK Government to hand over more and more meat inspection duties to the meat industry and dispense with proper independent inspection.**
>
> Source: Unison (trade union)

Tesco knew perfectly well that government inspection of food had been run down in recent years (see box). So it should have been making greater efforts to protect its customers (and its own reputation). It seems to have been very short-sighted in its approach to quality. It is likely to keep feeling the impact on its market share.

Questions (25 marks; 30 minutes)

1. Explain Tesco's performance at choosing effective suppliers. (9)

2. To what extent is quality of importance to a business such as Tesco? (16)

C. Extend your understanding

1. To what extent should quality management be solely a matter for the production department? (20)

2. To what extent is quality a major competitive issue in service businesses? (20)

Managing supply chains

Linked with: Analysing operational performance, Chapter 31; Improving quality, Chapter 32; Managing inventory, Chapter 34.

Definition

The supply chain is the complete sequence of stages involved in transforming raw materials into finished goods and getting them into the hands of customers.

33.1 Influences on the choice of suppliers

Cost

Cheaper supplies mean higher profit margins. The incentive to find a cheap supplier is huge for any firm; therefore, the price charged will be a key factor in the relationship between a firm and its suppliers. Large purchasers may almost be able to dictate prices to their suppliers. This is because the quantities they purchase may account for most of the supplier's output, giving a huge amount of power to the buyer. However, for small businesses with limited purchasing power, the supplier may have the upper hand. The lower the purchase price, the lower the buyer's variable costs and therefore the higher its gross profits.

Quality

There is likely to be a trade-off between the price charged by suppliers and the quality of their offering. The cheapest supplier may be one with a poor reputation for the quality of its products or service. Choosing to use a supplier with quality problems is likely to lead to operational problems. Poor-quality supplies can lead to machinery breakdowns, along with poor-quality output. This can lead to worsening customer complaints, guarantee claims or reputation. Choosing the cheapest supplier may sow the seeds of long-term problems for a business.

Reliability

Supplies at the right price and of a high quality may be of little use if they arrive late. It is important that a supplier can offer reliability to the purchaser. Failure to deliver on time can stop a manufacturing process or leave shop shelves empty. Suppliers' reliability will be easy to assess once a business has started working with them. However, a new business or a business sourcing new supplies may need to rely on word-of-mouth reputation to inform its choice.

Frequency

Depending on the type of business and the production system it uses, frequent deliveries may be needed from suppliers. Firms selling fresh produce will need to ensure that they are using suppliers that can supply and deliver frequently – probably as often as a new batch each day. Similarly, a firm that uses a just-in-time (JIT) production system will need very frequent deliveries to feed its production system without it having to hold stock (Honda, for example, requires hourly deliveries of parts to its Japanese car factories). For firms such as these, it makes sense to look for a local supplier; they are far more likely to be willing to deliver with a greater level of frequency.

Flexibility

In a similar way to ensuring the right frequency of supplies, many firms will need to find a supplier with the capacity to cope with widely varying orders. Businesses selling products with erratic demand patterns, caused by changes in the weather or fashion, will need to find suppliers that can meet their ever-changing needs. Probably the most common scenario is to ensure that suppliers have the spare capacity available to cope with sudden rush orders. A key to supplier flexibility is a short lead time (that is, there should not be too long a period between placing an order and receiving a delivery).

Payment terms

Most business transactions are on credit, not for cash. If Tesco wants to order 2,000 cases of Heinz Beans, the bill is unlikely to be paid for 30 or more days after the goods have been delivered. This gives time for the goods to be sold, providing the cash to make it easy to pay the bill. Small business start-ups will struggle to get the same terms. A newly opened corner shop will not be given credit by Heinz. The supplier will want to be paid in cash until the new business has shown that it can survive and pay its bills. So a new small firm has to pay up front, placing extra strain on its cash flow. This should not be a problem as long as it has been built into its start-up cash-flow forecast).

Real business

In the driver's seat

The results of the 14th annual automotive industry study on automakers' working relations with their suppliers show the US Big Three are once again falling behind their Japanese competitors, with Toyota, Honda and Nissan finishing 1-2-3 respectively in the top rankings. The survey revealed that:

● Toyota and Honda's efforts to improve supplier relations have paid off as they have regained their momentum and are ranked one and two, respectively, while extending their lead. Honda is the 'most preferred' customer among the suppliers.

● Nissan, the second most improved overall following Toyota, has taken over third place from Ford.

● After showing no real improvement in supplier relations for four years, Ford has slipped back to fourth place, having been passed by Nissan.

● For the first time in six years, Chrysler's overall ranking in supplier relations has fallen and the company is now ranked fifth, only one point above GM.

The real question behind the annual study is – why should they care? The answer is simple: for many years, the study has shown that automakers with the best rankings, specifically Toyota and Honda, receive the greatest benefit from their suppliers in a variety of areas including lower costs, higher quality, increased price reduction concessions, and supplier innovation.

Source: http://www.prnewswire.com/news-releases/2014-annual-automotive-oem-supplier-relations-study-shows-toyota-and-honda-on-top-nissan-displacing-ford-in-the-middle-chrysler-and-gm-falling-behind-258885661.html.

'All we are doing is looking at the timeline from the moment the customer gives us an order to the point when we collect the cash. And we reduce that timeline by removing non-value-added wastes.'
Taiichi Ohno, father of the Toyota Production System

33.2 Managing the supply chain efficiently

Some businesses enjoy telling their shareholders how tough they are with their suppliers: after all, the lower the supply cost, the higher the profit. Many firms encourage competition between rival suppliers by threatening to go elsewhere if the terms are not what they want. This approach has been important in building the hugely profitable business of many high-street stores, which find cheap goods by negotiating toughly in Cambodia, China or the Philippines.

An alternative approach was followed in the past by Marks & Spencer, and today by car firms such as Toyota and Honda. These companies build long-term relationships with their suppliers, in order to have a more efficient supply chain. There are many potential benefits from this approach, as discussed below.

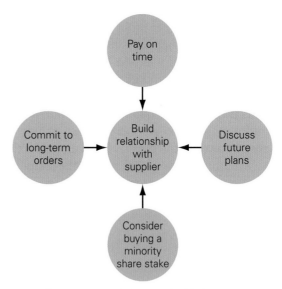

Figure 33.1 Logic chain: how to build strong relationships with suppliers

Working together on new product development

Developing new products involves many considerations. One of these will be how the product is to be manufactured, what materials will be used and what properties will be needed. Meanwhile, launching a new product will require careful production planning to ensure that consumers can get hold of the new product that the marketing department has told them about. The result is that suppliers have a major part to play in developing and launching new products. Many firms have recognised the importance of this and work hand in hand with their suppliers from the very earliest stages of developing a new product.

Flexibility

A strong relationship with a supplier should mean it is willing to make special deliveries if a business is running low on stock. A strong relationship may also allow some flexibility on payment. A toyshop may struggle to find cash in the months leading up to Christmas, so a trusting supplier may accept a delay in payment. This could be the lifeline required for the small firm. However, no supplier is likely to be able to sustain this generosity for a long period.

Sharing information to improve the efficiency of the supply chain

Large businesses with sophisticated IT systems have direct links between their cash tills and their suppliers. Cadbury knows at any hour of the day how many Twirls are selling in supermarkets. This enables Cadbury to plan its production levels (for example, pushing up output if sales are proving brighter than expected). The supermarket can even allow Cadbury to make the decisions about how much stock to produce and deliver on the basis of the information it is receiving.

'When you went into a Boston Chicken and ordered quarter-chicken, white, with mash and corn, when that was rung up it would signal all the way along the supply chain the need for more potatoes to be put on a truck a thousand miles away.' Stephen Elop, Microsoft vice-president

33.3 Matching supply to demand

Many factors can cause sales levels to fluctuate, including:

- fashion
- temperature and weather
- marketing activity
- competitors' actions.

Some of these are predictable; others less so. Sales forecasting can help in production planning, especially

for predictable changes in demand (such as higher swimwear sales in early summer than early winter). However, the fundamental issue is the same for most businesses: how to organise their operations to cope with demand variations.

Matching supply to demand is relatively easy when demand is highly predictable, as with sales of Heinz Tomato Ketchup. Seasonal sales variations are minor and the strength of the (£125 million) brand means that competitors' actions matter little. By contrast, think of sales of lawnmowers. These are extremely seasonal, with almost no one buying one in the winter (the grass doesn't grow!), but a burst of demand occurring when spring warms up to the point that the grass needs cutting.

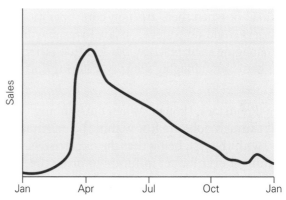

Figure 33.2 Lawnmower sales

Figure 33.2 shows a possible sales graph for lawnmowers – but imagine trying to match those monthly figures with production/supply: idle factories for half the year and then an incredible burst of activity when the weather improves. Surely it might be better to produce in the way shown in Figure 33.3. Line A shows steady production year-round. This would entail building up stocks throughout the winter, then selling them when demand arrives in the spring.

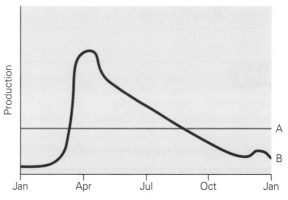

Figure 33.3 Possible production options

Advantages of Figure 33.2 (Match production to sales)	Advantages of Figure 33.3 (Constant production level)
• Minimal inventory (stock) levels so very little cash tied up	• Stable production so factory usage high (lower fixed costs per unit)
• No risk of overproduction (unsold stock if sales proved disappointing)	• Workers fully utilised year-round so labour costs per unit kept low
• Products are freshly made so quality is high (not an issue in this case!)	• Entering spring with high buffer stock, so customers will be supplied

Other ways to match supply to demand

1. Outsourcing (or subcontracting) means getting an outside company to produce for you.

This is valuable when there are predictable peaks in the workload or when there are 'non-core' operations that outsiders could do better. Top law firms may be great at managing their practice, but feel that others would be better at managing security, catering and cleaning.

There are downsides, though. When outsourcing is carried through, jobs are lost within the original company, with the risk being that the expertise is lost – making it ever harder in future to bring the work back in-house. Alternatively the outsourcing may be in part, that is, being used as a top-up for when demand exceeds the original factory's ability to supply.

When outsourcing there is a risk that the contractor cares little for 'your' customers and your reputation. Therefore it is important to get the contractor to sign up to a service agreement that sets out exactly what quality standards are required.

'If I start outsourcing all my navigation to a little talking box in my car, I'm sort of screwed. I'm going to lose my car in the parking lot every single time.'
Ken Jennings, US celebrity nerd

2. Hiring temporary and part-time staff

Temporary and part-time staff give extra flexibility to an employer. Temporary staff can be hired on fixed term contracts designed to last no longer than the expected busy period. Most tourist attractions keep very few full-time staff, relying instead on an army of summer temps to run their attractions. Part-time staff can be hired with contracts that include flexible working hours, offering employers the chance to call them in during busy periods. In recent years there has been a growing use of 'zero-hours contracts'. These promise staff no hours of work at all (and therefore no income); employers might contact zero-hours employees on a Thursday to let them know their work schedule for the following week. This gives huge benefits to the employer but no obvious advantages to the employee, who has no stability of income and therefore no chance of taking out a mortgage and little chance of saving.

Through the use of temporary and part-time staff, a company can reduce its fixed salary costs thus reducing the break-even point to a level that is sustainable during quiet periods. However, motivation, quality and customer service issues may arise with a workforce that may feel only loosely engaged with the company.

3. Producing to order

An important feature of modern operations management is recognising that customers will go to the producer that offers as close to a tailor-made product as possible. The term 'mass customisation' sums this up: production lines that combine the cost efficiency of mass production with the flexibility of tailor-making to each customer's specific requirements. On the Mercedes UK website the Car Configurator button allows customers to specify their precise requirements, to be built into the car at the factory. The uniquely specified Merc rolls off the line a couple of weeks later and is delivered to the customer.

> **Key terms**

> **Just-in-time (JIT):** ordering supplies so that they arrive 'just in time' (that is, just when they are needed). This means operating without reserves of materials or components held 'just in case' they are needed.

> **Lead time:** the time the supplier takes between receiving an order and delivering the goods.

> **Mass customisation:** producing flexibly on a mass production assembly line, giving the twin benefits of customer satisfaction and cost effectiveness.

> **Service agreement:** a contract between a company and its supplier that sets out exactly what is required by when and at what quality standards.

Five Whys and a How

Question	*Answer*
Why might it be a mistake to use short-term, low-cost contracts for supplies?	Because building a long-term relationship with the supplier can yield benefits in terms of quality and innovation
Why might outsourcing raise difficult ethical questions?	Because products are being made for you, but with terms and conditions that may be out of your sight and out of your control
Why do new, small firms find it hard to get trade credit from their suppliers?	New firms have a high failure rate, so it would be very risky for a supplier to give you goods on credit, perhaps later to find you in liquidation and unable to pay
Why might it be a mistake for a NHS hospital to outsource its cleaning services?	If the outside business was disconnected from the ethos of the hospital, quality standards might be low and disease might spread
Why may a business such as Cadbury choose to pay higher prices to buy Fairtrade supplies?	Perhaps for ethical reasons, but more probably because they think the image advantages outweigh the costs
How might mass customisation help a producer of racing bikes?	It would enable individual customer needs to be met while keeping production costs reasonably low

Evaluation: Managing supply chains

Evaluative themes relating to suppliers will centre on judgements that firms make as to which supplier to choose. This unit has covered a range of factors that need to be considered, but effective evaluation will come from a willingness to appreciate which factors are most important for the specific business. A retailer that sells high volumes of cheap products at low prices may be right to compromise on quality to use the cheapest suppliers. The reverse would be the case for a firm with a luxury image or targeting socially conscious consumers. Take care to work out which factors will be most important for the firm mentioned in the question.

Another judgement that should improve your answers is to determine who has the most power in the relationship between company and supplier. Larger firms tend to have more power; indeed there are concerns over the way Britain's huge supermarket chains treat small farmers. However, size may not be the only factor to consider. A supplier with a patent on a crucial component will need to be dealt with even if it fails to prove 100 per cent reliable.

Workbook

A. Revision questions

(30 marks; 30 minutes)

1. Explain why the cheapest supplier may not be the best choice. (4)

2. Identify two businesses for which daily deliveries may be absolutely crucial. (2)

3. Briefly explain two problems that may arise when a firm uses a supplier with poor levels of quality. (4)

4. Describe why attractive credit terms from a supplier will be particularly useful for a new business. (4)

5. Outline two reasons why a firm may choose to change its supplier of an existing component. (4)

6. Explain one benefit a mobile phone shop may receive by encouraging several suppliers to continually compete with each other for every month's order of components. (4)

7. What benefits could the mobile phone shop miss out on by not building a long-term relationship with its suppliers? (4)

8. Describe how a car manufacturer such as Volkswagen may benefit from including its component suppliers in the development process when designing a new car. (4)

B. Revision exercises
DATA RESPONSE
Operations management in a heatwave

Figure 33.4

The July 2013 British heatwave caused a delighted chaos in the ice cream business. In the first week, sales of single lollies and ice creams soared by 195 per cent year-on-year. And Yorkshire-based R&R ice cream (previously called Frederick's Dairies) reported a 300 per cent hike in sales. The managing director said: 'We are doing everything we can to fulfil the unprecedented demand... this hot weather has seen an uplift of 120 per cent on the forecast sales.' In fact customers of R&R's reported stock shortages as too little was delivered.

Needless to say, ice cream manufacturers know that sales in the summer months will be higher than in the winter. Typically, sales in June, July and August are four times higher than in the winter months. So production is ramped up in April, May and June to build up stock levels.

In addition to this predictable sales pattern comes the weather. To help match production to demand, Unilever (Walls) buys 10-day weather forecasts and plans accordingly. R&R, though, says: 'We think that weather forecast data is too expensive so we've stopped buying it. We have all our production facilities on one site in Skelmersdale. We can build stock up and react very quickly if the weather gets warm. We can make changes to our production schedule in a day.' Despite its forecasting, Unilever could not keep up with demand for its Ben & Jerry's brand, forcing it to source stock from its factories outside the UK.

Over the longer term, ice cream sales have been in decline. This accentuated the supply shock for the manufacturers. In July, Unilever's brand building director told *The Grocer* magazine: 'In the spring the sales team were pulling their hair out while the supply chain team were looking calm because stock levels were optimal. Now it's the other way round.' The worry for manufacturers is that consumer demand reacts quickly to worsening weather as well. Most supply chains struggle to keep up with this, so may be pushing out too much stock for a few days after the heatwave has subsided.

Questions (30 marks; 35 minutes)

1. Explain the approaches taken by Walls and R&R's to match ice cream supply to demand. (4)

2. Outline two operational objectives that would be suitable for an ice cream producer such as Walls. (4)

3. Explain one benefit and one drawback of a capital-intensive production strategy in the ice cream business. (6)

4. To what extent do you agree that lean production is the best operational strategy for ice cream manufacturers? (16)

C. Extend your understanding

1. To what extent is it unethical for a profitable retailer such as Sports Direct to hire part-time sales staff only on the basis of zero-hours contracts? (20)

2. To what extent should cost be the main influences on the choice of suppliers for a major retailer of your choice? (20)

Managing inventory

Linked with: Lean production, Chapter 28; Technology and operational efficiency, Chapter 30; Analysing operational performance, Chapter 31; Decision-making to improve operational performance, Chapter 35.

Definition

Inventory is the American term for stock, and its management is to ensure that supplies are ordered, delivered and handled to balance customer demand against the cost of holding stocks.

34.1 Types of inventory

Manufacturing firms hold three types of inventory. These are:

- raw materials and components: these are the stocks the business has purchased from outside suppliers; they will be held by the firm until it is ready to process them into its finished output

- work in progress: at any given moment, a manufacturing firm will have some items it has started to process, but that are incomplete; this may be because they are presently moving through the production process; it may be because the firm stores unfinished goods to give it some flexibility to meet consumer demand

- finished goods: once a product is complete, the firm may keep possession of it for some time; this could be because it sells goods in large batches or no buyer has yet come in for the product. For producers of seasonal goods such as toys, most of the year's production may be building stock in preparation for the pre-Christmas sales rush, a process known as producing for stock, or stockpiling.

The firm's costs increase if it holds more stock. However, this needs to be set against the opportunity cost of keeping too little stock, such as not being able to meet customer demand. One theory is that a firm should try to keep as little stock as possible at all times. This system, known as just-in-time, is covered in Section 34.6. The firm must keep control of all the different types of stock to ensure that it runs at peak efficiency.

'Substitute information for inventory' Anon

34.2 Influences on the amount of inventory held

A firm can hold too much or too little inventory. Both cases will add to the costs of the firm. Too much inventory can lead to:

- opportunity costs: holding the firm's wealth in the form of stock prevents it using its capital in other ways, such as investing in new machinery, or research and development on a new product; this may dent its competitiveness

- cash flow problems: holding the firm's wealth as stock may cause problems if it proves slow moving; there may be insufficient cash to pay suppliers

- increased storage costs: as well as the rental cost of the space needed to hold the inventories, the higher the stock value, the higher the cost of insurance against fire and theft

- increased finance costs: if the capital needs to be borrowed, the cost of that capital (the interest rate) will be a significant added annual overhead

- increased stock wastage: the more stock is held, the greater the risk of it going out of date.

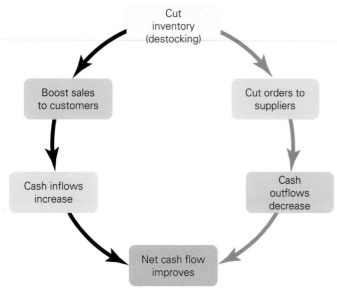

Figure 34.1 Logic chain: how destocking boosts cash

This does not, however, mean that the business is free to carry very low stocks. There are potential costs from holding too little inventory, including the following.

- Lost orders, if urgent customer orders cannot be met because there is too little finished goods stock
- Worker downtime if essential components have been delayed in arriving from suppliers (and the very low buffer has been used up already)
- The loss of the firm's reputation and any goodwill it has been able to build up with its customers.

The total cost of inventory to the firm will therefore be a combination of these factors. As the level of inventory grows, the costs of holding that stock will increase, but the costs of being out of stock decrease. The cost of holding stock will therefore look like Figure 34.2.

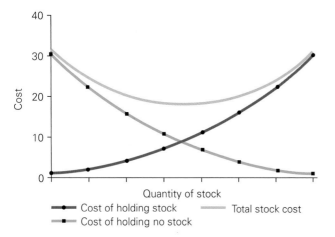

Figure 34.2 The cost of stockholding

For a firm, the optimum level of stock to hold will be where the total costs of holding stock are the lowest.

34.3 Inventory control charts

One way in which a firm analyses its stock situation is by using an inventory control chart. This line graph looks at the level of stock in the firm over time. Managers can see how stock levels are changing, and act quickly if slow sales have led to excessive stock levels.

A typical inventory control chart will look like that shown in Figure 34.3. On this chart there are four lines, which represent the levels described below.

- Stock levels: This line shows how stock levels have changed over the time period. As the stock is used up, the level of stock gradually falls from left to right. When a delivery is made, however, the stock level leaps upwards in a vertical line. The greater the rise in the vertical line, the more stock has been delivered.
- Maximum stock level: This shows the largest amount that the firm is either willing or able to hold in stock.
- Reorder level: This is a 'trigger' quantity. When stocks fall to this level a new order will be sent in to the supplier. The reorder level is reached some time before the delivery (shown by the vertical part of the stock level line). This is because the supplier will need some 'lead time' to process the order and make the delivery.
- Minimum stock level: This is also known as the buffer stock. The firm will want to keep a certain minimum level of stock so that it will have something to fall back on if supplies fail to arrive on time or if there's a sudden increase in demand.

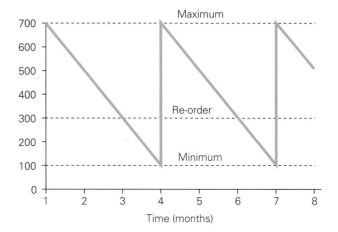

Figure 34.3 Stock control chart

Diagrams such as this, showing a neat and regular pattern to stockholding, will not happen in reality. Orders may arrive late and may not always be of the correct quantity. The rate of usage is unlikely to be constant. The slope of the stock level line may be steeper, showing more stock being used than normal, or shallower, showing a slower use of stock.

However, inventory control charts such as these give managers a clear picture of how things have changed, and show them what questions need to be asked. For example, perhaps suppliers are regularly delivering late. Managers will then know to ask if suppliers were taking longer than the agreed lead time, or if orders were being placed too late.

Figure 34.4 shows a more realistic stock control graph. It is based on actual sales of Nestlé Lion Bars at a newsagent in South West London.

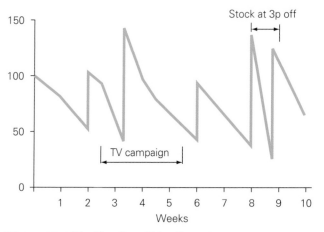

Figure 34.4 Weekly sales of Lion Bars at one newsagent

34.4 Buffer level of inventory

Buffer stocks are needed just-in-case something goes wrong. If warm weather sends customers rushing to buy ice creams, there's a serious chance of running out. So grocers try to keep a minimum number of ice creams in stock throughout the summer, just in case the sun bursts through.

Companies today love the idea of holding zero buffer stocks, but that is only possible if customers place orders and are willing to wait for delivery (as would be true of ordering a Mercedes with factory-fitted optional extras). Most companies need to set a buffer stock level and make sure to reorder early enough so that there's little or no chance of running out of stock.

'Inventory in work-in-progress hides inefficiencies. It's better to expose them by removing buffer stock.'
J.K. Liker, business author

34.5 Lead time and reorder levels

Lead time

This is the time between an order being placed and the supplies being delivered. This might be months, if the supplier company is based in China and the stock is too heavy to be flown to Britain. If so, the British company may have to hold quite a few of this part in stock, because it takes so long to get hold of another.

Alternatively the component may be made locally, available within hours, and available from more than one supplier. If so, it may only be necessary to have one day's worth of supplies in stock.

Reorder levels

When the level of inventory falls due to the sale or usage of stock, it may start to approach the buffer stock level. That, remember, is the minimum desired stock level and therefore the business wants the stock reordered early enough for it to arrive before the inventory sinks below that buffer stock level. The reorder level must be set, therefore, taking into account the rate of usage, the lead time for the stock item, and the level of the buffer stock.

Worked example

Reorder levels for a shop selling 6 items a week, with a buffer stock of 8, a reorder quantity of 18 and a supplier lead time of 1 week. Assumed starting point is 14 units of stock at the start of week 1.

Table 34.1 Inventory control at a shop selling sofas

Week	Inventory at start of week	Delivery from supplier	Usage of stock	Inventory at end of week
1	14	-	6	8
2	8	18	6	20
3	20	-	6	14
4	14	-	6	8
5	8	18	6	20
6	20	-	6	14

In the above example, the reorder level is 14, because when the stock level falls to 14 you need to phone the supplier asking for your next delivery of sofas in a week's time.

Reorder quantities

A further consideration is how much stock to order at any one time, that is, the reorder level. Large orders need only be made occasionally to keep sufficient stock levels, while smaller orders would have to be placed more regularly. The arguments for both of these are shown in Table 34.2.

Table 34.2 Large versus smaller orders

Advantages of many small orders	Advantages of few large orders
Less storage space needed	Lower cost per unit due to economies from buying in bulk
More flexible to changing needs	Avoids chance of running out of stock
Less stock wastage	Prevents machines and workers standing idle

Real business

RFID (Radio Frequency Identification) at Carlsberg

Brewers such as Carlsberg sell most of their beer and cider to pubs in 36-gallon aluminium kegs. The kegs are supposed to be sent back to the brewery by the pubs when they are empty. Unfortunately, in many cases they are not returned promptly, or they go missing.

In the past Carlsberg overcame this problem by purchasing extra kegs from their supplier. The problem with this cautious, just-in-case approach is cost. Each empty beer keg costs Carlsberg nearly £75. In early 2013 Carlsberg began fitting RFID tags to its latest product – Somersby Cider. The tags send digital information back to Carlsberg HQ. The tags have helped Carlsberg in two ways. First, fewer barrels are now going missing because Carlsberg now knows the precise locations of all its barrels. Second, the tags also tell Carlsberg how much cider is left in each barrel. This enables Carlsberg to better match supply with demand, ensuring that pubs don't run out of stock.

34.6 Just-in-time

Just-in-time (JIT) is a Japanese system of production; it is the attempt to operate with a zero buffer stock. At the same time, a system must be developed so that the costs and risks of running out of stock are avoided by the firm.

Establishing a JIT system is not something that can or should be achieved overnight. The risks of running out of stock are too great. Figure 34.5 shows how a firm might set out to achieve a JIT system in a carefully planned way. The diagram shows five phases, after which the firm would intend to continue with phases six, seven and thereafter, until it could get as close as possible to zero buffer stock. The five phases are as follows.

1. The firm orders 20,000 units of stock to arrive every third week.

2. Suppliers are asked to move to weekly deliveries, therefore only one-third of the quantity is ordered.

3. As Phase 2 has proved successful, there is no longer any need for such a high buffer stock. Stock levels are allowed to fall to a new, lower level.

4. With Phase 3 complete, the firm now moves to receiving deliveries twice a week. Therefore the order level is halved.

5. The suppliers have proved reliable enough to allow the buffer to be cut again…

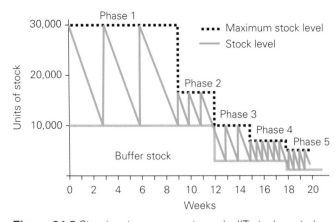

Figure 34.5 Step-by-step progress towards JIT stock control

Five Whys and a How

Question	Answer
Why is stock control especially important for some firms, such as greengrocers?	Too much stock would mean tired displays and high wastage levels; too little would mean frustrated customers
Why might an umbrella-seller want relatively high buffer stocks?	Because rain arrives erratically and high customer demand arrives instantly
Why is there a high opportunity cost to holding a large buffer stock?	Because all the money tied up in the stock could be used – profitably – elsewhere in the business
Why may JIT be the wrong approach for managing inventory at a hospital?	Because running out of stock may be a life-and-death matter – so buffer stocks are essential
Why should companies wanting to minimise their inventory look for suppliers with short lead times?	The faster the supplier can deliver, the less stock you need to hold as a buffer
How might the rise of online shopping affect decisions by retailers about inventory?	It gives suppliers a slight buffer between the customer order and the delivery time, making it easier to operate with minimal buffer stock

Key terms

Buffer stock: the desired minimum stock level held by a firm just in case something goes wrong.

Competitiveness: the extent to which a firm can stand up to – or beat – its rivals.

Opportunity cost: the cost of missing out on the next best alternative when making a decision (or when committing resources).

Stockholding costs: the overheads resulting from the stock levels held by a firm.

Evaluation: Managing inventory

Stock control is at the heart of many business operations. For retailers such as Zara, Topshop and Primark, the desire for a constant flow of new, fashion-orientated stock means huge pressure to clear away old inventory. Therefore, a JIT approach is ideal, with little or no buffer stock. In some cases it is quite helpful commercially to run out of stock, if it means that, next Saturday, shoppers come earlier to make sure they can get the must-have item. The thing that will not work is when customers go to a clothes shop and see tired, over-fingered stock that's outdated.

Yet there are still firms that believe mass production plus high inventories is the only way to be efficient. If that's what Cadbury says about making chocolate – even the highly seasonal Creme Egg – it would be arrogant to argue. So it is always important to keep an open mind about what is right for a specific company.

Workbook

A. Revision questions

(35 marks; 35 minutes)

1. Why may it be important to maintain good relationships with suppliers? (3)

2. State the three main categories of stock. (3)

3. Outline two factors that might lead to a fall in stockholding costs. (4)

4. Explain the difference between inventory reorder level and inventory reorder quantity. (4)

5. Sketch a typical stock control chart. (6)

6. State three costs associated with holding too much stock. (3)

7. Give three costs associated with running out of stock. (3)

8. What is meant by just-in-time stock control? (3)

9. Explain the meaning of the sentence in the text 'The purchaser's reputation is placed in the hands of the external supplier.' (3)

10. Why is inventory control of particular importance to an ice cream seller? (3)

B. Revision exercises

DATA RESPONSE 1

Ann Brennan established a bakery in Wigan twenty years ago. Although the firm is profitable, Ann is considering the introduction of modern techniques to help the company develop. In particular, she wishes to introduce information technology to improve communications between her five shops and the central bakery, and to help her manage her stock of raw materials more effectively.

Stocks of raw materials at the business are currently purchased in response to usage. For example, the bakery uses on average of 500 kg of flour per week. The most Ann wishes to hold at any time is 2,000 kg. She would be worried if the stock fell below 500 kg. An order takes one week to arrive, so Ann always reorders when her stock falls to 1,000 kg.

Questions (25 marks; 30 minutes)

1. What is meant by the following terms?
   a) reorder level (2)
   b) buffer stock (2)
   c) lead time. (2)

2. a) Draw a stock control graph for flour at Brennan's Bakery over a six-week period. (6)
   b) Draw a second graph showing the situation if twice the normal amount of flour were used in the fourth week. (6)

3. How might information technology be used to improve communication between Ann's shops and between the bakery and its suppliers? (7)

DATA RESPONSE 2

Is JIT always the best option?

In March 2011 a devastating earthquake and tsunami hit Japan. The effects of this natural disaster were arguably amplified by the widespread use of Just-In-Time production in Japan, whereby firms operate with very little, if any, buffer stock. This means that a whole production line will grind to a halt if just one component or raw material fails to be delivered by a supplier. The globalised nature of modern supply chains also meant that firms as far away as Britain and America suffered from the natural disaster in Japan. For example, Honda's factory in Britain quickly ran out of imported components from Japan, causing car production to halt in Swindon.

Fujitsu is one of the leading suppliers of semi-conductors in Japan. One of its Japanese factories was badly damaged by the 2011 earthquake, which reduced output. Despite this, Fujitsu was able to bounce back quickly. In less than three months production was back up to the pre-earthquake level. The key to Fujitsu's success was planning. Three years earlier, in response to another earthquake, the company developed an emergency response strategy. The strategy was based on creating additional capacity in other Fujitsu factories located in areas less susceptible to earthquakes. In 2011 Fujitsu wasted no time in implementing its plan, which worked.

Aside from acts of nature and war, manufacturers who want to be successful with JIT need to prepare for demand spikes (A demand spike is a sudden, unexpected upsurge in demand). Both Nintendo and Sony Corp. have had out-of-stock issues with their console systems, notably the PS4 in 2014. 'Just-in-time is OK, but if all of a sudden there is a surge in demand, you may not have the flexibility available to meet the demand,' says one noted business analyst.

C. Extend your understanding

1. 'The use of information technology makes stock control an automatic function, requiring little input from human beings.' To what extent do you agree with this statement? (20)

Questions (30 marks; 35 minutes)

1. Explain the one weakness of JIT that was revealed by the 2011 earthquake and tsunami in Japan. (5)

2. A noted business analyst has said that 'JIT is about meticulous planning'. How well did Fujitsu stand up to that test? Explain your answer. (5)

3. Explain one benefit to a business from operating JIT with a zero buffer stock level. (4)

4. To what extent might a JIT approach to stock management be appropriate to a business with demand 'spikes', such as Sony? (16)

2. Evaluate how important it might be for a retailer such as Next to move to a just-in-time system of inventory control. (20)

Decision-making to improve operational performance

Linked to: Technology and operational efficiency, Chapter 30; Analysing operational performance, Chapter 31; Improving quality, Chapter 32; Managing supply chains, Chapter 33; Managing inventory, Chapter 34.

> **Definition**
>
> Operational performance implies an evaluation of the effectiveness of the policies that relate capacity utilisation, stock and quality management to the corporate business objectives.

35.1 Introduction

Management guru Peter Drucker once wrote that there are only two real business functions: marketing and innovation. Oddly he failed to see that nothing in business matters unless there is sound operational performance. Nobody pays for the promise of a product; they pay for a finished, manufactured, delivered product of the right quality. Operations management matters and therefore the quality of operational decision-making has an important impact on competitiveness.

35.2 Operational decisions and competitiveness

In the 50/50 global duopoly market for aeroplanes, Boeing had gained a significant lead in the 250–300 passenger sector thanks to its innovative B787 plane. At the 2014 Farnborough Airshow, Airbus announced the decision to launch a new variation on its A330 aircraft called A330NEO. The wings would be redesigned and new, more fuel-efficient engines attached. And – crucially – the A330NEO would be priced 25 per cent below the $257 million list price for a B787. In this business battle for a sector worth $1 trillion over the next twenty years, operational excellence is a key factor.

In the market for aircraft, there are a series of key factors to consider when choosing between Airbus (Europe) and Boeing (US).

- Function: this is a combination of size (and therefore passenger capacity) and range; long-haul customers want to fly without a refuelling stop.

- Design: some planes are attractive to travellers, making them willing to pay a higher ticket price – which, in turn, helps the manufacturers charge higher prices.

- Economy: the most important element is fuel economy, as fuel accounts for about 30 per cent of all operating costs. Aircraft maintenance is also a big item, accounting for a further 12 per cent of costs

- Reliability: though when the competition is Airbus vs Boeing, no one really takes time over this – both have equally high quality standards

- Availability: if an airline places an order for a Boeing 787 in 2015, it cannot hope for delivery before 2022. This is largely because of supply constraints. In 2014 Boeing produced 787s at a rate of 10 per month. It will increase this capacity to 12 per month in 2016 and 14 by 2019. In the meantime there's a huge queue. So a Chinese airline needing more planes in the next year or so would struggle to get hold of 787s.

To boost its competitiveness the European manufacturer needs to tackle one or more of these issues. If it was able to boost the fuel economy of its aircraft, for instance, that operational step forward should help boost market share.

35.3 Operational decisions and the other business functions

In August 2014 the boss of the giant multinational Procter & Gamble (P&G) announced that the company planned to cut in half its huge brand portfolio. Culling perhaps 100 brands would enable the business to focus on the brands making perhaps 95 per cent of the company's profits. This is fundamentally an operational decision designed to help cut costs and therefore boost profit margins.

The knock-on effects, though, will impact the other business functions. If P&G sells higher volumes on fewer product lines, there will be more automation, perhaps leading to a round of redundancies. That will not only affect the human resources function, but also finance. The marketing department will also be affected by the halving of the product portfolio. Marketing staff will have to devise bold strategies to boost sales of the brands being retained.

In business, every decision by one department has a knock-on effect upon the other functions. This is why the job of co-ordination is such an important aspect of management. The table below shows the impact of other operational decisions.

Table 35.1 The impact of operational decisions

Operational decision	Impact on other functions
Build a factory extension to increase production capacity	Marketing must provide the confirmation from a forecast of future sales; finance must provide the capital and HR must plan the workforce flow
Outsource a component of production to an outside supplier	HR will need to consult with staff on whether to make redundancies or redeploy; finance will have to fund the exercise – possibly high short-term cash outflows on redundancy payments
To move to a Just-In-Time production strategy	Finance will benefit from improved cash flow; HR will have to plan for more frequent deliveries and more erratic production schedules

'There's nothing so useless as doing efficiently that which shouldn't be done at all.' Peter Drucker, business academic and writer

35.4 Impact on operations of market conditions and competition

In the period 1995–2007, the extremely low labour costs in China made it easy for UK companies to see the attractions of outsourcing to Chinese suppliers, or even building factories in the Far East. Since then the dramatic rise in industrial wages in China (up nearly twenty times in real terms since 1995), plus a strengthening of the Chinese currency, have altered the cost equation. Wages in China today are still much lower than in the West (around a fifth of UK levels), but

they now represent a significant cost. When transport costs and different productivity levels are factored in, the Chinese advantage is less clear-cut.

For one western company, Zara, this change in market conditions is pleasing because they have always kept supply close to their native Spain. This used to be a punishing strain on the company's competitiveness. Today it is far less so. In any case Zara always believed that there was a greater marketing advantage in being able to react quickly to changing fashions – by producing in Europe it could get new designs into UK shops more quickly than waiting for the boat from China.

'China is a great manufacturing centre, but it's actually mostly an assembly plant.' Noam Chomsky, philosopher.

Other market and competition factors affecting operations:

- In August 2014 Sony announced that PS4 sales had passed the 10 million mark, while Xbox One had sold half that figure. Although the higher demand for the Sony product was obvious, both consoles were still being held back by supply problems, nine months after launch. Competition for the highest quality suppliers and supplies is important in high technology markets
- Market demand and variability is another important factor. Some products have highly unpredictable demand, be it ice cream and the weather, clothing sales and changing fashions, toy sales and different fads or the randomising element that comes from a social media craze for a particular item. Operations managers have got to understand their product well enough to choose the right balance between capital-intensive (but inflexible) production and labour-intensive flexibility.

Real business

In Spring 2014 New Look suddenly found sales booming for one specific beachwear product: a kimono. Between April and August sales ran at 40,000 units a week (an amazing sales level). The company struggled but managed to keep supply levels up to capitalise on this unexpected demand. Clearly it's vital in the fashion business to keep supply lines very flexible. As a result, the company was able to sell £800,000-worth of kimonos a week, helping to boost New Look's April–June sales by 9 per cent and profits by 38 per cent. ⇨

Figure 35.1 The appeal of kimonos helped to boost New Look's profits in 2014

35.5 Ethical and environmental influences on operational decisions

In many companies Corporate Social Responsibility (CSR) lies within the public relations function of the business. Therefore it is understandable that many operations departments see ethical and environmental factors as 'outsourced'. When the Rana Plaza building collapse in Bangladesh killed 1,129 and injured 2,515 textile workers, the UK clothing chain Matalan was caught in the lights of media publicity (along with Primark, Asda and Debenhams). Matalan worsened its own position by dragging its feet about contributing to the victims' compensation fund. It seemed as if the company had neither taken its supply chain responsibilities very seriously, nor had it been quick to accept moral liability in the aftermath of the disaster.

Although there is little evidence that Matalan or Primark's sales are affected significantly by consumer concerns over the supply sources being used, it still could be hoped that some operations managers will push internally to get their companies to do more than is strictly necessary. For example, they could push to set up their own factory inspection teams to monitor what goes on at low-cost suppliers in countries that lack a government-financed inspection regime as exists in the UK.

Other ethical and environmental influences:

- Operations managers who have adopted the philosophy of lean production will see that not only can the approach aid long-term competitiveness and profitability but it will also lead to significant environmental benefits. After all, lean production is about the elimination of waste; lean producers want production to be right first time so that no materials need to be scrapped. Therefore a lean producer should be able to produce the same output as a mass producer, but using fewer materials.

- For ethics to mean anything, they must be given priority over profit rather than seen as a way to generate more business or to differentiate a brand. Therefore one should respect a business that opts into a Fairtrade agreement with suppliers purely because it sees it as morally correct. Is this always the case, though? How is it that Nestlé use the Fairtrade badge on its Kit Kats, yet ignores Fairtrade for other brands such as Yorkie and Quality Street?

35.6 Technological influences on operational decisions

It is important at the outset to be clear that however 'obvious' it is that new technology will have boosted labour productivity, the data shows something different. And not just for the UK, as America shows the same pattern: productivity over the past ten years has grown more slowly than in previous decades. See Figure 35.2.

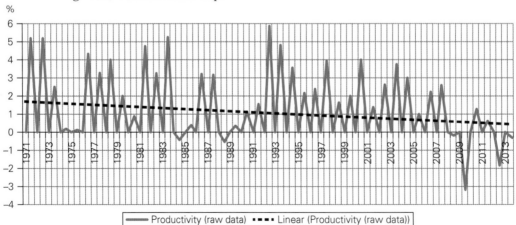

Figure 35.2 UK labour productivity 1971–2013

Annual percentage change in output per hour, in constant prices

Source: Organisation for Economic Co-operation and Development (OECD) 2014

The reality is that modern operations managers have to steer a tricky course between maximum efficiency and customer satisfaction. This is clear to see at any supermarket. At some you'll see half the checkouts open and a queue at every one. In this case labour productivity is being maximised – but at the cost of customers' time (and patience). At another supermarket more checkouts may be open, there may be less queuing, and the occasional 'idle' operator – sitting waiting for the next customer. Result? Happier customers but lower labour productivity figures (and maybe a smacked wrist from head office). So all the new technology in the world cannot prevent operations managers having to think hard about the proper balance between efficiency and customer satisfaction.

Other IT developments and their effect on operational decisions:

- The growth of online businesses creates a greater separation between the company and the production/operational process; for example ASOS doesn't need to ever touch a product. The order for a summer dress comes into the ASOS website together with the customer payment and feeds straight through to the supplier, who packs the item and posts it. In effect almost every aspect of operations is outsourced (except IT and purchasing)

- Better links with customers may be a consequence of new technology, though it could be argued that online relationships are weaker than face-to-face. Online gives opportunities (as on TripAdvisor) for suppliers to gain feedback from customers, and then reply to that feedback. That sounds good until you see that the company feedback looks evermore like a cut-and-paste exercise.

- Better links with suppliers can come about through a permanent EDI (Electronic Data Interchange) connection. This can be used to feed retail customer orders directly through to a factory, enabling the supplier to anticipate orders to come. This makes lean production much more viable.

- Better inventory control is made possible by more accurate data, for which RFID (Radio Frequency Identification) is the ideal technology. A study by Walmart showed that RFID reduced out-of-stocks by 30 per cent on low-selling items. In general, though, the big step forward came with barcodes and laser-barcode readers. Further improvements in inventory management will be relatively marginal.

'The first rule of any technology used in a business is that automation applied to an efficient operation will magnify the efficiency. The second is that automation applied to an inefficient operation will magnify the inefficiency.' Bill Gates, Microsoft founder

---

Key terms

Right first time: producing with 100 per cent accuracy so that there is no need for re-work (and, ultimately, no need for a quality control/inspection system).

Workforce flow: planning for the right combination of recruitment, training and productivity levels to meet future production requirements efficiently.

Evaluation: Decision-making to improve operational performance

In the 1990s the move by western companies to follow the Japanese towards lean production was hugely significant. It meant that, for a while, changes in operations were often of real importance in company competitiveness. In 2009 this culminated in America's auto giants General Motors and Chrysler both going under and needing to be bailed out by the US government. Only then were significant changes achieved.

Today, most of the big wins have already happened – until dramatic new technologies emerge, or until radical new ways of working come about. Therefore, if you consider any of the big global business battles: VW vs Toyota; Pepsi vs Coke; Unilever vs Procter & Gamble, the factors that sway market share are more to do with marketing or big strategic choices (Kellogg's buying Pringles for example) than to do with operations. James Dyson rightly points out that scientific and engineering expertise is needed to achieve innovation, but the more day-to-day aspects of operations management provide little scope for huge breakthroughs in competitiveness.

Five Whys and a How

Question	Answer
Why is this function called operations rather than 'production'?	Because 'production' sounds strange for the 80 per cent of UK business that is within the service sector
Why may the trend towards online retailing help the move to Just-In-Time stock management?	Whereas the customer *must* have the precise size and colour available when buying in-store, online ordering gives a day or two to obtain supplies
Why might an economic downturn make an operations manager's job easier?	Because it will be easier to negotiate deals with suppliers and there will be less pressure to get huge orders out to retail customers
Why might it be short sighted for a clothing retailer to ignore the working conditions of those within its supply chain?	Because the media likes to tell a story about business greed in ignoring the plight of those who create the products that generate the profits
Why might outsourcing to overseas suppliers prove a long-term mistake?	Even if unit costs are cut in the short term, future wage levels may rise as in China, reducing the cost advantages; and having suppliers close by gives the advantage of short lead times
How might a company measure the performance of a new operations manager?	By monitoring quantifiable data such as reject levels, customer satisfaction levels and stock value per £ of sales. But it's also important to consider qualitative factors such as morale in the factory and the distribution depots

Workbook

A. Revision questions

(35 marks; 35 minutes)

1. Explain how operational decisions might affect the competiveness of **one** of these companies:
   a) Urban Outfitters
   b) British Airways
   c) United Biscuits (McVities) (4)

2. Identify three aspects of operations management that might affect the reliability of a complex durable such as a car. (3)

3. Explain the possible impact on other business functions of an operational decision to 'reshore' production, that is, cancel an outsourced contract and bring production back to the UK. (6)

4. How might a retailer's operational decisions be affected if a new US competitor started offering a virtually identical product range to your own? (6)

5. Figure 35.2 shows that labour productivity has been falling in many of the recent years in the UK. How is this possible? (5)

6. Analyse the benefits of RFID that might explain Walmart's 30 per cent fall in out-of-stocks. (6)

7. In your own words, explain Peter Drucker's statement quoted on page 217. (5)

B. Revision exercises
DATA RESPONSE

Tesco and its suppliers

Tesco has had several years of difficult trading; that is, weak customer demand leading to falling market share and profitability. But buried within the company's website is some more data that could give senior management pause for thought. The graph below shows Tesco's own figures on the views of their own suppliers. And because the response rate from suppliers averages 50 per cent, it is possible that these figures overstate suppliers' attitude to the company.

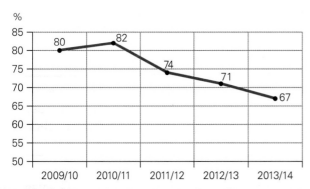

Figure 35.3 Tesco suppliers: 'I am treated with respect'

Source: *Tesco and Society* reports, from <u>www.tescoplc.com</u>

Perhaps the decline in the suppliers' relationship with Tesco can be related to the February 2013 public relations disaster in which a series of its own-label meat products proved to contain horsemeat. Ultimately, every business needs to manage its relationship with suppliers with as much care as it deals with customers.

Questions (35 marks; 40 minutes)

1. Describe the information given in the graph shown above. (5)

2. Explain why conclusions from the graph need to bear in mind the suppliers' response rate. (5)

3. Either Tesco knew that its products contained horsemeat, or it chose not to test the products. Analyse the ethics of this situation. (9)

4. To what extent might an increase in the use of technology solve the problem of Tesco's relationship with its suppliers? (16)

C. Extend your understanding

1. When I buy a chocolate bar I do not consider the working conditions of the West African cocoa farmers. Is it fair, therefore, to expect companies such as Primark to know every detail of the workers within the supply chain from raw cotton through to delivered clothing? Justify your answer. (20)

2. To what extent should the other business functions get involved in key operational decisions such as cutting capacity or moving away from a Just-in-Time system of inventory control? (20)

Chapter 36

Financial objectives

Linked to: Break-even analysis, Chapter 38; Profit and how to increase it, Chapter 41; Sources of finance, Chapter 43; Decision-making to improve financial performance, Chapter 44.

Definition

Financial objectives outline what the business wishes to achieve in financial terms during a certain period of time. Constraints are the internal and external factors that affect the firm's ability to achieve these objectives.

36.1 How are financial objectives set?

Financial objectives are determined by taking into account the overall company aims. They express the financial aspects of the overall company plan. They will be decided like any other business objective, by taking into account the internal position of the business and the external business environment. The internal aspects of the business, such as what the business is currently doing and what resources it has available, will determine what the business can achieve. This has to be put into the perspective of the external environment. The external environment will affect how easy it is to carry out the plans. An increase in sales is unlikely to be achieved in an economy that is going into recession.

What makes a good financial objective?

As with any other business objective, financial objectives should be SMART:

- Specific: they should be clearly defined so that all staff know and understand the aims

- Measurable: if the objective can be measured then it is possible to see if the target has been achieved

- Achievable: a good objective is challenging but it must be achievable. To set a target that is impossible is demoralising for staff and it could also create poor shareholder and public confidence if objectives are not met

- Realistic: any objective should make good business sense

- Timebound: financial targets usually relate to the company's financial year. They can also look further into the future.

'You read a book from beginning to end. You run a business the opposite way. You start with the end, and then you do everything you must to reach it.' Harold Geneen, fabled US businessman

36.2 Types of financial objective

It is generally assumed that all businesses operate in order to maximise profit. This is of course true to a certain extent. Why would people invest in a business if not to make profit? However, there are other considerations, as outlined below.

Return on investment

Companies (and people) put their capital at risk whenever they take it out of the bank and invest it in an asset or an activity. Sometimes the investment proves a success, such as Whitbread plc's brilliant purchase of Costa Coffee for £23 million in 1995. Today it's the second biggest coffee shop chain in China, quite apart from being Britain's No. 1. But sometimes the investment proves unwise, either producing disappointing profits or, like Morrisons' purchase of Kiddicare, significant losses.

Table 36.1 Return on investment: Sublime Costa to Ridiculous Morrisons'.

	Morrisons' buys Kiddicare	Whitbread buys Costa
Sum invested	£70 million	£23 million
Date of investment	Morrisons' paid this in 2011 for a fast-growing online retailer of kid's clothes	Bought in 1995 from the Costa brothers Bruno and Sergio, who founded Costa in London in 1971
Since then	In March 2014 Morrisons' writes the value of its assets down by £163 million to allow for the horror-show losses made by Kiddicare	
Latest information	Kiddicare is sold for £2 million in 2014 Morrisons' is glad to get rid of the business without further losses	In 2014 Costa's latest profit figure is £110 million
Implicit 2014 return on investment (ROI)	In 3 years £163m is lost, i.e. £54.3m a year. That's a ROI of -£54.3/£70 x 100 = *minus* 77.6 per cent a year	£110m/£23m x 100 = 478 per cent ROI

Financial safety

A key to long-term financial safety is to keep debt levels under control. A good rule of thumb is to say that no more than half a firm's financing should come from debt. Financial analysts are especially likely to check the long-term finances of a business, to see if long-term bank loans are more than half the total sum invested in the business in the long term. It would be a good financial target to say that 50 per cent should be the maximum allowable debt level for the business. This would help to avoid business collapses such as the RBS Bank in 2009 or La Senza retail outlets in 2014.

Capital structure objectives

To maximise the chance of long-term financial safety, directors need to think of the right capital structure for their business. This should be based on an assessment of the level of operational risks they face. Between 1997 and 2005 French Connection was the coolest young fashion brand in Britain, with its clever logo FCUK. Then the fashion-conscious moved on, leaving French Connection with eight years in the wilderness. Even in 2014 the business was still making operating losses. Fortunately for the company, founder and chief executive Stephen Marks had – during the

good times – made sure that the capital structure was super-safe. He reasoned that fashion businesses are inherently risky; therefore the long-term capital structure was based on zero debt. At the time it hit the rocks operationally, French Connection plc was debt-free and therefore could survive its operational difficulties. If its capital structure has been based on debt, the company would probably have collapsed during the 2009/10 recession.

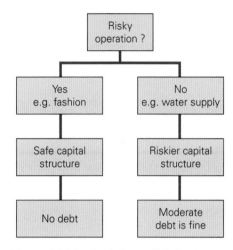

Figure 36.1 Logic chain: capital structure

Capital spending objectives

For businesses in fiercely competitive technological markets, a key to long-term success is to generate high enough profit margins to fund high levels of investment spending on capital equipment and on research and development (R&D). The spending on capital equipment enables the quality and efficiency of production to rise (think industrial robots), while spending on R&D can lead to product innovation. This is the world of Microsoft vs Sony vs Nintendo (games consoles) or Apple vs Samsung (phones, etc.).

To achieve the long-term market share desired by the directors, generous objectives may be needed for capital spending and spending on R&D.

Cost minimisation

A business may concentrate on minimising costs. Lowering costs will increase profitability. This may be a general overall aim, such as reducing fixed costs by 5 per cent, or it may be more specific, such as reducing wastage in the factory and therefore reducing material costs by 4 per cent. A strategy of cost minimisation may be necessary when times are hard (see Table 36.1).

Table 36.2 Cost-cutting strategies

To cut fixed costs	To cut variable costs
• Consider closing loss-making branches or factories • Consider moving the head office or main factory to a lower-cost location • Consider carefully whether a layer of management could be removed to reduce staffing costs	• Renegotiate with existing suppliers to try to agree lower prices • Look for new suppliers, perhaps from a low-cost country such as China • Redesign the goods to make them simpler and therefore quicker and cheaper to produce

36.3 Internal and external influences on financial objectives

There are many factors that will influence the way a firm sets its financial objectives. These can be categorised as internal and external constraints.

Internal influences

The ambitions of the leader

In 2014, the appointment of outsider Dave Lewis as Tesco chief executive came with a great deal of decision-making power. In the months leading up to his predecessor's sacking, many senior Tesco executives had left the company. So Dave Lewis could set the agenda and choose his own objectives. In fact he chose to take his time before deciding what the targets should be. As he was an outside appointment (from Unilever) City analysts were willing to give him that time.

Financial

Although it may seem strange to talk about internal finance as a constraint on financial objectives, it can play an important part. The pursuit of higher profit might be constrained by lack of cash flow, especially at times when demand is rising sharply.

Operational

A firm that is close to full capacity may find that it has fewer opportunities for improving the profitability of the business, unless it has the confidence and the resources to increase capacity, perhaps by moving to bigger premises.

'We want to become the fastest-growing company with the highest profit margins in the business of renting and leasing vehicles without drivers.' Robert Townsend, former Chairman of Avis car rentals

---

Real business

Table 36.3 Financial objectives of major businesses

Company	Financial objectives
Thornton's Chocolate plc	(2012) 'To boost operating margins to match the industry average within three years'; by 2013 margins had risen from 1.3 per cent to 3.3 per cent.
ASOS plc	'To achieve a £1 billion annual sales turnover.' In the 2014 financial year sales were over £955 million, so the target was in sight.
Marks & Spencer plc	'An online push to target the 19 million customers who shop at our stores, but shop elsewhere online' (May 2014)

External influences

Competitive environment

The plans of almost every business can be affected by the behaviour and reaction of competitors. A plan to increase profit margins by increasing prices may be wrecked if competitors react by reducing theirs.

Economic environment

The state of the economy plays a vital part in the ability of a business to meet its financial objectives. Higher taxes might reduce customers' disposable income and therefore spending, so financial objectives may not be met. The effect will depend on the business. Supermarket own-brand producers (of 'inferior goods') may do better, whereas branded goods may suffer.

Government

A firm may find its financial objectives limited by regulatory or legislative activity. Consumer watchdogs such as the Office of Fair Trading (OFT) have powers to fine businesses that they believe are not acting in the best interests of consumers. Legislation may also be introduced that increases business costs.

Building the outside in

Good business planning involves being aware of the possible external influences that may act as constraints. External constraints will always be subject to more uncertainty as they are outside the control of the business. It is therefore important when setting financial objectives that the business includes a series of 'what if' scenarios. This will prepare them for outside factors that may impede their progress.

36.4 The use of data for financial decisions

In new product development it can be argued that pure judgement may prove more successful than carefully researched 'facts'. Certainly that is what Apple says. If you look at Apple's accounts, however, you are left in no doubt that their finance director is as serious-minded as every other. In finance, decisions are made on the basis of data.

Apple's capital structure, therefore, will be decided upon after careful analysis of the company's accounts and those of rivals. Apple wants to stand out because of its products, not because its finances seem curious.

Every finance director will have daily information available to show the latest trends in profits, profitability, balance sheet health, cash flow and much more. All financial decisions are driven by data.

36.5 Ethical and environmental influences on financial decisions

In some businesses the pursuit of profit may cause conflict between the different groups with an interest in the business (the stakeholders), as in the following examples.

- The rise of interest in the environment has meant that costs have increased for many firms and therefore profit has been reduced. However, many firms have also discovered that they can make huge savings, such as by limiting waste.

- Some firms, most notably supermarket chains, are accused of driving the prices of their suppliers to the lowest possible level. Low supply costs increase profits. Businesses need to ensure that there is a balance between keeping costs low and maintaining the quality of the supplies. In the food chain, tough bargaining by supermarkets may cause unacceptable welfare conditions for animals such as chickens and piglets. This, in turn, may backfire, affecting the retailer's reputation.

- Taxation may be a consideration. Large multinational companies may deliberately reduce profit figures in one country in order to pay less tax, increasing profit figures in another where profits are taxed at a lower level.

They are able to do this by charging differential prices between subsidiaries in different countries. Such tax avoidance is legal, but arguably not ethical.

- Public image: a firm may choose to spend money on charitable concerns or sponsorship. This, as a cost, will reduce profit. However, it may well get a return on its investment through creating a better brand image or good public relations.

Key terms

Cash flow: the flow of cash into and out of the business.

External constraint: Something outside the firm's control that can prevent it achieving its objectives.

Full capacity: when the business is fully utilising all its assets.

Public limited company (plc): a company with limited liability and shares that are available to the public. Its shares are usually quoted on the stock exchange.

Stakeholders: groups with an interest in the success or failure of a firm's decisions and actions.

Evaluation: Financial objectives

There are advantages and disadvantages to setting tight financial objectives. Some people consider that objectives are vital to give direction to the business. A good set of objectives will enable plans for each sector of the business to be developed. Each individual within the organisation will then know the role that they are to play. Without objectives, the business may drift aimlessly.

Other people consider that objectives can stifle entrepreneurship and initiative. They feel that managers operate to satisfy the objectives but do not go beyond them. They also feel that they dampen risk-taking, which may prevent a business from taking the kind of leaps forward shown by Apple (iPhone, iPad) and Nintendo (Wii).

'Rapid growth is not necessarily the best measure of success. Indeed it is probably detrimental to most businesses.' Mark Spohr, US company president

Five Whys and a How

Question	Answer
Why might a small, fast-growing company focus its financial objectives on cash-flow objectives?	Because cash-flow difficulties are common among fast-growing firms
Why might a firm focus on financing higher R&D spending?	To stay competitive with other, perhaps overseas, high-technology companies
Why might employees think that senior management sees business ethics as subordinate to profit?	Because financial objectives that only mention profit or profitability implicitly suggest that ethics come second
Why may a firm's financial objectives seem impossible to achieve when a recession kicks in?	If the company mainly produces luxury goods it may be impossible, in the short term, to overcome falling sales and profits
Why might a plc keep its financial objectives secret?	Because it doesn't want competitors to plan accordingly: 'if they're focusing on cost minimisation we can increase our advertising spending and they won't follow us.'
How might a private school be affected by a capital structure based largely on debt?	Like any other business, a period of poor trading may cause the debts to accumulate, threatening the school's future

Workbook

A. Revision questions

(30 marks; 30 minutes)

1. What is meant by 'financial objectives'? (2)

2. Why is improving or maintaining profit likely to be the most important financial objective? (4)

3. Outline two examples of how stakeholder interests could affect the setting of business objectives. (4)

4. Outline two likely results for shareholders if profits fall. (4)

5. List and explain two possible internal constraints on achieving the financial objectives for a multinational chocolate producer. (6)

6. Discuss two external constraints that should be taken into account when financial objectives are set by *one* of the following businesses.
   a) Spotify (rapidly growing subscription service for streamed music)
   b) ASOS (rapidly growing online clothes retailer)
   c) Versace clothing. (8)

7. What government activity could act as a constraint on businesses achieving their financial objectives? Give an example. (2)

B. Revision exercises
DATA RESPONSE

Ethics and financial decisions at Glaxo

In July 2013 Gao Feng, the head of China's fraud unit, accused Glaxo Smith Kline (GSK) of bribing Chinese doctors to get them to buy GSK vaccines. GSK is one of Britain's largest pharmaceutical companies, so the London-based media were sceptical of these claims. Gao Feng, though, said: 'We found that bribery is a core part of the activities of the company. To boost their share price and sales, the company performed illegal actions.'

Later in the year, GSK implicitly accepted that up to £300 million in bribes had been paid in China. Later, further accusations of bribery by GSK staff emerged in Poland, Iraq, Jordan and Lebanon.

In July 2014 chief executive Sir Andrew Witty made it clear that the allegations were 'contrary to the values' he believed in. The company's 2013 Corporate Responsibility report spoke of 'our four core values: transparency, respect for people, integrity and patient-focus.' Unfortunately, as reported by the authoritative *Forbes* magazine: 'investors are still uneasy about the criminal probe by Chinese officials into allegations

that GSK executives engaged in widespread bribery. GSK executives have been accused of illegally paying doctors, hospitals and other medical organisations in an effort to increase sales of Glaxo products.'

Sir Christopher Gent, GSK Chairman, said in the 2012 annual accounts (the report immediately before the bribery crisis emerged): 'Ultimately the aim of our strategy is to deliver sustainable earnings per share growth (EPS) and improved returns to shareholders.' His objective of improved profits and higher dividends to shareholders could help explain the pressures on staff that might lead to fraudulent behaviour.

Questions (25 marks; 30 minutes)

1. Analyse the factors GSK might take into account when setting financial objectives for its next financial year. (9)

2. To what extent is it inevitable that profit comes into conflict with ethics in business today? (16)

C. Extend your understanding

1. Evaluate the importance of external influences on the financial objectives of a business such as easyJet. (20)

2. For a business such as BP, to what extent should environmental factors influence financial decisions? (20)

Chapter 37

Calculating revenue, costs and profit

Linked to: Break-even analysis, Chapter 38; Profit and how to increase it, Chapter 41.

Definition

Revenue is the value of total sales made by a business within a period, usually one year.

Costs are the expenses incurred by a firm in producing and selling its products, such as wages and raw materials.

Profit is made when a firm's sales revenue exceeds its total costs.

37.1 The measurement and importance of profit

Profit is measured by deducting all business costs from the revenues generated within a trading period – say six months. Business people sometimes say that 'revenue is vanity; profit is sanity'. In other words, making lots of sales feels great, but there is no business purpose in selling things unless profits are generated. Full details on measuring profit are covered in Section 37.4.

Profits are important for the following reasons:

- They provide a measure of the success of the organisation
- Profits are the best source of capital for investment in the growth of the business, for example, to finance new store openings or to pay for new product development
- They act as a magnet to attract further funds from investors enticed by the possibility of high returns on their investment.

'One of our most important management tasks is maintaining the proper balance between short-term profit performance and investment for future strength and growth.' David Packard, computer pioneer

However, it is not uncommon for a new business to fail to make profits in the first months – or even years – of trading. The need to generate profits becomes more important as time passes. A business ultimately needs to make profits to reward its owners for putting money into the enterprise.

Perhaps oddly, profit is also important to not-for-profit organisations such as charities. In the 2009 recession charitable giving in the UK fell by 11 per cent. A charity with important long-term programmes such as Oxfam would have needed to dip into their reserves to tide themselves over the fall in their income. Accumulated profits can insulate organisations from erratic factors, allowing them to keep achieving their stated objectives.

To understand profit fully, it is first necessary to look at revenues and costs.

37.2 Business revenues

The revenue received by a firm as a result of trading activities is a critical factor in its success. Entrepreneurs start their financial planning by assessing the revenue that they are likely to receive during the coming financial year. This can be calculated using this formula:

$$\text{Sales revenue} = \text{volume of goods sold} \times \text{average selling price}$$

A firm seeking to increase its revenue can plan to sell more or aim to sell at a higher price. Some firms may maintain high prices even though this policy depresses sales. Such companies, perhaps selling fashion or high-technology products, believe that in the long run this approach will lead to higher revenue and higher profits.

The term revenue is also sometimes referred to as 'turnover' or 'sales'.

Real business

Blackberry's falling revenue

In the three months ending 30 November Blackberry saw its revenue plunge from £1,660 million in 2012 'to £730 million in 2013. The reason for the 56 per cent fall in revenue was a collapse in phone sales from 3.7 to 1.9 million, plus a fall in the average price charged per Blackberry. The company had pinned everything on a new range of phones based on a new operating system, but it proved unable to dent sales of the iPhone and the Samsung Galaxy. As a consequence of the revenue decline, Blackberry made losses of £2.7 billion in its third quarter of 2013.

The other way to boost revenue is to charge a low price in an attempt to sell as many products as possible. In some markets this may lead to high revenues and profits. Firms following this approach are likely to be operating in markets in which the goods are fairly similar and consumers do not exhibit strong preferences for any brand. This is true of the market for young holidaymakers going to Spain or Thailand. Price competition is fierce as businesses seek to maximise their revenue.

Traditionally, companies printed price lists that might run for 12 months. These days online purchasing makes dynamic pricing more common; that is, allowing prices to rise and fall depending on demand and supply conditions. This is a way to maximise revenue, by charging high prices when demand is at its highest, but much more modest prices during periods of low demand. Football teams such as West Ham do something similar, offering 'Kids for a Quid' when their home game is against an unfashionable opponent such as Stoke City.

Real business

Price manipulation for maximised revenue

In a world increasingly dominated by online purchasing, businesses have the ability to vary prices to maximise revenue. This is quite open with airline prices where, for example, the easyJet Sunday 11.40 a.m. flight to Barcelona was priced at £98.99 for 28 December, £41.99 for 25 January, and £65.99 for 1 March 2015 (prices as at 16 December 2014). But it's less clear-cut with online purchasing of insurance, where the same car might cost £475 to insure on a Monday and £650 on a Tuesday, as the sellers try to reward those who can be bothered to shop around while simultaneously catching out the lazier shoppers. As the saying goes: let the buyer beware!

37.3 The costs of production

Costs are a critical element of the information necessary to manage a business successfully. Managers need to be aware of the costs of all aspects of their business for a number of reasons.

- They need to know the cost of production to assess whether it is profitable to supply the market at the current price.
- They need to know actual costs to allow comparisons with their forecasted (or budgeted) figures. This will allow them to make judgements concerning the cost-efficiency of different parts of the business.

Fixed and variable costs

This is an important classification of the costs encountered by businesses. This classification has a number of uses. For example, it is the basis for calculating break even, which is covered in Chapter 38.

Fixed costs

Fixed costs are any costs that do not vary directly with the level of output. These costs are linked to time rather than to level of business activity. Fixed costs exist even if a business is not producing any goods or services. An example of a fixed cost is rent, which is usually calculated monthly, but will remain the same whether business is great or awful that month. The landlord doesn't care; she or he just wants to be paid!

If a manufacturer can double output from within the same factory, the amount of rent will not alter, thus it is a fixed cost. In the same way, a seaside hotel has mortgage and salary costs during the winter, even though there may be very few guests. Given that fixed costs are inevitable, it is vital that managers work hard at bringing in customers to keep the fixed costs covered.

In Figure 37.1, you can see that the firm faces fixed costs of £50,000 irrespective of the level of output.

Other examples of fixed costs include the uniform business rate (local taxes), management salaries, interest charges and depreciation.

In the long term, fixed costs can alter. The manufacturer referred to earlier may decide to increase output significantly. This may require renting additional factory space and negotiating loans for additional capital equipment. Thus rent will rise as may interest payments. We can see that in the long term fixed costs may alter, but that in the short term they are — as their name suggests — fixed.

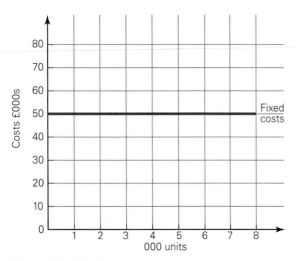

Figure 37.1 Fixed costs of £50,000 per year

Variable costs

Variable costs are those costs which vary directly with the level of output. They represent payments made for the use of inputs such as labour, fuel and raw materials. If our manufacturer doubled output then these costs would double. A doubling of the sales of innocent Strawberry Smoothies would require twice the purchasing of strawberries and bananas. There would also be extra costs for the packaging, the wage bill and the energy required to fuel the production line.

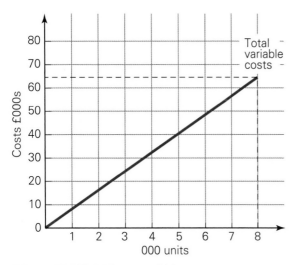

Figure 37.2 Variable costs of £8 per unit

The graph in Figure 37.2 shows a firm with variable costs of £8 per unit of production. This means that variable costs rise steadily with, and proportionately to, the level of output. Thus a 10 per cent rise in output will increase total variable costs by the same percentage.

However, it is not always the case that variable costs rise in proportion to output. Many small businesses discover that as they expand, variable costs do not rise as quickly as output. A key reason for this is that as the business becomes larger it is able to negotiate better prices with suppliers. Its suppliers are likely to agree to sell at lower unit prices when the business places larger orders.

Examples of some variable, fixed and hard-to-classify costs are given in Table 37.1.

Table 37.1 Some costs are easy to classify, some are hard

Variable costs	Fixed costs	Hard to classify
Raw materials	Rent	Delivery costs
Packaging	Heating and Lighting	Electricity
Piece-rate labour	Salaries	Machine maintenance costs
Commission (percentage on sales)	Interest charges	Energy

Total costs

When added together, fixed and variable costs give the total costs for a business. This is, of course, a very important element in the calculation of the profits earned by a business.

The relationship between fixed, variable and total costs is straightforward to calculate but has some important implications for a business. If a business has relatively high fixed costs as a proportion of total costs, then it is likely to seek to maximise its sales to ensure that the fixed costs are spread across as many units of output as possible. In this way, the impact of high fixed costs is lessened.

Real business

Paying the costs

In 2012 Scoop opened its third London ice cream parlour. The company intended to continue making all the ice cream at the original Covent Garden store, but deliver ice cream daily to the new branch at Gloucester Road (two miles away). This meant that all the fixed production costs would remain unchanged (rent on the floor space, the machinery and the professional ice cream maker's salary). Variable costs would increase by around 50 per cent, as long as the new parlour's sales matched the first two. These costs would be the ingredients, especially milk, cream and sugar; plus the cost of the electricity to run the ice cream-making machines. There would also be some brand new fixed costs: an extra refrigerated van plus the rent and the staff at the new premises. Overall, owner Matteo Pantani knew that he could increase his revenue by 50 per cent while total costs should increase by no more than 30 per cent. This should boost profit considerably.

37.4 Profits

Profit occurs when revenues are greater than costs. The key formula is:

Profit = total revenue – total costs

Calculating profits

Although the profit formula is simple (revenue – costs), it is easy to make mistakes when calculating the figures. The problems rarely come from calculating revenue; the hard part is getting total costs right. The following example may help:

> ### Worked example
>
> Gwen and John's pasta restaurant charges £10 for three courses and has an average of 800 customers per week. The variable costs are £4 per customer and the restaurant has fixed costs of £3,400 per week. To calculate profit:
>
> 1. Calculate revenue:
>   Price × no. of customers
>   £10 × 800 = £8,000
> 2. Calculate total costs:
>   Fixed costs + total variable costs (No. of customers × variable costs per meal)
>   £3,400 + (800 × £4 = £3,200)
> 3. Calculate profit:
>   Total revenue – Total costs
>   £8,000 – (£3,400 + £3,200) = £1,400 per week
>
> See the Workbook section for exercises to practise this very important skill.

'If you're not in business for fun or profit, what are you doing here?' Robert Townsend, the original business guru

37.5 Revenue, cost and profit objectives

In 2014 Italian café chain Carluccio's, with £120 million of sales from its 81 outlets, set itself the objective of doubling revenue within the next four years. This could be achieved by increasing its £1.5 million revenue per outlet or – more probably – by doubling the number of cafés it has. Having set that objective it can calculate how much capital will be required; work out how much it can generate from within the business; and then see how much might be needed from outside.

Carluccio's revenue objectives also make it possible (necessary, even) to set cost objectives. In other words, set maximum cost levels for the start-up cost of each new outlet plus cost objectives for the food costs, staff costs and overheads costs per outlet. From the revenue and cost objectives will come the calculation of likely profit (though the profit figure will depend a great deal on how successful the new outlets prove to be).

The purpose behind setting these objectives is to ensure that every manager in the business understands how they fit together. For a business such as Carluccio's there can be a serious gap between what head office thinks and knows, and what is known by the 81 operating stores. It can make it easier to delegate authority to the store managers if they are clear about the revenue, cost and profit objectives.

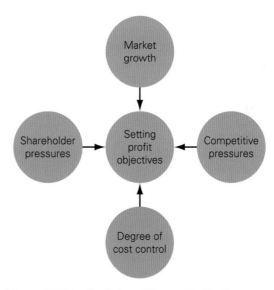

Figure 37.3 Logic chain: setting profit objectives

Five Whys and a How

Question	Answer
Why is it important for businesses to make a profit?	Because that provides the long-term capital for reinvestment and for business expansion
Why might a business want to separate its variable from its fixed costs?	Because it helps it to analyse the impact on profit of a change in demand or change in price
Why would a firm be worried if its revenue had slipped below its total costs?	Because it would be making operating losses; in the short-term that might be okay, but continual operating losses would force the company to close
Why might a business choose to lower its prices?	Because it feels that the increase in sales volume will outweigh the loss in revenue caused by the price cut, pushing total revenue up
Why might companies such as Aldi be willing to operate with low prices that provide low profits per item sold?	It's okay to have low profits per sale as long as you can sell masses of units. Aldi makes strong operating profits because its rate of sale is high
How does revenue differ from profit?	Revenue is just the value of sales, without taking costs into account. Profit includes the deduction of costs

Key terms

Dynamic pricing: using software that allows changing demand and supply levels to set ever-changing prices, as used by airlines and hotel chains.

Fixed costs: these costs do not vary as output (or sales) vary.

Piece-rate labour: paying workers per item they make; that is, without regular pay.

Profit margin: profit as a percentage of sales revenue.

Total costs: all the costs of producing a specific output level; that is, fixed costs plus total variable costs.

Total variable costs: all the variable costs of producing a specific output level; that is, variable costs per unit multiplied by the number of units sold.

Variable costs: the costs of producing one unit (can be known as unit variable costs).

Evaluation: Calculating revenue, costs and profits

When evaluating costs, revenues and profits for a new enterprise it is necessary to judge the likely accuracy of the forecast figures. It is also worth thinking about whether profits are the best measure of success for a new business. A successful first year of trading may see an enterprise gain a customer base and repeat orders by supplying at competitive prices. This may result in small profits initially while the business builds a reputation. Profits may become a more important measure of success in the longer term.

An assessment of the true worth of a business's performance as measured by its profits would also take account of the general state of the economy. Are businesses in general prospering, or is it a time of recession? They would also take into account any unusual circumstances such as, for example, the business being subject to the emergence of a new competitor.

Workbook

A. Revision questions

(30 marks; 30 minutes)

1. Why may a business initially receive relatively low revenues from a product newly introduced to the market? (3)

2. State two circumstances in which a company may be able to charge high prices for a new product? (2)

3. For what reasons may a firm seek to maximise its sales revenue? (4)

4. If a business sells 4,000 units of brand X at £4 each and 2,000 units of brand Y at £3 each, what is its total revenue? (4)

5. Outline two reasons why firms need to know the costs they incur in production. (4)

6. Distinguish, with the aid of examples, between fixed and variable costs. (4)

7. Explain why fixed costs can only alter in the long term. (3)

8. Give two reasons why profits are important to businesses. (2)

9. State one advantage and one disadvantage that may result from a business deciding to lower the proportion of profits it distributes to its owners. (2)

10. State two purposes for which a business's profits could be used. (2)

B. Revision exercises
DATA RESPONSE 1

(30 marks; 30 minutes)

1. During the summer weeks Devon Ice Cream has average sales of 4,000 units a week. Each ice cream sells for £1 and has variable costs of 25p. Fixed costs are £800.

   a) Calculate the weekly total costs for the business in the summer. (3)

   b) Calculate Devon Ice Cream's weekly profit in the summer. (3)

2. a) If a firm sells 200 Widgets at £3.20 and 40 Squidgets at £4, what is its total revenue? (3)

   b) Each Widget costs £1.20 to make, while each Squidget costs £1.50. What are the total variable costs? (3)

   c) If fixed costs are £300, what profit is the business making? (3)

3. 'Last week our sales revenue was £12,000, which was great. Our price is £2 a unit, which I think is a bit too cheap.'

   a) How many unit sales were made last week? (2)

   b) If a price rise to £2.25 cuts sales to 5,600 units, calculate the change in the firm's revenue. (4)

4. BYQ Co. has sales of 4,000 units a month, a unit price of £4, fixed costs of £9,000 and unit variable costs of £1. Calculate its profit. (4)

5. At full capacity output of 24,000 units, a firm's costs are as follows:

managers' salaries	£48,000
materials	£12,000
rent and rates	£24,000
piece-rate labour	£36,000

   a) What are the firm's total costs at 20,000 units? (4)

   b) What profit will be made at 20,000 units if the selling price is £6? (1)

DATA RESPONSE 2

Chalfont Computer Services Ltd

Robert has decided to give up his job with BT and to work for himself offering computer services to local people. He has paid off his mortgage and owns his house outright, so feels this is the time to take a risk. Robert has no experience of running a business, but is skilled in repairing computers and solving software problems. In the past Robert has repaired computers belonging to friends and family and is aware of the costs involved in providing this service. He believes that with the increase in internet usage there will be plenty of demand for his services. Robert has spoken to a few people in his local pub and this has confirmed his opinion. Robert needs to raise £10,000 to purchase equipment for his business and to pay for a new vehicle and intends to ask his bank for a loan.

The work Robert has already done allows him to forecast that the average revenue from each customer will be £40, while the variable costs will be £15. His monthly fixed costs will be £1,000. Table 37.2

Table 37.2 Estimates of number of customers

Month	Number of customers
January	40
February	50
March	60
April	82

gives Robert's estimates of the number of customers he expects to have.

Questions (20 marks, 25 minutes)

1. What is meant by the term 'variable costs'? (2)

2. Calculate Robert's forecast profits for his first three months' trading. (3)

3. Robert estimates that if he cut his prices by 10 per cent he would have 20 per cent more customers each month. Calculate the outcome of these changes and whether this would benefit Robert. (6)

4. Analyse the case for a bank lending Robert £10,000 on the basis of his forecast profits. (9)

C. Extend your understanding

1. In 2014 Tesco plc suffered a slide in its sales, with weekly data showing a 4 per cent decline compared with 2013. To what extent is it possible for a supermarket chain to rebuild its revenue without damaging its profit? (20)

2. When a rival surfing school opened next door, Jo's Surf School started to make weekly losses. To what extent would cutting variable costs restore Jo's Surf School's profitability? (20)

Chapter 38

Break-even analysis

Linked to: Calculating revenue, costs and profit, Chapter 37; Profit and how to increase it, Chapter 41.

Definition

Break-even analysis compares a firm's revenue with its fixed and variable costs to identify the minimum level of sales needed to cover costs. This can be shown on a graph known as a break-even chart.

38.1 Introduction

Businesses need to know how many products they have to produce and sell in order to cover all of their costs. This is particularly important for new businesses with limited experience of their markets.

Look at Table 38.1, which shows forecast revenue and cost figures for a new business.

Table 38.1 Forecast revenue and cost figures for a new business

Output of ties (per week)	Sales income (£ per week)	Total costs (£ per week)
0	0	10000
100	4000	11500
200	8000	13000
300	12000	14500
400	**16000**	**16000**
500	20000	17500
600	24000	19000

You can easily identify that 400 is the number of sales that must be achieved each week to break even. If sales are only 200 units the business will be making losses of a punishing £5,000 a week, so the break-even analysis is providing vital data.

To calculate the break-even point we need information on both costs and prices. Break-even can be shown on a graph or, more quickly, calculated in the following way.

38.2 Calculating break even

Calculating the break-even point for a product requires knowledge of:

- the selling price of the product
- its fixed costs
- its variable costs per unit.

Fixed costs are expenses which do not change in response to changing demand or output, such as rent and salaries. Variable costs will alter in relation to changes in demand and therefore output. A doubling of demand will double variable costs, but leave fixed costs the same.

The break-even output level can be calculated by the following formula:

$$\text{Break-even output} = \frac{\text{fixed costs}}{(\text{selling price per unit} - \text{variable cost per unit})}$$

Real business

Igloo ice cream costs 50p per unit to make and is sold for £2.50. The fixed costs of running the production process and the shop amount to £2,000 per week. Therefore the break-even output level is:

$$\frac{\text{Fixed costs}}{(\text{selling price per unit} - \text{variable cost per unit})} = \frac{£2,000}{£2.50 - 50p}$$

$$= 1,000 \text{ ice creams per week}$$

So although a £2 surplus per ice cream seems a lot of profit, it's only the 1001st ice cream that really makes £2. Before getting to the break-even point each ice cream sold is simply reducing the losses.

'(HMV) is now in danger of failing to break even in the full-year.' Nick Bubb, retail analyst (in December 2011, not long before the company collapsed into administration)

38.3 Contribution

In the above formula for break even, price *minus* variable costs is known as contribution. It is the surplus of £2 between the £2.50 selling price and the variable costs of 50p per unit.

Contribution per unit = selling price *minus* variable costs per unit

Total contribution = contribution per unit × quantity sold

So, in the above example, if 1,200 ice creams were sold, the total contribution would be: £2 × 1,200 ice creams = £2,400

Total contribution is a useful short-cut way to calculate profit, as:

Total contribution – fixed costs = profit

So,   £2,400 – £2,000 = £400 profit

38.4 Break-even charts

A break-even chart is a graph showing the revenue and costs for a business at all possible levels of demand or output. The break-even chart uses the horizontal axis to represent the output per time period for the business, for example, between 0 and 1,000 units a month. The vertical axis represents costs and sales in pounds.

Real business

Berry & Hall Ltd

Berry & Hall Ltd manufactures confectionery. The company is planning to launch a new sweet called Aromatics at a price of £5 per kg. The variable cost of production per kg is forecast at £3 and the fixed costs associated with this product are estimated to be £50, 000 a year. The company's maximum output of Aromatics will be 50,000 kg per year.

First, put scales on the axes. The horizontal output scale has a range from zero to the company's maximum output of 50,000 kg. The vertical axis records values of costs and revenues. For the maximum vertical value, multiply the maximum output by the selling price and then place values on the axis up to this figure. In this case it will have a maximum value on the axis of £250,000 (£5 × 50,000 kg). ⇨

Having drawn the axes and placed scales upon them, the first line we enter is fixed costs. Since this value does not change with output it is simply a horizontal line drawn at £50,000.

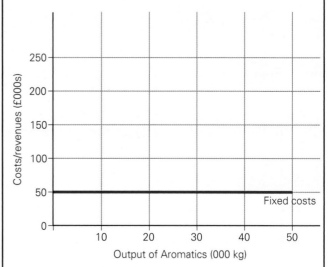
Figure 38.1 Fixed costs for Aromatics

Next, add on variable costs to arrive at total costs. Total costs start from the left hand of the fixed costs line and rise diagonally. To see where they rise to, calculate the total cost at the maximum output level. In the case of Aromatics this is 50,000 kg per year. The total cost is fixed costs (£50,000) plus variable costs of producing 50,000 kg (£3 × 50,000 = £150,000). The total cost at this level of output is £50,000 + £150,000 = £200,000.

This point can now be marked on the chart; that is, £200,000 at an output level of 50,000 kg. This can be joined by a straight line to total costs at zero output: £50,000. This is illustrated in Figure 38.2.

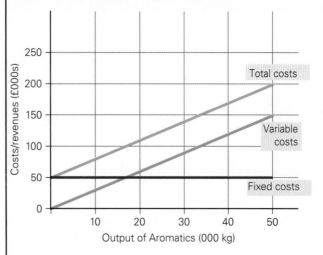
Figure 38.2 Fixed, variable and total costs for Aromatics

Finally, sales revenue must be added. For the maximum level of output, calculate the sales revenue ⇨

⇨

and mark this on the chart. In the case of Aromatics the maximum output per year is 50,000 kg; multiplied by the selling price this gives £250,000 each year. If Berry & Hall does not produce and sell any Aromatics it will not have any sales revenue. Thus zero output results in zero income. A straight diagonal line from zero to £250,000 represents the sales revenue (see Figure 38.3).

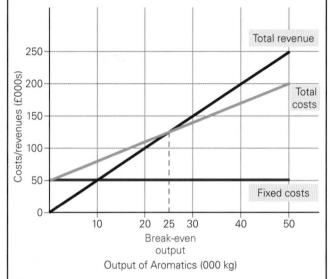

Figure 38.3 Break-even output for Aromatics

This brings together costs and revenues for Aromatics. A line drawn down from the point at which total costs and sales revenue cross shows the break-even output. For Aromatics, it is 25,000 kg per year. This can be checked using the formula method explained earlier.

38.5 Using break-even charts

Various pieces of information can be taken from break-even charts such as that shown in Figure 38.3. As well as the level of break-even output, it also shows the level of profits or losses at every possible level of output. Many conclusions can be reached, such as:

● Any level of output lower than 25,000 kg per year will mean the product is making a loss. The amount of the loss is indicated by the vertical distance between the total cost and the total revenue line

● Sales in excess of 25,000 kg of Aromatics per year will earn the company a profit. If the company produces and sells 30,000 kg of Aromatics annually, it will earn a profit of £10,000

● **The margin of safety.** This is the amount by which demand can fall before the firm starts making losses. It is the difference between current sales and the break-even point. If annual sales of Aromatics were 40,000 kg, with a break-even output of 25,000 kg, then the margin of safety would be 15,000 kg.

Margin of safety = sales *minus* break-even point

Margin of safety = 40,000 − 25,000

= 15,000 kg

The higher the margin of safety the less likely it is that a loss-making situation will develop. The margin of safety is illustrated in Figure 38.4.

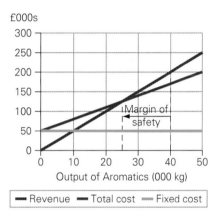

Figure 38.4 Margin of safety

Figure 38.4 shows how changes in business circumstances affect the break-even chart.

Table 38.2 How changes in business circumstances affect the break-even chart

	Cause	Effect
Internal factors	Extra launch advertising	Fixed costs rise, so total costs rise and the break-even point rises
	Planned price increase	Revenue rises more steeply; break-even point falls
	Using more machinery (and less labour) in production	Fixed costs rise while variable costs fall; uncertain effect on break-even point
External factors	Fall in demand	Break-even point is not affected, though margin of safety is reduced
	Competitors' actions force price cut	Revenue rises less steeply; break-even point rises
	Fuel costs rise	Variable and total cost lines rise more steeply; break-even point rises

38.6 The effects of changes in price, output and cost

On its own, a limitation of the break-even chart is that it's a static model. It doesn't show sales trends over time. Fortunately it can be a useful method for showing when changes are planned, for example, when the business is considering a price increase.

The main changes to consider are:

1. The impact on revenue, profits and break even of a change in price

2. The impact on revenue and profits of a change in demand, perhaps because the product has become more or less fashionable

3. The effect of a rise or fall in variable costs such as raw materials

4. The effect of a rise or fall in fixed costs, perhaps when a business chooses to 'downsize' to smaller, cheaper head office premises.

1. Price rise:

If a company increases its prices, its revenue line will rise more steeply than before. The line will start at the same point as before (0 sales = 0 revenue) but will rise to a higher revenue point at maximum output. This steepening of the revenue line will increase the profit potential at each level of output and lower the break-even point. So if you charge more, you don't need to sell as many to break even. This is shown in Figure 38.5.

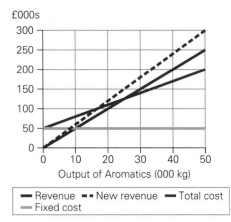

Figure 38.5 A rise in price; price increase to £6

2. A rise or fall in demand:

A change in demand has no effect on the lines of the break-even chart. It is simply that you have to read the change off the chart by drawing a line vertically up from the new sales quantity.

3. Rise in variable costs:

Between March and November the price of cocoa beans rose from $2,150 per tonne to $2,700. This 25 per cent increase would make the variable costs line rise more steeply, though it would start from the same point (zero). Naturally, if the variable costs rise, the total costs must also be affected. So if you are asked to show the effect on a break-even chart of a rise in variable costs, you must also adjust the total cost line. This is shown in Figure 38.6 – though in relation to Aromatics, not cocoa beans.

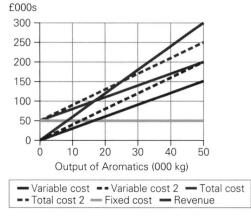

Figure 38.6 A rise in variable costs

4. Fall in fixed costs:

If a company's sales are falling it may be necessary to cut fixed costs in order to lower the break-even point. The fall in fixed costs will cut the total costs. All these things are indicated in Figure 38.7.

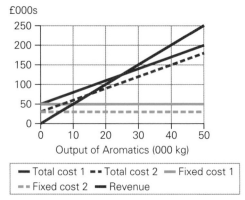

Figure 38.7 A fall in fixed costs

Summary of possible changes to the break-even chart to look out for:

1. **Prices can go up or down. If a price is increased, the revenue line starts in the same place but rises more steeply.**

2. **Fixed costs can rise or fall, so you may have to draw a new horizontal line. But** ⇨

remember that a change to fixed costs will also affect the total cost line.

3. Variable costs can rise or fall. An increase will make the variable cost line rise more steeply, though it will still start at the same point – at the fixed cost line. A change in variable costs will change the total costs line as well.

Note that each of these three changes will alter the break-even point.

'Because break-even points shift as conditions change, break-even analyses should be performed regularly, preferably on a quarterly basis.'
www.lplbatavia.com

38.7 The value of break-even analysis

Strengths

Break-even analysis is simple to understand. It is particularly useful for small and newly established businesses, where the managers may not be able to employ more sophisticated techniques. Businesses can use break-even to:

- estimate the future level of output they will need to produce and sell in order to meet given profit objectives
- assess the impact of planned price changes upon profit and the level of output needed to break-even
- take decisions about whether to produce their own products or components or whether to purchase from external sources.

Weaknesses

The weaknesses of break-even analysis are set out below.

- The model is a simplification. It assumes that variable costs increase constantly, which ignores the benefits of bulk buying. If a firm negotiates lower prices for purchasing larger quantities of raw materials then its total cost line will no longer be straight.
- Similarly, break-even analysis assumes the firm sells all its output at a single price. In reality, firms frequently offer discounts for bulk purchases.
- A major flaw in the technique is that it assumes that all output is sold. In times of low demand, a firm may have difficulty in selling all that it produces.

Five Whys and a How

Question	Answer
Why might a business want to calculate its margin of safety?	To know how much of a cushion it has between current (profitable) sales and the break-even point
Why might a sales revenue line pivot more steeply (to the left), even though it will start at £0 = 0 units?	Because there's been a price increase
Why might a cut in variable costs affect the total costs line?	Total costs consists of fixed costs plus variable costs, so of course a change in variable costs will change the total costs line
Why might it be useful to calculate profit using contribution instead of revenue minus total costs?	It's significantly quicker, and time has a substantial opportunity cost in exam conditions
Why might it be hard for a brand new business to use break-even analysis effectively?	Because the entrepreneurs cannot yet be sure of running costs or revenues – making the exercise a bit of a guess
How is the margin of safety calculated?	Sales volume *minus* break-even output

Key terms

Break-even chart: a line graph showing total revenues and total costs at all possible levels of output, or demand from zero to maximum capacity.

Fixed costs: fixed costs are any costs which do not vary directly with the level of output, for example rent and rates.

Variable costs: variable costs are those costs which vary directly with the level of output. They represent payments made for the use of inputs such as labour, fuel and raw materials.

Contribution: this is total revenue less variable costs. The calculation of contribution is useful for businesses that are responsible for a range of products.

Margin of safety: the amount by which current output exceeds the level of output necessary to break-even.

Evaluation: Break-even analysis

There is a risk of assuming that break-even charts tell you 'facts'. Break-even analysis seems simple to conduct and understand. That assumes the business knows all its costs and can break them down into variable and fixed. Tesco certainly can, but not every business is as well managed. Football clubs such as Sheffield Wednesday, Portsmouth and Darlington have hit financial problems partly because of ignorance of their financial circumstances. Similarly, few NHS hospitals could say with confidence how much it costs to provide a heart transplant.

Break-even analysis is of particular value when a business is first established. Having to work out the fixed and variable costs will help the managers to make better decisions, for example on pricing. As long as the figures are accurate, break-even becomes especially useful when changes occur, such as rising raw material costs. The technique can allow for changing revenues and costs and gives a valuable guide to potential profitability.

Key formulae

Break-even output: $\dfrac{\text{fixed costs}}{\text{contribution per unit}}$

Contribution per unit: selling price − variable costs per unit

Margin of safety: sales volume − break-even output

Total contribution: contribution per unit × unit sales

Workbook

A. Revision questions

(25 marks; 25 minutes)

1. What is meant by the term 'break-even point'? (2)

2. State three reasons why a business may conduct a break-even analysis. (3)

3. List the information necessary to construct a break-even chart. (4)

4. How would you calculate the contribution made by each unit of production that is sold? (2)

5. A business sells its products for £10 each and the variable cost of producing a single unit is £6. If its monthly fixed costs are £18,000, how many units must it sell to break even each month? (3)

6. Explain why the variable cost and total revenue lines commence at the origin of a break-even chart. (3)

7. What point on a break-even chart actually illustrates break-even output? (2)

8. Explain how, using a break-even chart, you would illustrate the amount of profit or loss made at any given level of output. (2)

9. Why might a business wish to calculate its margin of safety? (2)

10. A business is currently producing 200,000 units of output annually, and its break-even output is 120,000 units. What is its margin of safety? (2)

B. Revision exercises
DATA RESPONSE 1

An entrepreneur's first hotel

Paul Jarvis is an entrepreneur and about to open his first hotel. He has forecast the following costs and revenues:

- maximum number of customers per month: 800
- monthly fixed costs: £10,000
- average revenue per customer: £110
- typical variable costs per customer: £90

Some secondary market research has suggested that Paul's prices may be too low. He is considering charging higher prices, though he is nervous about the impact this might have on his forecast sales. Paul has found his break-even chart useful during the planning of his new business, but is concerned that it might be misleading too.

Questions (45 marks, 50 minutes)

1. a) Construct the break-even chart for Paul's planned business. (9)

   b) State, and show on the graph, the profit or loss made at a monthly sales level of 600 customers. (4)

   c) State, and show on the graph, the margin of safety at that level of output. (4)

2. Paul's market research shows that in his first month of trading he can expect 450 customers at his hotel.

   a) If Paul's research is correct, calculate the level of profit or loss he will make. (5)

   b) Illustrate this level of output on your graph and show the profit or loss. (3)

3. Paul has decided to increase his prices to give an average revenue per customer of £120.

   a) Draw the new total revenue line on your break-even chart to show the effect of this change. (3)

   b) Mark on your diagram the new break-even point. (1)

   c) Calculate Paul's new break-even number of customers to confirm the result shown on your chart. (6)

4. Paul is worried that his break-even chart may be 'misleading'. Do you agree with him? Justify your view. (10)

DATA RESPONSE 2

The Successful T-shirt Company

Shelley has recently launched the Successful T-shirt Company. It sells a small range of fashion T-shirts. The shirts are available in a range of colours and contain the company's logo, which is becoming increasingly desirable for young fashion-conscious people.

The shirts are sold to retailers for £35 each. They cost £16.50 to manufacture and the salesperson receives £2.50 commission for each item sold to retailers. The distribution cost for each shirt is £1.00 and current sales are 1,000 per month. The fixed costs of production are £11,250 per month.

The company is considering expanding its range of T-shirts and has approached its bank for a loan. The bank has requested that the company draw up a business plan including a cash-flow forecast and break-even chart.

Questions (25 marks, 30 minutes)

1. What is a break-even chart? (4)

2. Calculate the following:

   a) the variable cost of producing 1,000 T-shirts

   b) the contribution earned through the sale of one T-shirt. (4)

3. Shelley has decided to manufacture the shirts in Poland. As a result, the variable cost per T-shirt (including commission and distribution costs) will fall to £15 per T-shirt. However, fixed costs will rise to £12,000.

   a) Calculate the new level of break-even for Shelly's T-shirts.

   b) Calculate the margin of safety if sales are 1,000 T-shirts per month. (8)

4. Should Shelly rely on break-even analysis when taking business decisions? Justify your view. (9)

DATA RESPONSE 3

Start-up break-even analysis

On 27 September 2013 Mary's Garden opened in Raynes Park, South London. Oddly, Mary's Garden is a Japanese restaurant. It opened without any fanfare; without even putting a menu outside for passers-by. This was because, as at 1.30 that afternoon, 'we haven't decided on the prices yet'. Amazingly, at 7.30 that evening every table was taken.

The premises had been unused for more than a year, since an Indian restaurant closed down. Accordingly Mary's had been able to negotiate a stunningly low rent: £1,000 per month; business rates of £500 a month must be added, however. By Monday 30th, Mary had been able to estimate a probable average spend of £40 per customer, of which £15 goes on food costs and another £5 on other variable costs. With staffing costs of £5,000 a month and other monthly fixed costs amounting to £1,500, Mary's Garden has most of the information required for a break-even chart.

There remains one difficult issue, though; what is the maximum capacity level of the restaurant? Amazingly the current opening times are from 9.00 a.m. to 11.00 p.m.; it surely is the only Japanese restaurant in suburbia offering a breakfast menu. The restaurant itself is small, with just 25 seats. Theoretically it could fill them lots of times in 14 hours, but it seems wise to bet on a maximum of just 50 customers per day, 6 days a week, that is, 1,200 a month.

For break-even analysis the above is sufficient, but for real business insight there is one more critical variable: the actual level of customer demand. In conversation with Mary's son it emerged that no research has been done into this. My own local knowledge suggests that it should be full on Friday and Saturday evenings, a third full on Monday-Thursday and gain a smattering of breakfast and lunchtime customers (until this loss-making approach is stopped). Overall, my estimate is for 500 customers a month.

Questions (20 marks; 25 minutes)

1. Calculate the total:
   a) monthly fixed costs (1)
   b) variable costs per customer (1)
   c) contribution per customer (1)

2. Calculate the monthly:
   a) break-even number of customers (3)
   b) safety margin based on estimated customer numbers (2)

3. Outline three ways in which Mary's Garden's safety margin could be expanded. (6)

4. **a)** Calculate the monthly profit based on the estimated number of customers. (3)
   b) Calculate the monthly profit if customer numbers prove to be 50 per cent higher. (3)

C. Extend your understanding

1. To what extent might break-even analysis benefit a new small business offering Thai food for takeaway and delivery. (20)

2. To what extent would break-even analysis be of value when running a business such as Tesco or Primark or any other business you have researched? (20)

Chapter 39

Cash flow management and forecasting

Linked to: Cash flow versus profit, Chapter 42; Sources of finance, Chapter 43.

> **Definition**
>
> Cash flow is the flow of money into and out of a business in a given time period. Cash flow forecasting is estimating the flow of cash in the future.

39.1 The importance of cash flow management

Managing cash flow is one of the most important aspects of financial management. Without adequate availability of cash from day to day, even a company with high sales could fail. As bills become due there has to be the cash available to pay them. If a company cannot pay its bills, suppliers will refuse to deliver and staff will start looking for other jobs. Cash flow problems are the most common reason for business failure. This is particularly true for new businesses. It is estimated that 80 per cent of businesses that collapse in their first year fail because of cash flow problems.

Businesses need to continually review their current and future cash position. In order to be prepared and to understand future cash needs, businesses construct a cash flow forecast. This sets out the expected flows of cash into and out of the business for each month. In textbooks cash flows are normally shown for six months, but they can be done for any period of time. Most firms want to look 12 months ahead, so the cash flow forecast is constantly updated.

39.2 Constructing a cash flow forecast

To prepare a cash flow forecast businesses need to estimate all the money coming into and out of the business, month by month. These flows of money are then set onto a grid showing the cash movements in each month.

Cash in

In the example shown in Table 39.1 the business is a new start-up. The business will receive an injection of capital of £30,000 in March. The business will start production in April and will only receive cash when sales start in May. Cash inflows are expected to increase each month until reaching a maximum of £15,000 in August.

It is important that the income from sales is shown when the cash is received not when the sale is made.

Table 39.1 Example of cash inflow (March to August)

Month £s	March	April	May	June	July	August
Cash inflow						
Capital	30,000					
Sales			7,000	10,000	13,000	15,000
Total inflow	30,000	0	7,000	10,000	13,000	15,000

Outflow

In the example shown in Table 39.2:

- in March the firm will buy machinery for £23,000
- materials cost 50 per cent of the value of sales, but have to be paid in cash in the month before the sales take place, for example, £3,500 in April. In the early stages of a firm's life, suppliers are rarely willing to offer credit, so they have to be paid up front
- rent for the building costs £2,000 per month but the owner requires two months' rent in advance
- wages are estimated to be £2,000 per month and there are other expenses of £1,000 per month.

When these figures have been entered onto the grid the total expenditure can be calculated.

Table 39.2 Example of cash outflow (March to August)

Cash outflow £	March	April	May	June	July	August
Equipment	23,000					
Materials	0	3,500	5,000	6,500	7,500	7,500*
Rent	4,000	2,000	2,000	2,000	2,000	2,000
Wages		2,000	2,000	2,000	2,000	2,000
Other expenses		1,000	1,000	1,000	1,000	1,000
Total outflow	**27,000**	**8,500**	**10,000**	**11,500**	**12,500**	**12,500**

*assuming September sales of £15,000

Cash flow

The cash flow forecast can now be completed by calculating the following:

Monthly balance

This is cash inflow for the month minus cash outflow. It shows each month if there is a positive or a negative movement of cash. When outflow is greater than inflow the monthly balance will be negative. This is shown in brackets to indicate that it is a minus figure.

'A wise business owner once said: "Happiness is positive cash flow".' Quoted at www.freetaxquotes.com

---

Opening and closing balance

This is like a bank statement. It shows what cash the business has at the beginning of the month (opening balance) and what the cash position is at the end of the month (closing balance). The closing balance is the opening balance plus the monthly balance. For example, the business starts with £3,000 in the bank in April; a net £8,500 flows out during the month, so the closing bank balance is (£5,500).

The closing balance shows the overall state of the bank account at the end of the month.

The completed cash flow forecast is shown in Table 39.3

This shows that there is a negative cash balance from April onwards, though the accumulated position (the closing balance) is improving from the end of June.

As there is no such thing as negative money the cash flow forecast shows that action is needed to avoid problems in the early months. The easiest remedy would be to negotiate a bank overdraft.

Real business

Cash problems at Debenhams?

On 16 December 2013 department store chain Debenhams shocked its suppliers by sending them an email saying that sums owed would be reduced by 2.5 per cent. In other words, Debenhams would be going back on negotiated, agreed terms – and simply chopping an extra 2.5 per cent off the bills. And this would continue into the future. Several newspapers responded by questioning whether Debenhams was suffering a cash flow crisis, given that a pre-Christmas announcement such as this would inevitably generate bad publicity. Retail commentator Bill Grimsey said 'it means they have financial issues … a cash flow issue, a profit issue – or both.'

39.3 Analysing cash flow forecasts

There are three main ways to analyse a cash flow forecast:

1. Calculate the difference between the closing balance at the end of the period and the opening balance at the start. This gives a sense of what is happening over time. If the overall cash balances are building up, then cash inflows are greater than cash outflows and the situation is comfortable. If the balance is declining, urgent action may be necessary.

2. Use the monthly closing balance to assess trends in the data. If the closing balance from Table 39.3 is

Table 39.3 Example of a cash flow forecast

Month £'s	March	April	May	June	July	August
Cash inflow						
Capital	30,000					
Sales			7,000	10,000	13,000	15,000
Total inflow	**30,000**	**0**	**7,000**	**10,000**	**13,000**	**15,000**
Total outflow	**27,000**	**8,500**	**10,000**	**11,500**	**12,500**	**12,500**
Monthly balance	3,000	(8,500)	(3,000)	(1,500)	500	2,500
Opening balance	0	3,000	(5,500)	(8,500)	(10,000)	(9,500)
Closing balance	**3,000**	**(5,500)**	**(8,500)**	**(10,000)**	**(9,500)**	**(7,000)**

turned into a graph (see Figure 39.1) it helps highlight that the short-term plunge into the red seems, by July, to be stabilising into a steady recovery in the cash position of the business.

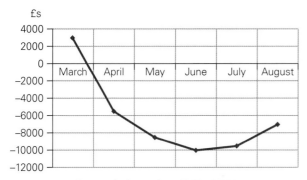

Figure 39.1 Closing balance from Table 39.3

3. Analyse the timings of cash inflows and outflows. Although some firms sell goods for cash, most provide customers with interest-free credit, for example, Cadbury selling to Tesco. The longer the customers take to pay, the longer the seller is without their cash. So any method of speeding up customer payments can boost a firm's cash flow. The sum of money outstanding from customers is known as 'receivables'. Logically, firms should want this figure to be as low as possible.

Firms not only have customers, they also have suppliers. When buying goods on credit, the longer the credit period you can negotiate from suppliers, the longer your cash will be sitting in your bank account. As it sits in your bank account, this money owed is known as 'payables'.

If a company has customers who pay in 30 days and suppliers who are paid in 30 days, businesses call this a 'cash-to-cash' figure of zero (which is fantastic). If customers take 60 days to pay but suppliers have to be paid in cash on delivery, that is a cash-to-cash figure of 60, which would put a strain on any business's cash flow position.

39.4 Cash flow objectives

For established, large businesses with many different products and numerous customers, cash flow is rarely an important issue. Many senior managers may never have heard the term mentioned in the workplace. The focus is much more on profits and profit margins.

For smaller firms, cash flow may be a daily concern, for example, will we have enough in the bank to pay this Friday's wage bill? This illustrates the first cash flow target for a small business: enough cash to meet all the expected bills in the coming months – with a bit to spare.

When small firms are growing, though, the objectives may become far more ambitious. Having opened a very successful tapas (Spanish snack) restaurant, it took brothers Eddie and Sam Hart five years to identify the right premises for their second outlet. Barrafina (2) opened in July 2014 in London's Covent Garden, and probably required close to a £1 million investment. Targeting the cash balance for that investment would be part of the reason it took them 5 years to complete their plan.

Real business

Late payments woes

A survey from the bank settlement organisation BACS showed that in April 2013 small businesses were owed £30.2 billion. This figure was up from £16 billion in 2007, before the recent recession. The same research showed that close to one million businesses said they were suffering from late payments. The Confederation of British Industry (CBI) followed this up by saying that 'Late payment is a serious issue for all businesses but particularly for smaller firms, as cash flow is their life blood. The reality is that few choose to act on late payment for fear of fall out with their customers'.

Source: several, including *The Guardian* 18 September 2013

'An important thing in business is to look after your suppliers. They must look after you, but you need them, so I always pay my bills on time.' Duncan Bannatyne, Dragon investor

39.5 Methods of improving cash flow

A business can improve its cash flow in several ways.

● Getting goods to the market in the shortest possible time; the sooner goods reach the customer, the sooner payment is received. Production and distribution should be as efficient as possible.

- Getting paid as quickly as possible; the ideal arrangement is to get paid cash on delivery. Most business, though, works on credit. Even worse, it is interest-free credit, so the customer has little incentive to pay up quickly. Early payment should be encouraged by offering incentives such as discounts for early payment.
- Debt factoring (see Chapter 43) It may be possible to speed up payments by factoring money owed to the business. The seller receives 80 per cent of the amount due within 24 hours of an invoice being presented. The factor then collects the money from the customer when the credit period is over and pays the seller the remaining 20 per cent less the factoring fees.
- Keeping stocks of raw materials to a minimum. Good stock management such as a just-in-time system means that the business is not paying for stocks before it needs them for production.

'There's nothing more important than cash flow. I lost my computer business when I was 29 because I gave credit to firms I didn't investigate (credit check).' Peter Jones, Dragon investor (worth £475 million, Sunday Times Rich List 2014)

Cash flow can also be improved by keeping cash in the business. Minimising short-term spending on new equipment keeps cash in the business. Things that the business can do include:

- Lease rather than buy equipment. This increases expenses but conserves capital.
- Renting rather than buying buildings. This also allows capital to remain in the business.
- Postponing expenditure, for example on new company cars.

Only as a last resort should a business ask its bank to increase its overdraft facility. A higher overdraft will not improve the cash flow – it just makes sure that negative cash flow can be managed temporarily.

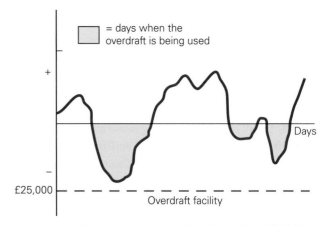

Figure 39.2 Daily cash balances for a firm with a £25,000 overdraft

Some methods that may be used to improve cash flow are set out in Table 39.4

Table 39.4 Ways to improve cash flow

Measure	Result	Drawbacks
Discounting prices	Increases sales	May undermine pricing structure
	Reduces stock	May leave low stocks for future activity
	Generates cash	
Reduce purchases	Cuts down expenditure	May leave business without means to continue
Negotiate more credit	Allows time to pay	May tarnish credit reputation
Delay payment of bills	Retains cash	Will tarnish credit reputation
Credit control – chase debtors	Gets payments in, and sooner	May upset customers
Negotiate additional finance	Provides cash	Interest payments add to expenditure
		Has to be repaid
Factor debts	Generates cash	Reduces income from sales
	A proportion of the income is guaranteed	Costs can be high
Selling assets	Releases cash	Assets are no longer available
Sale and leaseback	Releases cash	Increases costs – lease has to be paid
	Asset is still available	Company no longer owns asset

Five Whys and a How

Question	Answer
Why is it important to ask who constructed the cash flow forecast?	Because unconscious bias may have slipped in, e.g. an entrepreneur's optimism may make the cash inflow projections unrealistic
Why may it be a concern if a company's sales are dominated by one large customer	Because any disagreements about the invoice may lead to payment delays – which may be crippling if the bulk of cash inflow is due from that one customer
Why is cash flow often referred to as 'the lifeblood' of the business?	Partly because it's *that* important to business survival and partly because, like blood, you only think about it when something's gone wrong
Why is it important to distinguish between slow payment and slow sales as causes of cash flow problems?	Slow payment is a purely cash-related issue that can be sorted out between accounts departments; slow sales may be a far more long-term problem – and will involve the marketing department.
Why should a business analyse the causes of a cash problem beforé opting to increase its overdraft limits	Because overdrafts are expensive and all they do is cover over the cash flow problems, they don't solve them
How should a business make its estimates for future cash inflows and outflows?	By being pessimistic with the cash inflows (keep them low) and also with the cash outflows (be pessimistic; suspect they'll be quite high)

Key terms

Best case: an optimistic estimate of the best possible outcome, for example if sales prove much higher than expected.

Cash flow forecast: estimating future monthly cash inflows and outflows, to find out the net cash flow.

Debt factoring: obtaining part-payment of the amount owed from a factoring company. The factoring company will then collect the debt and pass over the balance of the payment.

Overdraft: short-term borrowing from a bank. The business only borrows as much as it needs to cover its daily cash shortfall.

Worst case: a pessimistic estimate assuming the worst possible outcome, for example sales are very disappointing.

'The fact is that one of the first lessons I learned in business was that balance sheets and income statements are fiction; cash flow is reality.' Chris Chocola, businessman

Evaluation: Cash flow management and forecasting

There is no doubt that cash flow management is a vital ingredient in the success of any small business. For a new business, cash flow forecasting helps to answer key questions:

- Is the venture viable?
- How much capital is needed?
- Which are the most dangerous months?

For an existing business the cash flow forecast identifies the amount and timing of any cash flow problems in the future. It is also useful for evaluating new orders or ventures.

Nevertheless, completing a cash flow forecast does not ensure survival. Consideration needs to be given to its usefulness and limitations. It must be remembered that cash flow forecasts are based on estimates of amounts and timing. When preparing cash flow forecasts, managers need to ask themselves 'what if?' A huge mistake is to only look at one forecast. It is far better to look at best case and worst case possibilities. The firm needs to be continually aware of the economic and market climate and its current cash position.

Workbook

A. Revision questions

(30 marks; 30 minutes)

1. What is meant by 'cash flow'? (2)

2. Why is it important to manage cash flow? (4)

3. What is a cash flow forecast? (3)

4. Explain two limitations of cash flow forecasts. (4)

5. Give two reasons why a bank manager may want to see a cash flow forecast before giving a loan to a new business. (2)

6. How could a firm benefit from delaying its cash outflows? (3)

7. What problems could a firm face if its cash flow forecast proved unreliable? (3)

8. Outline three ways in which a business can improve its cash flow situation. (6)

9. What internal factors could affect a firm's cash flow? (3)

B. Revision exercises

DATA RESPONSE 1

(18 marks; 20 minutes)

A business is to be started up on 1 January next year with £40,000 of share capital. It will be opening a designer clothes shop. During January it plans to spend £45,000 on start-up costs (buying a lease, buying equipment, decorating, and so on). On 1 February it will open its doors and gain sales over the next five months of: £12,000, £16,000, £20,000, £25,000 and £24,000 respectively. Each month it must pay £10,000 in fixed overheads (salaries, heat, light, telephone, and so on) and its variable costs will amount to half the revenue.

Complete the cash flow table below (Table 39.5) to find out:

1. the company's forecast cash position at the end of June

2. the maximum level of overdraft the owners will need to negotiate with the bank before starting up.

Table 39.5 Cashflow table

	Jan	Feb	Mar	Apr	May	June
Cash at start						
Cash in						
Cash out						
Net cash flow						
Opening balance						
Closing balance						

DATA RESPONSE 2

Cash problems at a pound store

PoundLandline was quickly a media success after opening day publicity, due to a row between the online start-up and the long-established Poundland retail chain. As the row spread over social media, opening day sales through PoundLandline were eight times higher than the budget. At 3 p.m. the site crashed – incapable of dealing with all the hits to its website. Founders Sonia and Colin had set the site up with an expectation of selling 8,000 items a day at £1 each, leading to annual revenue of £2.8m but with slim gross margins and therefore gross profit of £420,000. With fixed overheads of £200,000 (covering the warehouse rental and other costs), they anticipated a very satisfactory net profit.

The problem now was the cost of fixing the website crash. They needed extra bandwidth and a more robust site. Although Colin was a very good programmer, he needed to hire in extra expertise. Their budget had 'been too tight for contingency allowances' according to Sonia, so this was a strain on cash flow. A second issue was that high sales would mean speedy purchasing of extra stock – and paying for it. There was much to be done.

An underlying problem faced by the two entrepreneurs had been the unhelpful attitude of the banks. Despite TV advertisements boasting how much they help small firms, Sonia and Colin had found them unwilling to commit to the slightest risk. Therefore they refused to give bank loans and would

only provide an overdraft when guaranteed by the security of Sonia's flat. If things went wrong, even though the business was PoundLandline Ltd, Sonia could end up homeless. As shown in the cash flow forecast, the pair had needed to invest £54,000 to get the business up and running. That was the limit of their financial resources.

So now, with customers desperate to shop at the first online pound store, the entrepreneurs had a cash flow problem – on Day 1 of Month 1! The carefully constructed cash flow forecast was already being disrupted.

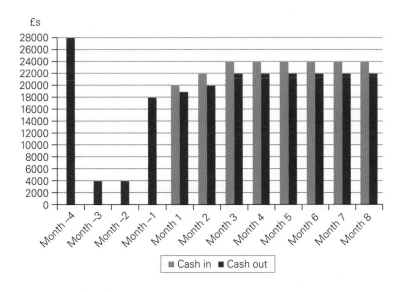

Figure 39.3 Cash flow forecast for PoundLandline Ltd

Questions (25 marks; 25 minutes)

1. a) Explain two reasons for the Day 1 cash flow problems at PoundLandline Ltd. (8)

   b) Explain whether Sonia and Colin could be blamed for these causes of the cash flow difficulties. (5)

2. Given the situation the business was in by the end of Day 1, discuss what the entrepreneurs could do to overcome their cash flow problems. (12)

C. Extend your understanding

1. Evaluate the importance of cash flow forecasting for a new retail business. (20)

2. 'Cash flow management is important for small companies but not for large companies.' To what extent do you agree with this statement? (20)

Chapter

40

Budgets and budgeting

Linked to: Financial objectives, Chapter 36; Cash flow management and forecasting, Chapter 39; Sources of finance, Chapter 43.

Definition

A budget is a target for costs or revenue that a firm or department must aim to reach over a given period of time. An income budget sets a floor, that is, a minimum target, while an expenditure budget sets a ceiling, for example, a maximum target for costs.

40.1 How to construct a budget

Budgeting is the process of setting targets, covering all aspects of costs and revenues. It is a method for turning a firm's strategy into reality. Nothing can be done in business without money; budgets tell individual managers how much they can spend to achieve their objectives. For instance, a football manager may be given a transfer expenditure budget of £20 million to buy players. With the budget in place, the transfer dealing can get under way.

A budgeting system shows how much can be spent per time period, and gives managers a way to check whether they are on track. Most firms use a system of budgetary control as a means of supervision. The process is as follows:

1. Make a judgement of the likely sales revenues for the coming year.

2. Set a cost ceiling that allows for an acceptable level of profit.

3. The budget for the whole company's costs is then broken down by division, department or by cost centre.

4. The budget may then be broken down further so that each manager has a budget and therefore some spending power.

In a business start-up, the budget should provide enough spending power to finance vital needs such as building work, decoration, recruiting and paying staff, and marketing. If a manager overspends in one area, she or he knows that it is essential to cut back elsewhere. A good manager gets the best possible value from the budgeted sum.

'The budget is our guide. It tells us what we're supposed to do for the year. We couldn't get along without it.' Jim Bell, US factory manager

Real business

The BP disaster

On 23 March 2005 a huge explosion at BP's Texas oil refinery killed 15 people and injured more than 180. Most were the company's own staff. After an enquiry, the chairwoman of the US Chemical Safety Board reported that 'BP implemented a 25 per cent cut on fixed costs from 1998 to 2000 that adversely impacted maintenance expenditures at the refinery'. The report stated that 'BP's global management' (the British Head Office) 'was aware of problems with maintenance spending and infrastructure well before March 2005'. Yet they did nothing about it. The chairwoman delivered the final critique:

'Every successful corporation must contain its costs. But at an ageing facility like Texas City, it is not responsible to cut budgets related to safety and maintenance without thoroughly examining the impact on the risk of a catastrophic accident.' BP confirmed that its own internal investigation had findings 'generally consistent with those of the CSB'.

In 2010, there was an echo of this disaster when an explosion on a BP well in the Gulf of Mexico killed 11 people and caused the biggest oil spill in American history. By 2014 the costs associated with this had forced BP to sell off more than $42 billion of assets, wiping out a fifth of the value of the company. Cost cutting can be costly.

Source: Adapted from *Topical Cases*, www.a-zbusinesstraining.com

40.2 Setting budgets

Setting budgets is not an easy job. How do you decide exactly what level of sales are likely next year, especially for new businesses with no previous trading to rely on? Furthermore, how can you plan for costs if the cost of your raw materials tends to fluctuate? Most firms treat last year's budget figures as the main determinant of this year's budget. Minor adjustments will be made for inflation and other foreseeable changes. Given the firm's past experience, budget setting should be quite quick and quite accurate.

'Any jackass can draw up a balanced budget on paper.' Lane Kirkland, former US trade union president

For start-ups, setting budgets will be a much tougher job. They are fundamental to the business plan, but as heavyweight boxing champ Mike Tyson once said: "Everyone has a plan until they get punched in the mouth". To succeed, the entrepreneur will need to rely on:

● a 'guesstimate' of likely sales in the early months of the start-up

● the entrepreneur's expertise and experience, which will be better if the entrepreneur has worked in the industry before

● the entrepreneur's instinct, based on market understanding

● a significant level of market research.

Real business

Budgeting helps but is not easy for start-ups

Stanford University research into 78 business start-ups showed that firms with budgeting systems were more likely to survive and experience significant growth rates. They reported that budgeting systems allowed senior staff access to the information needed when making decisions. However, they acknowledged the difficulties in setting budgets for new start-ups. They point out that, for a new company, predicting the future is hugely unpredictable and setting 12-month budgets is likely to be unrealistic.

The best criteria for setting budgets are:

● to relate the budget directly to the business objective; if a company wants to increase sales and market share, the best method may be to increase the advertising budget and thereby boost demand

● to involve as many people as possible in the process; people will be more committed to reaching the targets if they have had a say in how the budget was set.

'(Budgets) must not be prepared on high and cast as pearls before swine. They must be prepared by the operating divisions.' Robert Townsend, the original business guru

Simple budget statements

An example of a simple budget statement may look like that shown in Table 40.1.

Table 40.1 Example of a budget statement

	January	February	March
Income	25,000	28,000	30,000
Variable costs	10,000	12,000	13,000
Fixed costs	10,000	10,000	11,000
Total expenditure	20,000	22,000	24,000
Profit	5,000	6,000	6,000

This information is only of value if it proves possible for a manager to believe that these figures are achievable. Only then will she or he be motivated to try to turn the budget into reality.

40.3 Budgetary variances

Variance is the amount by which the actual result differs from the budgeted figure. It is usually measured each month, by comparing the actual outcome with the budgeted one. It is important to note that variances are referred to as adverse or favourable – not positive or negative. A favourable variance is one that leads to higher than expected profit (revenue up or costs down). An adverse variance is one that reduces profit, such as costs being higher than the budgeted level. Table 40.2 shows when variances are adverse or favourable.

Table 40.2 Adverse or favourable variance?

Variable	Budget	Actual	Variance	Fav/Adv
Sales of X	150	160	10	Favourable
Sales of Y	150	145	5	Adverse
Material costs	100	90	10	Favourable
Labour costs	100	105	5	Adverse

The value of regular variance statements is that they provide an early warning. If a product's sales are slipping below budget, managers can respond by increasing marketing support or by cutting back on production plans. In an ideal world, slippage could be noted in March, a new strategy put into place by May and a recovery in sales achieved by September. Clearly, no firm wishes to wait until the end-of-year to find out that things went badly. An early warning can lead to an early solution.

40.4 Analysing budgets and variances

When significant variances occur, management should first consider whether the fault was in the budget or in the actual achievement. In January 2014 Nintendo announced to shareholders that it was cutting the sales budget for its Wii U from 9 million units to 2.8 million in the period to the end of March 2014. That's a cut of about 70 per cent! Nintendo's management decided that its budget was at fault and it would not therefore blame its marketing managers. The launch of the PS4 had been known about, but Nintendo never expected it to be as successful as it was.

When adverse variances occur, senior managers are likely to want to hear an explanation from the responsible 'line manager'. He or she will need to have a clear explanation of what has gone wrong. Clearly, if recession has hit sales throughout a market, it will be easy to explain adverse income variances. Far tougher is when the blame lies with falling market share rather than market size.

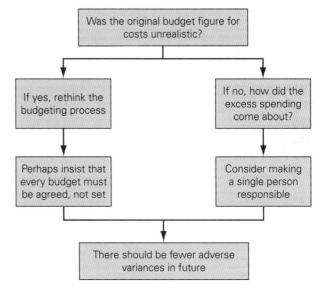

Figure 40.1 Logic chain: making variance analysis more effective

Five Whys and a How

Question	Answers
Why are budgets used in most organisations?	To keep costs under control while allowing some degree of delegation of power
Why may over-optimistic revenue budgets be demoralising?	Because managers feel they're being set up to fail
Why might an adverse cost variance be forgivable?	If it's a new product or a new technique, there's a learning curve for staff to climb
Why might it be wise to reset budgets during the middle of a financial year?	If variances have been high, perhaps the original budgets were wrongly set – so now's the time to try to get them right
Why should positive variances be investigated?	Because you need to understand why things have gone well in order to achieve the same again.
How are variances calculated?	By comparing the actual to the forecast data

Key terms

Adverse variance: a difference between budgeted and actual figures that is damaging to the firm's profit (for example costs up or revenue down).

Criteria: yardsticks against which success (or the lack of it) can be measured.

Delegated: passing authority down the hierarchy.

Expenditure budget: setting a maximum figure for what a department or manager can spend over a period of time. This is to control costs.

Favourable variance: a difference between budgeted and actual figures that boosts a firm's profit (for example, revenue up or costs down).

Income budget: setting a minimum figure for the revenue to be generated by a product, a department or a manager.

Profit budget: setting a minimum figure for the profit to be achieved over a period of time.

Zero budgeting: setting all future budgets at £0, to force managers to have to justify the spending levels they say they need in future.

Evaluation: Budgets and budgeting

The sophistication of budgeting systems is usually directly linked to the size of a business. Huge multinationals have incredibly complex budgeting systems. For a small business start-up, any budgeting system will be quite simple. Most will rely on a rough breakdown of how the start-up budget is to be divided between the competing demands. There is, however, no doubt that budgeting provides a more effective system of controlling a business's finances than no system at all.

Budgets are a management tool. The way in which they are used can tell you a lot about a firm's culture. Firms with a culture of bossy management will tend to use a tightly controlled budgetary system. Managers will

have budgets imposed upon them and variances will be watched closely by supervisors. Organisations with a more open culture will use budgeting as an aid to discussion and empowerment.

Whatever the culture, if a manager is to be held accountable for meeting a budget, she or he must be given influence over setting it, and control over reaching it. Budgets are set for future time periods and analysis of actual against budgeted performance can take place only after the event. This is true of all financial monitoring and leads to doubts as to its effectiveness as a planning tool. Measures such as market research may be far more reliable in predicting future performance.

Workbook

A. Revision questions

(40 marks; 40 minutes)

1. Explain the meaning of the term 'budgeting'. (2)

2. List three advantages that a budgeting system brings to a company. (3)

3. Why is it valuable to have a yardstick against which performance can be measured? (3)

5. Briefly explain how most companies actually set next year's budgets. (3)

6. Why should budget holders have a say in the setting of their budgets? (3)

7. Complete the budget statement shown in Table 40.3 by filling in the gaps: (8)

Table 40.3 A budget statement

	January	February	March	April
Income	4200	4500	4000	
Variable costs	1800		2000	1800
Fixed costs	1200	1600		1600
Total costs		3600	4100	
Profit				600

8. How could a firm respond to an increasingly adverse variance in labour costs? (4)

9. Explain what is meant by a 'favourable cost variance'. (3)

10. Look at Table 40.4, then answer the following questions.

Table 40.4 Budgeted and actual figures for May and June

| | May | | June | |
	Budgeted	Actual	Budgeted	Actual
Revenue	3500	3200	4000	4200
Variable costs	1000	900	1200	1500
Fixed costs	1200	1200	1300	1100
Total costs	2200	2100	2500	2600
Profit				

a) Calculate the budgeted and actual profit figures for both months. (2)

b) Identify a month with:
  i) a favourable revenue variance
  ii) an adverse fixed cost variance
  iii) an adverse variable cost variance
  iv) a favourable fixed cost variance
  v) an adverse total cost variance
  vi) an adverse revenue variance
  vii) a favourable total cost variance
  viii) an adverse profit variance
  ix) a favourable profit variance. (9)

B. Revision exercises
DATA RESPONSE 1

Table 40.5 Variance analysis

| | January | | | February | | |
	B	A	V	B	A	V
Sales revenue	140*	150	10	180	175	?
Materials	70	80	(10)	90	95	?
Other direct costs	30	35	(5)	40	40	0
Overheads	20	20	0	25	22	?
Profit	20	15	(5)	?	18	?

All figures in £000s

Questions (20 marks; 20 minutes)

1. What are the five numbers missing from the variance analysis shown in Table 40.5? (5)

2. Examine the financial strength or weakness in this data, from the company's viewpoint. (9)

3. Explain the ways a manager might set about improving the accuracy of a sales budget. (6)

DATA RESPONSE 2

Table 40.6 Budget data for Clinton & Collins Ltd (£000s)

| | January | | February | | March | | April | |
	B	A	B	A	B	A	B	A
Sales revenue	160	144	180	156	208	168	240	188
Materials	40	38	48	44	52	48	58	54
Labour	52	48	60	54	66	62	72	68
Overheads	76	76	76	78	76	80	76	80
Profit	(8)	(18)	(4)	(20)	14	(22)	34	(14)

Questions (30 marks; 30 minutes)

1. Use the data given in Table 40.6 to explain why February's profits were worse than expected. (5)

2. Why may Clinton & Collins Ltd have chosen to set monthly budgets? (5)

3. Explain how the firm could have set these budgets. (4)

4. The directors of Clinton & Collins Ltd knew that the recession was causing problems for the firm but were unsure as to whether things were improving or worsening. To what extent does the data suggest an improvement? (16)

DATA RESPONSE 3

Chessington World of Adventures

In April 2014 Chessington World of Adventures opened up for its summer season. The newly appointed merchandise manager (in charge of all non-food sales) was given his sales budget for the year. It had been set 4 per cent higher than for 2013. He thought the budget was quite ambitious, especially when a wet April and May meant that there were fewer visitors in the early part of the season. Then the period July to August saw hot, dry weather and the turnstiles were 'buzzing' again. As a hot day at Chessington can boost crowds by 50 per cent, the merchandise manager did not need to make any effort to meet his budget.

Questions (25 marks, 25 minutes)

1. Outline two other ways in which management might have constructed the sales budget for 2014. (4)

2. Explain one problem that might arise if the merchandise manager's pay was linked to sales figures. (5)

3. To what extent are budgets worthwhile in a business such as Chessington? (16)

C. Extend your understanding

1. 'Budgeting systems can often be demotivating for middle managers'. To what extent do you agree with this statement? (20)

2. To what extent is it true to suggest that budgets are the most important financial documents for most managers? (20)

Chapter

41

Profit and how to increase it

Linked to: Calculating revenue, costs and profit, Chapter 37; Break-even analysis, Chapter 38; Sources of finance, Chapter 43.

Definition

Gross profit is the difference between selling price and the direct costs generated by the goods sold. Operating profit is the profit left after all fixed and variable operating costs have been deducted from revenue.

41.1 Gross profit, operating profit and profit for the year

Profit can be calculated in many different ways. For most business purposes, though, it is enough to know gross profit, operating profit and profit for the year. Table 41.1 shows a simplified version of Ted Baker plc's 2014 accounts, to help show how these three levels of profit are calculated.

41.2 Gross profit and gross profit margin

The gross profit of a business is an absolute number, for example, £10,000. The number is calculated by deducting direct costs from sales revenue. Is £10,000 a good level of profit or not? To find out, it is helpful to measure the profit in relation to the sales revenue. This is the gross profit margin:

$$\text{Gross profit margin} = \frac{\text{gross profit}}{\text{sales revenue}} \times 100$$

For example, if the gross profit is £10,000 and the sales are £40,000 the gross profit margin is:

$$\frac{£10,000}{£40,000} \times 100 = 25 \text{ per cent}$$

Having turned the profit figure into a percentage, a comparison can be made with the profitability achieved by other companies. Comparing fashion retailers Ted Baker plc and SuperGroup plc, for example: the former made a 2014 gross margin of 61.5 per cent while SuperGroup's margins were 59.7 per cent. Both figures are remarkably high, confirming the strength of the Ted Baker and SuperDry brand names. Needless to say, Ted Baker's is a little more impressive than SuperGroup's – and both are hugely better than the original calculation of 25 per cent.

41.3 Operating profit and operating profit margin

When City and media analysts are evaluating companies, the number they focus on is operating profit, and then take that as a percentage of revenue to

Table 41.1 Ted Baker plc's 2014 accounts

Accounting item	Figure (£ millions)	Method of calculation	Comment
Revenue	322.0		The value of all the sales made in the financial year
Cost of sales	(123.5)		The cost of the clothes Ted buys in
Gross profit	**198.5**	Revenue – Cost of sales	
Fixed overheads	(159.0)		Cost of running the stores + head office
Operating profit	**39.5**	Gross profit – Fixed overheads	
Net financing cost	(0.6)		
Corporation tax	(10.0)		Unlike some, Ted pays his taxes
Profit for the year	**28.9**	Operating profit – Financing and tax	

calculate the operating profit margin:

$$\text{Operating profit margin} = \frac{\text{operating profit}}{\text{sales revenue}} \times 100$$

For example, if the operating profit is £3,000 and the sales are £40,000 the operating margin is:

$$\frac{£3,000}{£40,000} \times 100 = 7.5 \text{ per cent}$$

Having turned the profit figure into a percentage, a comparison can be made with the profitability achieved by other companies, or looking at one company over time. In 2014 Ted Baker plc had an operating margin of 12.3 per cent. Sainsbury's, by contrast, had a 2014 operating margin of just 3.3 per cent. As the businesses operate in different types of retailing, it would be unfair to conclude that Ted Baker is better run than Sainsbury's.

Real business

If a business cannot make a reasonable operating profit it has no chance of long-term survival. A good example is Blockbuster UK. In its 2010 financial year it made an operating profit that was less than 1 per cent of its sales. Then, with sales falling as the DVD market declined, operating profits of £1.7m slipped to losses of £8.5m in 2011 and £11.2m in 2012 before collapse in 2013. The final Blockbuster stores were closed by early 2014.

41.4 Ratio analysis

The calculations of profit margins undertaken above can come under the heading 'ratio analysis'. This is a technique used by accountants to analyse business in comparison with a close rival, or to investigate the performance of a business over time. A ratio is simply a comparison of one piece of numerical data with another. In the case of profit margins, these comparisons are shown in percentage terms.

Table 41.2 shows how ratio analysis allows questions to be asked, and sometimes answered. It provides data on Tesco plc over time, and then shows Tesco versus Sainsbury and Morrisons'. Over time, it is clear that Tesco's profitability has fallen steadily. Nevertheless, in 2014, despite Sainsbury's steady improvement in its operating profit margin, Tesco remained significantly more profitable. As for Morrisons', in 2014 it made operating losses rather than profits. So, at that time, there were positives in Tesco's ratio analysis as well as negatives.

Table 41.2 Trading profit margins in the UK grocery market

	Tesco (UK only)	Sainsbury's	Morrisons'
2009	6.65 per cent	3.0 per cent	4.6 per cent
2010	6.2 per cent	3.1 per cent	5.3 per cent
2011	6.15 per cent	3.2 per cent	5.5 per cent
2012	5.8 per cent	3.2 per cent	5.5 per cent
2013	5.2 per cent	3.25 per cent	5.2 per cent
2014	5.0 per cent	3.3 per cent	(0.55 per cent)

41.5 Profit for the year

After every possible cost has been deducted, including interest charges and tax bills, the resulting figure is the profit for the year (also known as 'earnings'). The profit for the year is important because it leads to a huge boardroom decision: the directors must decide how much of that profit to pay out in dividends to shareholders and how much to leave in the business for reinvestment. In the case of Next plc, about one third of the profit for the year is paid out as dividends, leaving two thirds to finance the growth of the business. By contrast, in 2013 Tesco paid out nearly all its profit in dividends. So, at a time when it needed capital to invest in repositioning its shops, it gave nearly all its capital away to its shareholders. Short-termism in the extreme.

Ted Baker in 2014 kept about half of its profit for the year (after paying the other half out as dividends). At first that £15 million would sit in the bank account, boosting the firm's cash position. Then, if management chose to do it, the capital could be taken from the current account to buy new shop leaseholds, or a new distribution centre or to pay for a new advertising campaign. However the money is spent, it's reasonable to see it as an investment in Ted Baker's future growth prospects.

41.6 What is a good net profit margin?

The typical net profit margin in an industry will vary from one sector to another. Net profit margins from selected 2013 company accounts are shown in Table 41.3. The food retail market, for example, is very competitive and the profit per sale (the profit margin) is likely to be quite low (for example, 5 per cent). However, provided you can sell a high volume of items your overall net profits can still be high. You may make relatively little profit per can of beans, but provided you sell a lot of beans your overall profits may still be high.

In the case of luxury items such as SuperDry clothes or Rolex watches the profit margin is likely to be much higher. However, although the profit per sale is relatively high, this does not automatically mean the profits are high –that depends on how many items you sell.

Table 41.3 Net profit margins from selected 2013 plc accounts (half-year figures)

	Sales (£ million)	Underlying net profit (£ million)	Profit margin (%)
Tesco	31,914	1,466	4.6
Sainsbury's	12,684	400	3.2
SuperGroup	192	18	9.4

'I generally disagree with most of the very high margin opportunities. Why? Because it's a business strategy trade-off: the lower the margin you take, the faster you grow.' Vinod Khosla, Indian billionaire entrepreneur

'Market leadership can translate directly to higher revenue, higher profitability, greater capital velocity, and correspondingly stronger returns on invested capital.' Jeff Bezos, founder of Amazon.com

41.7 Methods of improving profits

To increase profits a business must:

1. increase revenue
2. decrease costs
3. do a combination of 1 and 2.

To increase revenue a business may want to consider its marketing mix. Changes to the product may mean that it becomes more appealing to customers. Better distribution may make it more available. Changes to promotion may make customers more aware of its benefits. However, the business needs to be careful that rising costs do not swallow up the rise in sales revenues.

To reduce costs a business may examine many of the functional areas (such as marketing, operations, people and finance):

● Could the firm continue with fewer staff?
● Could money be saved by switching suppliers?
● Do the firm's sales really benefit from sponsoring the opera?
● Are there ways of reducing wastage?

Essentially, a business should look for ways of making the product more efficiently (for example, with better technology) by using fewer inputs or paying less for the inputs being used. However, a business must be careful that when it reduces costs, the quality of service is not reduced. After all, this might lead to a fall in sales and revenue. Cutting staff in your coffee shop may cut costs, but if long queues form it may also reduce the number of customers and your income. Managers must weigh up the consequences of any decision to reduce costs.

Real business

Vietnam as a production base

Average wages in Vietnam are lower than those of two of its neighbours: Thailand and China. Vietnamese factory workers earn just two thirds of what their colleagues in China take home (about 65p an hour compared with £1 in China).

Companies such as Foxconn, which assembles consumer electronics and phones for big-brand companies like Apple and Sony, operate on very low profit margins and so try to find the lowest cost location they can. This makes Vietnam very attractive as a production base. Even high profit margin businesses such as Nike are shifting production to Vietnam, simply to keep costs down and therefore margins up.

41.8 Methods of increasing profitability

Profitability (as opposed to 'profits') is a relative term. It is mainly measured using the operating profit margin. To increase operating profits in relation to sales a business could do the following.

Increase the price

Increasing the price would boost the profit per sale, but the danger is that the sales overall may fall so much that the overall profits of the business are reduced. (Notice the important difference again between the operating profit margin and the overall level of profits; you could make a high level of profit on one can of beans relative to its price, but if you only sell one can your total profits are not that impressive!). The impact of any price increase will depend on the price elasticity of demand; the more price elastic demand is, the greater the fall in demand will be, and the less likely it is that a firm will want to put up its prices.

Cut costs

If cutting costs can be done without damaging the quality in any significant way then this clearly makes sense. Better bargaining to get the supply prices down or better ways of producing may lead to higher profits per sale. However, as we saw above, the business needs to be careful to ensure that reducing costs does not lead to a deterioration of the service or quality of the product.

Five Whys and a How

Question	Answer
Why might Sainsbury's want to compare its gross profit margin to that of Tesco?	To see which is creating a wider gap between costs paid to suppliers and prices charged to customers
What's the difference between gross profit and operating profit?	Fixed overheads
Why is 'profitability' looked at separately from 'profit'?	Because profit is an absolute (number) whereas profitability is a relative figure (e.g. as a percentage of revenue)
Why is 'profit for the year' so important to companies?	Because it pays for dividends and reinvestment; both are crucial for financing long-term growth
Why is it important to fair, long-term competition that every company should pay the same percentage rate of corporation tax?	If Ted Baker pays up but rivals find ways to avoid tax, in the long run the competitors will keep more profit for the year, be able to invest more, and therefore have an unfair advantage
How might a struggling firm attempt to increase its operating profitability?	By squeezing supply costs a bit more or by acting on fixed overhead costs, e.g. moving its head office to somewhere smaller and cheaper

Key terms

Corporation tax is a levy on the incomes of companies, that is, you pay a percentage of your pre-tax profit.

Fixed overheads are the indirect costs that have to be paid however the business is performing, for example, rent and salaries.

Evaluation: Profit and how to increase it

A difficulty with questions about poor profits is that it's easy to provide responses that are too obvious. Sainsbury's has a significantly lower profit margin than Tesco. But is it worth pointing out that Sainsbury's could look for bulk-buying discounts on its supplies? Surely it will be doing that already.

A good answer needs to look beyond the obvious to consider, perhaps, that Sainsbury's may have to address its head office (fixed overhead) costs in order to boost its margins to match those of Tesco.

Workbook

A. Revision questions

(30 marks; 30 minutes)

1. What is meant by 'revenue'? (2)

2. What is meant by 'operating profit'? (2)

3. Does an increase in price necessarily increase revenue? Explain your answer. (5)

4. How could a company jeopardise its future by paying out generous dividends to shareholders? (4)

5. Is profitability measured in pounds or percentages? (1)

6. What is the formula for the operating profit margin? (2)

7. Explain two ways of increasing profits. (4)

8. Why may cutting costs end up reducing profits? (4)

9. Outline one way in which operating profit might be affected by a decision within:
   a) the marketing function (3)
   b) the operations function. (3)

B. Revision exercises

DATA RESPONSE 1

SOFA-SOGOOD Ltd is a retailer of sofas. It had been experiencing a 'very slow' summer. Revenues had been falling and costs had been pushed up by pay increases, higher rent costs and higher interest payments on debts. As a result, net profits had fallen by 20 per cent on last year. Renis, the managing director, was very disappointed that revenue had fallen because he had cut prices by 5 per cent and had expected customer numbers to increase sharply. Once it became clear that this discounting policy was not working, he imposed a pay freeze on everyone in the company and a policy of non-recruitment. If any staff member left, she or he would not be replaced.

Questions (25 marks; 30 minutes)

1. Distinguish between revenue, costs and net profit. (3)

2. Explain why a fall in price might not have led to an increase in revenue. (4)

3. Apart from the methods mentioned in the text, analyse two other actions SOFA-SOGOOD could take to improve its profitability. (9)

4. Analyse the implications for the business of the staffing cost-saving actions taken by Renis. (9)

DATA RESPONSE 2

Measuring and increasing profits: Padrone Pizza

The news that the economy recovered in 2013 just made Pat more depressed. For the last 5 years his business (Padrone Pizza) had been sinking and sinking, caught up in a whirlwind of local competition driven by promotional discounting. 85 per cent of all his takings were now through some kind of promotion: 2-for-1; £5 Mondays; Häagen Dazs Wednesdays and so on. Five years ago he made £6 gross profit for every £10 of sales; now, in early 2014, he made just £2.50 on every £10 – and that's before counting all the fixed overheads: rent, rates, energy bills and advertising.

Over Christmas he'd talked it over with his dad and his 15-year-old daughter. She'd been full of ideas,

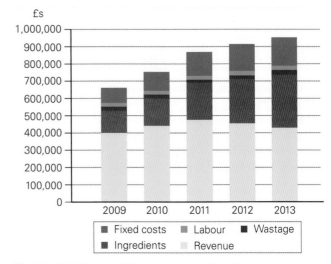

Figure 41.1 Padrone Pizza: revenue and costs

some from her GCSE Business course, but most from her knowledge of the local area and people. One phrase of hers kept coming back into Pat's mind: "Kids in class love boasting about the big pizza deals they've had last night; you need them talking about the pizza, not the deal." But how, given that every type of pizza was offered by his six local competitors? And what about other ways of improving profits?

C. Extend your understanding

1. In 2014 Next plc's retail business enjoyed operating profit margins of 15.6 per cent. Marks & Spencer plc had operating margins of 6.7 per cent. To what extent might price increases be the right way to boost M&S profits to match that of Next? (20)

Questions (25 marks; 25 minutes)

1. Calculate the profits made by Padrone Pizza in 2009 and in 2013. (4)

2. **a)** Outline three ways you can see to increase Pat's profit. (6)

   b) Discuss which one would be the best approach. Construct strong arguments in favour of your recommendation. (15)

2. In 2014 Snapchat boosted user numbers to more than 200 million people, but had not found a way to generate revenue, let alone profit. Discuss the difficulties for a new app in turning usage into profit. (20)

Chapter 42

Cash flow versus profit

Linked to: Cash flow management and forecasting, Chapter 39; Profit and how to increase it, Chapter 41; Sources of finance, Chapter 43.

Definition

Cash flow is the movement of cash into and out of a firm's bank account. Profit is when revenue is greater than total costs.

42.1 Introduction

A year ago a busy bar in Wimbledon closed down. Regulars were surprised, shocked even, that such a successful business had failed. The business was operating profitably, but the owners had become too excited by their success. Their investment in two new bars elsewhere in London had drained too much cash from the business, and the bank had panicked over the mounting debts. It forced the business to close. A profitable business had run out of cash.

To understand how cash differs from profit, the key is to master profit. On the face of it, profit is easy: total revenue *minus* total costs. Common sense tells you that revenue = money in and costs = money out. Unfortunately that's far too much of a simplification.

42.2 Distinction between cash flow and profit

To understand the difference, it is helpful to break it down into its two components.

1. Distinguishing revenue from cash inflows

Revenue is *not* the same as money in. Revenue is the value of sales made over a specified period: a day, a

month or a year. For example, the takings at a Topshop outlet last Saturday: £450 of cash sales, £2,450 on credit cards and £600 on the Topshop store card (£3,500 in total). Note that the cash inflow for the day is just £450, so revenue is not the same as 'cash in'.

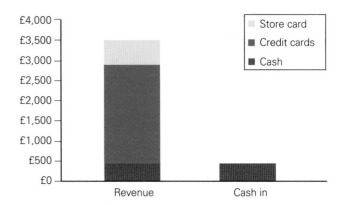

Figure 42.1 Saturday takings at a clothing outlet

Whereas revenue comes from just one source (customers), cash inflows can come from many sources. It is not limited to trading. Selling an old warehouse for £600,000 does not generate revenue, but it does bring in cash. Similarly, taking out a bank loan could not be classed as revenue, but it does put cash into your bank current account.

So cash inflows *can* be part of the revenue, but they do not have to be. Therefore cash and revenue are not the same. Examples of differences between cash inflows and revenue are given in Table 42.1.

Table 42.1 Differences between cash inflows and revenue

Financial item	Cash inflow	Revenue
Cash sales made to customers	✔	✔
Credit sales made to customers	✘	✔
Capital raised from share sales	✔	✘
Charge rent on flat upstairs	✔	✔
Take out a £20,000 bank loan	✔	✘
Carry out a **sale and leaseback**	✔	✘

'Revenue is vanity; profit is sanity; cash is King.' Anon

2. Distinguishing costs from cash outflows

The same distinction applies to costs and cash outflows. There are many reasons why a firm might pay out cash. Paying for the business's costs is only one of them. For example, the firm may pay out dividends to its shareholders, or it may repay a bank loan, or it may buy a piece of land as an investment.

In the case of the Wimbledon bar, the £200,000 annual profit gave the owners the confidence to buy leases on two new premises. They put together a business plan for expansion and received a £90,000 bank loan plus an £80,000 overdraft facility from a high street bank. They then hired architects and builders to turn the premises into attractive bars. Unfortunately, building hitches added to costs while delaying the opening times. The first of the new bars opened without any marketing support (there was no spare cash) and with the second of the bars still draining the business of cash, the bank demanded to have its overdraft repaid. As there was no way to repay the overdraft, the business went into liquidation.

So, a profitable business may run out of cash, simply because it expands too ambitiously, perhaps unluckily. There are other reasons why a profitable business might run into negative cash flow. These are set out below.

Seasonal factors

A firm that is generating sufficient revenue to cover its costs over a 12-month period might still hit short-term cash flow problems. This is a particularly difficult problem for new small firms. A new bicycle shop opens in the spring and may enjoy an excellent first 6 months' trading. The owners may get excited at the good profit level, buy a new van and have a much-needed holiday. They would have expected the winter half-year to be fairly poor for bike sales, but may be shocked by the level of decline. By February they may run out of cash and be unable to pay their staff. If only they had known the pattern of demand, the owners could have saved money in the first half of the year; but a fundamentally profitable business may close down due to a cash flow crisis.

Problems with credit periods

If a firm gives credit periods to its customers, there is risk from a long delay to a credit payment. For example, a builder who has put a great deal of money into renovating a large house finds that the client keeps

delaying the final payment. The more serious the builder's cash flow problems become, the stronger the position of the client. So a profitable business may be thrown into a cash crisis that could threaten its survival. Examples of differences between cash outflows and costs are given in Table 42.2.

Table 42.2 Differences between cash outflows and costs

Financial item	Cash outflow	Costs
Cash payments to suppliers	✔	✔
Purchases from suppliers on credit	✗	✔
Paying out wages	✔	✔
Repayment of bank loans	✔	✗
Tax bill received but not yet paid	✗	✔
Buying freehold property*	✔	✗
Paying the electricity bill	✔	✔

*Because a £500,000 property is worth £500,000, an accountant would not treat it as a cost.

42.3 Analysing the difference between cash flow and profit

The key is to appreciate that cash flow and profit are different aspects of the same thing. Cash flow and profit are linked, but they are not the same. Good financial planning requires an estimate of the likely profitability of a course of action. It then requires a careful forecast of the flows of cash in and out of the business. Profitability shows the long-term value of a financial decision; cash flow shows the short-term impact of that decision on the firm's bank balance.

Real business

Trish decides to open a beauty salon. She estimates that annual fixed overheads will be £160,000 and annual revenues £300,000 offset by variable costs at 20 per cent of revenue (£60,000).

In other words annual profit should be: £300,000 − (£160,000 + £60,000) = £80,000

The start-up costs of opening the salon are expected to be £60,000, so the business will be profitable from year 1.

However, there are some important cash flow issues to consider: first, how long will it take before the salon opens its doors (and cash starts flowing in)? Second, will the business *really* start at a revenue level equivalent to £300,000 per year (£25,000 per month), or will it take many months before sales rise to a satisfactory level?

Figure 42.2

Table 42.3 shows the cash flow position of the business, assuming that it takes three months to prepare the beauty salon (building work, decoration, and so on) and that it will take four months before regular custom has built up fully. The forecast is for the first eight months.

Table 42.3 Cash flow forecast for new beauty salon

All figures in £000s	1	2	3	4	5	6	7	8
Cash at start	0	(20)	(40)	(60)	(64)	(64)	(59)	(51)
Cash in	0	0	0	10	15	20	25	25
Cash out	20	20	20	14	15	15	17	17
Net cash	(20)	(20)	(20)	(4)	(0)	5	8	8
Cumulative cash*	(20)	(40)	(60)	(64)	(64)	(59)	(51)	(43)

*This is the firm's bank balance at the end of each month.

As you can see, even after eight months the business still has a serious cash flow problem. If the figures remain the same, it will be another six months before cumulative cash flow (the bank account) becomes positive. So the 'profitable' first year (and any accountant would confirm that the year is profitable) ends in the red.

The reason is simple. The cash investment to set up the business all takes place at the start, before the salon can generate a penny of cash inflow. The cash flow problem is because the cash outflow occurs before the cash inflows arrive. Therefore, the bank must be kept informed, so that it is willing to keep the business afloat. Unless the overdraft requirements are clear, and predicted, the bank manager may lose faith and demand all loans to be repaid.

'Every calculation of net profit reflects choices from competing theories of accounting… Profit is an opinion, cash is a fact.' Alex Pollock, American Enterprise Institute

42.4 Difficulties improving cash flow

Company cash flow is dominated by credit. Few companies pay cash: they buy on credit; and few sell for cash: they sell on credit. Therefore the biggest difficulty is if a company loses its financial credibility. If other businesses fear that a business will close it will surely do so. Suppliers will no longer give credit, so more cash is needed simply to keep in business; and if customers are increasingly worried about your survival, they'd prefer to go elsewhere.

It's critical, therefore, to avoid any suggestion that you are struggling financially. So if you need to improve cash flow you need to do it with subtlety. Beware of demanding shorter credit periods from your customers – or longer ones from suppliers. This is a reason why companies try to improve their cash flow position by cutting inventories or by speeding up their production programme.

Table 42.4 Difficulties improving cash flow

Business factor	How to boost cash flow	Difficulty in practice
1. Credit from suppliers	Delay payment to them	They may lose confidence in your solvency – and demand cash on delivery
2. Credit to customers	Cut credit period	Risk that they will go off and find a more generous supplier
3. Short of working capital	Use debt factoring	Fees take quite a slice of the profit, so it's hard to carry on for long
4. Use your assets	Sell underperforming assets for cash	There's a risk the business will end up with few assets for the future

42.5 Difficulties improving profit

Profit can be improved in one of three ways: raise prices (if price elasticity isn't too high), raise sales volumes or cut costs. In reality each will be difficult because the business will already have done what is necessary to optimise revenues and profits. Therefore, prices will already be set at the 'right' level and costs will already have been driven down as low as

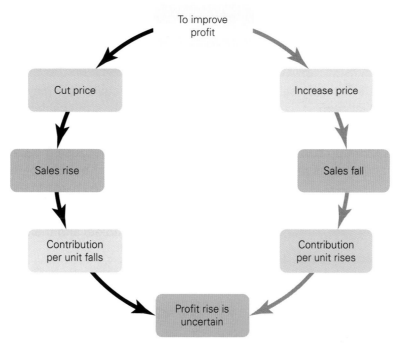

Figure 42.3 Logic chain: difficult to increase profit

makes sense. It's unwise, therefore, to make it sound easy to improve profit.

In practice the main difficulties are:

1. Raising prices: for price elastic products this inevitably cuts revenue, as the percentage fall in sales outweighs the percentage price rise. But even for price inelastic products there can be concerns. If other companies can see that one high-priced brand is making big profit margins, they will be attracted to compete. So pushing the price up provides a nice short-term boost to profit but perhaps at the cost of a future decline in market share.

2. Boosting sales volumes: the problem here is that either it is done by cutting prices (which will make it very

hard to boost profits) or the strategy will require some addition to costs, for example, extra advertising spending, the launch of a new flavour, or a flashy competition with prizes in Hawaii. Careful analysis is required to demonstrate that boosting sales volumes will end up improving profit

3. Cutting costs: it may seem obvious that you should look for a cheaper supplier, but every business is always on the look-out for that; so there's a risk that a cheaper supplier will have negatives such as: poorer quality, worse delivery reliability or perhaps – in some months' time – a scandal about child labour. Similarly, cutting fixed overhead costs by moving to a cheaper location may mean losing key staff – or stirring some hostile press coverage.

Evaluation: Cash flow versus profit

Especially for small firms, every significant decision needs to be assessed in terms of cash flow as well as profit. The cash flow forecast predicts the impact on the bank balance and may show the need for extra overdraft facilities to be negotiated. Or, if the firm's cash position is already weak, it may be safer to postpone the proposal.

Yet cash flow is no substitute for calculating profit. A cash-rich business idea (such as insurance) may

inevitably lead to **insolvency** if the business is not profitable. Getting cash inflows at the start seems great, but will turn into a nightmare if the cash outflows eventually start flooding in.

Remember, then, that cash flow and profit are not the same. Cash flow measures the short-term and profit shows the longer-term financial result of a decision. Clever managers look at both before they proceed.

Five Whys and a How

Question	Answer
Why may a shoe shop's Saturday sales be different from its cash inflows?	Because some customers may use credit cards, which delays the cash inflows by several working days
Why is taking out a £20,000 bank loan a cash inflow, but not counted as revenue?	It's a cash inflow because the £20,000 is credited to the bank account but it's not revenue; revenue is just the value of sales made in the trading period
Why might a profitable business face a cash flow crisis?	Because it's inefficient at collecting sums owed by customers (payables) and therefore runs out of cash
Why should an overdraft be a last resort if a company faces a cash flow problem?	Because the interest charges will eat away part of the company's profit; far better to solve the cash flow problem, e.g. cut inventory (stock) levels
Why do small firms have to focus upon cash flow rather than profit?	Their cash-to-cash position is usually poor because customers want plenty of credit while suppliers give little or no credit
How may seasonal factors disrupt the cash flow of a profitable business?	Acutely seasonal sales create highly seasonal cash inflows, making it hard to manage financially during the slack part of the year

Key terms

Dividends: annual payments to shareholders from the profits made by the company. It is the equivalent of the interest paid to those who lend money.

Insolvency: inability to pay the bills, forcing closure.

Negative cash flow: when cash outflows outweigh cash inflows.

Sale and leaseback: selling the freehold to a piece of property then simultaneously leasing it back, perhaps for a period of 20 years. The owner gives up tomorrow's valuable asset in exchange for cash today.

'Banks only deal with those that don't need them.' Robert Townsend, Avis boss and business author

Workbook

A. Revision questions

(20 marks; 25 minutes)

1. Explain in your own words why cash inflow is not the same thing as revenue. (3)

2. Look at Table 42.1. Explain why taking out a £20,000 bank loan generates a cash inflow but not revenue. (3)

3. Give two reasons why a profitable business could run out of cash when it expands too rapidly. (2)

4. Look at Table 42.2. Explain why 'purchases from suppliers on credit' is treated as a cost, yet not as a cash outflow. (3)

5. Identify whether each of the following business start-ups would be cash-rich or cash-poor in the early years of the business.

   a) A pension fund, in which people save money in return for later pay outs. (1)

   b) Building a hotel. (1)

   c) Starting a vineyard (grapes can only be picked after 3 to 5 years). (1)

6. Look at Table 42.3. Use it and the accompanying text to explain why the cash flow of the beauty salon is different from its profit. (4)

7. Why is it important for a small business to look both at profit and cash flow? (2)

B. Data response

Investment Dragon Peter Jones on cash and profit

Managing your cash in a focused manner is fundamental to survival, let alone success. Businesses are more likely to fail because they run out of cash – not because they're unable to generate a profit. You can have a lorry load of orders with the promise of untold profits in the pipeline, but if you don't have the cash to make and sell your products in the first place, and you are unable to pay your immediate bills, your business will fold.

Cash flow is a common hurdle for small and start-up enterprises. For that reason, it is important to **strengthen cash flow** from the outset.

Monitor profit and **avoid over-commitment.** One common mistake entrepreneurs make is that they see a run-rate of business and immediately start to incur costs. They'll rent an office, take on new lease commitments, buy a new car. These monthly payments can result in losing sight of the real cash that's generated through the business.

Grow the business organically and **keep costs down**, especially if you can't access bank finance. Focus on keeping costs to a bare minimum. Forget the office; work from home. Forget the car; use public transport. Grow the business, grow a pot of cash and then invest in the business. Using that money to reinvest is vital.

Reinvest profits wisely. It is important to:

● Understand what your start-up and on-going costs are. Be realistic. It is better to overestimate expenditure and time and underestimate revenue than fall short of revenue and overspend.

● Evaluate and monitor profit continually.

● Reinvest your profit. That way, you'll scale the business far quicker than if you use the profit to rent another office building or buy a car. It's how you spend the profit that's important. Entrepreneurs always spend profit on the business. Successful entrepreneurs invest that profit on the right areas to maximise growth and enhance existing offerings.

Source: www.peterjones.com

Questions (25 marks; 30 minutes)

1. Explain why, in the first paragraph, Peter Jones seems to be suggesting that cash flow is more important than profit for a small business. (5)

2. By 'run-rate' Peter Jones means the revenue generated by the business once it is up and running. Why does he think an entrepreneur should wait before spending at this rate? (6)

3. Growing 'organically' means from within; that is, not rushing to buy up other businesses. Organic growth is usually at a slow enough pace to cope with cash flow pressures. Analyse why rapid growth can cause big cash flow problems. (9)

4. Explain why it is 'better to overestimate expenditure and time and underestimate revenue'. (5)

C. Extend your understanding

1. When recession hits, wise financial managers focus more on cash flow and less on profit. Discuss why that might be the case. (20)

2. 'In the long run net cash flow and profit must be related. But in the short term they can differ wildly.' To what extent do you agree or disagree with this statement? (20)

Chapter
43

Sources of finance

Linked to: Different business forms, Chapter 2; Issues in understanding forms of business, Chapter 3; Financial objectives, Chapter 36; Decision-making to improve financial performance, Chapter 44.

Definition

All businesses need money. Where the money comes from is known as the 'sources of finance'.

43.1 The need for finance

Starting up

New businesses starting up need money to invest in long-term assets such as buildings and equipment. They also need cash to purchase materials, pay wages and to pay the day-to-day bills such as water and electricity. Inexperienced entrepreneurs often underestimate the capital needed for the day-to-day running of the business. Generally, for every £1,000 required to establish the business, another £1,000 is needed for the day-to-day needs.

Growing

Once the business is established there will be income from sales. If this is greater than the operating costs, the business will be making a profit. This should be kept in the business and used to help finance growth. Later on, the owners can draw money out, but at this stage as much as possible should be left in. Even so, there may not be enough to allow the business to grow as fast as it would like to. It may need to find additional finance and this will probably be from external sources such as bank loans.

Other situations

Businesses may also need finance in other circumstances, such as a cash flow problem. A major customer may refuse to pay for the goods, causing a huge gap in cash inflows. Or there may be a large order, requiring the purchase of additional raw materials. In all these cases businesses will need to find additional funding.

43.2 Internal sources of finance

Internal finance comes from within the business and its resources. The most important is profit, that is a surplus of revenue over costs. That surplus will start by accumulating in the company bank account, and then will typically be spent, perhaps on buying new machinery, new vehicles or on a launch advertising campaign in a new country. Nothing soothes a difficult cash situation better than profit. It is also the best (and most common) way to finance investment into a firm's future. Research shows that over 60 per cent of business investment comes from reinvested profit.

Another internal source of finance is from within the company's working capital, that is the cash spent on building inventory and in credit provided to customers. If that investment can be cut, cash will be generated. In the case of Ted Baker plc in 2014, it had £80 million tied up in stocks (inventory) and £35 million owed to it by customers. If it was able to halve its stock levels it could boost its cash holdings by £40 million; and halving the figure for customer receivables would generate £17.5 million of cash. That's a lot of potential finance generated from within the business.

43.3 External sources of finance

If the business is unable to generate sufficient funds from internal sources then it may need to look to external sources. There are two sources of external capital: loan capital and share capital.

Loan capital

The most usual way is through borrowing from a bank. This may be in the form of a bank loan or an overdraft. A loan is usually for a set period of time. It may be short term – one or two years; medium term – three to five years; or long term – more than five years. The loan can either be repaid in instalments over time or at the end of the loan period. The bank will charge interest on the loan. This can be fixed or variable. The bank will demand collateral to provide security in case the loan cannot be repaid.

An overdraft is a very short-term loan. It is a facility that allows the business to be 'overdrawn'. This means that the account is allowed to go 'into the red'. The length of time that this runs for will have to be negotiated. The interest charges on overdrafts are usually much higher than on loans. Fortunately the interest charges only apply to actual debts instead of the facility itself. For firms that use the overdraft as a way of smoothing short-term cash variations, the interest payments can be quite small.

Share capital

As an alternative to debt, if the business is a limited company it may look for additional share capital. This could come from private investors or venture capital funds. Venture capital providers are interested in investing in businesses with dynamic growth prospects. They are willing to take a risk on a business that may fail, or may do spectacularly well. They believe that if they make ten investments, five can flop, and four do 'OK' as long as one does fantastically. Peter Thiel, the original investor in Facebook, turned his $0.5 million investment into just over $1,000 million, making a profit of 199,900 per cent between 2004 and 2012!

Once it has become a public limited company (plc), the firm may consider floating on the stock exchange. For smaller UK businesses this will usually be on the Alternative Investment Market (AIM).

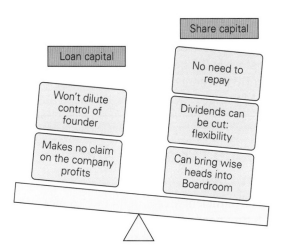

Figure 43.1 The value of share capital

Financing growth

How do rapidly growing small firms finance their growth? To find an answer to this question, Hamish Stevenson from Templeton College, Oxford, looks each year at 100 of the fastest growing UK firms. One of these is The Gym Group, which offers low-cost memberships for 24-hour gyms. Its sales grew from £1 million in 2008/9 to £22.6 million in 2012/13. The business started in 2007 with venture capital backing. Founder John Treharne had already built and sold a profitable chain of health clubs. Therefore, he was able to persuade venture capital company Bridges Ventures to provide £20 million of start-up equity in exchange for a substantial share stake. When the business required more capital to fulfil a plan of growing from 38 to 74 gyms by the end of 2015, another venture capital group invested a further £50 million in June 2013.

The Gym Group's easy access to capital contrasts with many others. As many as 54 of the 100 fastest growing firms financed all their early growth from a combination of personal savings and reinvested profits, that is, with no external funding at all.

43.4 Advantages and disadvantages of sources of finance

Internal sources

The advantages and disadvantages of internal sources of finance are set out below.

Retained (reinvested) profit

From any profits generated by the business most companies pay out about half as an annual dividend to the shareholders, ploughing the other half back into the business to help it grow. The advantage of reinvested profit is that it does not have an associated cost. Unlike loans it does not have to be repaid and there are no interest charges. The disadvantage is that there may be too little profit to allow the business to grow to its full capability.

Cash squeezed out of day-to-day finances

By cutting stocks, chasing up customers or delaying payments to suppliers, cash can be generated. This has the advantage of reducing the amount that needs to be borrowed. However this is a very short-term solution and if the cash is taken from day-to-day capital for a purpose such as buying long-term assets, the firm may find itself short of cash flow.

Debt factoring

One way to squeeze capital from day-to-day finances is by the use of debt factoring. A company that sells goods on credit can arrange that its bank take over the invoicing, giving the seller 80 per cent of the value of the sale immediately, then collecting the payment from the customer. Having taken its own commission, the bank then hands over the remaining sum to the seller (probably around 16 per cent). So the seller has most of the cash immediately, to help build the business, and does not have to chase the payment from the customer. It receives about 96 per cent of the value of the sale. The bank does the legwork but keeps a cut of about 4 per cent for itself.

External sources

The advantages and disadvantages of external sources of finance are set out below.

Bank overdrafts

This is the commonest form of borrowing for small businesses. The bank allows the firm to overdraw up to an agreed level. This has the advantages that the firm only has to borrow when and as much as it needs. It is, however, an expensive way of borrowing, and the bank can insist on being repaid within 24 hours.

The old saying holds: 'Owe your banker £1,000 and you are at his mercy; owe him £1 million and the position is reversed.' – John Maynard Keynes, British economist and author.

Trade credit

This is the simplest form of external financing. The business obtains goods or services from another business but does not pay for these immediately. The average credit period is two months. It is a good way of boosting day-to-day finance. A disadvantage could be that other businesses may be reluctant to trade with the business if they do not get paid in good time.

Bank loan

A bank loan is usually for a period of 2–5 years and is therefore classified as medium-term finance. It is an excellent form of finance for a new, growing business because there is no need to repay any capital until the contract says so – usually at the end of the period.

Venture capital

This is a way of getting outside investment for businesses that are unable to raise finance through the stock markets or loans. Venture capitalists invest in smaller, riskier companies. To compensate for the risks, venture capital providers usually require a substantial part of the ownership of the company. They are also likely to want to contribute to the running of the business. This dilutes the owner's control but brings in new experience and knowledge. The term 'dragon' became a well-known term for a venture capital provider, thanks to the BBC TV series *Dragon's Den*.

'One thing I'm so grateful for is sidestepping the usual venture capital, private equity route. My friends who have gone that way are many times beholden to their boards of directors, to 'sell' ideas to a team.' Blake Mycoskie, founder TOMS Shoes

---

A modern version of venture capital is 'crowdfunding'; it's a way of getting small investors to put money into a new business – often with an incentive such as to get a sample product or service in return for their investment. It works via the internet and works most effectively when the sponsors use social media to promote their business. In the UK, Seedrs and Kickstarter are two of the best-known sponsors of crowdfunding.

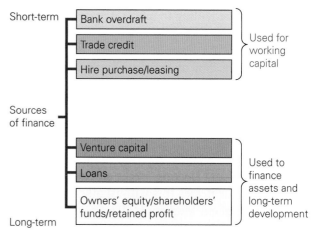

Figure 43.2 Short- and long-term sources of finance

'62.4 per cent of venture capital investments were completely lost while 3.1 per cent of the investments accounted for 53 per cent of the profits for roughly 600 investments.' Mahendra Ramsinghani, business author

---

43.5 Finance for short- and long-term uses

Businesses need sufficient access to finance to meet current and future needs. This is a major issue for new firms and for those that are expanding rapidly. When a business expands without sufficient finance it is known as 'overtrading'.

The key is to match the type of finance to its use. A distinction is made in company financing between short- and long-term finance (see Figure 43.2). Short-term finance is usually considered to be for less than one year. Medium-term is one to five years. Long-term finance is longer than five years.

Short-term finance should not be used to finance long-term projects. Using short-term finance such as overdrafts puts continual pressure on the company's cash position. An overdraft should only be used to cope with ups and downs in cash flow. By its very nature,

growth is a long-term activity, so appropriate long-term finance should be sought to fund it.

Another key aspect of appropriate finance is that businesses should find the right balance between 'equity' and debt. Equity means share capital, which is safe and stable, as shareholders need not be paid a dividend if times are tough. Debt-based finance such as an overdraft or loan is more risky. Even when business is poor the bank still expects to be paid interest on the loan, plus – with an overdraft – the bank may demand that the overdraft is repaid immediately.

Five Whys and a How

Question	Answer
Why might a business finance expansion using debt rather than equity?	Issuing more equity dilutes the value of shares, putting the founders' control of the business at risk
Why might debt factoring be a mistake for some types of business?	Banks take a cut of about 4 per cent of the value of the sale; if the business has low profit margins (say, 8 per cent) this would halve the sellers' profit
Why might a bank refuse to lend to a business?	It may doubt the firm's ability to repay, i.e. see it as too risky; or the bank may think it can make more profit elsewhere, e.g. property speculation
Why might a business collapse from overtrading (growing too fast)?	If sales increases outstrip the firm's capital base, it can run out of cash and slide into administration
Why do venture capital companies invest in some businesses but not others?	Venture capitalists seek huge potential gains, therefore they love 'scalability': a high potential for the business to grow massively
How might crowdfunding prove harmful to a new small business?	Getting a bank loan for £250,000 is simple to administer; 50,000 crowdfunders investing £5 each could become an administrative nightmare

Key terms

Angel investors: investors who back a business before it's opened its doors, taking a full equity risk, that is, if it fails the angel investor will lose everything.

Collateral: an asset used as security for a loan. It can be sold by a lender if the borrower fails to pay back a loan.

Crowdfunding: instead of getting one angel investor to finance a £50,000 start-up, crowdfunding looks for many small investors, perhaps each investing an average of £100 (so 500 such investors will be needed).

Overtrading: when a firm expands without adequate and appropriate funding.

Public limited company (plc): a company with limited liability and shares which are available to the public. Its shares can be quoted on the stock market.

Share capital: business finance that has no guarantee of repayment or of annual income but gains a share of the control of the business and its potential profits.

Stock market: a market for buying and selling company shares. It supervises the issuing of shares by companies. It is also a second-hand market for stocks and shares.

Venture capital: high-risk capital invested in a combination of loans and shares, usually in a small, dynamic business.

Evaluation: Sources of finance

Raising finance is a perfect example of the different skills required by business people. When starting out, the personality of the entrepreneur is likely to be of critical importance, as **angel investors** must decide, in part, whether they want to work with this person. Later on, when the start-up has progressed to the point of needing more capital for expansion, the need is for an organised person with thorough records of cash flow and profit. At first, charisma counts; now it's competence that matters. Not many people have both qualities, so it's important to hire wisely, and to delegate to someone who has skills you lack.

Whatever the situation, debt should still be taken as a threat to any business. Advisors tell firms to borrow more when times are good, but good turns to bad amazingly quickly, which can leave over-stretched companies floundering. Debt always means risk; but of course some risks are well worth taking.

Workbook
A. Revision questions

(30 marks; 40 minutes)

1. Describe the problem caused to a company if a major customer refuses to pay a big bill. (3)

2. Why do banks demand collateral before they agree to provide a bank loan? (2)

3. Outline two ways in which businesses can raise money from internal sources. (4)

4. What information may a bank manager want when considering a loan to a business? (4)

5. Explain briefly the benefits to a manufacturing business of using debt factoring instead of an overdraft. (4)

6. Outline two sources of finance that can be used for long-term business development. (4)

7. Explain why a new business could find it difficult to get external funding for its development? (5)

8. Outline one advantage and one disadvantage of using an overdraft. (4)

B. Revision exercises
DATA RESPONSE 1

Indian in China?

Posting to www.chinasuccessstories.com:

Hi everyone, I am from India and wish to open a quick takeaway and a small restaurant or café but with Indian snacks and food in Nanjing, near the International University. I would like to know about:

1. the rules and regulations

2. the approximate budget

3. the minimum area requirement

4. the real estate prices in an area like Shanghai Lu, Nanjing.

Please contact me by leaving a comment here.

Thank you,

Karishma

Hi Karishma,

You have to know that the life expectancy of a new foreign restaurant on Nanjing Road is between three and six months, in 50 per cent of cases. Many foreigners open restaurants without complying with all the rules… Be ready to have enough funds to survive for one year minimum without any revenues. If you want I could give you contacts with very good companies that could help you for all legal aspects. Good luck, and I will come to your restaurant!

Paul Martin

Questions (30 marks; 30 minutes)

1. Explain to Karishma the implications for start-up financing of Paul Martin's reply. (5)

2. Analyse the circumstances in which Karishma should proceed with her idea, if she were able to obtain the start-up finance. (9)

DATA RESPONSE 2

Kickstarter

In recent years crowdfunding has become an alternative to traditional market research and also a different way to finance a start-up. The Kickstarter website helps a creative business idea to be put to the public, asking for start-up capital in exchange for a free 'taste' of the product.

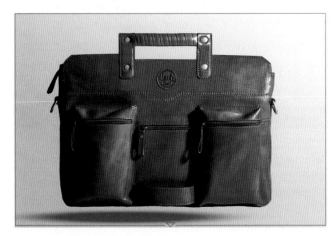

Figure 43.3 The Boombox bag

One successful 2014 start-up was Chivote, a producer of leather bags and accessories. It raised £20,000 through Kickstarter by offering products in exchange

C. Extend your understanding

1. While at University you develop a game for mobiles based on tractors, farms, rabbits and foxes – and everyone loves it. Your parents lend you £4,000 and you have £2,000 but you estimate that it'll cost about £20,000 simply to get the game ready for use and to get it some publicity. To what

3. To what extent should Karishma be looking for share rather than loan capital to finance her start-up? (16)

for investment. A £7 investment received a leather nametag in return, while £240 yielded a Boombox bag.

Crowdfunding uses online technology and social media to replace the traditional role of banks.

Chivote has another unusual aspect to its business. It sources its leather goods from a small partnership of craftsmen which works as a partner instead of a supplier to Chivote. This is another way to help minimise the capital needed to start up the business. Usually a new business would have to pay cash up front for supplies; the partnership ensures that normal credit terms can smooth the cash flow requirements.

Questions (30 marks; 35 minutes)

1. Explain the benefit to cash flow of having a supplier who offers credit terms instead of cash-only. (5)

2. Analyse the benefits of crowdfunding compared with traditional venture capital funding when starting a business such as Chivote. (9)

3. A weakness of crowdfunding might be that it's effective only with consumer-friendly, attractive products or services. To what extent is that a problem? (16)

extent might venture capital be the best way to finance the start-up of your business? (20)

2. For the founder of a rapidly growing small business, how important is it to keep 51-plus per cent of the share capital? Justify your answer. (20)

Chapter
44

Decision-making to improve financial performance

Linked to: Financial objectives, Chapter 36; Cash flow management and forecasting, Chapter 39; Profit and how to increase it, Chapter 41; Sources of finance, Chapter 43.

Definition

Financial performance means measuring the achievements of the business in relation to the financial objectives set.

44.1 Introduction

Financial performance can be measured in many ways. Entrepreneurs in the Dragon's Den are trying to obtain finance; later they'll be hoping for break even and in the longer term profit will become the key form of measurement. This chapter looks at the constraints that can prevent companies from finding it easy to meet their financial objectives.

44.2 Financial decisions and competitiveness

Whenever possible, finance directors like to compare their own firm's financial performance with that of a direct competitor. A good case in point is the competition between two fashion clothing businesses: Ted Baker plc and SuperGroup plc (aka SuperDry). As shown in Table 44.1 both companies could learn from this comparison. SuperGroup is doing brilliantly to convert a lower gross margin into a higher operating margin (implying tighter control of fixed overhead costs). Ted Baker can take huge pride in its recent growth rate, especially for e-commerce.

In terms of financial decisions, SuperGroup might consider heavier investments into its website – perhaps it needs to catch up with Ted. For Ted Baker, perhaps serious thought is needed about the overhead costs; for example, should Ted move its headquarters to somewhere cheaper?

Table 44.1 Financial performance at Ted Baker plc and SuperGroup plc

	Ted Baker plc	SuperGroup plc
Revenue 2014	£322 m	£431 m
Revenue growth re: 2013	+26.7 per cent	+19.6 per cent
E-commerce growth 2014	+55.7 per cent	+26.7 per cent
Gross profit margin	61.7 per cent	59.7 per cent
Operating profit margin	12.3 per cent	14.3 per cent

Among other financial decisions that might affect business competitiveness are:

- Borrowing more: this is a quick and easy way to add capital to a business that is growing, or one that needs a dramatic change in strategy. Unfortunately it runs the medium- to long-term risk that the indebted capital structure will create significant operational risks. Growth can evaporate if customer taste turns sour and dramatic changes in strategy are – by definition – risky. A severely weakened balance sheet can undermine a company's competitiveness.

- Cutting costs: removing a whole layer of store management, as Asda and Morrisons' did in Spring 2014, may cause short-term disruption to both operations and HR, but all in the cause of stronger long-term competitiveness. Where price competition is as fierce as in grocery retailing, keeping costs down (especially fixed overheads) will always be a critical success factor.

- Boosting cash flow: recently ASOS stretched its time to pay suppliers from 43 days in 2012 to 59 in 2013; taking an extra half a month to pay enables the company to keep nearly £20 million extra in its bank account. That helps finance growth, though competitiveness may be worsened if suppliers start to show preference for other retailers (for example, with stock of newly launched product lines).

'Competitive prices may result in profits which force you to accept a rate of return less than you hoped for.' Alfred Sloan, CEO, General Motors

Real business

A massive restructuring by the supermarket chain Asda has put 4,100 management jobs in consultation. It is thought thousands of middle managers will leave the company rather than accept alternative lower-paid jobs. The restructuring comes as the grocer realigns itself to deal with the growing popularity of online shopping and home delivery.

'We haven't updated our structure for five to six years,' said Asda's chief operating officer, Mark Ibbotson. 'We believe we are about 18 months ahead of our competitors. They're all going to have to do this at some point.'

Ibbotson is tasked with finding £1 billion of cost savings over the next five years as a fierce battle on price continues among the nation's largest supermarkets.

As part of the restructuring Asda has created in-store e-commerce manager roles and will devote more staff to services such as click-and-collect and grocery home delivery.

Source: Several, including *The Grocer*, *The Guardian* and *RetailWeek*

44.3 Financial decisions and the other business functions

No department is as central as finance. Its decisions affect and are affected by every other function. If marketing decides to run a '20 per cent off' price promotion that unexpectedly doubles demand, finance will need to find the cash for buying the extra supplies and to pay the overtime bill. Figure 44.1 shows this.

What most finance directors hate most is unexpected surprises. This is why they are so keen on budgeting, which requires staff to plan ahead and then record any variations from the planned income or expenditure.

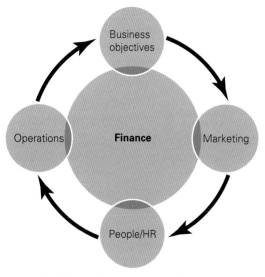

Figure 44.1 Logic chain: finance at the core

44.4 Impact on finance of market condition and competition

Following its scandal-ridden era from 2007–2013 Barclays Bank announced in 2014 that 15,000 jobs would go that year, and that the medium-term plan was to cut staff from 140,000 worldwide to 100,000. These huge job cuts reflected the bank's worsening revenue position and its withdrawal from some of its highest-risk banking sectors. In this case, then, worsening market conditions dictated the finance department's demand for cost cuts. Perhaps sadly, in the case of Barclays, there was no additional competitive pressure facing it or other high street banks. Despite all the banks' failings and the low esteem in which they were held, most people remained reluctant to switch their current account.

Perhaps it's fair to say that bad times place finance at the heart of every business decision. A bigger test comes in good times. If sales and profits are rising, marketing and R&D people may push harder for bigger budgets – and it may be difficult to stop this happening. Those finance departments that 'succeed' in good times are probably managing to persuade directors that it's time for shareholders to get some significant rewards. In 2014 Apple Inc. spent $30 billion in cash to buy shares back from its stockholders. This boosts the share price (which, handily, can boost bonus payments for directors) but at the cost of the firm's cash flow position.

Overall, the finance function tends to want to keep on-going costs as low as possible, so that profit margins are as high as possible. They tend not to mind share buy-backs because they are a one-off expenditure rather than an on-going one.

And competition? The typical finance manager wants as little of it as possible. So any proposal to buy up direct competitors will always get a good hearing – and probably enthusiastic backing from the company's bankers. Competition is a threat to profit margins and a threat to a secure, easy life for the company. The last thing finance staff want to see is a price war.

'Cost accounting is the number one enemy of productivity'. Johnson and Kaplan, business writers

---

44.5 Ethical and environmental influences on financial decisions

Those working in finance tend to have a pragmatic view of ethical or environmental issues. In other words they want to see them pay their way. So an environmental programme based on recycling and waste minimisation can get the support of the finance function if its advocates can prove that cost reductions will make the proposal profitable. Similarly, a move to Fairtrade supplies (such as Nestlé/Kit Kat in 2010) needs to justify itself in terms of the value it adds to consumers' perception of the brand. In other words, it's okay to add half a penny to the costs if the price can be pushed up a full penny. For a business to make a genuine move towards ethical practices it would be essential that the finance department got instructions from on high (the chief executive or the board). Then co-operation will happen.

Another important aspect of modern finance is tax 'planning', that is, the deliberate act of tax avoidance. In the UK there has been a successful effort to point the finger of blame at US companies, especially those in the technology sector. Starbucks, Amazon, Apple, Google and many others have been picked out. In fact there are many British firms or organisations that deserve huge criticism, including Vodafone, the Virgin group and perhaps the whole of the private equity sector (owners of Boots, Pret A Manger, many energy companies and

much, much more). Ultimately, the tax-dodging deals are done by senior finance executives. And if you think that tax avoidance is ethically neutral, how can it be fair that a tax-paying company such as Ted Baker should have to compete with a rival fashion retailer that rigs things to pay little or no tax. A level playing field is an important underpinning to an effective market.

44.6 Technological influences on financial decisions

Currently crowdfunding is a fashionable approach to capital raising, especially for businesses with a consumer-friendly business proposition. From Seedrs in the UK to M-Changa in Kenya, this is seen as a valuable application of online technology to financial needs. In fact the approach can be dated at least as far back as Mozart in the 1700s, raising money to fund three concerts in Vienna. But the crowdfunding of today is unquestionably an online process.

More fundamental, perhaps, are the financial implications of key strategic decisions about whether to function via 'bricks' or 'clicks'. Setting up a network of shops or physical outlets implies huge fixed operating costs and therefore a high break-even point. Having only a digital/online presence cuts those costs dramatically and therefore brings the break-even down. Much though this would please finance managers, the downside is that it may be much harder to build sales virtually than physically.

Real business

Future Ad Labs is a UK business focused on intelligent targeting of advertising to users of hand-held devices. Having achieved funding from Seedrs in 2012, it obtained an extra $1 million from venture capital and angel investors in 2013 and then returned to Seedrs in 2014 to raise more finance via convertible shares. A sceptic would worry about all this capital-raising (How about making some profit, guys?), but because Future Ad Labs specialises in high technology online and social media advertising, investors have been happy to support its cash-hungry growth.

Five Whys and a How

Question	Answer
Why might new, low-cost Chinese competition help boost a UK firm's competitiveness in the long term?	It would force the UK firm to rethink its costs and perhaps encourage operations to become more efficient
Why might finance professionals believe finance is the most important business function?	Success in business is measured by profit and loss, so it's understandable to see finance as all-important
Why might finance professionals care less about ethical standards than managers in HR or marketing?	Because the finance executives feel only distantly involved in decisions that might include price fixing or tax avoidance
Why don't finance professionals take into account the external costs and benefits of the company's actions?	Because only the government can calculate based on social benefits and costs; business organisations just look at their internal costs and benefits
Why may high debts represent a risky capital structure?	Because, if things go wrong, high debts mean high interest payments and therefore a threat to cash flow
How might operations management be affected by big cutbacks in the budgets allocated by finance?	A short-term cutback in investment spending might be followed by a longer-term need to cut capacity so as to boost capacity utilisation

Evaluation: Decision-making to improve financial performance

Day by day, staff working within finance will rarely see those from other functions. Finance staff are busy gathering data on what has happened to revenue and costs, and projecting forward to try to anticipate what's going to happen over the coming months. The single most important period of time for working with other departments is when budgets are to be agreed. Then finance staff will try to identify budget claims that are unwarranted. In addition, there will occasionally be major changes to strategy (perhaps marketing or operations) which require a very different financial approach. The best finance director will be the one that knows when to stop saying no. Bold strategies need bold financial decisions.

'Business is a good game – lots of competition and a minimum of rules. You keep score with money.'
Nolan Bushnell, computer game pioneer

Workbook

A. Revision questions

(25 marks; 25 minutes)

1. Look at the data in Table 44.1. Give two possible reasons why Ted Baker's gross profit margin is greater than SuperGroup's. (2)

2. If a company is enjoying rising profits at a time when the economy is booming, what might it do to check on the strength of its performance? (5)

277

3. Briefly explain why Barclays had to cut its staff numbers so dramatically in 2014. (3)

4. Explain how a firm's competitiveness might be affected if it ends up adopting too risky a capital structure. (4)

5. Briefly explain the inter-relationship between finance and the other functional areas. (4)

6. What might be the implications of a business deciding to outsource its finance department? (4)

7. Why might crowdfunding be a good alternative to bank borrowing when a company wishes to raise more capital? (3)

B. Revision exercises
DATA RESPONSE

Change of strategy at Hovis

Figure 44.2 Hovis white loaf

In 2006 UK food giant Premier Foods plc paid £2 billion to take over Hovis bakeries. The stock market was impressed, boosting the Premier share price by 10 per cent in a day. Yet when Michael Clarke took over as chief executive at Premier Foods in August 2011, he described the business as 'virtually broken'. Huge debts plus poor trading had cut the value of Premier shares by 98 per cent. The prime cause was Hovis.

In March 2012 Premier announced a £259 million pre-tax loss after writing down the value of its bread division (Hovis). Fierce price competition meant that trading profits for the bread division fell by 90 per cent in 2011/12 to £3.4 million. With Premier weighed down by more than £1 billion of debt, Clarke decided it was time to tackle the Hovis problem.

In 2011 the Hovis strategy had been to build market share by boosting advertising spending using cycling star Victoria Pendleton as the face of the brand. This increased sales by a higher percentage than the bread market as a whole, yet did not prevent the 90 per cent profit slide mentioned above. When the profit figures came through, the marketing plan was deemed to

have failed. So, for 2012, Clarke decided that cost minimisation was required.

The first signal came in October 2012 when Premier announced that it was withdrawing from a £75 million contract to supply bread to the Co-op retail chain. This supply contract (two-thirds Hovis branded, one third Co-op own brand) was described by Premier as a 'high-cost, low-margin retail partnership'. The purpose behind the cancellation became clear a month later when Premier announced the closure of two bakeries and the removal of 130 distribution routes, leading to 900 job losses (10 per cent of bread division staffing).

The company announced that: 'The bread contract loss takes volume out and that is a catalyst for us to be able to make changes and manage the bread business in a different way... The move forms part of a long-term strategy to drive efficiency.'

Later, in November 2012, the managing director of Premier's bakery arm resigned. He had only been in the job for a year, but perhaps he was unwilling to be part of a switch from market-share growth to severe cost cutting. The cutbacks associated with the Co-op contract are unlikely to be the last.

Figure 44.3 Hovis Best of Both loaf

Meanwhile, Premier's big rival Allied Bakeries says it is delighted to pick up the Co-op contract on the same terms as those rejected by Hovis. In other words Allied thinks it can make money from the deal. A City analyst commented that 'Allied anticipates the benefits of marginal economies from the Co-op deal... It is fair to say that Allied is more efficient than Hovis and so has more ammunition at hand.' Can Premier really strengthen itself by strengthening the market-share position of its rivals? Time will tell.

C. Extend your understanding

1. It is sometimes said that in Germany businesses revolve around engineers, but in Britain they revolve around accountants. To what extent might this be a disadvantage to Britain? (20)

Questions (25 marks; 30 minutes)

1. For a business such as Premier Foods plc, analyse the factors that might lead to a decision to focus on cost minimisation. (9)

2. Examine one alternative financial strategy that Premier Foods might adopt. (7)

3. Analyse how the finance department might have judged that the 2011 Hovis marketing plan was unprofitable. (9)

2. 'Many financial measurements which are useful and valid in static situations are strategic traps in growth situations.' Bruce Henderson, Boston Consulting Group. To what extent do you agree with this statement? (20)

Setting human resource (HR) objectives

Linked to: Motivation and engagement in theory, Chapter 46; Managing the human resource flow, Chapter 49; Analysing human resource performance, Chapter 51; Decision-making and improved human resource performance, Chapter 52.

Definition

Human resource management is a common term for the personnel function. HR professionals think of their role as central to the overall goals of the business, and set their HR objectives accordingly.

45.1 Human resource objectives

The management of people (otherwise known as human resource management) involves a wide range of activities. The overall aim is to maximise the contribution of employees on an individual and group level to the organisation's overall objectives. To do this, specific goals need to be met. These HR objectives will be derived from the targets of the business as a whole.

'Management by objectives works if you know the objectives. Ninety per cent of the time you don't.' Peter Drucker, business writer/guru

Employee engagement and involvement

As shown in Figure 45.1, companies simply cannot assume that hiring and training staff is enough. According to Gallup Poll, only 13 per cent of staff worldwide are fully engaged in their job. If they aren't engaged and interested, they will never give 100 per cent.

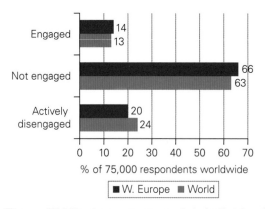

Figure 45.1 Employee engagement study, October 2013
Percentage of 75,000 respondents worldwide
Source: Gallup Poll Worldwide

The problem is that there is no reason to suppose that HR professionals have any real solution to this problem. 'Employee engagement' is little different from 'motivation', but even though it has been known for fifty years that motivation can best be addressed through job enrichment, the HR approach is quite different. Nor is this a surprise. Job enrichment requires jobs to be redesigned, with high division of labour replaced by giving people a complete unit of work. Yet this is outside the scope of HR professionals, who couldn't possibly advise an operations manager about how to lay out a factory or a supermarket checkout. So the HR approach is to pretend that employee engagement can be achieved through financial devices and bureaucratic devices such as staff appraisal. Professor Herzberg, whose theories are discussed in Chapter 46, would see little value in any of this. Given the prevalence of HR departments today, the 'engaged' figure of 13 per cent is a clear pointer to the need for a different approach.

'British management doesn't seem to understand the importance of the human factor.' Charles, Prince of Wales

Talent development

For many businesses, the key to long-term success is training and motivation of the staff as a whole. In some circumstances, though, it is understandable that the focus may be on the talented few rather than the entire staff. Southampton FC has been a leading light in football talent development, having consistently devoted a large chunk of budget to developing youth players. The result, from Gareth Bale and Theo Walcott through to Luke Shaw, has generated enough transfer cash to justify the policy.

For other businesses, graduate 'fast-track' schemes have long existed, with the view that those with extra talent should be given every opportunity for career progression as rapid as their talents allow. There is a risk, though, that the focus on the talented few could seem to come at the expense of the majority. This is unlikely to help morale.

In 2014 the Chartered Institute of Personnel Development (CIPD) published research showing that the median annual training budget per employee in Britain is £286 (down from £303 in 2013). With such a tiny figure, the idea of switching it away from the majority towards the 'talented' could negatively affect the teamwork and culture of an organisation.

Training

Professor Herzberg once said that 'the more a person can do, the more you can motivate them.' Therefore training people to be able to do more, and do it with confidence, represents a big potential step forward for a business. Yet there is scant evidence that UK firms understand this fully. They like to blame schools and universities for failing to prepare students for the world of work, but their own reluctance to train is quite odd. Figure 45.2 shows data from America and Britain that

Figure 45.2 Employer annual spend on training UK vs USA
Source: CIPD and ASTD

paints British employers in a poor light. British government data in 2014 suggested a UK productivity gap of about 30 per cent compared with America. Perhaps it is time to address this – starting by spending more on training.

Diversity

The Greggs website (http://corporate.greggs.co.uk/greggs-at-a-glance/main-board) includes photographs of the executive directors of Greggs plc.The non-executive directors include three women, but decisions in business are driven through by executive directors, so these are the ones who count. Excellent a company though Greggs has long been, it is striking to see the lack of diversity by age, gender and race. Surely, given that Greggs' customers are a cross-section of British consumers, the boardroom would benefit from some voices other than those of middle-aged, white blokes.

This is why some companies have set themselves the objective of diversifying their middle and senior management teams. They have been encouraged by statements such as this, by David Tyler, Sainsbury's chairman: 'Shareholders benefit when boards have a diversity of skills, background and experience. That's the way the most effective boards tend to be composed – with both men and women playing a full part.' The UK organisation '30 Per Cent Club' wants to see women making up at least 30 per cent women of board directors. This focus on female representation risks sidelining race as an issue. In 2014 two-thirds of Britain's Top 100 companies had no non-white full-time executive board members. The case for diversity is clear; the drive to achieve it is less so.

Figure 45.3 In 2014 two-thirds of Britain's Top 100 companies had no non-white full-time executive board members.

Alignment of values

Business author Jim Collins has said that businesses spend too long worrying about their new mission or vision. They would be stronger if they spent more time aligning staff to the organisation's core values. He cites the US company 3M (famous for Post-it Notes), which has long had at its centre: sponsoring innovation, protecting the creative individual and solving problems in a way that makes people's lives better.

Collins suggests that firms should work at identifying their core values, then make sure that every employee sees these values as central to decision-making throughout the business. Accordingly, recruitment and induction training should focus on making sure that there is a true fit between staff and the values. This should not only ensure that ethical issues are tackled in a consistently moral way, but should also help build a sense of purpose throughout the staff – which may help with motivation and retention levels.

Real business

US giant 3M is proud of its first patent from its operation in India. India's massive textile industry had long sent discarded cotton threads to landfill. Now 3M's technology allows handloom weavers to transform the threads into floor-cleaning cloths, creating jobs for local residents – and providing a commercial incentive for recycling.

The number, skills and location of employees

Organisations are continually changing in terms of the work being done and the way it is done. This reshaping requires changes in the human resource input. For example, it may require more people, greater flexibility or different skills. The human resource function is responsible for making sure the business has the right number of people at the right time, with the right skills and attitudes. A lack of appropriate staff can lead to delays for customers, rushed and poor-quality work, and an inability to accept some contracts. By comparison, if the human resource requirements are met, a business is more likely to be able to provide a high-quality service and fulfil the expectations of customers. Achieving the right number of staff may be relatively easy if you can simply recruit more people when you need them. However, it can also be a very long-term process that involves enormous planning. In the case of the health service, for example, there is a very long training period for doctors and surgeons. The NHS has to plan years in advance for the number of doctors it will need.

A further factor is the location of staff. HR departments like staff to be willing to work in Portsmouth for six months, then move to Manchester. For many staff this flexibility is impossible, so careful planning is required to make sure that Manchester has the right manager at the right time.

45.2 Internal and external influences on HR objectives and decisions

Internal influences

The recent history of a business often provides insight into its corporate and HR objectives. The German industrial giant Siemens was involved in a series of bribery scandals in 2005. Its response was to appoint a new boss from outside the company (Peter Loescher). He encouraged the company to develop a bureaucratic style of 'ethical tick boxes' which made staff reluctant to take responsibility for decisions. This undermined the efficiency of the business, leading to poor engineering project management, contract losses and the dismissal of Loescher in 2013.

In addition to recent history, other internal influences are:

- the past experiences, character and ambitions of any newly appointed chief executive
- any financial pressures felt by the business, for example, cash flow problems requiring a quick fix
- changing marketing objectives, such as the decision by Aldi to move upmarket in the UK in 2011. This would have forced a change in recruitment and training from an HR perspective.

External influences

Few external influences are more important in HR than the economy. When economic growth is sustained for a few years and unemployment is falling, HR departments have to work hard to attract the best recruits, especially graduates. If a recession takes hold, HR objectives revert to efficiency maximisation, involving redundancies, a switch to temporary and part-time working, and outsourcing (which usually means lower wage rates).

In addition to economic factors, other external influences are:

- whether the business is a stock market-quoted plc or a large family-run business. This affects the timescales for HR and other objectives; for example, the bosses of under-pressure businesses such as Marks & Spencer have to fulfil shareholders' half-yearly expectations regarding sales and profit performance. This is not helpful for long-term HR planning.
- The social and ethical climate: sometimes the media and the public seem to develop huge concern for specific issues such as Fairtrade supplies; HR objectives must take these things into account (though it would be a lot more impressive if ethical concerns were a consistent business feature).
- Legal factors may have an effect. In 2014 the Labour opposition warned that it might feel the need to legislate to enforce greater ethnic diversity in Britain's boardrooms. In Norway, legally enforceable quotas have taken female board representation from 9 per cent in 2003 to over 40 per cent by 2014. British businesses always warn of terrible consequences from employment legislation; Norway's experience suggests it would be relatively painless.

45.3 HR strategies: soft and hard HRM

Hard HRM

While all organisations undertake the various activities involved in managing human resources (such as recruitment, selection and training) the attitude and approach of managers towards employees can differ significantly. At one extreme is hard HRM. This regards employees as a necessary if unwelcome cost; people are an input required to get the job done, but add little to the overall value created by the business. With this approach managers see themselves as the 'thinkers'; they develop the best way of doing things and employees are expected to get on with it. This fits with the 'scientific management' approach of F. W. Taylor (see Chapter 46).

Hard HRM usually adopts a top-down management style in which employees are directed and controlled. Employees are expected to fit in with the design of the organisation. Managers and supervisors instruct

them and then monitor their actions. Jobs tend to be broken down into relatively small units so that one person does not have much control over the process and a replacement can easily be recruited, selected and trained. This type of approach can often be seen in call centres, where the work of operatives is very closely monitored, or in highly controlled outlets such as McDonald's.

The hard approach to HRM has many benefits, such as:

- the outcomes should be predictable because employees do as they are told
- employees should be easily replaceable
- managers retain control for decision-making and this reduces the risk of major errors being made.

However, the disadvantages of this approach include:

- a possible failure to build on the skills, experience and insights of the employees; this can lead to dissatisfied employees and low morale
- a danger that the organisation as a whole is at risk because it relies so heavily on the senior managers; if they make mistakes the business as a whole could fail because there is no input from lower levels.

'"Top" management is supposed to be a tree full of owls hooting when management heads into the wrong part of the forest. I'm still unpersuaded they even know where the forest is.' Robert Townsend, author of *Up the Organisation*

Soft HRM

By comparison, the soft HRM approach takes the view that employees can add a great deal of value to an organisation, and the business should develop, enhance and build on their interests, skills and abilities. Under a soft approach managers see themselves more as facilitators. They are there to coach and help employees to do their job properly, perhaps by ensuring sufficient training is provided and that the employee can develop in his or her career.

The advantages of a soft approach to HRM are that:

- the organisation is building on the skills and experience of their employees; this may enable the business to be more creative, more innovative and differentiated from the competition
- the organisation may be able to keep and develop highly skilled employees with expectations of a career within the business
- individuals throughout the business are encouraged to contribute, which may make the organisation more flexible and adaptable to changing market conditions.

The disadvantages of a soft HRM approach may be that:

- time is taken in discussion and consultation rather than 'getting the job' done

- employees may not have the ability or inclination to get involved; they may just want to be told what to do and be rewarded for it. In this case a soft approach to HRM may be inappropriate and ineffective.

Five Whys and a How

Question	Answer
Why might a business set out clear HR objectives?	To make sure they match the corporate objectives and to make sure that the HR plans/strategies match the HR objectives
Why might the HR objectives be affected by the recent history of the business?	Recent trading or public image difficulties will affect the objectives and decisions made within HR
Why might a company talk about diversity but do little more than appoint diverse non-executive directors?	Because companies care about public relations (PR) and therefore want to avoid embarrassment, yet they perhaps fail to see the operational benefits that might result from true diversity
Why might Marks & Spencer benefit if it had younger, more ethnically diverse executive directors?	They might help the business realise how much it has to do to break free from its current image as a shop for middle-aged, middle class, white Britain
Why might a business need to switch from a soft to a hard approach to human resources?	In a situation of crisis, tough decisions have to be made, and made quickly. Even if these decisions are regretted later on, they may be needed for survival
How would a manager interested in talent development set about solving a long-term problem of staff engagement?	By delegating to a talented young manager the task of looking at the problem and possible solutions

Key terms

Hard HRM: when managers treat the human resource in the same way they would treat any other resource (for example, ordering more one week, and less the next). In such a climate, employee relations are likely to be strained and staff may see the need for trades union involvement.

Line managers: staff with responsibility for achieving specific business objectives, and with the resources to get things done.

Soft HRM: when managers treat the workforce as a special strength of the business and therefore make sure that staff welfare and motivation are always top priorities.

Staff appraisal: a regular (perhaps annual) meeting between employee and line manager to discuss past performance and future business and career objectives.

Evaluation: Setting human resource (HR) objectives

Human resource management is one of the functions of a business. The overall approach to HRM (for example, soft versus hard) and specific HRM decisions (for example, to recruit or train) will be linked to the objectives and strategy of the business as a whole. A decision by a business to downsize or to expand abroad, for example, will have major implications for the HRM function. At the same time, the HRM resources of a business will influence the strategies a business adopts.

'Once people feel challenged, invigorated and productive, their efforts translate into profits.'
Ricardo Semler, maverick businessman

Workbook

A. Revision questions

(30 marks; 30 minutes)

1. What may be the effects of managing human resources in the same way as all the other resources used by a business? (4)

2. Identify three important features of the job of a human resource manager. (3)

3. Some people think that schools should stop teaching French and instead teach Mandarin (Chinese). If a school decided to do this, outline two implications for its training programme. (4)

4. A fast-growing small business might not have a human resources manager. The tasks may be left up to the line managers. Examine two reasons in favour of creating a human resources management post within such a business. (6)

5. Outline two ways in which a human resources manager may be able to help increase productivity at a clothes shop. (4)

6. Analyse the circumstances in which it might be appropriate for a manager to adopt a 'hard HRM' approach. (9)

B. Revision exercises
DATA RESPONSE

Hard and soft HRM

While Google is famous for its 'soft HRM' approach based on wonderful working conditions and time off to pursue personal projects, IT giant Yahoo has adopted a different tack with its 12,000 staff. In early 2014, tech blog *AllThingsD* reported that Yahoo staff were reeling from 600 recent firings as a result of a 'stack-ranking' system adopted by new chief executive Marissa Mayer. Stack-ranking is known more commonly as 'rank and yank'.

Of all the possible 'hard HRM' strategies, none was more famous than 'rank and yank,' as practised at General Electric USA (GE) during the 20-year rule of chief executive Jack Welch. It required managers to create an annual ranking of staff performance in each division of a business; the bottom 5 per cent would automatically be fired and the next 5 per cent would have to fight for their jobs. The top 20 per cent would get generous bonuses. Welch claimed that this was one of his most successful schemes, at the heart of GE's growth between 1981 and 2001. The case in favour was simple: it ensured that all staff felt at all times that they had to perform to their best – coasting was not an option. The case against was that it encouraged cronyism, that is, staff 'sucking up' to their bosses, to try to avoid a low ranking.

Yahoo's move is all the more surprising because IT giant Microsoft was abandoning stack ranking at exactly the same time. Soon after Microsoft fired boss Steve Balmer in Autumn 2013, the new chief executive announced the ending of this long-standing HR approach. A US magazine article on Balmer in 2012 (called 'Microsoft's lost decade') highlighted stack ranking as a major contributor to the company's difficulties in competing with Apple, Google and Samsung. The journalist wrote that 'Every current and former Microsoft employee I interviewed – every one – cited stack ranking as the most destructive process inside Microsoft'. The typical comment by staff was that the program pitted staff against each other, hampering collaboration and focusing staff on internal instead of external competition.

For Yahoo, the adoption of stack ranking might go down as one of the classic business mistakes. The company has been responsible for quite a few. As one of the earliest internet companies it was valued at $128 billion in early 2000. Fourteen years on it has a value of less than a third of that figure. Its greatest mistake was in 2006. It had agreed to buy a young software business for $1 billion from Mark Zuckerberg. When Yahoo tried to cut the price to $850 million Zuckerberg walked away. Today Facebook is worth $140 billion. It could have been Yahoo's.

Questions (25 marks; 30 minutes)

1. Explain how the HR strategy known as 'stack ranking' might help achieve the HR objectives at a large business such as Yahoo. (5)

2. Explain one possible reason why new boss Marissa Meyer may have decided to harden Yahoo's approach to human resources management. (4)

3. To what extent might the adoption of stack ranking damage the effectiveness of employer/employee relations at Yahoo? (16)

C. Extend your understanding

1. To what extent would you agree that a 'hard HRM' approach is the right way to run a supermarket branch where 50 per cent of the staff are part-time students? (20)

2. In 2014 Tesco announced that it planned to open a supermarket chain in India, one of the world's fastest growing economies. To what extent will Tesco's success or failure in India depend upon a successful HR strategy? (20)

Motivation and engagement in theory

Linked to: Motivation and engagement in practice, Chapter 47; Analysing human resource performance, Chapter 51; Decision-making and improved human resource performance, Chapter 52.

Definition

To Professor Herzberg, motivation occurs when people do something because they *want* to do it; others think of motivation as the desire to achieve a result.

46.1 Introduction

A study by the Hay Group found that just 15 per cent of UK workers consider themselves 'highly motivated'. As many as 25 per cent say they're 'coasting' and 8 per cent admit to being 'completely demotivated'. In the same survey, employees felt they could be 45 per cent more productive if they were doing a job they loved. Poor management is part of the problem, as 28 per cent say they would be more productive with a better boss.

The Hay Group calculates that if the under-performance was tackled successfully, the value of UK output would rise by more than £350 billion a year. So motivation matters.

46.2 F.W. Taylor and scientific management

Although there were earlier pioneers, a good starting point for the study of motivation is F.W. Taylor (1856–1917). As with most of the other influential writers on this subject, Taylor was American. Much business practice in America, Europe, Japan and the former Communist countries is still rooted in his writing and work.

A recent biography of Taylor is titled *The One Best Way*; this sums up neatly Taylor's approach to management. He saw it as management's task to decide exactly how every task should be completed, then to devise the tools needed to enable the worker to achieve the task as efficiently as possible. This method is evident in every McDonald's. Fries are cooked at 175 degrees for exactly three minutes; then a buzzer tells employees to take them out and salt them. In every McDonald's there is a series of dedicated, purpose-built machines for producing milkshakes, toasting buns, squirting chocolate sauce, and much else. Today, 120 years after his most active period working in industry, F.W. Taylor would feel very much at home ordering a Big Mac.

So, what was Taylor's view of the underlying motivations of people at work? How did he make sure that the employees worked effectively at following 'the one best way' laid down by managers?

Taylor believed that people work for only one reason: money. He saw it as the task of the manager to devise a system that would maximise efficiency. This would generate the profit to enable the worker to be paid a higher wage. Taylor's view of human nature was that of 'economic man'. In other words, people were motivated only by the economic motive of self-interest. Therefore, a manager could best motivate a worker by offering an incentive (the 'carrot') or a threat (the 'stick'). Taylor can be seen as a manipulator, or even a bully, but he believed his methods were in the best interests of the employees themselves.

Taylor's influence stemmed less from his theories than his activities. He was a trained engineer who acted as a very early management consultant. His methods were as follows.

- Observe workers at work, recording and timing what they do, when they do it and how long they take over it (this became known as time and motion study).
- Identify the most efficient workers and see how they achieve greater efficiency.
- Break the task down into small component parts that can be done quickly and repeatedly (high division of labour)
- Devise equipment specifically to speed up tasks.

- Set out exactly how the work should be done in future. 'Each employee,' Taylor wrote, 'should receive every day clear-cut, definite instructions as to what he is to do and how he is to do it, and these instructions should be exactly carried out, whether they are right or wrong.'

- Devise a pay scheme to reward those who complete or beat tough output targets, but that penalises those who cannot or will not achieve the productivity Taylor believed was possible; this pay scheme was called piece rate – no work, no pay.

As an engineer, Taylor was interested in practical outcomes, not in psychology. There is no reason to suppose he thought greatly about the issue of motivation. The effect of his ideas was profound, though. Long before the publication of his 1911 book *The Principles of Scientific Management*, Taylor had spread his managerial practices of careful measurement, monitoring and – above all else – control. Before Taylor, skilled workers chose their own ways of working and had varied, demanding jobs. After Taylor, workers were far more likely to have limited, repetitive tasks; and to be forced to work at the pace set by a manager or consultant engineer.

Eventually workers rebelled against being treated like machines. Trades union membership thrived in factories run on Taylorite lines, as workers wanted to organise against the suffocating lives they were leading at work. Fortunately, in many Western countries further developments in motivation theory pointed to new, more people-friendly approaches.

'In our scheme, we do not ask the initiative of our men. We do not want any initiative. All we want of them is to obey the orders we give them, do what we say, and do it quick.' F.W. Taylor, *The Principles of Scientific Management*, 1911

Real business

More than 100 years after F.W. Taylor's book was published, 2013 saw a wave of criticism of the working conditions at Amazon.com's distribution depots in Britain and Germany.

Many staff work under zero-hours contracts that provide no guaranteed income but can still have to walk up to 15 miles during a shift, while toilet breaks are monitored and timed. It is also claimed they can be sacked and re-hired.

Former staff at Amazon's warehouse in Rugeley, Staffordshire, told newspaper reporters that they were hired for 12 weeks before being sacked and re-employed so that the company did not have to give them the same rights as full-time employees.

An investigation by Channel 4 News found that employees are tracked using GPS tags while inside the warehouse. A BBC Panorama reporter concluded that the work was much harder physically than seemed reasonable. If staff are found to breach any of the company's rules, such as talking to colleagues or leaving work early, they can be dismissed on a 'three strikes and you are out' basis.

F.W. Taylor would have agreed with Amazon's desire for full control of workers' actions, but would have made more effort to make sure that the job requirement represented a 'fair day's work'.

'Direction and control are of limited value in motivating people whose important needs are social and egotistic.' Douglas McGregor, author of *The Human Side of Enterprise*.

46.3 Maslow and the hierarchy of needs

Abraham Maslow (1908–70) was an American psychologist whose great contribution to motivation theory was the 'hierarchy of needs'. Maslow believed that everyone has the same needs, all of which can be organised as a hierarchy. At the base of the hierarchy are physical needs such as food, shelter and warmth. When unsatisfied, these are the individual's primary motivations. When employees earn enough to satisfy these needs, however, their motivating power withers away. Maslow said: 'It is quite true that humans live by bread alone – when there is no bread. But what happens to their desires when there is bread?' Instead of physical needs, people become motivated to achieve needs such as security and stability, which Maslow called the safety needs. In full, Maslow's hierarchy consisted of the elements listed in Table 46.1.

'What a man can be, he must be. This need we call self-actualisation.' Abraham Maslow, psychologist

---

Table 46.1 Maslow's hierarchy of needs: implications for business

Maslow's levels of human need	Business implications
Physical needs, e.g. food, shelter and warmth	Pay levels and working conditions
Safety needs, e.g. security, a safe structured environment, stability, freedom from anxiety	Job security, a clear job role/description, clear lines of accountability (only one boss)
Social needs, e.g. belonging, friendship, contact	Team working, communications, social facilities
Esteem needs, e.g. strength, self-respect, confidence, status and recognition	Status, recognition for achievement, power, trust
Self-actualisation, e.g. self-fulfilment; 'to become everything that one is capable of becoming,' wrote Maslow	Scope to develop new skills and meet new challenges, and to develop one's full potential

Ever since Maslow first put his theory forward (in 1940) writers have argued about its implications. Among the key issues raised by Maslow are the following.

- Do all humans have the same set of needs? Or are there some people who need no more from a job than money?

- Do different people have different degrees of need? For example, are some highly motivated by the need for power, while others are satisfied by social factors? If so, the successful manager would be one who can understand and attempt to meet the differing needs of her/his staff.

- Can anyone's needs ever be said to be fully satisfied? The reason the hierarchy diagram (see Figure 46.1) has an open top is to suggest that the human desire for achievement is limitless.

Figure 46.1 Maslow's hierarchy of needs

Maslow's work had a huge influence on the writers who followed him, including Fred Herzberg. The hierarchy of needs is also used by academics in many subjects beyond Business Studies, notably Psychology and Sociology.

46.4 Herzberg's 'two factor' theory

The key test of a theory is its analytic usefulness. On this criterion, the work of Professor Fred Herzberg (1923–2000) is the strongest by far.

The theory stems from research conducted in the 1950s into factors affecting workers' job satisfaction and dissatisfaction. It was carried out on 200 accountants and engineers in Pennsylvania, USA. Despite the limited nature of this sample, Herzberg's conclusions remain influential to this day.

Herzberg asked employees to describe recent events that had given rise to exceptionally good feelings about their jobs, then probed them for the reasons why. 'Five factors stand out as strong determiners of job satisfaction,' Herzberg wrote in 1966, 'achievement, recognition for achievement, the work itself, responsibility and advancement – the last three being of greater importance for a lasting change of attitudes.' He pointed out that each of these factors concerned the job itself, rather than issues such as pay or status. Herzberg called these five factors 'the motivators'.

The researchers went on to ask about events giving rise to exceptionally bad feelings about their jobs. This revealed a separate set of five causes. Herzberg stated that 'the major dissatisfiers were company policy and administration, supervision, salary, interpersonal relations and working conditions.' He concluded that the common theme was factors that 'surround the job', rather than the job itself. The name he gave these dissatisfiers was 'hygiene factors'. This was because fulfilling them would prevent dissatisfaction, rather than causing positive motivation. Careful hygiene prevents disease; care to fulfil hygiene factors prevents job dissatisfaction.

To summarise: motivators have the power to create positive job satisfaction, but little downward potential. Hygiene factors will cause job dissatisfaction unless they are provided for, but do not motivate. Importantly, Herzberg saw pay as a hygiene factor, not a motivator. So a feeling of being underpaid could lead to a grievance; but high pay would soon be taken for

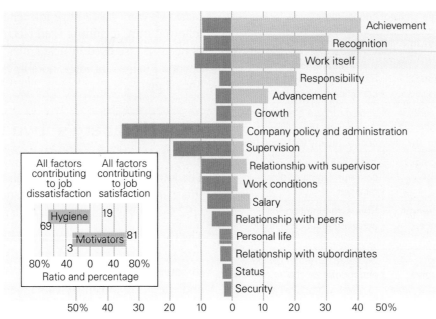

Figure 46.2 Comparison of satisfiers and dissatisfiers

granted. This motivator/hygiene factor theory is known as the 'two factor theory' (see Table 46.2).

Table 46.2 Herzberg's two factor theory

Motivators (can create positive satisfaction)	Hygiene factors (can create job dissatisfaction)
Achievement	Company policy and administration (the rules, paperwork and red tape)
Recognition for achievement	Supervision (especially being over-supervised)
Meaningful, interesting work	Pay
Responsibility	Interpersonal relations (with supervisor, peers, or even customers)
Advancement (psychological, not just a promotion)	Working conditions

Movement and motivation

Herzberg was keen to distinguish between movement and motivation. Movement occurs when somebody does something; motivation is when they *want* to do something. This distinction is essential to a full understanding of Herzberg's theory. He did not doubt that financial incentives could be used to boost productivity: 'If you bully or bribe people, they'll give you better than average performance.' His worries about 'bribes' (carrots) were that they would never stimulate people to give of their best; people would do just enough to achieve the bonus. Furthermore, bribing

people to work harder at a task they found unsatisfying would build up resentments, which might backfire on the employer.

Herzberg advised against payment methods such as piece rate. They would achieve movement, but by reinforcing worker behaviour, would make them inflexible and resistant to change. The salaried, motivated employee would work hard, care about quality and think about – even welcome – improved working methods.

'Our goal should be minimum standardisation of human behaviour.' Douglas McGregor, author *The Human Side of Enterprise*, 1960

46.5 The use of non-financial methods of motivating employees

Although the UK's banking sector seems convinced of the need for financial incentives to achieve high performance, few in key industries such as advertising or aircraft design and manufacture would agree. Most people believe that motivation is as much about psychology as money. One of the reasons why Herzberg's work had such an impact on business is because he not only analysed motivation, he also had a method for improving it. The method is job enrichment, which he defined as 'giving people the opportunity to use their ability'. He suggested that, for a job to be considered enriched, it would have to contain the following.

A complete unit of work

People need to work not on just a small repetitive fragment of a job, but on a full challenging task. Herzberg heaped scorn upon the 'idiot jobs' that resulted from Taylor's views on high division of labour.

Direct feedback

Wherever possible, a job should enable the worker to judge immediately the quality of what she or he has done; direct feedback gives the painter or the actor (or the teacher) the satisfaction of knowing exactly how well they have performed. Herzberg disliked systems that pass quality inspection off onto a supervisor: 'A man must always be held responsible for his own quality.' Worst of all, he felt, was annual appraisal, in which feedback is too long delayed.

Direct communication

For people to feel committed, in control and to gain direct feedback, they should communicate directly – avoiding the delays of communicating via a supervisor or a 'contact person'. This leads to an important conclusion: that communications and motivation are interrelated.

'Blue collar and white collar call upon the identical phrase: "I'm a robot."' Studs Terkel, much-missed US journalist (from his book *Working*, 1974)

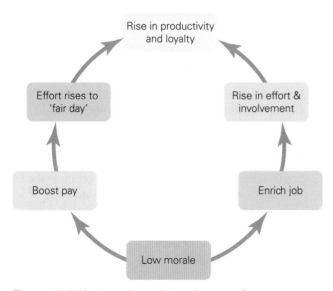

Figure 46.3 Herzberg logic chain: take care of hygiene factors and motivators

46.6 The value of theories of motivation

Herzberg's original research has been followed up in many different countries, including Japan, Africa and Russia. His main insight was to show that unless the job itself was interesting, there was no way to make working life satisfying. This led companies such as Volvo in Sweden and Toyota in Japan to rethink their factory layouts. Instead of individual workers doing simple, repetitive tasks, the drive was to provide more complete units of work. Workers were grouped into teams, focusing on significant parts of the manufacturing process, such as assembling and fitting the gearbox, and then checking the quality of their work. Job enrichment indeed. Some key quotes from Professor Herzberg are given in Table 46.3.

Table 46.3 Key quotes from Professor Herzberg

On the two factor theory:	'Motivators and hygiene factors are equally important, but for different reasons.'
On movement:	'If you do something because you want a house or a Jaguar, that's movement. It's not motivation.'
The risks of giving bonuses:	'A reward once given becomes a right.'
The importance of training:	'The more a person can do, the more you can motivate them.'
The importance of always treating staff fairly:	'A remembered pain can lead to revenge psychology... They'll get back at you some day when you need them.'
On communication:	'In industry, there's too much communication. And of course its passive... But if people are doing idiot jobs they really don't give a damn.'
On participation:	'When participation is suggested in terms of control over overall goals, it is usually a sham.'

As with all theories, though, both Maslow and Herzberg have their critics. With Maslow, the questions concern the existence of any hierarchy – certainly no research has been able to prove this idea. Yes his five sets of needs are well chosen, but don't different people perhaps have different hierarchies of those needs? In Herzberg's case the most common criticism is that his original research was conducted on a small sample size (200) and just on middle-class employees: accountants and engineers.

As mentioned above, the ultimate test is how well a theory performs in the real world. Herzberg's remains a marvellous way to predict disasters (the misuse of financial bonuses in the banking sector) and a successful way to run a business.

Five Whys and a How

Question	Answer
Why did trade unions dislike F.W. Taylor with his financial incentives and 'one best way'?	They disliked the shift in power towards management and hated being 'deskilled'; doing the same repetitive task every day
Why do theorists such as Herzberg distinguish motivation from morale?	Morale can be high if the future looks bright and job security is strong – that doesn't mean that motivation will be high; motivation is doing a good job because you want to
Why might 'esteem needs' be hard to provide in some workplaces?	It might be hard in some jobs that society rates lowly, such as bin collecting or road sweeping
Why does Herzberg think financial incentives aren't motivating?	He accepts that they incentivise and therefore can generate some 'movement' – but to him, motivation comes from within
Why may companies find it difficult to provide a 'complete unit of work'?	Some tasks can be completed far more efficiently with high division of labour, so a complete unit of work can seem an indulgence
How could you increase the motivation of England's national football team?	Recruit players who love playing, give them plenty of responsibility – perhaps to discuss and plan tactics – and let them do the pre- and post-match interviews

Key terms

Division of labour: subdividing a task into a number of activities, enabling workers to specialise and therefore become very efficient at completing what may be a small, repetitive task.

Hygiene factors: 'everything that surrounds what you do in the job', such as pay, working conditions and social status; all are potential causes of dissatisfaction, according to Herzberg.

Job satisfaction: the sense of well-being and achievement that stems from a satisfying job.

Piece rate: paying workers per piece they produce (for example, £2 per pair of jeans made).

Productivity: output per person (that is, a measure of efficiency).

Trades union: an organisation that represents the interests of staff at the workplace.

Evaluation: Motivation and engagement in theory

Most managers assume they understand human motivation, but they have never studied it. As a result they may underestimate the potential within their own staff, or unthinkingly cause resentments that fester.

The process of managing people takes place in every part of every organisation. So every manager should be aware of motivation theory. In some cases, ignorance leads managers to ignore motivation altogether; they tell themselves that control and organisation are their only concerns. Other managers may see motivation as important, but fail to understand its subtleties.

For these reasons, there is a case for saying that the concepts within this unit are the most important in the whole subject. Certainly it is true to say that Taylor, Maslow and Herzberg are studied from Russia to Japan and Angola to Zimbabwe.

Further reading

Herzberg, F. (1959) *The Motivation to Work*. Wiley International.

Maslow, A.H. (1987) *Motivation and Personality*. HarperCollins (1st Edition, 1954).

Workbook

A. Revision questions

(30 marks; 30 minutes)

1. Which features of the organisation of a McDonald's could be described as Taylorite? (3)

2. Explain the meaning of the term 'economic man'. (3)

3. Explain how workers in a bakery may be affected by a change from salary to piece rate. (3)

4. Which two levels of Maslow's hierarchy could be called 'the lower-order needs'? (2)

5. Describe in your own words why Maslow organised the needs into a hierarchy. (3)

6. State three business implications of Maslow's work on human needs. (3)

7. Herzberg believes pay does not motivate, but it is important. Why? (4)

8. How do motivators differ from hygiene factors? (3)

9. What is job enrichment? How is it achieved? (3)

Choose one answer from the four choices in each of the following questions:

10. If staff absenteeism is increasing, is it likely to be because: (1)

a) Hygiene factors are over-rewarded	b) Wage increases are outstripping inflation	c) There's too much self-actualisation	d) Division of labour is too high

11. Herzberg's 'hygiene factors' relate best to: (1)

a) Taylor's focus on the 'one best way'	b) Maslow's concept of self-actualisation	c) Taylor's idea of self-actualisation	d) Maslow's physiological needs

12. Maslow's idea of 'self-actualisation' means: (1)

a) Striving to get a promotion	b) Finding just what you're capable of	c) Getting the money rewards you deserve	d) Finally enjoying true self-esteem

B. Revision exercises
DATA RESPONSE

Tania was delighted to get the bakery job and looked forward to her first shift. It would be tiring after a day at college, but £52 for eight hours on a Friday would guarantee good Saturday nights in future.

On arrival, she was surprised to be put straight to work, with no more than a mumbled: 'You'll be working packing machine B.' Fortunately, she was able to watch the previous shift worker before clocking-off time, and could get the hang of what was clearly a very simple task. As the 18.00 bell rang, the workers streamed out, but not many had yet turned up from Tania's shift. The conveyor belt started to roll again at 18.16.

As the evening wore on, machinery breakdowns provided the only, welcome, relief from the tedium and discomfort of Tania's job. Each time a breakdown occurred, a ringing alarm bell was drowned out by a huge cheer from the staff. A few joyful moments followed, with dough fights breaking out. Tania started to feel quite old as she looked at some of her workmates.

At the 22.00 meal break, Tania was made to feel welcome. She enjoyed hearing the sharp, funny comments made about the shift managers. One was dubbed 'Noman' because he was fat, wore a white coat and never agreed to anything. Another was called 'Turkey' because he strutted around, but if anything went wrong, got into a flap. It was clear that both saw themselves as bosses. They were not there to help or to encourage, only to blame.

Was the bakery always like this, Tania wondered? Or was it simply that these two managers were poor?

Questions (30 marks; 35 minutes)

1. Analyse the working lives of the shift workers at the bakery, using Herzberg's two factor theory. (9)

2. If a managerial follower of Taylor's methods came into the factory, how might she or he try to improve the productivity level? (5)

C. Extend your understanding

1. Followers of F.W. Taylor and Professor Herzberg each set about increasing the motivation of teachers. To what extent do you think that followers of Taylor would be the more successful? (20)

3. Later on in this (true) story, Tania read in the local paper that the factory was closing. The reason given was 'lower labour productivity than at our other bakeries'. The newspaper grumbled about the poor attitudes of local workers. To what extent is there justification in this view? (16)

2. To what extent might it be successful if Tesco's new boss applied Maslow's hierarchy of needs to the whole workforce? (20)

Motivation and engagement in practice

Linked to: Motivation and engagement in theory, Chapter 46; Analysing human resource performance, Chapter 51; Decision-making and improved human resource performance, Chapter 52.

Definition

Assessing how firms try to motivate their staff and how successful these actions are. In this context, companies take 'motivation' to mean enthusiastic pursuit of the objectives or tasks set out by the firm.

47.1 Introduction

There are two main variables that influence the motivation of staff in practice:

1. the financial reward systems

2. job design and enrichment.

These will be analysed with reference to the theories outlined in Chapter 46.

The chapter will then look at how businesses choose and assess the effectiveness of reward systems.

'My best friend is the one who brings out the best in me.' Henry Ford, founder of Ford Motors

47.2 Financial methods of motivation

Piece rate

Piece rate means working in return for a payment per unit produced. Pieceworkers receive no basic or shift pay, so there is no sick pay, holiday pay or company pension.

Piecework is used extensively in small-scale manufacturing, for example, of jeans or jewellery. Its attraction for managers is that it makes supervision virtually unnecessary. All the manager needs to do is operate a quality control system that ensures the finished product is worth paying for. Day by day, the workers can be relied upon to work fast enough to earn a living wage.

Disadvantages of piece rate

Piecework has several disadvantages to firms, however, including the following.

● Scrap levels may be high, if workers are focused entirely on speed of output.

● There is an incentive to provide acceptable quality, but not the best possible quality.

● Workers will work hardest when they want higher earnings (probably before Christmas and before their summer holiday). This may not coincide at all with seasonal patterns of customer demand.

● Worst of all is the problem of change; Herzberg pointed out that 'the worst way to motivate people is piece rate…it reinforces behaviour.' Focusing people on maximising their earnings by repeating a task makes them very reluctant to produce something different or in a different way (they worry that they will lose out financially).

'I have never found anybody yet who went to work happily on a Monday that had not been paid on a Friday.' Tom Farmer, Kwik-Fit founder

Real business

Most football clubs have signed expensive new players who subsequently fail to perform on the pitch. In 2013 Liverpool decided to overcome this problem by offering new signings lower basic salaries offset by lucrative performance-related bonuses. According to Managing Director Ian Ayre, 'From the football club's perspective, our view has to be that people are rewarded for contributing towards what we achieve. As long as contracts are structured in that way then everyone wins.' That year Liverpool went on to enjoy one of their highest finishes in the Premier League.

Performance-related pay

Performance-related pay (PRP) is a financial reward to staff whose work is considered above average. It is used for employees whose work achievements cannot be assessed simply through numerical measures (such as units produced or sold). PRP awards are usually made after an appraisal process has evaluated the performance of staff during the year.

The usual method is outlined below.

1. Establish targets for each member of staff/management at an appraisal interview.

2. At the end of the year, discuss the individual's achievements against those targets.

3. Those with outstanding achievements are given a Merit 1 pay rise or bonus worth perhaps six per cent of salary; others receive between zero per cent and six per cent.

'Motivating people over a short period is not very difficult. A crisis will often do just that, or a carefully planned special event. Motivating people over a longer period of time, however, is far more difficult. It is also far more important in today's business environment.' John Kotter, management thinker

---

Lack of evidence for benefits of PRP

Despite the enthusiasm they have shown for it, employers have rarely been able to provide evidence of the benefits of PRP. Indeed the Institute of Personnel Management concluded in a recent report that: 'It was not unusual to find that organisations which had introduced merit pay some years ago were less certain now of its continued value... it was time to move on to something more closely reflecting team achievement and how the organisation as a whole was faring.'

This pointed to a fundamental problem with PRP: rewarding individuals does nothing to promote teamwork. Furthermore, it could create unhealthy rivalry between managers, with each going for the same Merit 1 spot.

Why do firms continue with PRP?

So why do firms continue to pursue PRP systems? There are two possible reasons:

1. to make it easier for managers to manage/control their staff (using a carrot instead of a stick)

2. to reduce the influence of collective bargaining and therefore trades unions.

Commission

Commission is a bonus earned on top of a basic salary, usually in line with a specific achievement such as meeting a sales target. It might be that a member of staff is expected to generate £80,000 of sales a year, and for every £1,000 above that total a commission will be paid of £50. That five per cent rate of commission might enable the individual to boost income considerably by the end of the year.

Commission is used widely to incentivise staff in clothes shops, furniture shops and other outlets where it can take effort and skill to clinch a sale. Note that it would be incorrect to write about commission as a 'motivator'. In Professor Herzberg's terms, commission is simply a hygiene factor.

Salary schemes

According to Professor Herzberg, 'the best way to pay people is a salary.' He considered every attempt to 'motivate' people through financial incentives doomed to fail – simply because people would be incentivised to do the wrong thing – again and again. This proved true in the 2008/09 financial crisis, when the mayhem in the financial sector was often the result of faulty financial incentives (such as encouraging excessive risk-taking in the short-term).

To Herzberg, then, paying the 'right' salary is the goal. He warned against underpaying people every bit as much as overpaying. And was also a fan of non-incentivised benefits such as company pensions and holiday and sick-pay schemes – to apply to all staff within the organisation.

47.3 Job design and enrichment

Professor Herzberg defines job enrichment as 'giving people the opportunity to use their ability'. A full explanation of his theory is outlined in Chapter 46.

How can job enrichment be put into practice? The key thing is to realise the enormity of the task. It is not cheap, quick or easy to enrich the job of the production line worker or the supermarket checkout operator. Herzberg's definition of job enrichment implies giving people 'a range of responsibilities and activities'. To provide job enrichment, workers must have a complete unit of work (not a repetitive fragment), responsibility for quality and for self-checking, and be given the opportunity to show their abilities.

Full job enrichment requires a radical approach. Take a conventional car assembly line, for example. As shown in Figure 47.1, workers each have a single task they carry out on their own. One fits the left-hand front door to a car shell that is slowly moving past on a conveyor belt – every 22 seconds. Another worker fits right-hand front doors, and so on. Job enrichment can be achieved only by rethinking the production line completely; coming up with a new job design.

Figure 47.1 A traditional production line

Figure 47.2 shows how a car assembly line could be reorganised to provide a more enriched job. Instead of working in isolation, people work in groups on a significant part of the assembly process. An empty car shell comes along the conveyor belt and turns into the Interior Group Area. Six workers fit carpets, glove boxes, the dashboard and much else. They check the quality of their own work; then put a rather impressive-looking vehicle back on the conveyor belt. Not only does the teamwork element help meet the social needs of the workforce, but there are also knock-on effects. The workers can be given a time slot to discuss their work and how to improve it. When new equipment is needed, they can be given a budget and told to go out to meet potential suppliers. In other words, they can become managers of their own work area.

Figure 47.2 An enriched 'team-working' line

Such a major step would be expensive. Rebuilding a production line may cost millions of pounds and be highly disruptive in the short term. There would also be the worry that team-working could make the job

more satisfying, yet still be less productive than the boring but practical system of high division of labour.

'Motivation is everything. You can do the work of two people, but you can't be two people. Instead, you have to inspire the next guy down the line and get him to inspire his people.' Lee Iacocca, successful boss of Chrysler Motors

---

47.4 Choice and assessment of financial and non-financial reward systems

Research regularly shows that financial reward systems are extremely difficult to get right. Think of it in relation to your class. If the teacher had £1,000 to hand out as financial rewards to the students 'that deserved it most', what would be the result? Possibly a well-motivated class if the teacher manages to satisfy everyone, but probably a bit of a disaster as various students feel the rewards are unfairly distributed.

This points to an important influence on financial reward systems: can the rewards be clearly related to the quantity and quality of work done? In a clothes factory making jeans, it may be that paying piecework (such as £2 per pair) works effectively at incentivising staff to work hard. If I produced 40 pairs earning £80, while you produced 70 pairs earning £140, I might be disappointed, but I wouldn't call it unfair.

Other important influences on the choice of whether to use financial or non-financial reward systems include:

- The results of careful measurement of past reward systems – what was the impact of financial incentives the last time they were used?
- The timescale being considered; if there are urgent requirements for production over the next six months, financial incentives might be effective, but in the long run you want people to want to give of their best, all the time
- The level of change the business faces; financial incentives are very difficult to change, because some staff will already do well out of them and fear lower earnings if there is change.

Ultimately, assessing financial and non-financial reward systems is extremely difficult when the job is complex. Surgeons, for example, do far more than just operate on patients. So if a measurement system looks solely at operations per day, it will fail to capture the real job, from training new doctors to talking to patients. Systems that claim to do so should be treated with scepticism. Human resource professionals are keen to find measurable solutions to complex problems, but research suggests that this is near impossible.

In well-run businesses, a clear sense of purpose and the freedom to act responsibly and collaboratively is usually the best way to have motivation in practice.

Five Whys and a How

Question	Answer
Why might bonus payments fail to motivate?	They provide incentives, but Herzberg says motivation comes from within, i.e. doing something because you want to. If there's a financial incentive, that only achieves movement*
Why may the payment of piece rate make it hard to achieve change in the workplace?	Those with high earnings on the old system will fear change – and all staff will have been conditioned to do one thing repeatedly
Why is empowerment more powerful than delegation?	Delegation passes down the hierarchy the power to do things; empowerment gives the power to decide what to do
Why do you think that HR departments love performance-related pay?	Because it gives them a role and a degree of control. Pay everyone a salary, and who needs an HR department?
Why would F.W. Taylor be thrilled to see that performance-related pay is still a powerful force in the 21st century?	Taylor believed that workers should be under the tight control of management; PRP can achieve this by forcing staff to do what they're told in order to maximise their pay
How might performance-related pay for teachers affect lessons in future?	It may make them more formulaic, with all teachers focused solely on maximising grades

*For the difference between movement and motivation, remember the English football team at the 2014 World Cup.

Key terms

Division of labour: subdividing a job into small, repetitive fragments of work.

Job design: having designed a new product, it is time to design the jobs needed to make the product. Merely subdividing it into repetitive work fragments will be unmotivating, so design the job with people in mind.

Motivation: to Professor Herzberg, it means doing something because you want to do it. Most business leaders think of it as prompting people to work hard.

Evaluation: Motivation and engagement in practice

When writing about financial incentives, there is a serious risk of over-simplification. The reality is that using money to try to motivate people often proves a dreadful mistake (as Herzberg always made clear). Exaggerated commissions or performance-related pay can lead sales staff to oversell goods or services which may cause customers huge difficulties later on, such as cosmetic surgery or questionable investments. Also, within the workplace, serious problems can arise: bullying to 'motivate' staff into working harder, or creating a culture of overwork which leads to stress.

Fortunately, there are many businesses in which the management of motivation is treated with respect: companies which know that quick fixes are not the answer. Successful motivation in the long term is a result of careful job design, employee training and development, honesty and trust. It may be possible to supplement this with an attractive financial reward scheme, but money will never be a substitute for motivation.

'There is no room for criticism on the training field. For a player – and for any human being – there is nothing better than hearing "well done". Those are the two best words ever invented in sports.' Sir Alex Ferguson, former manager of Manchester United

Workbook

A. Revision questions

(40 marks; 45 minutes)

1. 'Job design is the key to motivation.' Outline one reason why this may be true, and one reason why it may not. (4)

2. Look at the famous saying by Lee Iacocca on page 297. Explain in your own words what he meant by this. (3)

3. How *should* a manager deal with a mistake made by a junior employee? (4)

4. State three reasons why job enrichment should improve staff motivation. (3)

5. Distinguish between job rotation and job enrichment. (4)

6. How does 'empowerment' differ from 'delegation'? (4)

7. Identify three advantages to an employee of working in a team. (3)

8. State two advantages and two disadvantages of offering staff performance-related pay. (4)

9. What could be the implications of providing a profit share to senior managers but not to the workforce generally? (5)

10. What problems may result from a manager bullying staff to 'motivate' them? (6)

B. Revision exercises
DATA RESPONSE 1

Fifty per cent of primary teachers and 52 per cent of secondary teachers believe that incremental pay rises should depend at least in part on performance. This was the finding of a survey of over 1000 teachers on behalf of The Sutton Trust. But the survey conducted by The National Foundation for Educational Research found that a large minority favoured the old system of linking pay to length of service. Schools are required to link pay progression to classroom performance for teachers in the first five years of their career, under a government initiative introduced in September 2014. Teachers have previously had yearly incremental rises.

In the US teachers receive bonuses depending on their pupils' progress, but evidence that the approach can improve learning outcomes is inconclusive. Professor Steven Higgins of Durham University's School of Education said the evidence was not convincing. 'Attracting the best teachers and retaining them, for which pay may be a significant component, is more important than rewarding teachers on the basis of their pupils' recent test scores or their observed lesson performance.' Research has suggested that observing

lessons is 'not a reliable way of identifying teacher effectiveness, so any system which relies only on observation or test scores or even a combination is likely to be flawed,' according to Professor Higgins.

Christine Blower, general secretary of the National Union of Teachers, opposes performance-related pay for teachers on the grounds that it is less transparent and open to biased judgments.

Source: Adapted from bbc.co.uk

Questions (30 marks; 35 minutes)

1. Why does the government appear to believe that teachers are motivated by money? (3)

2. Apart from money, identify and explain two other factors which might motivate teachers. (6)

3. Explain one method the government might use to measure the individual performance of teachers. (5)

4. To what extent might teacher performance be affected by a switch to performance-related pay? (16)

DATA RESPONSE 2

An October 2013 study finds 'emotional factors' are strongest motivators in the workplace.

Bonuses are not the top motivator for employees, according to a study into what makes workers most productive by the Institute of Leadership and Management (ILM).

The survey of more than 1,000 workers found that only 13 per cent of people agreed that a bonus would have an effect on their motivation, however having a good basic salary and pension was viewed as an important incentive by almost half of the respondents.

In fact, the top motivator was 'job enjoyment' according to 59 per cent of respondents, while other emotional factors such as good working relationships and fair treatment also rated highly in the survey. More than two-fifths of the respondents cited 'getting on with colleagues' as a key motivator, while just over a fifth agreed that 'how well they are treated by their managers' affected motivation, with a further fifth saying that higher levels of autonomy motivated them.

The ILM said the findings suggested that the £36.9 billion spent on performance bonuses in the UK last year had 'no impact on the motivation and commitment levels of the vast majority of recipients'.

The survey highlights how important good managers are to ensuring happy and motivated staff. When asked to identify one thing that would motivate them to do more, 31 per cent of employees said 'better treatment from their employer', 'more praise' and 'a greater sense of being valued'. However, while the majority of managers (69 per cent) said they 'always give feedback' to their staff, just 23 per cent of employees agreed.

'Understanding your employees and what makes them tick is vital in having a happy and motivated workforce,' said Charles Elvin, chief executive of the ILM. 'In the past year UK companies have collectively spent an astronomical amount on financial incentives for their staff. But this report is telling us there are far more effective, and cost-effective, ways to motivate people. These include giving regular feedback, allowing people to have autonomy in a role, the opportunity to innovate and improved office environments.'

Source: www.cipd.co.uk

Questions (25 marks; 30 minutes)

1. From the passage:
   a) Outline two points that fit into the category called 'motivators' by Herzberg. (4)
   b) Outline two points that fit into the category called 'hygiene factors' by Herzberg. (4)

2. The ILM implies that 'the £36.9 billion spent on performance bonuses' was a waste of money. Explain two possible reasons why businesses might persist with staff bonuses despite the evidence provided here. (8)

3. Use the evidence provided in the text to examine how a manager might improve the workplace performance of one of the following: a school cleaner; a full-time employee at Tesco; or a bus driver. (9)

C. Extend your understanding

1. To what extent do you agree with the view that there is no one ideal method to motivate staff, because everyone is different? (20)

2. To what extent are financial reward systems important in the motivation of young, part-time staff at a business such as Nando's chain of chicken restaurants? (20)

Improving organisational design

Linked to: Analysing human resource performance, Chapter 51; Decision-making and improved human resource performance, Chapter 52.

Definition

Organisational design means creating the formal hierarchy that establishes who is answerable to whom throughout the organisation. When presented as a diagram, it shows the departmental functions plus the vertical and horizontal links that represent the formal communications system.

Table 48.1 Examples of management layers

Military	Business
Captain	Senior Manager
Lieutenant	Manager
Sergeant	Team Leader
Corporal	Supervisor
Foot soldier	Shop-floor worker

'If a sufficient number of management layers are superimposed on top of each other, it can be assured that disaster is not left to chance.' Norman Augustine, US chief executive

48.1 Introduction

As organisations became larger and more complex, early management thinkers such as F.W. Taylor and H. Fayol considered how to structure an organisation. Both saw the function of organisations as converting inputs, such as money, materials, machines and people, into output. Therefore, designing an organisation was like designing a machine, the objective being to maximise efficiency.

Taylor and Fayol based their thoughts largely on the way an army is organised. The key features of the hierarchy would be:

- To break the organisation up into divisions with a common purpose. In business, this was usually the business functions: marketing, finance and so on.
- Every individual would answer to one person: their line manager
- No manager would be overloaded with too many subordinates, so the span of control was kept low.
- To achieve low spans of control, it was necessary to have many management layers. Examples of management layers are shown in Table 48.1.

48.2 The growing business

In the early stages of a new business, there are often only one or two people involved. When the business is so small the day-to-day tasks are carried out by the owner/s. No formal organisation is needed as communication and co-ordination will be carried out on an informal, face-to-face basis. However, as the business grows and more people become involved, the firm will need to develop a more formal organisational structure. This will show the roles, responsibilities and relationships of each member of the firm. This is often illustrated through an organisational chart. This is a diagram that shows the links between people and departments within the firm. They also show communication flows/channels, lines of authority and layers of hierarchy. Each of these terms will be explained later in the chapter.

When Matteo Pantani founded Scoop ice cream in Covent Garden in 2007, he only employed part-time staff at the counter to serve the ice cream and take the money. Matteo made the ice cream and ran the business. He did not need to think about a 'hierarchy' or a 'structure'. But the organisational structure that existed in 2007 is shown in Figure 48.1.

As the business grew, he opened a second outlet in 2010, in Brewer Street, Soho, and a third in South Kensington in 2012. This meant he needed managers to run the other outlets, while Matteo was largely at Covent Garden. By mid-2014, the organisational hierarchy looked like the one shown in Figure 48.2.

The point, of course, is to appreciate how much more complex a hierarchy becomes as the business grows.

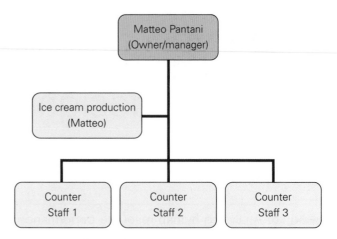

Figure 48.1 Scoop: old organisational structure

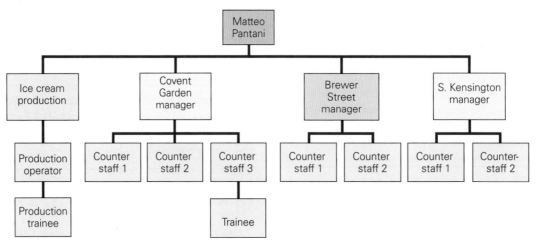

Figure 48.2 Scoop: new organisational structure

48.3 Influences on organisational design

This section will examine the main areas of theory associated with organisational structure and how it is designed. To help clarify, references will be made to the above chart (Figure 48.2).

Levels of hierarchy

These show the number of different supervisory and management levels between the bottom of the chart and the top of the hierarchy. Figure 48.2 shows that at Scoop there are now four levels of hierarchy. In an organisation such as Tesco plc, which employs more than 500,000 staff, it is easy to see how there might be 25 levels of hierarchy. The problem that will cause is extremely slow (and unreliable) communications between the top and bottom of the organisation. TV programmes such as *Undercover Boss* consistently show how hard it is for the chief executive to understand the problems faced by those on the shop floor.

Span of control

This describes the number of people directly under the supervision of a manager. Matteo has the widest span of control, as he has four staff under him directly. If managers have very wide spans of control, they are directly responsible for many staff. In this case they may find that there are communication problems, or the workers may feel that they are not being given enough guidance. The ideal span of control will depend upon the nature of the tasks and the skills and attitude of the workforce and manager. (See Table 48.2)

'Every company has two organisational structures: the formal one is written on the charts; the other is the living relationship of the men and women in the organisation.' Harold Geneen, US management guru

Chain of command

This shows the reporting system from the top of the hierarchy to the bottom; that is the route through which information travels throughout the organisation. In an

Table 48.2 Advantages and disadvantages of a narrow span of control

Advantages	Disadvantages
Allows close management supervision; this is vital if staff are inexperienced, labour turnover is high or if the task is critical, e.g. manufacturing aircraft engines	Workers may feel over-supervised and therefore not trusted; this may cause better staff to leave, in search of more personal responsibility
Communications may be excellent within the small, immediate team, e.g. the boss and three staff	Communications may suffer within the business as a whole, as a narrow span means more layers of hierarchy, which makes vertical communications harder
Many layers of hierarchy means many rungs on the career ladder, i.e. promotion chances arise regularly (though each promotion may mean only a slightly different job)	The narrow span usually leads to restricted scope for initiative and experiment; the boss is always looking over your shoulder; this will alienate enterprising staff

organisation with several levels of hierarchy the chain of command will be longer and this could create a gap between workers at the bottom of the organisation and managers at the top. If information has to travel via several people there is also a chance that it may become distorted.

'Every management layer you can strip away makes you more responsive.' John Whitney, US academic

Delegation

This means passing authority (power) down the hierarchy, to give greater responsibility to junior managers or staff. It should therefore be seen as a democratic process. Sadly, some bosses simply pass down the tasks they do not want to tackle. Passing on the dull or difficult stuff should not be confused with delegation.

Influences on delegation include the attitude of management towards its workforce. If there is mistrust, then delegation will never be genuine. Assuming trust exists, it may still be important that the junior staff are highly trained. No one wants to be delegated power without the knowledge and therefore confidence that they are able to get the job done.

Centralisation and decentralisation

This describes the extent to which decision-making power and authority is delegated within an organisation. A centralised structure is one in which decision-making power and control remains in the hands of the top management levels. A decentralised structure delegates decision-making power to workers lower down the organisation. Many organisations will use a combination of these approaches, depending upon the nature of the decision involved. For example, in many schools and colleges, the decisions concerning which resources to use will be decentralised; that is, taken by teachers as opposed to the senior management team. Other decisions, concerning future changes in subjects being offered, may be centralised; that is, taken by senior managers.

Influences on centralisation versus decentralisation are primarily internal; that is, within the business. Often they represent alternatives that look rosier if the opposite approach has proved disappointing. Therefore there is a risk that a company in difficulties will lurch from one approach to the other – and perhaps back again. The Waterstones bookshop chain has suffered from this. It was set up by founder Tim Waterstone as a decentralised, locally-oriented chain of stores. When bought by W.H. Smith, book buying and store layouts were centralised. Today they are back with a more localised, decentralised approach.

'It's a paradox that the greater the decentralisation, the greater the need for both leadership and explicit policies from the top management.' Bruce Henderson, chief executive, Boston Consulting Group

48.4 Influences on job design

Professor Herzberg believed that worker motivation would improve only when some vertical barriers were broken down within hierarchies. His idea of job enrichment was that jobs should be redesigned to give people a range of activities and responsibilities at work. Explicitly he wanted 'self-checking', effectively meaning scrapping supervisory roles and therefore cutting a tall hierarchy down to size.

This work was developed further by US academics Richard Hackman and Greg Oldham. Writing in the 1970s they described Herzberg's two factor theory as 'by far the most influential behavioural approach to work redesign' and set out to build on it. They developed a model that looked beyond the analysis of job-related factors to consider three aspects of what they termed 'the job characteristics model'. These were:

1. Core job characteristics, that is, the factors involved at the heart of the job.

   These included skill variety, task variety, task significance, autonomy (personal independence) and feedback. All five characteristics could be

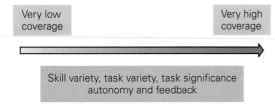

Very low coverage ➡ Very high coverage

Skill variety, task variety, task significance autonomy and feedback

Figure 48.3 Core job characteristics

measured against a scale from very low coverage to very high (see Figure 48.3)

2. Psychological states

This aspect of the theory focuses on people rather than the job. In effect it asks: what are the core factors affecting an individual worker's psychological state? Hackman and Oldham suggest three:

● meaningfulness in the job itself

● responsibility for work outcomes

● knowledge of the results of the work.

The greater the level of one or (preferably) all these three, the more positive and more relaxed will be the individual's psychological state.

3. Outcomes

Unlike Herzberg, Hackman and Oldham build the consequences into the theory. The core job characteristics and the psychological states both impact upon the workplace outcomes. These outcomes can and should be measured. They consist of:

● employee motivation

● employee performance, for instance productivity

● employee job satisfaction

● plus the practical measurements: absenteeism and labour turnover.

The whole of the job characteristics model can be illustrated as:

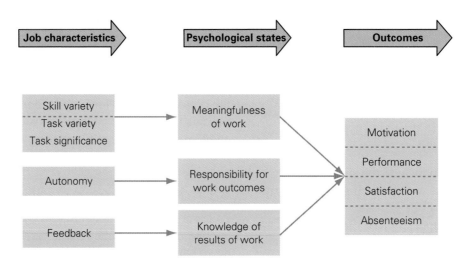

Figure 48.4 Job characteristics model
Source: Adapted from Hackman and Oldham, 1975

'Lots of jobs are not so well designed. They demotivate people rather than turn them on.'
Hackman and Oldham, US academics

48.5 The value of changing job and organisational design

Following the publication of Herzberg's theory the US giant AT&T experimented with job redesign, focusing especially on job enrichment. 'These studies appear to demonstrate, for a diversity of jobs, that job enrichment can lead to beneficial outcomes both for the individuals involved and for the employing organisation.' (Hackman and Oldham, 1980)

An important result of improved job design is that stress levels are reduced. Stress is associated with lack of control of the employee's environment; so improved job control is an important target. With lower stress levels, absenteeism and labour turnover figures tend to improve.

Changing organisational design is a much more difficult problem. To an extent, job design can be tackled one person at a time. By definition a change in organisational design affects everyone. That might involve 500,000 staff (Tesco) or over 1.3 million staff (the NHS). Some companies lurch from decentralisation to centralisation and then back again (Waterstones); others such as Unilever change vertical structure from functional (marketing, finance, etc.) to divisional

(Foods division; Cosmetics division, etc.) and then back again. No criticism is implied; it is simply that company bosses desire a perfect organisational structure, but none exists. Every large business suffers severe problems of communication, co-ordination and motivation. The occasional change to the organisational design may improve things temporarily, but there is no magical solution to the problems of size.

Five Whys and a How

Question	Answer
Why is organisational structure so important?	Because, however keen and competent the staff, large organisations can operate slowly, frustratingly and bureaucratically if the organisational structure is wrong
Why might there be benefits from widening an organisation's span of control?	A wider span means fewer layers of hierarchy are needed. This would allow delayering to take place – which saves money and can improve vertical communication
Why might Asda and Morrisons' both have decided (in 2014) to remove a layer of supervisory management from all their stores?	Perhaps both felt the need to cut fixed overhead costs given the market share gains achieved by the discounters Aldi and Lidl.
Why do firms such as Google usually start with an informal management hierarchy, but firm it up when the business has grown?	Because a formal structure is unnecessary when everyone knows/can talk to the boss or bosses. Once Google had 20,000 staff that was no longer possible.
Why are businesses so scared of the word 'bureaucracy'?	Because it suggests slowness and complacency that firms believe only happens in government departments
How might a large plc improve its performance by improving its organisational structure?	Usually, the flatter the structure the better the business. This also serves as a warning against growing too big (through takeovers)

Key terms

Delayering: removing a management layer from the organisational structure.

Line manager: a manager responsible for meeting specific business targets, and responsible for specific staff.

Matrix management: where staff work in project teams in addition to their responsibilities within their own department. Therefore, staff can be answerable to more than one boss.

Span of control: the number of staff who are answerable directly to a manager.

There is no 'ideal' organisational structure or span of control. What works for one business may fail in another, even if both are the same size. In case studies there will usually be hints about whether the structure is working. A flat hierarchy may be at the heart of an innovative business, or there may be signs that staff lack direction and have low morale. A tall hierarchy may be at the centre of a focused, career-orientated workforce, or it may be bureaucratic and incapable of a quick decision. The judgement is yours.

Workbook

A. Revision questions

(30 marks 30 minutes)

1. What is meant by the chain of command? (2)

2. Define 'span of control'. (2)

3. Some theorists believe that the ideal span of control is between three and six. To what extent do you agree with this? (5)

4. Explain two implications of a firm having too wide a span of control. (4)

5. Explain what an organisational chart shows. (4)

6. Why is it important for a growing firm to think carefully about its organisational structure? (4)

7. State three possible problems for a business with many levels of hierarchy. (3)

8. What is meant by the term 'accountable'? (2)

9. What do you think would be the right organisational structure for a hospital? Explain your answer. (4)

B. Revision exercises
DATA RESPONSE 1

These questions are based on the Scoop organisation charts (Figure 48.1 and Figure 48.2)

Questions (20 marks; 25 minutes)

1. Explain why communication might be harder in the larger Scoop of 2010. (6)

2. Should the Brewer Street counter staff be allowed to contact ice-cream production directly; for example, if they see they are running out of vanilla ice cream? Explain your reasoning. (6)

3. Explain two ways in which Matteo may find his management responsibilities more difficult when he opens his third Scoop outlet. (8)

DATA RESPONSE 2

Management changes at ailing Morrisons' could see 2,000 jobs axed

UK supermarket chain Morrisons' has revealed plans to cut over 2,000 jobs in an overhaul of its management structure. The move, which will reduce layers of management across the firm's 500 UK stores, is expected to primarily affect middle managers.

The move follows similar cost-cutting measures by Morrisons' main rivals Tesco, Sainsbury's and Asda, which are all facing competitive pressure from low-cost supermarkets Aldo and Lidl, as well as from upmarket chains such as Waitrose.

Morrisons', which has run trials of the new leaner management structure, said it had led to better performance. Currently each store has a manager, deputy manager and multiple assistant deputy managers covering broad product categories (such as fresh food). Individual departments (such as green groceries, meat or fish) are led by supervisors reporting to them.

Many of these old posts will now be eliminated to make way for team leaders who will spend most of their time on the shop floor and be responsible for the management of a smaller number of merged departments.

Adapted from *The Guardian* and bbc.co.uk

DATA RESPONSE 3

Chicken Little

Peter (known as 'Paxo') Little set up his free-range chicken farm in the early 1990s. At the time it was an unusual move, especially on the grand scale envisaged by Paxo. His farm had the capacity to produce 250,000 chickens every 45 days; that is, 4 million birds a year. Since then the business has grown enormously, to a turnover of £25 million today.

But Paxo is getting concerned that his business is not as efficient as it used to be. As managing director, he finds that he rarely hears from junior staff; not even the quality manager's five staff, who used to see him regularly. As he said recently to the operations director, 'The communication flows seem like treacle today, whereas they used to be like wildfire.'

Fortunately, the boom in demand for free range and organic produce has helped the business. So even though the team spirit seems to have slipped away, profits have never been higher. Unfortunately, the marketing director repeatedly talks about rumours

Questions (25 marks; 30 minutes)

1. Describe how Morrisons' organisational chart will change following the restructuring. (4)

2. Explain the probable thinking behind Morrisons' decision to change its management structure. (5)

3. To what extent do you think the changes are guaranteed to improve Morrisons' profitability. (16)

that a huge Dutch farming business is about to set up poultry farms in Britain. That could 'set the cat among the chickens'; in other word, provoke quarrelling and dissension.

Questions (25 marks; 30 minutes)

1. **a)** What is the managing director's span of control? (1)

   b) Comment on the strength and weaknesses of this organisational structure. (4)

   c) How important does human resources seem within this business? (2)

2. Examine why vertical communications may not be as effective today as they were in the past at Chicken Little. (9)

3. Examine the ways in which the factory manager may benefit or suffer from the organisational structure shown in Figure 48.5. (9)

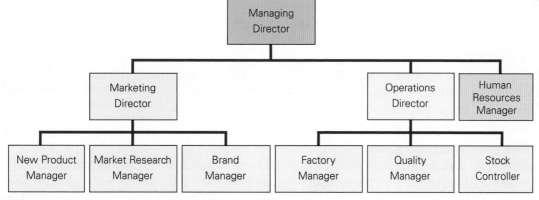

Figure 48.5 Organisational structure of Chicken Little farms

C. Extend your understanding

1. To what extent is a business of your choice moving towards – or moving away from – a centralised management approach? (20)

2. Organisational hierarchies were originally modelled on the army, with many ranks and clarity about who was the boss of whom. To what extent is this approach out-of-date in a business world dominated by online sales and online businesses? (20)

Managing the human resource flow

Linked to: Analysing human resource performance, Chapter 51; Decision-making and improved human resource performance, Chapter 52.

Definition

The flow of labour and skills into, within and out from an organisation. Assessing these flows is the first step towards devising an effective human resource (workforce) plan.

49.1 The human resource (workforce) plan

Human resource planning is about thinking ahead so that staff have the right balance of the right skills in each year into the future. In 2013 Fulham FC started the season with the oldest squad in the Premier League (by far). At the season end the club was relegated. A succession of managers had failed to develop an effective workforce plan. The key components of human resource planning are set out below.

- Audit what you have at the moment; how many staff and what their skills are. Ideally, this audit would include aspirations (for example, staff who say 'I'd love to travel' or 'I've always wanted to learn a foreign language').

- Analyse the corporate plan to turn plans into people. For example, if Sainsbury's corporate plan says '20 new stores to be opened in Britain in the next two years', the workforce plan can be set: 20 new stores, each staffed by 200 people = 8,000 new staff needed.

- Take into account the changes on the way from here to there. How many will leave to retire, have kids or just to have a career change? Some football teams age together; eleven 29 year olds may be great, but four years later there will be a problem.

- Calculate the gaps that need to be filled between now and two years' time. This can be done through the following sum:

  Staff needed in 2 years *minus* staff now *plus* staff leaving between now and then = extra staff required

An example of a human resource plan by UK grocery chain Tesco is given in Table 49.1

Table 49.1 Components of a human resource plan for Tesco

UK grocery chain Tesco, investigating opening stores in India	
1. Audit current staff, to find out their skills	How many current staff speak Hindi, and how many have significant, recent local knowledge?
2. Identify the workforce needs in 2 years' time, based on the corporate plan	How many staff will be needed in the UK in 2 years' time, broken down by skill and seniority; and how many will be needed in India?
3. Estimate employee loss through natural wastage	Research into HR records to find how many of the 500,000 staff will be retiring; if the labour turnover is 10 per cent, 50,000 people need to be recruited just to maintain the present situation.
4. Calculate the gaps between what exists now and what will be needed in 2 years – then plan to fill them	If Tesco plans 10 new store openings in the UK plus 10 in India, it may need 8,000 new staff in addition to the 50,000 needed to replace leavers. These 58,000 must be divided up to plan for how many Hindi speakers, how many butchers, bakers, accountants, etc. are needed

Having completed this process (which should be done carefully, with full consultation with every senior manager), it is time to put it into practice. The process of human resource planning includes recruitment and selection, training and development, and planned redundancies.

49.2 Recruitment

A human resource plan emphasises quantity (the right number of people with the right skills) plus quality (the soft skills shown by staff, such as the ability to collaborate and communicate). The plan provides a structure within which effective recruitment can take place. Within this, the character and personalities of the new staff should be treated as of equal importance as their skills and aptitudes.

'If each of us hires people smaller than we are, we shall become a company of dwarfs.' David Ogilvy, advertising guru

The recruitment process may be triggered by a number of events, including retirement or finding employment elsewhere. At this point, it would be worth analysing the vacant job role. Do all of the responsibilities associated with the vacant job still need to be carried out or are some redundant? Could the remaining duties be reorganised amongst the existing employees? Alternatively, additional workers may need to be recruited in order to support a firm's expansion strategies, or employees with new skills may be required to help develop new products or new markets.

Once the firm has established its human resources requirements, the next step is to consider the nature of the work and workers required in order to draw up a job description and a person specification. Both documents have an important influence on both recruitment and selection; not only can they be used to draw up job advertisements, but also to assess the suitability of the candidates' applications.

'Mediocrity knows nothing higher than itself; but talent instantly recognises genius.' Sherlock Holmes (Arthur Conan Doyle), *The Valley of Fear*

49.3 Training and development

Training is the process of instructing an individual about how to carry out tasks directly related to his or her current job. Development involves helping an individual to realise his or her full potential. This concerns general growth in personal skills, for example in public speaking or in assertiveness, and is not related specifically to the employee's existing job.

Even before training kicks in, new recruits will have been put through an induction programme. That should provide insights into working methods within the business, plus a clear understanding of the firm's aims, objectives and key strategies.

The four key objectives of training and development are as follows.

1. To help a new employee reach the level of performance expected from an experienced worker. This initial preparation upon first taking up a post is known as 'induction' training. It often contains information dealing with the precise nature of the job, layout of the firm's operating facility, health and safety measures, and security systems. An attempt may also be made to introduce the individual to key employees and give an impression of the culture of the organisation. The firm's induction training should aim to drive each employee along their own personal learning curve as quickly as possible (see Figure 49.1).

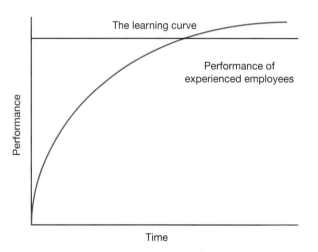

Figure 49.1 Objective of induction training

2. To provide a wide pool of skills available to the organisation, both at present and in the future (see Figure 49.2).
3. To develop a knowledgeable and committed workforce.
4. To deliver high-quality products or services.

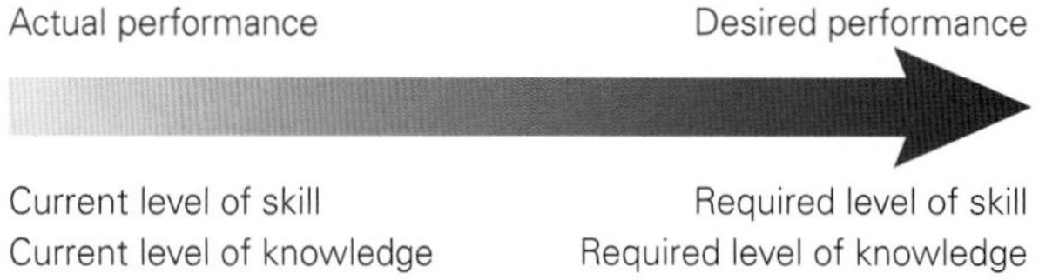

Actual performance   Desired performance

Current level of skill   Required level of skill
Current level of knowledge   Required level of knowledge

Figure 49.2 The training gap

Two types of training

1. On-the-job training

For this method of training employees are not required to leave their workplace but actually receive instruction while still carrying out their job. This means that workers can receive training while remaining productive to some extent. Common methods include mentoring, coaching and job rotation.

2. Off-the-job training

For off-the-job training employees leave their workplace in order to receive instruction. This may involve using training facilities within the firm, for example seminar rooms, or those provided by another organisation, such as a university, college or private training agency. Although this will inevitably involve a temporary loss of production, it should allow the trainee to concentrate fully on learning and perhaps allow access to more experienced instructors than those available within the workplace.

Table 49.2 Training: benefits and costs

Training	
Benefits	**Costs**
It increases the level and range of skills available to the business, leading to improvements in productivity and quality.	It can be expensive, both in terms of providing the training itself and also the cost of evaluating its effectiveness.
It increases the degree of flexibility within a business, allowing it to respond quickly to changes in technology or demand.	Production may be disrupted while training is taking place, leading to lost output.
It can lead to a more motivated workforce by creating opportunities for development and promotion.	Newly-trained workers may be persuaded to leave and take up new jobs elsewhere (known as **poaching**), meaning that the benefits of training are enjoyed by other businesses.

'Train everyone – lavishly… You can't overspend on training.' Tom Peters, business writer

49.4 Redeployment

Even in the most successful businesses, changes in market demand or in technology can make certain tasks or responsibilities redundant. For example,

since 2007 there has been a 40 per cent cut in university modern foreign language courses. In such circumstances, many specialist languages teachers will lose their jobs. Some, however, may have general skills (or other teaching specialisms) that enable them to be redeployed. In other words, switched from their redundant job to another post for which there are future prospects.

Redeployment has several benefits for the organisation:

- saves the cost of redundancy payments
- helps internal morale, as staff see the organisation trying its best to avoid redundancy
- avoids recruiting from outside, when existing employees already understand the culture and procedures within the business – thereby avoiding the induction learning curve shown in Figure 49.1.

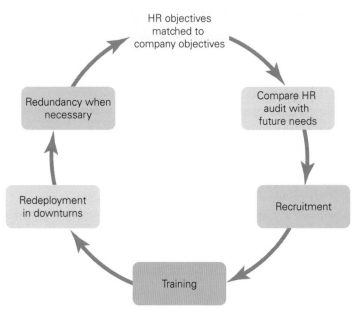

Figure 49.3 Logic chain: human resource flow

49.5 Redundancy and dismissal

Human resource plans are as important in downturns as in the good times. Whereas it may be necessary to dismiss an incompetent employee at any time, redundancies only occur when there is a reduced need for staff – usually because sales are declining or technology is changing labour requirements. Human resource managers are the ones who have to cope with the difficult task of selecting those to be made redundant – and then informing them.

Lloyds Bank

In January 2014 Lloyds announced that it would be shedding 1,400 jobs in Britain. Over 1,000 job roles would be axed, including more than 600 staff who provide face-to-face support to small businesses. In their place would be more work for Lloyds' call centres. In addition, more than 300 staff would be transferred to work for a service supplier to the banking group.

Within the workforce plan Lloyds expected that up to two-thirds of the job reductions would come from voluntary redundancies. This might mean that the HR department would have to make fewer than 400 compulsory redundancies.

Five Whys and a How

Question	Answer
Why may it be hard to ensure that the human resource flow fits with a new business strategy?	Because company employees develop ways of thinking and working that can be hard to change. Can Marks & Spencer staff change to become more like Pret A Manger? Hum.
Why should companies take plenty of time deciding on their staff recruitment – even for shop floor workers?	Because customers are more likely to come into contact with 'ordinary' staff than with managers, so the attitude and competence of shop floor staff is vital to competitiveness
Why might management with a Taylorite approach to staff only be interested in skills rather than attitudes?	Because F.W. Taylor emphasised that financial incentives dictate behaviour; therefore all you need is competent people incentivised by well-structured bonus payments (Herzberg disagrees)
Why may staff redeployment prove more expensive than redundancy plus fresh recruitment?	Redeployment from teaching German to teaching Economics may cost more in training than the cost of redundancy plus recruiting a new, young economist
Why is poaching thought damaging to the economy?	The more companies poach staff, the lower the incentive for any company to induct and train new people – so the productive potential of the economy is weakened
How might Tesco improve its human resource flow?	By clarifying exactly what its corporate plans are, making it easier for HR to decide exactly what skills and attitudes are needed from staff in future

Key terms

Job description: a statement of what the job tasks and duties are, that is, the job itself (rather than describing the right person for the job).

Induction training: familiarises newly appointed workers with key aspects of their job and their employer, such as health and safety policies, holiday entitlement and payment arrangements. The aim is to make employees fully productive as soon as possible.

Person specification: an account of the qualifications, attributes and experience required from a successful candidate for the post.

Poaching: persuading staff to leave the company that trained them, thereby getting fully trained staff without paying the training cost (Premier League clubs are often accused of this by lower league teams).

Soft skills: personal qualities such as warmth, openness, willingness to act on criticism and empathy.

Human resource flow emphasises that business organisations are on a continuous journey of change and development but also disappointment. The key thing is that HR decisions must fit in with the aims, ethos and strategy laid down for the business as a whole. Pret A Manger is a great example, because its recruitment and training practices are all focused on its company-wide plan: good, safe food but outstanding service. Other organisations continue to view training as an avoidable expense, choosing to cut training budgets when under pressure to cut costs, or to poach employees already equipped with the necessary skills from other firms. New employees can bring a number of benefits, including fresh ideas and approaches to work. Yet however excellent the staff, there can still be a need for redeployment or even redundancy if market trends move against the business.

Workbook

A. Revision questions

(30 marks; 30 minutes)

1. Explain the idea of human resource flow. (3)

2. Outline two reasons why a business may need to recruit new employees. (4)

3. Briefly explain the difference between a job description and a person specification. (4)

4. Outline two factors that would influence the method of recruitment used by a business. (4)

5. Outline two reasons why a firm should provide induction training for newly recruited employees. (4)

6. Briefly explain why poaching may lead to a skills gap in the UK labour market. (3)

7. Outline two possible disadvantages of redeploying staff instead of making them redundant. (4)

8. Explain the difference between redundancy and dismissal. (4)

B. Data response

Recruiting people with a passion at Pret A Manger

According to Pret A Manger, talent management is one of the biggest challenges for firms operating in the fiercely competitive UK hospitality industry. The company has grown steadily since its set up in 1986 but still retains a strong entrepreneurial character, despite employing over 5,000 people. Its workers are chosen from a wide pool of recruitment, in order to reflect its customer base. In 2014, around 70 per cent of vacancies at the company were filled within four days.

Job candidates undergo an initial screening interview and are selected on the basis of their personal qualities and passion for customer service, rather than their hospitality skills. Personal qualities include a genuine smile and an eagerness to learn and to progress. Those candidates that pass successfully through the interview stage complete a 'joiner experience day', where they are paid to work in a Pret A Manger store close to where they live. At the end of this, the store team vote on whether or not the candidates should be appointed.

Source: Adapted from multiple sources including Pret A Manger

Questions (25 marks; 30 minutes)

1. Analyse two benefits of Pret A Manger's approach to recruitment. (9)

2. Evaluate the importance of effective recruitment and selection for a company like Pret A Manger? (16)

C. Extend your understanding

1. Stamford Software Solutions, a medium-sized IT company based in the south-east of England, needs to recruit a new sales manager. Evaluate how the company should do this. (20)

2. According to a recent report, UK employers spend an estimated £33 billion in total each year on training, yet one third of employers provide no training at all. To what extent are damaging consequences inevitable for firms who choose not to train their staff? (20)

Improving employer–employee relations

Linked to: Managing the human resource flow, Chapter 49; Analysing human resource performance, Chapter 51; Decision-making and improved human resource performance, Chapter 52.

Definition

The relationship between staff and management is on a spectrum that has complete trust at one end and 'them and us' mistrust at the other.

50.1 Introduction

The relations between bosses and workers will be effective if communications are good and there is a sensible amount of give-and-take between them. They will be bad if there is a lack of trust, leading to restricted communication and the tendency to make demands rather than conduct conversations. In a perfect world, adults would behave in an adult manner towards each other. But just as no family is perfect, neither is any individual business organisation. The key is not to be perfect, but to be better than most.

Research into staff engagement in 2014 found a close correlation between 'trusting your boss' and employee commitment. The 8 per cent who trusted bosses 'to a very great extent' were the happiest of all at work. The 67 per cent who trusted 'to a great or moderate' extent were the second most engaged group.

There are three main areas to consider within the heading 'effective employer–employee relations':

1. good communications
2. methods of employee involvement
3. the causes and solutions to industrial disputes.

Real business

ACAS

ACAS (the Advisory Conciliation and Arbitration Service) is Britain's most important, independent voice on the workplace. Over forty years it has developed a view of what it thinks is the 'model workplace'. The ACAS model includes the following six themes:

1. ambitions, goals and plans that employees know about and understand
2. managers who genuinely listen to and consider their employees' views, so everyone is actively involved in making important decisions
3. people to feel valued so they can talk confidently about their work, and learn from both successes and mistakes
4. work organised so that it encourages initiative, innovation and working together
5. a good working relationship between management and employee representatives that in turn helps to build trust throughout the business
6. formal procedures for dealing with disciplinary matters, grievances and disputes that managers and employees know about and use fairly.

Source: www.acas.org.uk

50.2 Good communications

The importance of effective communication

Effective communication is essential for organisations. Without it, employees may not know what to do, why they are supposed to do it, how to do it or when to do it by. Similarly, managers have little idea of how the business is performing, what people are actually doing or what its customers think. Communication links the activities of all the various parts of the organisation. When it's effective it ensures everyone is working towards a common goal and enables feedback on performance. This could help staff feel they have a real input into key business decisions.

'We provide our Partners with the knowledge they need to carry out their responsibilities effectively as co-owners of the Partnership.' John Lewis constitution, 2014

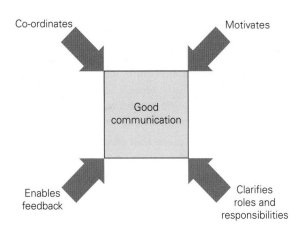

Figure 50.1 Good communication

Effective communication is also vital for successful decision-making. To make good decisions, managers need high-quality information. If they do not know what their shop floor staff know about customers and competitors, their decision-making will be faulty. Good communication provides managers with the information they need, in a form they can use, when they need it.

Good-quality information should be:

● easily accessible
● up to date
● cost effective.

How to manage and improve employer–employee communications and relations

In a well-run organisation with effective delegation and consultation, good communication will flow from the top and to the top. If vertical communications are weak, frustrated staff may look for a trades union to represent their views to management. The overall business leader can do many things to help, as outlined below.

● Have a chat with every new member of staff; this may be impossible for the boss of Tesco's 510,000 employees, but is perfectly possible in most cases.

● Take regular initiatives to meet with staff; some retail bosses go out every Friday to two or three different stores to discuss problems with shop-floor staff

● If staff know that their complaints or suggestions are being addressed, they will be happy to keep contributing their thoughts. Most staff want their workplace to be efficient, to allow them to do as good a job as possible; inefficiency is frustrating for all.

50.3 Influences on employer– employee relations

In addition to the importance of effective engagement and good communications, employer–employee relations are influenced by:

● The underlying demand conditions faced by the business. If revenue is growing strongly it's easy for the whole staff to feel optimistic about job security and promotion prospects. Staff will know that the employers (represented by senior managers) will have a shared view of the optimistic prospects for the business and therefore its staff

● The level of skill required by the producers of the product or service being sold. There can be a risk of a 'them and us' divide opening up if the management see the workforce as low-skilled. A 'them and us' divide implies a serious rift in communication and trust, with a likelihood of solidarity building up among shopfloor staff in opposition to management. It is important to appreciate that one or both sides can be at fault in these circumstances

● Conditions in the broader labour market. If the economy is booming, demand for labour can be high enough to make staff push hard for perhaps overly-ambitious improvements to their pay and conditions of service. At such times faultlines can appear between employers and employees.

50.4 Value of good employer– employee relations

In 2014, in a very difficult grocery market, Asda decided to cut overhead costs by stripping out a layer of middle-management in the stores. This meant thousands of jobs were lost, with most individuals being offered an alternative, lower-paid and lower-status job instead. Naturally this was hugely unpopular, but because of an underlying pattern of good employer–employee relations in the business, staff quite quickly got on with working within the new structure. There was no apparent impact of these changes on Asda's market share.

Good relations are valuable because staff and management have to get along in the long term for the business to do well. As changing external market conditions can force change (including redundancies) on a business, a degree of trust is hugely valuable. Staff will accept a difficult short-term if they believe that staff and management are headed in the right direction. That is why it can be so disruptive to have senior executives paying themselves huge salaries and bonuses. Good employer–employee relations needs to be based on the belief that 'we're all in it together'.

50.5 Methods of employee involvement

Intelligent bosses realise that success depends on the full participation of as many staff as possible. Football managers typically use the club captain as the representative of the players. Small firms may have an informal group consisting of one person from each department; monthly meetings are used as a way to raise issues and problems, and discuss future plans. In larger firms, more formal methods are used to ensure that there is a structure to allow an element of workplace democracy. Alternatively the organisation's staff may be represented by a trades union.

50.6 Trades unions

What is a trades union?

A trades union is an organisation that employees pay to join in order to gain greater power and security at work. The phrase 'unity is strength' is part of the trades union tradition. One individual worker has little or no power when discussing pay or pensions with a large employer. Union membership provides greater influence collectively in relations with employers than workers have as separate individuals.

Some people assume that union membership is only for people in low-status jobs. In fact, although trades unions are in decline in Britain, some powerful groups of 'workers' remain committed to membership. For example, the PFA (Professional Footballers' Association) includes almost all Premiership players, and more than 75 per cent of airline pilots belong to their union BALPA.

Traditionally, unions concerned themselves solely with obtaining satisfactory rates of pay for a fair amount of work in reasonable and safe working conditions. Today the most important aspect of the work of a trades union is protecting workers' rights under the law. Far more time is spent on health and safety, on discrimination and bullying, on unfair dismissal and other legal matters than on pay negotiations. One other important matter today is negotiations over pension rights. Recently, many companies have cut back on the pension benefits available to staff; the unions fight these cutbacks as hard as they can.

'Collective bargaining' remains an important aspect of union activity. This means that the union bargains with the employers on behalf of all the workers. In April 2014 a one-year wrangle between the Post Office and the Communication Workers' Union resulted in agreement to pay rises of up to 7.3 per cent.

'Let's deliver fair pay for all with a living wage, new wages councils, and action to tackle greed at the top.' Frances O'Grady, TUC General Secretary, 2014

Union recognition

'Recognition' is fundamental to the legal position of a trades union. In other words, management must recognise a union's right to bargain on behalf of its members. Without management recognition, any actions taken by a union are illegal. This would leave the union open to being sued. Until recently, even if all staff joined a union, the management did not have to recognise it. Why, then, would any company bother to recognise a union?

- It is helpful for managers to have a small representative group to consult and negotiate with. Collective bargaining removes the need to bargain with every employee individually.

- In situations of potential difficulty, such as relocation, union officials can be consulted at an early stage about causes, procedure and objectives. This may give the workforce the confidence that management are acting properly and thoughtfully. It promotes consultation rather than conflict.

- Trades unions provide a channel of upward communication that has not been filtered by middle managers. Senior managers can expect straight talking about worker opinions or grievances.

Today, UK employers with 21-plus staff members must give union recognition if more than 50 per cent of the workforce vote for it in a secret ballot (and at least 40 per cent of the workforce takes part in the vote).

'Strong, responsible unions are essential to industrial fair play. Without them the labour bargain is wholly one-sided.' Louis Brandeis, lawyer, 1856-1941

50.7 Other methods of employee involvement

Works council

A works council is a committee of employer and employee representatives that meets to discuss company-wide issues. Although works councils have worked well in Germany they have not been so popular in the UK. However, under European Union legislation larger companies that operate in two or more EU countries must now set up a Europe-wide works council. Works councils will usually discuss issues such as training, investment and working practices. They will not cover issues such as pay, which are generally dealt with in discussions with trades union representatives.

Employee groups

Employee groups are organised by the business but with representatives elected by the staff. These are little different from a works council, but because they are the invention of the business (that is, the management) they lack real credibility. Staff may suspect that management frown upon those who raise critical issues. In a similar way, some school councils are vibrant and meaningful, while others are largely ignored by the school management.

Employee co-operatives

These range from huge organisations such as the John Lewis Partnership to the 150 staff at Suma. Because all staff are part-owners of the business, all have a right to have their voices heard at every stage in the decision-making process. Inevitably, the board of directors includes representatives from ordinary shop-floor workers, ensuring that everyone's voice is heard.

Figure 50.2

Five Whys and a How

Question	Answer
Why might a company turn to ACAS?	To benefit from its credibility as an independent body that helps resolve industrial disputes
Why might employees become disengaged in the workplace?	Their jobs may be too repetitive or too pressurised, or they may no longer trust in the word/s of management
Why might customer service be worse at an employee co-operative than at an ordinary company?	Staff may be too focused on themselves and care too little about customers
Why might a company voluntarily offer recognition to a trade union?	As a mechanism for gaining good communication from every part of the business
Why might a trade union ask for arbitration to resolve a dispute with management?	They presumably feel confident in their case and therefore happy to see an independent 'judge' decide on the right resolution to the dispute
How might a conciliation process be conducted?	By inviting both sides to a meeting, but allowing the conciliator to act as a go-between – helping to get people talking

Key terms

Arbitration: when an independent person listens to the case put by both sides, then makes a judgement about the correct outcome.

Conciliation: an independent person encourages both sides in a dispute to get together to talk through their differences. The conciliator helps the process but makes no judgements about the right outcome.

Feedback: obtaining a response to a communication, perhaps including an element of judgement (for example, praise for a job well done).

Vertical communications: messages passing freely from the bottom to the top of the organisation, and from the top to the bottom.

Evaluation: Improving employer–employee relations

Good relations are built on shared goals, on trust and on good communications. Yet they are always fragile. One instance of hypocrisy can ruin years of relationship building. A boss may claim to be acting for the good of all the staff, yet switch production from Britain to Asia (James Dyson), or cut pension benefits to staff while keeping them intact for directors. In the long term, some firms really stick by the view that 'our people are our greatest asset', while others just pretend. Staff will learn which is which. Where they find they cannot trust their bosses, joining a trades union becomes a sensible way to get greater protection and greater negotiating power. Union representation will make the employer–employee relationship more formal, and occasionally more fractious. Yet trades union representation can help to move a business forward. It is wrong to jump to the conclusion that unions are 'trouble'. Real trouble comes when employers and employees have no relationship at all.

Workbook

A. Revision questions

(30 marks; 30 minutes)

1. Explain why good communications within a firm are important. (3)

2. Explain why feedback is important for successful communications. (3)

3. State three actions a firm could take in order to improve the effectiveness of communication. (3)

4. Explain why good communication is an important part of motivating employees. (4)

5. Why might a company choose to accept strike action in preference to settling a dispute? (3)

6. How could a business benefit from a successful works council? (4)

7. Why may an employee co-operative have better employer–employee relations than a public company? (5)

8. Why is it so important to a union to gain recognition from employers? (5)

B. Revision exercises

DATA RESPONSE

There have been over 100 arrests at McDonald's corporate headquarters in Illinois, as a national debate on pay inequality gains momentum. Protesters converged on the Oak Brook corporate campus outside Chicago to demand a minimum wage of $15 (£9.60) per hour and the right to unionise. Organisers said 2000 people had attended the rally, which occurred the day before a vote by shareholders at the giant fast-food chain on executive pay. Don Thompson, the chief executive of McDonald's earned close to $10 million in total compensation in 2013.

The US Bureau of Labor Statistics says median hourly wages for fast-food workers is $8.83 (£5.65). Research by a NY think tank has suggested that in 2013 CEOs in the fast-food industry earned 1000 times what their workers did. Jessica Davis is one of 3.5 million fast-food and counter workers in the US. The 25-year-old McDonald's crew trainer has two children and earns $8.98 per hour (£5.75) at a Chicago McDonald's. She said Don Thompson was earning his millions on the backs of working mothers and fathers. 'We need to show McDonald's that we're serious and that we're not backing down.'

'Fifteen dollars is unrealistic, but we know that the minimum wage will increase over time,' a McDonald's spokeswoman was quoted as saying. She said the company and its franchisees were monitoring the minimum wage debate.

Mary Kay Henry, president of the Service Employees International Union (SEIU) said it was time for the McDonald's Corporation 'to stop pretending that it can't boost pay for the people who make and serve their food.' She was among those arrested at the McDonald's protest.

Source: Adapted from Reuters.com

Questions (30 marks; 35 minutes)

1. Outline one reason why McDonald's customers might care about the pay levels of the company's staff. (2)

2. The famous banker J.P. Morgan once said that the highest earner in a company should earn no more than twenty times that of the lowest earner. At McDonald's today the differential is 1,000 times. Explain one reason in favour and one against McDonald's approach. (8)

3. Evaluate the implications for McDonald's of the successful unionisation of its workers. (16)

C. Extend your understanding

1. To what extent do you agree that effective communications are at the heart of successful business management? (20)

2. 'Good managers welcome trades unions as a way of improving workplace performance.' To what extent do you agree with this statement? (20)

Analysing human resource performance

Linked to: Setting human resource (HR) objectives, Chapter 45; Motivation and engagement in practice, Chapter 47; Managing the human resource flow, Chapter 49; Decision-making and improved human resource performance, Chapter 52.

Definition

Staff costs are usually between 25 and 50 per cent of a firm's total costs. So firms try to measure the performance of their people objectively (that is, in an unbiased way). Calculations such as staff productivity can be used to measure the success of initiatives such as new working methods.

51.1 The need to measure performance

Managers require an objective, unbiased way to measure the performance of personnel. The firm needs to be able to see several things:

- Is the workforce fully motivated?
- Is the workforce as productive as it could be?
- Are the personnel policies of the business helping the business to meet its goals?

It is not possible to measure these things directly. How, for example, can the level of motivation of workers be measured accurately? Instead, a series of indicators are used which, when analysed, can show the firm if its personnel policies are contributing as much to the firm as they should.

There are two main performance indicators used to measure the effectiveness of a personnel department. They are:

1. labour productivity
2. labour turnover.

51.2 Labour productivity

Calculating labour productivity

Labour productivity is often seen as the single most important measure of how well a firm's workers are doing. It compares the number of workers with the output that they are making. It is expressed through the formula:

$$\frac{\text{Output per period}}{\text{Number of employees per period}}$$

For example, if a window cleaner employs ten people and in a day will normally clean the windows of 150 houses, then the productivity is:

$$\frac{150}{10} = 15 \text{ houses per worker per day}$$

Any increase in the productivity figure suggests an improvement in efficiency. The importance of productivity lies in its impact on labour costs per unit. For example, the productivity of AES Cleaning is 15 houses per worker per day; MS Cleaning achieves only 10. Assuming a daily rate of pay of £45, the labour cost per house is £3 for AES but £4.50 for MS Cleaning. Higher productivity leads to lower labour costs per unit. And therefore leads to greater competitiveness both here and against international rivals.

Figure 51.1

'There was a time when people were "factors of production" managed little differently from machines or capital. No more. The best people will not tolerate it.' Robert Waterman, business writer

Real business

The UK's largest recruitment firm is 'on the front foot for the first time in years' says its boss. Perhaps white-collar recruitment group Hays can teach Britain's economic policymakers a thing or two. While they fret about the country's low productivity, the UK's biggest recruitment firm has been investing heavily to ensure it becomes more productive.

That effort is now paying off, according to chief executive Alistair Cox, and helped Hays post a forecast-beating pre-tax profit, up 10 per cent at £62.5 million, as it delivered first-half results yesterday. 'We've had a diligent focus on productivity,' said Mr Cox. 'As a recruiter, we're the ultimate people business. We've brought in quality people, we've trained them, managed them, equipped them to do the job as best as is possible. We're the only recruiter to bother investing in technology.'

Cynics might argue that he's taking the credit for an improving global economy that's actually driving the performance. However, credit where credit's due: net income rose by just 1 per cent to £363.4 million, so the 10 per cent profit increase was impressive. During the half-year in question, total operating costs fell by just over 1 per cent.

Source: adapted from *The Telegraph*, 27 February 2014

'We have always found that people are most productive in small teams with tight budgets, time lines and the freedom to solve their own problems.' John Rollwagen, chief executive, Cray Research

Employee costs as a percentage of turnover

Another way to look at the impact of productivity on the finances of a business is to calculate staff costs as a percentage of sales revenue, that is, turnover. This would help show how serious might be the impact of inefficiency. Figure 51.2 shows that labour costs are twice as high in relative terms at British Airways as they are for Ryanair. This might be a serious problem if Ryanair and BA were in head-to-head competition. In fact, customers are willing to pay a slightly higher price for a BA ticket than for a Ryanair one, so it's not too serious an issue.

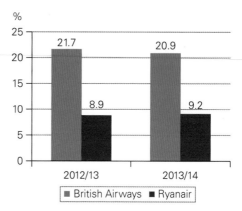

Figure 51.2 Employee costs as a percentage of turnover
Source: Company accounts

51.3 Labour turnover

Measuring labour turnover

This is a measure of the rate of change of a firm's workforce. It is measured by the ratio:

$$\frac{\text{number of staff leaving the firm per year}}{\text{average number of staff}} \times 100$$

So a firm which has seen 5 people leave out of its staff of 50 has a labour turnover of:

$$\frac{5}{50} \times 100 = 10 \text{ per cent}$$

As with all business data, it is best to find comparative data, either from a rival business or how the figure has changed over recent years, and then to look for the reasons behind the data.

Factors affecting labour turnover

If the rate of labour turnover is increasing, it may be a sign of dissatisfaction within the workforce. If so, the possible causes could be either internal to the firm or external.

Internal causes

Internal causes of an increasing rate of labour turnover could be:

- A poor recruitment and selection procedure, which may appoint the wrong person to the wrong post. If this happens, then eventually the misplaced workers will wish to leave to find a post more suited to their particular interests or talents.

- Ineffective motivation or leadership, leading to workers lacking commitment to this particular firm.

- Wage levels that are lower than those being earned by similar workers in other local firms. If wage rates are not competitive, workers are likely to look elsewhere to find a better reward for doing a similar job.

External causes

External causes of an increasing rate of labour turnover could be:

- More local vacancies arising, perhaps due to the setting up or expansion of other firms in the area.
- Better transport links, making a wider geographical area accessible for workers. New public transport systems enable workers to take employment that was previously out of their reach.

Consequences of high labour turnover

Negative effects

A high rate of labour turnover can have both negative and positive effects on a firm. The negative aspects would be:

- the cost of recruiting replacements
- the cost of training replacements
- the time taken for new recruits to settle into the business and adopt the firm's culture
- the loss of productivity while the new workers learn the new ways of working (reach the peak on their learning curve).

Positive effects

On the positive side, labour turnover can benefit the business in several ways:

- new workers can bring new ideas and enthusiasm to the firm
- workers with specific skills can be employed rather than having to train up existing workers from scratch
- new ways of solving problems may be identified by workers with a different perspective, whereas existing workers may rely on tried and trusted techniques that have worked in the past.

On balance, then, there is a need for firms to achieve the right level of labour turnover, rather than aiming for the lowest possible level.

Another way of measuring the loyalty and commitment of staff is to look at labour retention rates. This calculation is based on exactly the same raw data as labour turnover, but uses the information differently.

Formula for labour retention:

$$\frac{\text{staff not leaving in the past year}}{\text{average number of staff employed in the year}} \times 100$$

51.4 Using data for human resource decision-making and planning

Productivity and labour turnover data provide the firm with a commentary on its performance. Poor productivity and high labour turnover might suggest poor management in the workplace. For the most effective comparisons, good managers analyse the figures to identify:

- changes over time (this year versus last)
- how the firm is performing compared with other similar firms (or perhaps benchmarking against the best performers in the sector)
- performance against targets, such as a 20 per cent improvement on last year.

Each of these comparisons will tell the firm how it is performing in relation to a yardstick. This will indicate to the firm where it is performing well and where it may have a problem. The firm must then investigate carefully the reasons for its performance before it can judge how well its personnel function is operating.

For example, labour productivity may have fallen during the previous 12 months. Closer investigation may show that the fall was due to the time taken to train staff on new machinery installed at the start of the year. Figures may show that productivity in the last six months has been climbing satisfactorily. An apparent problem was actually masking an improvement for the firm.

Key terms

Benchmarking: measuring yourself against the best, or sometimes against the average of businesses within your industry.

Culture: the accepted attitudes and behaviours of people within a workplace.

Labour productivity: output per person.

Labour turnover: the rate at which people leave their jobs and need to be replaced.

Five Whys and a How

Question	Answer
Why might productivity fall during a period when sales are rising?	Management might get complacent, recruiting more staff than the revenue increase warrants
Why does rising productivity tend to push labour costs per unit down?	Because employees' wages are being spread over more units of output
Why might staff retention figures improve during a recession?	Staff are scared to risk unemployment, so they stay put even if they get little satisfaction from their jobs
Why might a company's labour turnover figures have worsened steadily over the past four years?	There may be a new management approach that puts more pressure on staff, encouraging increasing numbers of them to look for work elsewhere
Why might the Chancellor of the Exchequer be concerned if UK productivity figures failed to rise?	The Chancellor would worry, because without productivity gains our economy has no prospects for sustained economic growth; rising efficiency makes it easier to export, and easier to fight off imported goods
How might a head teacher view a big rise in labour turnover since his or her arrival?	It depends on how highly he or she rates the staff; if she's not keen then she should be delighted they're going

Evaluation: Analysing human resource performance

Performance ratios such as labour turnover raise questions. They do not supply answers. Follow-up staff surveys or chats may be needed to discover the underlying problems. Figures such as these give the firm an indication of what issues need addressing if the firm is to improve its position in the future, but this must be taken within the context of the business as a whole. A high labour turnover figure may have been the result of a deliberate policy to bring in younger members of staff who may be more adaptable to a changing situation in the workplace.

It must be remembered that these figures are all looking to the past. They tell the firm what has happened to its workforce. Although this has a strong element of objectivity, it is not as valuable as an indication of how the indicators may look in the future.

Workbook

A. Revision questions

(20 marks; 20 minutes)

1. Define the following terms:
   a) labour productivity   b) labour turnover.   (4)

2. Why could an increase in labour productivity help a firm to reduce its costs per unit?   (3)

3. In what ways could a hotel business benefit if labour turnover rose from 2 to 15 per cent per year?   (4)

4. Some fast food outlets have labour turnover as high as 100 per cent per year. What could be the effects of this on the firm?   (4)

5. How might a firm know if its human resource strategy was working effectively?   (5)

B. Revision exercises

DATA RESPONSE 1

A firm has the data shown in Table 51.1 on its human resource function.

Table 51.1 Data held by a firm on its human resource function

	Year 1	Year 2
Output	50,000	55,000
Average no. of workers	250	220
No. of staff leaving the firm	12	8
Working days per worker – possible	230	230
Average no. of staff absent	4	3

Questions (15 marks; 15 minutes)

1. Calculate the following ratios for both years:
   a) labour productivity
   b) labour turnover   (6)

2. Analyse the questions these figures could raise in the minds of the firm's management.   (9)

DATA RESPONSE 2

Turner's Butchers is a chain of three shops in a large town in the North of England. The shops are all supplied with prepared and packaged produce from Turner's Farm, owned by the same family.

The management is particularly concerned at present by the differing performance of the three shops. In particular, they feel there may be a problem with the personnel management in the chain. The concerns were highlighted recently in a report looking at various indicators of personnel effectiveness.

The key section of the report is shown in Table 51.2.

Questions (28 marks; 30 minutes)

1. Briefly outline your observations on each of the three shops in terms of their personnel management.   (6)

Table 51.2 Key section of a report on indicators of personnel effectiveness

Workforce performance data per shop			
	Grayton Road	St. John's Precinct	Lark Hill
Staff (full-time)	8	6	7
Labour turnover (per cent)	25	150	0
Absence rate (per cent)	5	12	1
Sales per employee (£000s)	14	15	18

2. Analyse the factors that may have contributed to the problems.   (7)

3. Taking the business as a whole, make justified recommendations as to how any problems could be tackled by the management.   (15)

DATA RESPONSE 3

Employers face high staff turnover in 2014

A fifth of employees plan to quit their job this year, according to a survey from the Institute of Leadership and Management (ILM). The study, of 1,001 workers, found that of the staff who are preparing to change job, 16 per cent want to leave because they do not feel valued. Of this group, the vast majority would like a similar job (40 per cent) or a different post (39 per cent) at a new company, while one in 10 would like to start their own business.

However, in addition to the fifth of workers planning to leave, a further 31 per cent are unsure about whether they will stay in their current role,

suggesting employers face high staff turnover in the coming months.

Charles Elvin, ILM's chief executive, said: 'The New Year is always a popular time for workers to look ahead and think about how they can progress. Our findings show that UK employees are beginning to reassess the job market and look into a range of new opportunities, from starting a new job to developing a new business.

'The survey illustrates just how crucial it is that workers feel valued in the workplace. As many workers like to make a change at this time of year, it is important that organisations adapt to this phase by offering the chance to learn new skills and opportunities to progress wherever possible.'

The survey also asked employees about their workplace resolutions for the New Year. Most respondents (31 per cent) said improving their work/life balance was a top priority for 2014. This was closely followed by a desire to receive more training or attain a new qualification (28 per cent), to become a better manager (13 per cent), and be more productive at work (11 per cent). The ILM said that the findings revealed a desire to improve the standards of leadership in organisations, with 19 per cent hoping to improve their own leadership skills this year and 17 per cent hoping for more transparent leadership from their boss.

'The survey reinforces the importance of leadership to workers in the UK, and in particular the desire for greater transparency in the workplace,' Elvin added. 'This should be an important consideration for both current managers and those looking to improve their leadership skills.'

Source: http://www.cipd.co.uk/pm/peoplemanagement/b/we-blog/archive/2014/01/07/employers-face-high-staff-turnover-in-2014-survey-suggests.aspx

Questions (25 marks; 30 minutes)

1. Explain the fall in labour turnover during the recent recession. (4)

2. Explain the reasons for the expected rise in labour turnover during the recent recession. (5)

3. To what extent should high labour turnover always be a cause for concern for managers? (16)

C. Extend your understanding

1. 'Human resource ratios raise questions. Good managers make sure they answer them.' To what extent do you agree with this statement? (20)

2. Evaluate the ways in which a firm may respond to an increasing rate of labour turnover. In your answer, refer to one retail business and one other organisation you have researched. (20)

Decision-making and improved human resource performance

Linked to: Setting human resource (HR) objectives, Chapter 45; Motivation and engagement in theory, Chapter 46; Managing the human resource flow, Chapter 49; Analysing human resource performance, Chapter 51.

Definition

Human resource performance implies an evaluation of the effectiveness of the policies that relate labour productivity, turnover and engagement to the corporate business objectives.

52.1 Introduction

People are a resource of the business. Like any other resource they have to be managed. Many organisations claim their people are 'our most important asset' and that HR management makes a significant difference to business success. All too often, though, staff are treated like a cost, not an asset.

'You have got to have an atmosphere where people can make mistakes. If we're not making mistakes we're not going anywhere'. Gordon Forward, President, Chaparral Steel

52.2 Human resource decisions and competitiveness

A huge number of decisions and circumstances affect competitiveness. Among the great British business successes of recent times (Jaguar Land Rover, especially the Evoque; Costa Coffee; aircraft and aero-engine manufacture, especially Rolls Royce; ASOS; Primark) it is hard to see human resources at their heart. The most important factors have been strategic decisions, for instance Costa taking on Starbucks in China, and ASOS having the courage to develop internationally while still growing in Britain.

Despite this, these companies could not have enjoyed success if their people had been alienated or misdirected from the organisations' objectives. Therefore it is valid to see human resources as a key factor. In the case of Jaguar Land Rover (JLR) the most important HR decisions have related to flow. In other words, having identified the remarkable sales boom it has been vital to recruit, train and retrain staff quickly enough to keep up with demand. As a result of that HR success, the business can enjoy the fruits of the boom in demand for its products (see Table 52.1).

Table 52.1 Sales of Jaguar Land Rover cars (almost all UK made, then exported)

Sales in units	2005	2009	2010	2011	2012	2013	2014 (est)
China JLR sales*	n/a	15,000	26,126	42,063	73,347	95,200	118,000**
Total JLR sales	n/a	195,663	232,839	274,280	357,773	425,000	476,000
China per cent share of JLR sales	1 per cent	7.60 per cent	11.20 per cent	15.30 per cent	20.50 per cent	22.40 per cent	24.80 per cent
China ranking (out of JLR sales)	12th	6th	4th	3rd	1st	1st	1st
Total JLR employee numbers	n/a	17,529	16,384	17,255	20,887	24,913	28,000

*At an average price of £70,000.

**This sales level represents £8.3 billion of retail sales in China

Source: All data from JLR accounts and press releases

Of course, successful HR decisions can affect competitiveness. In 2003 James Dyson decided to separate the engineering and design part of his business from the manufacturing. Production headed east while R&D stayed in Wiltshire. Perhaps, by focusing HR efforts on the highly skilled part of the business it made it easier for Dyson Appliances to become one of the most profitable consumer goods companies in the world.

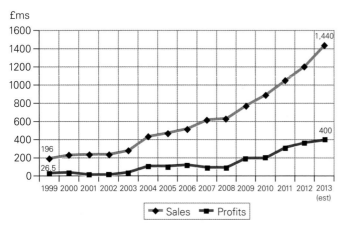

£ms

Figure 52.1 UK's most competitive private limited company: Dyson sales and profits

Source: various newspaper reports

52.3 Human resource decisions and the other business functions

Whereas there are plenty of marketing directors and finance directors in Britain's boardrooms, it is difficult to find many human resource directors. Unilever was one of the first to boast having an HR director, but today the 'Chief HR Officer' is one of fifteen members of the Unilever Leadership Executive, but not on the Board. Among other UK businesses (HSBC Bank; Associated British Foods – owners of Primark; BP and Sainsbury's) the same is true. Chief finance officers are at the top table; the HR people are rarely so.

The implication is that it is naïve to think that HR departments make decisions that the other business functions have to follow. The reality is more likely to be that the board decides on general aims and objectives; that these are firmed up into an overall corporate strategy by the chief executive and his or her team – then the functional areas have to play their part in making things happen.

The relationship between HR and operations or marketing, therefore, has to be collaborative not dominating. If the plan is to reposition Ryanair as a customer-friendly airline, HR will play an important part in organising the retraining and perhaps changing

the recruitment criteria. But it will all be in conjunction with what the operations managers want and what the finance function says can be afforded.

52.4 Impact on HR of market conditions and competition

The key impact on HR decisions comes from the labour market. If jobs are plentiful, HR departments have to focus hugely on staff recruitment and retention. This ensures that issues such as flexible working are tackled with people in mind instead of the company.

When times are tough, HR managers focus on flexibility from the company's viewpoint. There is no better example than the zero hours contract. This is an employment contract promising nothing, in which staff may be contacted with short notice to be told when and for how long they are working the following week. For the company, this effectively turns a fixed cost into a variable one; but the very thing that makes this great for the boss makes it lousy for the worker, especially if she or he has obligations such as a mortgage.

There is a tendency to assume that it's the personality of the HR boss that determines whether a 'hard HR' or 'soft HR' approach is taken. In fact it's often a function of market and competitive conditions. During times of recession, many more firms will adopt a 'hard' HR approach – simply because they can get away with it. A surprise in the 2009 recession was that exactly the same tendency affected the public sector. Given fairly tough public spending cuts, the problem shifted from the private to the state sector. Figures for 2014 showed zero-hours contracts were used by 17 per cent of private sector firms but in 25 per cent of public sector contracts.

Ultimately, competition is the key factor affecting HR performance. The great Japanese business writer Kenichi Ohmae once said that: 'Without competitors there is no need for strategy'. Here, the competition in question is the battle to hire and keep the best people. When the labour market is buoyant, the brightest graduates can expect lavish inducements from prime employers such as management consultants and investment banks. In late 2008, Aldi was offering newly graduated recruits a starting salary of £40,000 plus a company car, to try to compete for the best. With the benefit of hindsight it may well have been a very shrewd move.

In another famous quote from a famous man, Karl Marx once described 'the unemployed as the reserve army of capitalism'. He meant that unemployment made it easier for companies to get their way in the labour market, because the competition from that 'reserve army' meant that HR departments did not have to try so hard.

'Our goal should be to minimise standardisation of human behaviour.' Douglas McGregor, author, *The Human Side of Enterprise*

52.5 Ethical and environmental influences on HR decisions

People like to think that the ethical environment for business is improving, perhaps because companies make more of an effort to sound concerned. Sadly in many areas of business there is little evidence of improvement. A good example is the banking sector. Every one of Britain's high street banks has been found guilty of a series of mis-selling and market-rigging scandals. When individual employees have tried to stem the tide, they have been swept aside. At Lloyds Bank a whistleblower HR manager (Ian Taplin) tried between 2005 and 2010 to get senior managers at the bank to take seriously his evidence that bank employees were persuading its poorer customers to pay more for life insurance than richer ones. Instead of taking an interest in their customers, Lloyds made three offers to pay Taplin off (with gagging clauses) and then fired him anyway. This is in no way exceptional; many other corporate whistleblowers have suffered the same fate (even more shockingly, the same is true in the public sector, notably the NHS).

If you are working in an organisational culture where truth and fairness come second to getting things done (maximising your personal bonus or achieving your NHS targets), the logical thing is to lie low – and perhaps start looking for another job. Regrettably often,

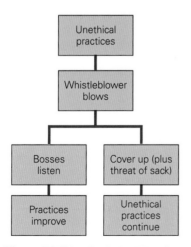

Figure 52.2 Logic chain: risks of whistleblowing

whistleblowers have found it impossible to get another job in their chosen profession.

Environmental influences on HR perhaps focus mainly on transport factors. In London the number of people cycling to work rose by 144 per cent between 2001 and 2011 (these are census figures that won't be updated until 2021!). Much of the reason for this increase was a government scheme offering tax incentives to firms to encourage cycling. The reality, though, is that such schemes were pushed by HR departments that could see fitness benefits for staff together with environmental benefits for the City. Outside London, cycling numbers also rose between 2001 and 2011, as follows: Bristol +94 per cent, Manchester +83 per cent and Newcastle +81 per cent.

(Source: Office for National Statistics, March 2014)

(Referring to homeworking): 'It's against corporate culture not to have people on site. Executives want to own their employees.' Margrethe Olsen, company director

52.6 Technological influences on HR decisions

There is a tendency to assume that information technology will grow ever greater in importance in every aspect of business. In fact the CIPD's 2014 report on Learning and Development in the UK says that: 'E-learning may have reached its peak, as fewer predict growth of e-learning (2014: 23 per cent, 2013: 29 per cent, 2012: 24 per cent, 2011: 30 per cent). Respondents found e-learning to have a bigger gap between use and effectiveness than any other L&D (learning and development) practice.' So whereas there had been a move towards online training courses, HR professionals believe that boom is now over.

Other important technological influences on HR decisions include:

- the ever developing improvements in international communications, which makes it more possible to interview overseas recruits online, and to discuss common problems with HR departments in different parts of the world
- the impact of real technological change, for instance if a high street seller decides to switch to online selling. There would probably be redundancies, retraining and new recruitment needed to carry out such a strategy.

Five Whys and a How

Question	Answer
Why might competitiveness falter if HR is mismanaged?	HR has to plan ahead however long is necessary to make sure that the right staff, with the right motivation are available at the right time
Why might senior HR managers find it hard to affect overall business strategy?	HR is seen in firms as a service department – getting the right staff at the right time – HR staff rarely have board-level input into strategy
Why is HR not regarded more highly in business?	It has rarely been possible to show the effect of great HR on sales/profits (though Pret A Manger is an example of a business that's got it right)
Why might a moral individual put up with unethical practices at work?	For simple reasons of need: mortgage to be paid; kids to be fed; and lack of self-confidence to look for another job
Why may new technology start to threaten HR jobs in the future?	If unmanned computer-controlled delivery vans are the future, why would HR jobs be required?
How much does an HR director earn?	According to Reed 2014, £80,003 a year, compared with £91,000 a year for finance directors

Key terms

Whistleblower: an employee who reveals unethical or risky practices that line managers have been trying to keep quiet. The secrets may be passed up the hierarchy or (if that has no effect) be revealed to the media/outside world.

Zero-hours contract: an employment contract that promises nothing more than a last minute offer of work for the following week. This is flexibility for employers at the cost of uncertainty for employees.

Evaluation: Decision-making and improved human resource performance

Human resource management it easy to put on a pedestal, because motivation theory is such a compelling part of a business course. Sadly for HR professionals, their tasks are less exciting, though no less important than that. Getting things right is a management art – far removed from clever decision-making. HR professionals make sure that the directors' wishes can be achieved, cost-effectively and competently. In modern business, people who get things right are not necessarily given the opportunities they deserve.

Workbook

A. Revision questions

(30 marks; 30 minutes)

1. A new pizza place opens two doors from yours and some of your staff switch to the new employer. Outline two ways an HR manager should react to this situation. (4)

2. Identify three aspects of HR management that get easier when there's a recession. (3)

3. If an HR manager suspects that one of the staff has won a large contract using bribery, what might she or he do? (4)

4. Explain the reasons for a multinational business operating in 35 countries around the world holding all HR management meetings in English. (6)

5. Analyse why online training courses may be less successful than face-to-face ones. (6)

6. Explain two reasons why an HR director would make a good future managing director of the whole company. (8)

B. Revision exercises
DATA RESPONSE

Barclays Bank – Ethics and HR

Over a period of perhaps 10 years, Barclays Bank developed a culture that damaged the interests of an extraordinary range of its stakeholders, including retail customers, business customers and the wider community. The bank has been at the centre of extreme tax avoidance plans, the Libor rate-fixing scandal, the PPI mis-selling scandal and much else. What was once a straightforward high street bank became dominated by the casino culture of investment banking. In 2013 its staff were the next stakeholders to suffer – with a wave of job losses.

> ## Our culture
>
> **Our culture evolves as the world in which we live and work changes. Sitting still is simply not an option so we are always looking at ways to improve ourselves and better serve all our customers.**
>
> **The result is a culture where everyone is encouraged to stretch themselves, take responsibility for their actions and challenge the status quo by coming up with fresh ideas.**
>
> Source: Barclays website 24/2/13

Following a parliamentary inquiry into banking standards in July 2012, Lord McFall, a member of the committee, said there is 'no hint' Barclays are thinking of changing their culture following the Libor rate-fixing scandal. Lord McFall said the bank's apology was 'nothing more than a futile gesture'. Eventually, in July 2012 the Bank of England leaned on Barclays to get rid of its highly-paid boss Bob Diamond.

At first, Bob Diamond's successor, Antony Jenkins, kept a low profile. Only in February 2013 did he emerge with a round of press conferences and media interviews to announce his new vision for Barclays. Above all else, he claimed to be 'shredding' the Barclays culture of the past, and would instead build the new culture around 'the bank's new values – respect, integrity, service, excellence and stewardship.'

On 12 February *The Guardian* reported that: 'The new boss of Barclays has attempted to break from the bank's scandal-ridden recent past by announcing plans to pull out of controversial businesses that speculate on food prices, specialise in "industrial scale" tax avoidance schemes and use the bank's money to bet on markets.'

Antony Jenkins, promoted to the top job last year when Bob Diamond was forced out in the wake of the Libor-rigging scandal, had vowed to shut down businesses that were unethical, regardless of the profits they generate for the bank. However, he stepped back from the most radical reform by insisting the investment bank – which generates 60 per cent of the bank's total profits – would remain a 'very large part and an important part of the group.' He said changing the bank's culture and rebuilding its reputation would take five to 10 years.

Some 3,700 jobs are to be axed as the bank retrenches from troubled businesses in continental Europe to focus on the UK, US and Asia after a six-month review of 75 individual business lines. Some 1,600 investment banking jobs have gone in the last six weeks alone. The bank's shares jumped 9 per cent to 327p on the measures to cut costs and avoid the most radical options for reform.

In a room emblazoned with the bank's new values – respect, integrity, service, excellence and stewardship – Jenkins insisted: 'This is not window dressing or PR. They define the work we will do and the work we won't do.'

'There will be no going back to the old ways of doing things,' said Jenkins. He is linking the pay and bonuses of the bank's 125 top staff to his new 'values' this year. All employees will have their pay linked to them next year.

Independent analyst Louise Cooper was asked by *The Guardian* just what Barclays would have to do to achieve culture change: 'I believe strongly that corporate culture is set by executives and management – their behaviour and attitudes implicitly tell employees what is acceptable and important and how to behave. Standards and morality trickle down an organisation. If a firm has been proven to be highly toxic then bosses must leave. That is the first rule. It is very difficult to reprimand an employee for bad or illegal behaviour when it's been previously sanctioned, even encouraged or copied from bosses. Nothing can change without executives leaving.

'Secondly, the new team must publicise there has been a change from the old world order. This is what the new boss at Barclays has done. He has sent a clear message to staff that if they don't like the new morality then they should leave. This is also important for clearing out the middle managers who refuse to adapt.

'Thirdly, follow the advice of the [former] New York mayor Rudy Giuliani and adopt a "zero tolerance policy". The new standards of behaviour must be rigorously enforced. Fourthly, reward those who embrace the new rules and penalise those who don't – the carrot and the stick.

'And finally, for those seeking to make the changes, it is important to realise it is a long process. It is a sad comment on human nature that bad behaviour spreads like wildfire through an organisation and yet good behaviour takes forever to develop. Leaders get the organisations they deserve.'

Source: Adapted from guardian.co.uk

Questions (30 marks; 35 minutes)

1. Explain the importance of 'the carrot and the stick' in the theories of either F.W. Taylor or Professor Herzberg. (5)

2. Analyse the implications for HR managers of '3,700 jobs' being axed in the near future. (9)

3. To what extent may a 'zero-tolerance policy' make it possible for the HR department to eliminate unethical behaviour throughout the bank? (16)

C. Extend your understanding

1. Mr Mao Chinese takeaway has grown to 30 outlets in the North West and plans to go national. At present it has no HR department. How important is it to establish a human resource function within the business? Justify your answer. (20)

2. In the hotel business fierce price competition can encourage a company to cut costs, cut back on employee benefits and outsource important business functions. An alternative is to offer a differentiated product and encourage staff to give great service. To what extent is a hotel likely to succeed by using the second approach? (20)

Acknowledgements

Every effort has been made to trace the copyright holders of material reproduced here. The authors and publishers would like to thank the following for permission to reproduce copyright illustrations.

Fig. 1.6 © Philippe Huguen/AFP/Getty Images; Fig. 6.1 © Fotum – Fotolia; Fig. 10.2 © Suzanne Kreiter/The Boston Globe via Getty Images; Fig. 11.3 © innocent drinks; Fig. 11.5 © Clynt Garnham Food & Drink/Alamy; Fig. 12.1 © Tomohiro Ohsumi/Bloomberg via Getty Images; Fig. 12.3 © Robert Wilkinson/Alamy; Fig. 14.2 © Jeanette Dietl – Fotolia; Fig.15.1 © Asife – Fotolia; Fig. 16.6 © Tom Bourdon/Alamy; Fig. 17.2 © Henry Schmitt – Fotolia; Fig. 17.4 © Oli Scarff/Getty Images; Fig. 17.5 © Newscast-Online Limited/Alamy; Fig. 18.1 © Photoshot; Fig. 19.5 © Sonu Mehta/Hindustan Times via Getty Images; Fig. 20.5 courtesy of Taisun Foods & Marketing Co. Ltd; Fig. 22.5 © Richard Levine/Demotix/Press Association Images; Fig. 23.4 © Bernardo De Niz/Bloomberg via Getty Images; Fig. 23.5 © Sunil Saxena/Hindustan Times via Getty Images; Fig. 24.3 © Eranga Jayawardena/AP/Press Association Images; Fig. 27.2 © WavebreakMediaMicro – Fotolia; Fig. 27.4 © Photofusion/REX; Fig. 28.2 © Denis Doyle/Bloomberg via Getty Images; Fig. 30.1 © Oleksiy Maksymenko/Alamy; Fig. 30.2 © Martina Berg – Fotolia; Fig. 30.4 © Bas Czerwinski/EPA/Corbis; Fig. 30.6 © Piero Cruciatti/Alamy; Fig. 33.4 © Viktor - Fotolia; Fig. 35.1 © Silvia Olsen/REX; Fig. 42.2 © WavebreakMediaMicro – Fotolia; Fig. 43.3 © Chivote; Fig. 44.2 © ACORN 1/Alamy; Fig. 44.3 © Simon Dawson/Bloomberg via Getty Images; Fig. 44.5 © Michael Blann/Getty Images; Fig. 50.2 © INSADCO Photography/Alamy; Fig. 51.1 © Picture-Factory – Fotolia

Crown copyright material is licensed under the Open Government Licence v1.0

Index

outsourcing 217
robotics 187
sports footwear 144
Chocola, Chris 247
Chomsky, Noam 217
Clinton, Hilary 11
co-operatives 10
Coca-Cola 44
collateral **271**
commission 296
commodities 74
communication
  with employees 313–14
  and motivation 291
  with stakeholders 62
  with suppliers 188
competition 23, 44–5, 86, 141, 156
Competition and Markets
    Authority 79, **83**
competitive markets 73–7
competitive structure 23
competitiveness **201**, **213**
  and financial decisions 274–5
  and human resource decisions 325–6
  and marketing 76
  and operational decisions 216
  and opportunity costs 209
complementary goods **145**
component supply 175
computer-aided design (CAD) 186
Conan Doyle, Arthur 42, 309
conciliation **317**
confidence intervals 94–5
Confucius 69
consumer attitudes 113
consumer demand 25, **27**
consumer goods 131
consumer profiles 113
consumer usage 113
contribution 236, **240**
convenience goods 131
corporate objectives 4–5, **5**, **83**
corporation tax **259**
correlation 99–100
Cosby, Philip 197
cost minimisation 223–4
costs
  and cash outflows 263
  definition 228
  operational objectives 161–2
  of production 142, 229–30, 231
  and supply chains 203
Covey, Stephen 79
credit periods 263
creditors 8, **12**
criteria **253**
CRM (customer relationship
    marketing) 68
crowdfunding 270, **271**, 273, 276
culture **321**
customer relationship marketing
    (CRM) 68

customer taste 23
Cutler, Laurel 42
data gathering 101–2
data use, operational decision-
    making 193
Debenhams 244
debt factoring 246, **247**, 270
decentralisation 303
decision-making
  and financial performance 274–7
  human resources 321
  influences on 44–5
  intuitive 42, 45
  and operational performance 216–19
  and price elasticity 107
  and risk 43–4
  role of managers 32
  scientific 42–3, 45
  see also marketing decision-making
decision trees 48–52
delayering **305**
delegation 4, **5**, 36, **253**, 297, 303
Dell Computers 10, 197
Dell, Michael 10
demand 86–7, 205–6 *see also* price
    elasticity of demand
democratic leadership 36, **39**
demographic factors 26
demographic segmentation 117–18
dependability, operational
    objectives 162
design 75, 174
design technology 186–7
development 309–10
digital marketing 66–8, 85–6, 157
direct feedback 291
direct online distribution 149
discretionary income **27**
dismissal 310
disruptive change 23, **27**
distribution channels 148–9
diversity, management teams 281–2
dividend cover 18, **19**
dividends 16, 18, 263, **266**
division of labour 287, **292**, 297, **298**
dogs, portfolio analysis 137, **138**
Domino's pizza 171
downtime **182**
Drucker, Peter 1, 3, 31, 38, 87, 92, 174,
    216, 217, 280
dynamic pricing 68, 229, **232**
e-commerce 149, 157
e-learning 327
early adopters **145**
economic climate 22, **27**
economies of scale **124**
EDI (electronic data interchange)
    188, 219
Edwards Deming, W. 67, 197, 198
efficiency 161, **165**, 167
Eisenhower, Dwight 36, 129
elasticity of demand 106–9

electronic data interchange (EDI) 188, 219
Elop, Stephen 205
emergency purchases 129–30
employee co-operatives 316
employee costs 319, 320
employee engagement 280,
    287–92, 295–8
employee groups 316
employee involvement 314, 315–16
employee motivation 168–9
employees
  location 282
  numbers of 282
  skills 282
employer–employee relations 313–17
empowerment 297
engagement 280, 287–92, 295–8
entrepreneurs 3, **5**, 6
environmental influences
  financial decisions 276
  financial objectives 225
  HR decisions 327
  marketing 69–70
  operational decisions 218
environmental issues 26
environmental objectives, operational
    objectives 162–3
equity 271 *see also* share capital
ethical influences
  decision-making 44
  financial decisions 276
  financial objectives 225
  HR decisions 327
  marketing decisions 69
  operational decisions 218
ethical objectives 5
ethics 69–70
Evans, J. 116, 117
excess capacity **182**
expected values 50, **52**
expenditure budget 251, **253**
extension strategies 135–6, **138**
external constraints **109**, 224
external influences
  affecting business 22–8
  break-even charts 237–9
  decision-making 44–5
  financial objectives 224
  HR decisions 282–3
  labour turnover 321
  on marketing mix 157
  on marketing objectives 82
  operational objectives 164
extrapolation 100–1
failures 23
Fairtrade 26
Fanning, Cynthia 175
Farmer, Tom 295
favourable variances 251, **253**
Fayol, Henri 30–1, 301
feedback 113, 219, 314, **317**
Ferguson, Alex 298